It's a tale that doesn't seem like it wou
improbable proposition of a ten-mile reef of gold in the middle of the
continent, a cabal of scheming investors, a farrago of poor planning
and preposterous publicity, the fiasco of the prematurely celebrated
triumph of technology over unforgiving terrain, a dead prospector —
and no gold. The Central Australian Gold Exploration Company
had it all, and **Lasseter's Last Ride** *was in the stores before the*
final chapter of the real-life debacle had closed. It was a runaway success.

Angus & Robertson sold three million copies of Ion Idriess' sixty books before he died in 1979. In his lifetime he was Australia's most popular author. But in 1931 he was living on his wits as a journeyman journalist and looking for an angle to finish a book about a hyped-up gold prospecting expedition. He found it in sorcery, which he used to infill the gaps between the few facts and fanciful descriptions of lands and peoples he had never seen. Idriess' fictional account of the last months of the life of Harold Bell Lasseter gave birth to a legend that repeats in dozens of books, films, poems, paintings, podcasts, websites and exhibitions, is memorialised in the names of a highway and a casino, and has spawned searches and scams that continue a century on. Idriess was probably surprised at its success and chose not to tamper with a winning formula when inconvenient material emerged. To do that he had to control the evidence and continued to insist on his narrative's *unimpeachable adherence to fact.* *Reef Madness* exposes how Idriess confected his first successful book and why the story of a failed prospector became a quintessentially Australian myth.

THE AUTHOR

Born in Perth, Western Australia, Ernest Hunter trained as a public health physician and psychiatrist in the United States. After returning to Australia in the 1980s he worked for more than three decades in remote northern Australia, most of that time being in Cape York and the Torres Strait. He has published several hundred articles and monographs in the academic and popular press and is author of *Aboriginal Health and History: Power and Prejudice in Remote Australia* (Cambridge University Press, 1993), and *Vicarious Dreaming: On Madman's Island with Jack Idriess* (ETT, 2019). He lives with his wife, Trish Fagan, in Kewarra Beach north of Cairns – overlooking a different kind of reef.

COVER IMAGE

Hugh Sawrey was the founder of the Australian Stockman's Hall of Fame in Longreach and a prolific artist. Through the 1960s and '70s he spent time in Central Australia where he was a close friend of Iris Harvey, founder of Arunta Gallery. Sawrey left a rich legacy of impressions of the region and its stories including *Lassiter's Last Ride* [sic], painted in 1967 directly on the wall of a station homestead west of Alice Springs. One of several artists' mural imaginings in that now deserted building, it was found by a Lasseter-lands traveller in August 2021. With the permission of Anthony Sawrey, the artist's son and author of *A Thousand Miles Beyond: The Equine Paintings of Hugh Sawrey* (2020).

REEF MADNESS

Digging Up the Dirt on an Australian Myth

ERNEST HUNTER

ETT IMPRINT
Exile Bay

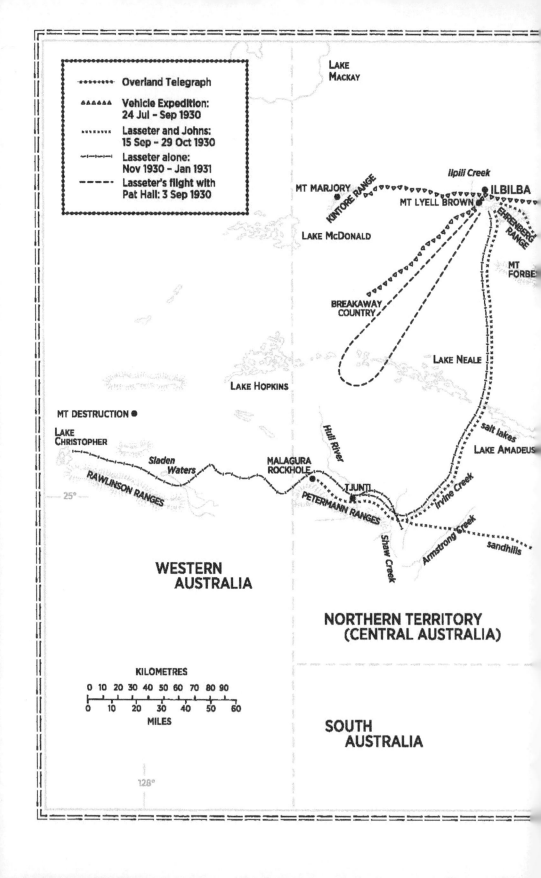

Legend

- •••••••• Overland Telegraph
- ▲▲▲▲▲▲ Vehicle Expedition: 24 Jul – Sep 1930
- ········ Lasseter and Johns: 15 Sep – 29 Oct 1930
- ┤–┤–┤– Lasseter alone: Nov 1930 – Jan 1931
- – – – – Lasseter's flight with Pat Hall: 3 Sep 1930

LAKE MACKAY

Ilpili Creek

MT MARJORY

KINTORE RANGE

MT LYELL BROWN

ILBILBA

EHRENBERG RANGE

LAKE McDONALD

MT FORBE

BREAKAWAY COUNTRY

LAKE NEALE

LAKE HOPKINS

MT DESTRUCTION

LAKE CHRISTOPHER

salt lakes

LAKE AMADEUS

Sladen Waters

Hull River

MALAGURA ROCKHOLE

TJUNTI

RAWLINSON RANGES

Irvine Creek

25°

PETERMANN RANGES

Shaw Creek

Armstrong Creek

sandhills

WESTERN AUSTRALIA

NORTHERN TERRITORY (CENTRAL AUSTRALIA)

KILOMETRES

0 10 20 30 40 50 60 70 80 90

0 10 20 30 40 50 60

MILES

SOUTH AUSTRALIA

128°

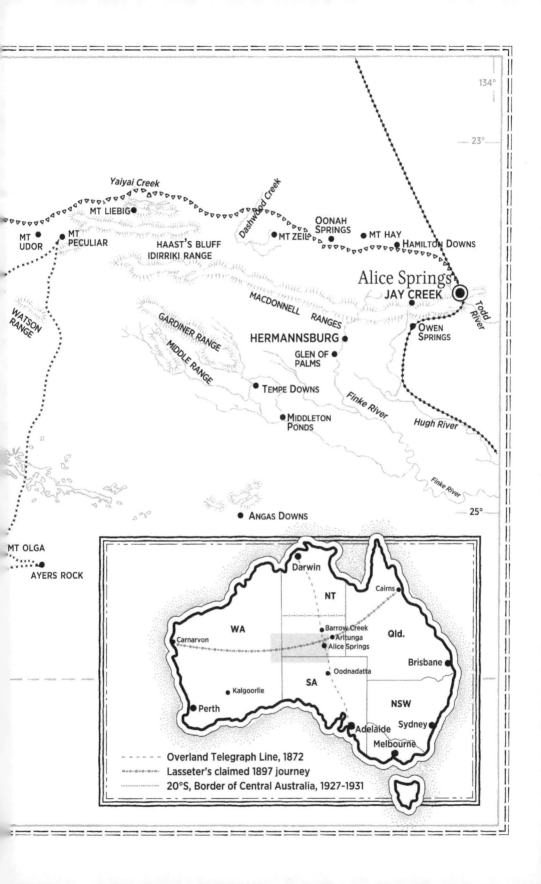

134°

23°

Yaiyai Creek

MT LIEBIG ●

MT UDOR ●   MT PECULIAR ●   *Dashwood Creek*   OONAH SPRINGS   ● MT HAY

MT ZEIL ●   ● HAMILTON DOWNS

HAAST'S BLUFF
IDIRRIKI RANGE

Alice Springs
JAY CREEK ●

WATSON RANGE

MACDONNELL   RANGES

Todd River

GARDINER RANGE

HERMANNSBURG ●   OWEN SPRINGS ●

GLEN OF PALMS ●

MIDDLE RANGE

TEMPE DOWNS ●

Finke River

MIDDLETON PONDS ●

Hugh River

Finke River

25°

● ANGAS DOWNS

MT OLGA ●

AYERS ROCK ●

● Darwin

● Cairns

NT

WA   ● Barrow Creek
Carnarvon   ● Arltunga
             ● Alice Springs

Qld.

● Oodnadatta   Brisbane ●

SA

● Kalgoorlie   NSW

Perth ●   Sydney ●

● Adelaide
    Melbourne ●

- - - - Overland Telegraph Line, 1872
●-●-●-● Lasseter's claimed 1897 journey
—·—·— 20°S, Border of Central Australia, 1927-1931

CONTENTS

FOREWORD

Australian history is always picturesque. Indeed, it is so curious and strange that it is itself the chiefest novelty the country has to offer, and so it pushes the other novelties into second or third place. It does not read like history, but like the most beautiful lies, and all of a fresh sort, not the mouldy old stale ones. It is full of surprises, and adventures, and incongruities, and contradictions, and incredibilities, and they are all true.

Mark Twain.

Short of cash, Mark Twain toured Australia between September 1895 and January 1896 lecturing to packed venues. The following year his pithy observations of the Australian colonies on the cusp of Federation appeared in *Following the Equator: A Journey Around the World*. That was the same year that, three decades later, Harold Bell Lasseter claimed to have crossed the continent as a teenager, finding a gold-laden reef along the way. Mark Twain wouldn't have been surprised that a lot of people thought it was true, or that those *beautiful lies* initiated a train of events that rumble on a century later and are now history, legend and myth. His whimsical reflection has been much quoted, including as the epigraph to Ernestine Hill's collection of northern Australia tales, *The Territory*. Hill was more than passingly familiar with gold rumours and rushes in Central Australia and, as a journalist around the same time that the first expeditions were searching for Lasseter's reef, her impetuous reporting fuelled overly-optimistic expectations of finds at The Granites.[1] She knew the area and the Lasseter story, met some of the key players and was a contemporary of the man who, more than anyone else, was responsible for transmuting Lasseter's *beautiful lies* into legend – Ion Idriess. They both contributed to *Walkabout* magazine, were stablemates at Angus & Robertson, and were among a small set of authors who defined a particular genre of mid-century, outback, *middlebrow* writing.[2]

As journalists they intuitively understood that their readers yearned for escape and were willing to suspend disbelief – embracing beautiful lies as truth so long as they were wrapped in a good story. That's probably why she prefaced *The Territory* with Mark Twain's words and, almost as an afterthought, acknowledged the artifice of her fellow journalist and Centralian legend-maker: *Strange to say, legends of the Territory eventually come true, always with the exception of Lasseter's literary Reef, that "cave of gold" that, long before Ion Idriess made drama of a long-drawn desert ride to death, was a novel founded largely on the fictions of King Solomon's Mines.*[3]

Ion Llewellyn Idriess survived Ernestine Hill by seven years and died in a Mona Vale nursing home in 1979. In his lifetime more than three million copies of some sixty titles were sold and, for a generation, he was Australia's most popular author. While he wrote a dozen books on military themes and others lobbying for major investment to unlock the economic potential of Australia's north, he made his name by building on two decades as an anonymous, journeyman magazine writer recording folksy vignettes of frontier life. As with Ernestine Hill some of it was true – and a lot was not. An example is his third book, *Lasseter's Last Ride*, which made his name and defined his career, an account of the last months of the life of Harold Bell Lasseter, who died in remote Central Australia in 1931. In retrospect it's a tale that doesn't seem like it would be a winner; an improbable proposition of a ten-mile reef of gold in the middle of the continent, a cabal of scheming investors, a farrago of poor planning and preposterous publicity, the fiasco of the prematurely celebrated triumph of technology over unforgiving terrain, a dead prospector – and no gold. The Central Australian Gold Exploration Company had it all, and *Lasseter's Last Ride* was in the stores before the final chapter of the real-life debacle had closed. It was a runaway success.

The appeal of *Lasseter's Last Ride* at that time is understandable. The Depression was driving the newly unemployed from cities to the bush – for work if it could be found, or for a lucky break. Everyone was a fossicker and many were sustained by rumours of finds that were as incredible as they were touted. But not all; the largest nugget ever found in Australia, the Golden Eagle, was being toured through the Eastern

States. For those hungry for distraction and hope, *Lasseter's Last Ride* provided both; the pluck and persistence of prospectors wrapped in a fanciful fabric of tribal exotica, and the lode located – but lost. The tragedy Idriess set up was Lasseter's demise despite reaching his goal. But why this fictional story took on the patina of myth resulting in dozens of expeditions searching for Lasseter's Lost Reef, is another matter. To be lost it had to have been found in the first place and, even though Lasseter's claim that he had stumbled on a gold reef while crossing the continent in 1897 was proven to be a lie, searches continue today – nine decades later.

Reef Madness: Digging up the Dirt on an Australian Myth, is the backstory to *Lasseter's Last Ride* and describes how Idriess wrote and revised the book that launched his career and an industry – there are magazine articles, books, poems, television programs, films, podcasts, websites, and the ill-fated prospector's name is preserved in signs for a highway and a casino. While the discourse has shifted from contesting the veracity of Lasseter's claims and Idriess' account, to disentangling the elements of the resulting myth, the means by which it was birthed by Idriess have not been explored. This work draws on Idriess' personal papers, archival sources, published material, and interviews with a range of informants with diverse interests in Lasseter and Idriess – collectors, traders, researchers, writers, publishers, prospectors, film-makers, webmasters, and relatives of both men.

Reef Madness was born of coincidences – passing comments about Lasseter and mental illness, a chance find in a bookstore, and a recently completed project that drew on the works of Ion Idriess. That project resulted in *Vicarious Dreaming: With Jack Idriess on Madman's Island*, in which the north Queensland writings of the younger Idriess were used as a device to tell a story about the history of coastal Cape York. Having worked in remote Indigenous communities of that region for three decades I emphasised the Aboriginal and Torres Strait Islander past and presence across all the terrains in which those tales of the last few centuries unfolded. I chose not to assume an Indigenous voice or represent an Aboriginal or Torres Strait Islander view. The same applies in ***Reef Madness.*** Aboriginal people are a constant and essential presence in ***Lasseter's Last Ride*** but are used as a plot device to support contemporary views of native peoples and to respond to appetites for the exotic which were current at the time. However, this is a story of a myth that is quintessentially *whitefella business.*[4] It is about avarice, vanity, dishonesty, betrayal and gullibility. And it starts with corporate greed, political posturing and spin. However, as with ***Vicarious Dreaming*** I have sought to identify that all the sites through which the narrative weaves and my research has taken me have an Indigenous past and present. I have also attempted to demonstrate how Idriess and his contemporaries used Indigenous people and cultures as a resource, commodifying a primitive exotic for what was a receptive readership.

Ion Idriess was a complicated figure. In relation to Aboriginal and Torres Strait Islander Australians, who figure prominently in many of his books, it can be argued that he was ahead of his time. He was probably the first author to write about Indigenous Australians as resistance heroes, for instance in ***Nemarluk*** and ***Outlaws of the Leopolds.*** However, even these fighters are presented as tragic remnants, and the wider frame of his interests relates to the colonial project. To that extent he was not only echoing the beliefs and attitudes of his time, he was reinforcing them. And as he aged he was less in touch with the times through which he continued to write. Some of his later works from the 1960s, such as ***Our Living Stone Age*** and ***Our Stone Age Mystery***, repackaged and repurposed material he had collected decades earlier and were out of step with where the nation was in grappling with race relations and Aboriginal rights through a time of dramatic social transformations. Idriess remained stuck in the frontier world of remote Australia which he had left toward the end of the 1920s to take up residence in Sydney – his base for the rest of his life.

Like ***Vicarious Dreaming***, ***Reef Madness*** was conceived in a book-store. It is about how one book became the *urtext* of a myth. Its author had been at Gallipoli, crucible for the most powerful and enduring national myth, and the account of his experience there, and in Egypt and Palestine – ***The Desert Column*** – can be counted as one of the best books by an Australian soldier of the First World War. It was published a year after ***Lasseter's Last Ride*** and a dozen more titles were released before the next War. Among those are Idriess' better writing, ***Men of the Jungle*** and ***Drums of Mer***, and his biggest sellers ***Flynn of the Inland*** and ***The Cattle King***. ***Lasseter's Last Ride*** is not Idriess at his best; it was written in a hurry and he took enormous liberties – some for plot and narrative consistency, others to protect sources and self-interest. That it has gone through more than 45 editions[5] since 1931 speaks to the degree to which its message continued to resonate with a popular readership. While he could not have realised until after the fact, with ***Lasseter's Last Ride*** Idriess had found an enduring sweet spot – ***Reef Madness*** explains how that happened.

A NOTE ON NAMES AND TERMS

Ion Llewellyn Idriess was a Sydneysider; he was born in Waverley in 1889, died in Mona Vale in 1979, and a banksia marks where his ashes were placed in the Northern Suburbs Cemetery in North Ryde. But he is remembered for tales from elsewhere and for much of his early adult life he was known as Jack, and it is as Jack that he appears in many of his books, from ***Madman's Island*** (1927) to ***My Mate Dick*** (1962). He was also known by other bush names including *Cyclone* which, according to Idriess, was conferred by Aboriginal contacts in his fossicking days around Cooktown before the First World War. By that time he was already an accomplished writer, his observations of bush life appearing in magazines under various pseudonyms, the best known of which was as *Gouger* in the *Aboriginalities* pages of *The Bulletin*. Others included *Up Top*, *Sea Nomad*, *I.L.I.*, *G.L.I.*, *Bill Ion*, *I.I.* and *Two Eyes*.[6]

In the Alice Springs Memorial Cemetery the plaque on a squat sandstone effigy identifies that the remains interred below are those of Lewis Harold Bell Lasseter. He had also been a writer and contributed to local newspapers as *The Gleaner*. It was minor stuff and although Idriess was the author, much more has been written about Lasseter. But for most of his life, from his birth in Bamganie, Victoria, he was Lewis Hubert Lasseter; it was as Lewis Hubert Lasseter that he married Florence Elizabeth Scott in the United States in 1903 and enlisted – twice – in Melbourne and Adelaide in 1916 and 1917 respectively. But in 1924 it was as Lewis Harold Bell Lasseter that he bigamously married Louise Irene Lillywhite in Melbourne. Confusingly, he has been referred to by other names including Harold Frederick Bell, Lance Harold Bell Lasseter, Possum, Das Lasseter and Frederick Harold Bell. In *Lasseter's Last Ride* Idriess refers to his subject as *Lasseter*, or in dialogue as *Harry* – which is also how Lasseter signed off in his last letters to Irene Lasseter written in the month before he died and which were found near his body and, seven months later, buried in a cave.

Idriess' account is about the prospecting expedition that set out with Lasseter as a member and of which he was the sole casualty. It starts with a story told and retold by Lasseter that eventually got a bite in the Australian Workers' Union (AWU) offices in Sydney in March 1930 and resulted in the setting up of the Central Australian Gold Exploration (CAGE) Syndicate, which segued into the CAGE Company, the Directors of which launched two expeditions. Lasseter was with the First Expedition from July 1930. His body was located by Bob Buck on 29th March 1931 near Shaw Creek, and Buck returned to Alice Springs with various items found nearby including a small set of notes and a letter to his wife, Irene. Buck was the leader of the Second Expedition which set out later that year to locate the reef that Lasseter claimed, in messages sent to the Directors in September 1930, to have sighted. It was during this Second Expedition that a larger cache of documents was discovered buried in a cave at a place now known as Tjunti near Hull Creek. Via Idriess, part or all of it ended up in the vaults of Angus & Robertson in Sydney. Across the decades since, the events, players and found materials have become confused in the retelling. In *Reef Madness* the terms CAGE Syndicate, CAGE Company and CAGE Directors are used with the two expeditions referred to as the First CAGE Expedition and Second CAGE Expedition. The documents found in March 1931 by Buck near Lasseter's body at Shaw Creek after the First CAGE Expedition, which were drawn on by Idriess for the first edition of *Lasseter's Last Ride* in September 1931 are identified as such. The larger cache unearthed in the cave at Tjunti in October 1931 by the Second CAGE Expedition and which – largely because of Idriess – has come to be known as Lasseter's diary is referred to as *The Diary*, selections of which were incorporated into three additional chapters to *Lasseter's Last Ride* from 1932.

Idriess wrote *Lasseter's Last Ride* in Sydney. He scavenged personal accounts, reports, photographs and archival material – but he had never been to Central Australia. His descriptions of the country were not first-hand; the terrain and locations were described from secondary sources. Idriess sought narrative flow rather than accuracy – there are almost no dates in *Lasseter's Last Ride* and later research has demonstrated the limitations of his understanding of the country. To bolster authenticity he incorporated place names mentioned by Lasseter in the two batches of notes found in 1931 that relate to his last wanderings. Some, such as Lake Christopher, are clear but others, for instance Winter's Glen, which had been named by Ernest Giles over five decades earlier, are not. Finally, there are certain place names that are different to those of later authors including members of the First CAGE Expedition. The most important is the base for the Expedition at what Idriess calls Ilbilba in the Ehrenberg Range. Other versions are Ilbilla, Ilbpilla and Ilpili. Taylor's Creek figures prominently in the Idriess story but is elsewhere referred to as Yaiyai Creek (sometimes YaiYai or Aiai Creek) which is used hereafter. Idriess recounts events at Mount Marjory (the term used in this book) in the Kintore Range near the border with Western Australia which was a major narrative station although other writers have used Mount Marjorie for what is now Mount Leisler – Yunytjunya. The site of Lasseter's Cave at Tjunti is sometimes Tjuunti (Kulpi Tjarranya). Regardless of its rendering in English it is a Pitjantjatjara word. All of the locations in this saga were – and are – known in Pintupi, Luritja or other Aboriginal languages, including Uluru and Kata Tjuta. These Anangu names are now more widely known, but at the time of the CAGE Expeditions – and until recently – were referred to as Ayers Rock and the Olgas. The settlement of Stuart – in Arrernte, Mparntwe – was better known for a repeater station on the Overland Telegraph that was close to a waterhole found in a dry riverbed during construction in 1871. Alice Springs was named for the wife of Charles Todd, the project leader, whose name was given to the river.[7] The town that grew around it, Stuart, became capital of Central Australia from 1927 to 1931 and it was only in 1933 that the name was officially changed to Alice Springs. These are the terms used by members of the CAGE Expeditions and Idriess and, with respect to traditional owners, are used in this book. For the tribal names of those individuals identified decades later as having met with the Expedition at Ilbilba, and who were with Lasseter in his last months, the rendering of Billy Marshall-Stoneking is used. Quotes retain the original terms and spelling. The most comprehensive synthesis of locational information related to the Lasseter story, with a history of the early exploration and mapping of remote central Australia, is the detailed XNATMAP submission compiled by Paul Wise.[8]

Lewis Hubert (Harold Bell) Lasseter
1880 - 1931.

Ion Llewellyn (Jack) Idriess
1889 -1979.

ACKNOWLEDGEMENTS

As for *Vicarious Dreaming* Trish Fagan, my wife, enabled this work. I am grateful to Jim Bradly, Tom Thompson, and Beverley Eley for Idriess guidance. In relation to Lasseter I am indebted to Robert Ross, particularly for his detailed chronology of the Expedition in the *Sullivan's Diary* section of the website – *Lasseteria*. In alphabetical order, other informants who have given their time and knowledge are: Barry Allwright, Alison Anderson, Peter Bridge, John Chapman, Rob Coutts, Desmond Clacherty, Chris Clark, Clive English, Paul Feain, Alan Foskett, David Hewitt, Garry Holmes, Murray Hubbard, Bob Lasseter, Wendell Peacock, Trevor Potts, Duncan Quarterman, Nicolas Rothwell, Lesley Synge and Luke Walker. The Mitchell Library and the digitised records of the National Library of Australia and the National Archives of Australia were heavily relied on, and I offer my thanks to all those involved in supporting and securing these national treasures.

Images have been sourced from the Angus & Robertson Archives in the Mitchell Library and the three relevant digitised collections relating to the CAGE Expeditions also in the Mitchell: 1) *1930 'CAGE' expedition led by Lasseter, Central Australian Gold Exploration [and the later search for him]*; 2) *John Bailey collection of photographs showing Bob Buck leading the expedition to recover Lasseter's body in Central Australia*, which is largely from the Second Expedition, and; 3) *Errol Hampton Coote photographs, 1929 to 1932*. Other newspaper collections and websites are identified. The chapter header images of covers from Idriess' books were provided by Idriess' current publisher, Tom Thompson. Images and/or permission to use other covers were obtained from authors and/or publishers (Peter Bridge of Hesperian Press, Luke Walker of Scribble Films, Chris Clark, John Chapman, Jim Bradly, Gary Gregor and Beverley Eley). The remain-ing photographs were taken by the author with the permission of the subject or owner, and in Alice Springs by Marcus Tabart. Cameron Emerson-Elliott referenced the maps in *Lasseter's Last Ride* for that to *Reef Madness*.

Ion Idriess.

Harold Lasseter.

CHAPTER 1

Adelaide

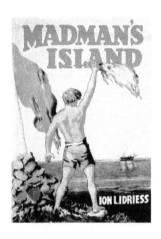

A band of natives guided Buck to where Lasseter lay under a canopy of dried bushes, his false teeth on the ground beside him. They had served him well, for he had used them as "Kaditcha." Buck scratched his head thoughtfully.

"The natives would never dare touch those teeth" he said, "but it beats me why the crows haven't carried them away."

The boy nodded.

Ion Idriess 1931.[9]

It started with dental before it slipped sideways to mental – and then on. I tried to imagine a doomed prospector using false teeth for sorcery. Even recognising fiction masquerading as fact it grated – but it's classic Idriess, and maybe that's why I remembered it. *Lasseter's Last Ride* was a digression while I was reading his tales of Cape York and the Torres Straits set in the years before and after the First World War. I used those stories – and Idriess – as devices to scaffold an historical fiction and it was his first book that set the scene. *Madman's Island* was published in 1927 as a work of fiction – and it flopped. By the time the revised version appeared in 1938, the one he claimed was the true story of being stranded with a deranged prospector on Howick Island in 1920, he was on a roll. And that started with his third book, which came out in September 1931 – *Lasseter's Last Ride* – his account of the last months of the life of the man born as Lewis Hubert but who died as Harold Bell Lasseter, the story that launched Idriess' career and birthed a myth.

A century on from whatever really happened on Howick Island I was slowly getting over the three years of Idriess-immersion it had taken to write *Vicarious Dreaming: On Madman's Island with Jack Idriess.* I was left with a bookcase filled with cracked-spine early-editions, not to mention e-space crammed with downloads from Trove and obscure websites, and files and backups of notes, quotes, letters and logs. So – 2019 resolution to self – *no more Idriess.* That was the mantra each time I approached a book-shop and, pretty much, it worked – until the closing days of October 2019. It was late morning as I turned from the shisha-scented, early summer heat of downtown Adelaide into Station Arcade to find O'Connell's Bookshop and, against my better judgement, ended up at the Idriess stack. Familiar dustjackets and titles, including a 1933 edition of *Lasseter's Last Ride.* On the same shelf were related items of *Lasseteria* – a term I'd soon understand – and among them a facsimile copy of *The Diary* buried by Lasseter and unearthed by the Second Expedition sent to figure out what had happened. Right next to it was *Lasseter Did Not Lie!* by Austin Stapleton, published a half-century after Idriess's foundation account, and *Lasseter: The Making of a Legend* by Billy Marshall-Stoneking.

It was probably the author's name that prompted me to slide it out of the press of Lasseter titles. *Billy Marshall-Stoneking* seemed to be chan-nelling a high-sierra shaman and, as I learned later, that intuition wasn't far off the mark. Maybe a bit of sloppy shelving – a different Lasseter and another legend. But it wasn't and, as soon as I opened it, the maps had me in their thrall. I've always been mesmerised by charts – *Vicarious Dreaming* was as much a meditation on maps as a story about Cape York. Palimpsest-like, their lines and letters tell tales in time as well as terrain; their markings refract earlier imaginings. Marshall-Stoneking's maps are scattered though the text, detailed small-scale sections of a journey that are very different from the untitled chart on the flyleaf of *Lasseter's Last Ride* that is centred on Lake Amadeus, with Mount Unapproachable to the north-west and Mount Olga and Ayers Rock to the south. Idriess' map has no route markings – for the vehicle expedition or for Lasseter after he and a chance-met German *dogger* headed south with five camels in the middle of September 1930. And other than Arltunga, there are no Indigenous names.[10]

That's not the case for Marshall-Stoneking's book which, as I later understood, is an attempt to locate the Lasseter story in Aboriginal space. But that's not why – against my resolution – I put that book into a *to be considered* pile. It was because I happened to glance at page 190 and a comment by a Pintupi informant, someone who had been present when Lasseter's bush grave was relocated in the 1950s and his skeleton exhumed and taken to Alice Springs. It had initially been interred where he died at the end of March 1931 by Robert Buck, a struggling pastoralist who was catapulted by that event and Idriess' portrayal of him as a *legendary Centralian bushman* into a Lasseter career. The Pintupi man was Nosepeg Tjupurrula and in the 1980s he told Marshall-Stoneking – who knew that Buck had presented a number of items as proof of having found the body, including the dead prospector's dentures – that three decades earlier he had seen: *"Not false teeth! True one! Inside."*[11] I flipped through **Lasseter's Last Ride** and on page 226 found: *Lasseter lay under a canopy of dried bushes, his false teeth on the ground beside him.*

Without thinking more about it I added those three books to a res-olution-breaking pile and returned to the Holiday Inn Express. As my computer struggled to connect to the hotel network I thought the internet would resolve the dental dilemma. But it only took seconds to realise that anything to do with Lasseter cascades thousands of hits. Not just historical; despite dozens of failed expeditions to find his *lost reef* and compelling evidence that it had never been found in the first place, the commentaries and blogs make it clear that the search continues. But there's plenty about the man and from the National Archives I found that Harold Bell Lasseter had been born in Victoria and raised as Lewis Hubert Lasseter, and had been medically discharged from the Australian Military Forces during the First World War twice without completing training. In October 1916 he was ruled medically unfit at the Seymour camp in Victoria because of defective eyesight. The medical report is clear that there was no military liability for health problems, including what must have been existing poor dentition, as against the question: *Is the loss of teeth the result of wounds, injury, or disease directly attributable to active service,* is recorded: *not so due.* His dentition receives more attention in the records of his second enlistment, in Adelaide in 1917, where on 10th September he was declared *DENTALLY FIT* against a stamp stating *ARTIFICIAL DENTURE SUPPLIED,* with another, nearby specifying *LOWER.*[12]

So, he had false teeth, but they may not have lasted long because the next day he was admitted to hospital: *Suffering from a scalp wound & unconscious.* In another file is a letter by Lasseter written three years later from Gippsland. He was applying for assistance from the Repatriation Fund and gave his account of the events, which he linked to his discharge: *the day prior to embarkation I was laid out by a gang of larrikins who had been taken into camp when men were scarce. I got my head broke & was dis-charged in consequence.*[13] That was not how it was seen by those doing the discharging; against *Disease or Disability* is *Mentally deficient.* A few lines later the *essential facts of the history of the disability* records: *Has marked hallucinations, wants to join flying corps as a friend is coming to present him with an aeroplane.* In the same hand his *present condition* is glossed: *Has peculiar manner & is constantly talking.* Several pages later, under *the pathological condition present at the time of examination by the Board,* the presumptive diagnosis is given as: *neurotic condition with hallucinations.* And on the final page under *Summary of causes or invaliding* – the last entry – *mentally deficient pre-existing, Discharge Medically Unfit, Incapacity nil.* On 30th October 1917 Lewis Hubert Lasseter was out of the military again – with false teeth.

While the issue of whether Lasseter had dentures was sorted, the problem presented by Nosepeg Tjupurrula's comments remained. But a different issue was now in play – Lasseter's state of mind. That triggered recollections of comments from two psychiatric colleagues, one of whom connected to Adelaide. The first was Robert Kaplan, a Wollongong-based psychiatrist and author of much that teeters on the edge of the apocalyptic and bizarre. Rob had attended the Sydney launch of *Vicarious Dreaming* in early 2019, a small gathering of friends and in-laws with a few ring-ins, including Rob, who told me over after-launch drinks that he'd recently published a book with a chapter that might be of interest, and a pdf copy arrived a few days later. In *Dark Tales of Illness, Medicine and Madness: The King who Strangled his Psychiatrist* the relevant chapter is *Harold Lasseter: Flying too close to the sun.*[14] I'd saved it, unread, and there it was – *Lasseter/Kaplan* – on my computer desktop.

Coincidentally, years earlier Rob and I had written obituaries for a colleague, John Cawte, who had been responsible for the development of ethnopsychiatry in Australia in the 1970s. A third was written by another colleague, Barry Nurcombe, and as I shifted Rob's article to a new file – *Lasseter story* – where it joined the military records and a dozen or so other downloads, I remembered a dinner conversation with Barry in Cairns not long after the Sydney launch. I was talking about Idriess in north Queensland when Barry commented: *You know John Cawte read Lasseter's Last Ride and contacted Idriess. Told him that he had evidence Lasseter was delusional. Idriess didn't want to talk about it or wasn't interested.* John Cawte, Ion Idriess – it wasn't a connection I'd ever conceived. Their lives overlapped but Idriess was born around four decades earlier than John, who was drawn to more cerebral fare than Idriess produced and wouldn't have approved of how he repackaged Aboriginal ethnographies. And I was over Idriess; the comment was stored – but not lost.

With the sounds of Adelaide's traffic filtering up from the street I was turning over the possibilities. John Cawte was only six when Lasseter died – they never met. But from writing John's obituary I knew that he began his career in the 1950s in Adelaide, and from skimming Lasseter's military records I knew that Adelaide was where he spent his second sojourn in the military and where he was discharged. Then, on an ancestry website, I found a piece written by his daughter, Lillian Agnes (Ruby) in 1960.[15] Lasseter had married her mother, Florence Elizabeth Scott, in the United States in 1903 and they returned to Australia in 1909, arriving in Adelaide where his older sister, Lillian, had settled. Maybe the connection was Adelaide, and John had found psychiatric records dating back to 1909 or 1917.

To check that out I did a quick search of South Australia's historical health databases. *Colonial Lunatic Asylum, Adelaide and Parkside Lunatic Asylums, Parkside Mental Hospital and Glenside Hospital, 1845-1981* seemed a good place to start. But after four phone calls the best I could do, despite nearly a century since Lasseter might have been in a civilian hospital, were templates for a release of information to be signed by next of kin, and a freedom of information application. Maybe it was fortunate that before I entered that maze I read the two documents by psychiatrists that I already had. The first was Rob Kaplan's chapter, which reprises the essentials of the expedition and of Lasseter's early life. Various neuropsychiatric labels are tried on but, in the end, Rob opts for a more prosaic explanation:

> *Lasseter was a compulsive liar, but the big one devoured him. His great failure has become part of the defining mythology of Australia. And now he is commemorated by a cave, a highway, a grandiose tombstone in Alice Springs, a casino, an ever-replenishing coterie of believers (including Dick Smith) and a story that never seems to end. At least 13 expeditions have set out to find the treasure, but constantly failed.*[16]

The defining mythology of Australia – Rob credits Idriess and the highly fictionalised **Lasseter's Last Ride** for that. I wasn't surprised; his stirring but sanitised depictions of north Queensland history and its characters that I sifted for **Vicarious Dreaming** is much the same. I was beginning to realise that it wasn't Lewis – or Harold – Lasseter, the person with whatever faults he may have had, or the frantic scouring of remote and unforgiving lands in the middle of the continent then and since that is interesting. It was, and is, less and more; it's why this story transmuted from mundane misadventure to myth and the role of the alchemist – Ion Idriess. The second document by a psychiatrist brought me full circle. I remembered that at the end of his career John Cawte had written **The Last of the Lunatics**, a reflection on his early years as a young clinician at Adelaide's Enfield Receiving Hospital through the final decades of asylums in Australia; I had a pdf copy on my computer and there, on page 150, was a reference – the only one – to Harold Lasseter:

The legend of Lasseter's lost gold-reef in the dead heart of Australia is perhaps the best known tale of the imposition of internal riches on distant deserts. In 1893 an Afghan camel driver found the apparently insane Harold Lasseter wandering in the desert. Lasseter claimed he had found a gold-reef to surpass all reefs, some thousand miles west of Alice Springs. In 1930, he led an expedition in search of his El Dorado. The seventy-two camels in the expedition all died of thirst, and the aircraft and truck broke down. Impatiently Lasseter pressed ahead of the party, and perished. His body was eventually found in the Petermann Range country south-west of Alice Springs on the Western Australian border. The historical incident has been dramatized in **Lasseter's Last Ride**, *by Ion L. Idriess. Delusions and overvalued ideas may have a vivid, almost hallucinatory quality and, when projected into the desert, elicit El Dorado behaviour from the subject. How much exploratory or pioneering activity is performed on the basis of distant placement of internal objects, seeking legendary wealth?*[17]

Even after just a half day of internet sleuthing I knew John had some of the facts wrong, but while his take on Lasseter is different to Rob Kaplan's two decades later, both are based on stories about stories. I'd found dozens of others online and in a quasi-fugue state as Adelaide's evening sounds replaced the shrill turbulence of commuter chaos, I ordered most of them – the *Lasseter story* file was about to grow. And the trajectory had shifted again; I was confident that John Cawte did not see clinical information about Lasseter. If he had it would be in the text – maybe that was Barry's source. But regardless, for both Rob and John, **Lasseter's Last Ride** was centre stage. As I shut down my laptop to head out into the Adelaide night I was scaffolding a new project. Not about whether Harold Lasseter had a pre-existing mental health problem, or about Harold Lasseter at all. I was back travelling with Ion Lewellyn Idriess again, musing over the making of myth.

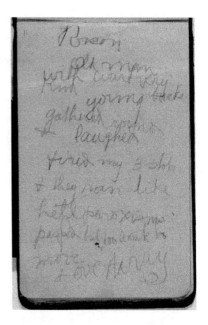

On 30th October 1917
Lewis Hubert Lasseter was out
of the military again …

… *The Diary buried by Lasseter and
unearthed by the Second Expedition
sent to figure out what had happenened.*

… *after he and a chance-met German dogger headed south with five camels in the middle
of September 1930.*

CHAPTER 2

Witnesses

One day I was advised by Mr. Jack Gilchrist, the counter attendant, that Lasseter was anxious to discuss a mining proposition with me, he further considered that I should grant him an interview. I left instructions that when Lasseter called again, to direct him to my office. He was a short thick-set person, about 5 feet 3 inches high, dark complexion and well-spoken. I formed the opinion that Lasseter had been well-educated. At this time he was shabbily dressed. "Well", I said, "I have been advised you are interested in gold-mining". He replied. "Yes, I have a proposition for you, Mr Bailey".

John Bailey, 1947.[18]

Books began appearing in my letter box about a week after I returned to Cairns and kept coming for two months. Beneath three shelves crammed with the Idriess afterglow of **Vicarious Dreaming** there is now a row in which every second spine shares the dead man's name: **Lasseter's Gold**; **Lasseter Did Not Lie!**; **Lasseter: The Making of a Legend**; **Lasseter's Dream of Millions**; **The Search for Harold Lasseter**; **The Truth about Lasseter**; **On Lasseter's Trail** – and **Lasseter's Last Ride**. I quickly realised that reading as they arrived – the most recent and easily sourced before earlier accounts that were harder to find – overlaid current understandings and values on those of the 1930s, and lost the incremental unfolding of the events, the narrative and the aftermath. So I reversed the strategy, re-reading the first account – *Lasseter's Last Ride*. But I didn't get much past Herbert Basedow's glowing commendation of the author and the work. He left no doubt that he believed the story as told: *That Lasseter's original discovery was not a myth I have not the slightest doubt. The high opinion I personally formed, after a careful geological study of the area, might be gauged by referring to a recent report of mine in the Journal of the Geographic Society of London (1929).*[19]

Herbert Basedow was no slouch when it came to remote Australia and quite a catch for Idriess. Born a year after Lasseter and post-deceasing him by two, he was variously a medical practitioner, anthropologist, geologist, politician, entrepreneur, explorer and, briefly, Chief Protector of Aborigines in the Northern Territory. He knew Central Australia and the area where Lasseter died; he was part of the first Donald Mackay expedition in 1926 that went to the Petermann Ranges by camel. Just four years later Mackay's first Aerial Survey expedition in early 1930 employed Bob Buck and Albert Paul Johns to set up a landing strip at Ilbilba in the Ehrenberg Range west of Alice Springs, which the First CAGE Expedition used as its base from August of that year. That's where Johns, the last European to see Lasseter alive, left him in November – four months before Buck found the prospector's body 300 kilometres to the south-west. And Basedow also had first-hand experience of the local tribal populations – he was an acknowledged expert when it came to native peoples and published *The Australian Aboriginal* in 1925 which was, for its time, a major contribution to a very thin field.

No slouch, and neither was Idriess, they would have gotten along just fine, and probably shared the Kiplingesque imperial melancholy that was typical of the times – *The white man's burden*. In the foreword Basedow reflected that:

Among the names of the intrepid little band of our West-Central pio-

neers (apart from Lasseter) who have made the greatest human sacrifice in the interests of colonization, might be mentioned those of Gibson, George, Warman, and Frayne. These men sleep peacefully in the one great grave of heroes, beneath the sacred vault of Heaven, and on the glorious bosom of their ever watchful Mother Nature.

Basedow concluded the foreword: *Mr Idriess' book adds another illuminating but tragic page to the annals of Australian exploration, which in years to come will supply a useful link to literature dealing with the history of the foundation and development of our Commonwealth and Empire.* Idriess' dedication echoes that theme: *To the pioneer spirit which never dies.* From reading more than thirty of his books I'm familiar with the sentiment and style. *Chapter 1 – Lasseter's story* is true to form and begins: *He was a little man but you looked at him twice; he was so short, so broad, his blue eyes so determined. He walked into the office of the Australian Workers union in Macdonell House, Pitt Street, Sydney. In that busy office he had to wait his turn among a crowd of shearers who were signing on for work in distant country sheds. But Lasseter was used to waiting: he had waited years.* That was enough, I decided that Idriess could wait. **Lasseter's Last Ride** may have birthed the legend but Idriess wrote it without having been there. I decided I had to find first-hand accounts.

To do that I surveyed the contents of the Lasseter shelf, which generated a number of general categories. First were the voices of people who played a part in the events – *Witnesses.* The second group was made up of commentaries on a subset of those accounts, each promoting a particular text – *Corroborators.* A set of more recent books shifted the focus to Lasseter's backstory; what is known about his earlier life and what that says about the claims he made, on the basis of which the Expedition was funded – *Sleuths.* The fourth category is a small group presenting a compromise position based on an alternative reading of Lasseter's backstory which preserves the reef but shifts the locus – *Decoders.* Which left a fifth category that has as its subject the mythopoeic text, **Lasseter's Last Ride** *– Mythbusters.*

Witnesses: who

In a forensic investigation witness evidence needs to be weighed up: what was the proximity and extent of involvement; how much time elapsed between event and report; potential conflict of interest in the outcome of the inquiry, and; the credibility or trustworthiness of the source. In relation to Lasseter there are accounts by eight men who were party to events around the Central Australian Gold Exploration (CAGE) Syndicate, which became the CAGE Company, that funded the First CAGE Expedition; three from the beginning, three for part of the Expedition, and two whose involvement was indirect.

John Bailey, the President of the Central Branch of the Australian Workers Union, was approached by Lasseter in March 1930 with a story about a gold reef he had found in the middle of the continent three decades earlier. While Bailey didn't go on the Expedition, he became the Chairman of the CAGE Syndicate that found the funding for it. Errol Coote was a journalist who happened to be with John Bailey and Bailey's son, Ernest, on that day. He had learned to fly and became the pilot for the Expedition. Fred Blakeley was an experienced miner and bushman, and had crossed the country by bicycle in 1908. He became the leader of the Expedition and it didn't hurt that his brother, Arthur, was the Federal Labor Member for Darling and, at that time, the Minister for Home Affairs in the Scullin Ministry formed in October 1929, just as the Wall Street Crash cascaded into the Great Depression. With Home Affairs came responsibility for Territories which included, from 1927, Central Australia and North Australia, and Arthur Blakeley oversaw their merger back into a single Northern Territory effective June 1931, six months before the Scullin government was dissolved.

Those three were there from the birth of the CAGE Syndicate, the other five were not, but three of them were involved in the Expedition. The youngest member was Philip Lawrence Taylor. Born just outside London in the first year of the new century, in 1919 he joined the De Havilland Aircraft Company and came to Australia with the founder to establish a branch in Melbourne, which was subsequently transferred to Sydney just as the Depression was biting. When Taylor was about to leave for England he was asked by his boss if he was interested in joining an expedition to Central Australia as a driver-mechanic. He was a late inclusion to replace Charles Lexius Burlington who, despite or because of knowing a lot about mining, aeroplanes and maps, was objected to by both Lasseter and Coote. Taylor met Coote in Parkes and flew on with him to Alice Springs to join the rest of the team. Just two years older was John Matthew Blakiston-Houston, an Eton-educated military man. Sixteen at the outbreak of the First World War, by its end he was a veteran of the Tank Corps. Remaining in the military, he spent the first half of the 1920s in Egypt and India including experience in the Himalayas, and in 1929 became Aide-de-Camp to Viscount Stonehaven who was Australia's Governor General from 1925 to 1930. While waiting to return to England, Blakiston-Houston heard about an opportunity to visit Central Australia and his chances were increased by having met Coote during flying lessons. He only had a month to spare, two weeks of which were lost when the expedition leaders missed their train from Sydney, but he was present for the first fortnight from Alice Springs.

The last participant to leave an account was Albert Paul Johns.[20] A late entry recruited to continue with Lasseter when the rest of the First CAGE Expedition abandoned the search for the reef and returned to Alice Springs in September 1930, Johns was a German national who had arrived in Central Australia in 1929. He had worked briefly at Hermannsburg where another witness, Pastor Friedrich Wilhelm Albrecht, a Polish-born Lutheran missionary, had been based since 1926. Finally, Walter Smith was an experienced and respected bushman who knew the area and met Lasseter in Alice Springs just before the Expedition set out in July 1930. He told his story to Dick Kimber, a historian of Central Australia.

Witnesses: when

Between the events and the accounts there is a span of nearly half a century. Philip Taylor kept a diary throughout the expedition, which was destroyed in a fire near Ayers Rock on 8th November 1930. However, he began again from 25th November and that record was eventually given to the Mitchell library, but also included in Philipp Scherer's ***Camel Treks in the Outback***[21] in 1994, twelve years after Taylor had died. But Taylor left another and very specific record of issues aeronautical, which he wrote from the Expedition's base at Ilbilba on 6th January 1931. That report was to Colonel H.C. Brinsmead, the Director of Civil Aviation. Errol Coote wrote up his version soon after the expedition and it was first published as ***Hells Airport*** in 1934.[22] In the Mitchell Library, Paul Johns' unsigned account, ***Lasseter's Reef***[23] was probably written by Ernestine Hill but appeared, barely changed, under his name as articles in *The Sun*[24] in 1934 and *The Sydney Mail*[25] in 1935.

Three of the accounts date from the late 1940s. John Bailey's unpublished manuscript, *The History of Lasseter's Reef* was completed just before he died in September 1947.[26] That year John Blakiston-Houston donated his memoirs up to 1945, with a chapter on his involvement in the First CAGE Expedition, to the Liddell Hart Military Archives in London.[27] Expedition leader Fred Blakeley's version, ***Lasseter's Dream of Millions***, wasn't published until 1972, ten years after his death. The original drafts dated from 1936 and a version completed in late 1938[28] was submitted to Angus & Robertson but, with obvious challenges to the narrative of their bestseller, ***Lasseter's Last Ride***, it was declined. Blakeley continued to work on it and was assisted from the 1940s until his death by Mary Mansfield, who saw it to publication in 1972 – ironically by Angus & Robertson.[29] Blakeley's ambivalence about releasing his account is clear from the conditions he gave to the Mitchell Librarian, Phyllis Mander Jones, on 1st June 1948. As a result, his statement was placed in a *RESTRICTED* file and only removed in 1983: *Mr Blakeley gave me the following about Lasseter after I had undertaken not to make them available at present. Some of them are probably known from other sources but as given here they are not to be used while Lasseter's descendants might be injured by them or until 100 years have elapsed.*[30] The draft that eventually became ***Lasseter's Dream of Millions*** probably dates from the 1940s or '50s, not long after John Bailey's record. Both men were dead when Pastor Albrecht's recollections appeared as *On Lasseter's trail* in the ***Lutheran Almanac*** in 1964 (somewhat reprised in Adelaide's *Sunday Mail* three years later[31]), and Dick Kimber recorded Walter Smith's reminiscences of outback life in the Centre in the early 1980s. This appeared in 1986 as **Man from Arltunga: Walter Smith Australian Bushman**.

Witnesses: prejudice

Impartiality is impossible for those telling their own stories, and when responsibility, reparation and reputation are in play the key variable is the degree of self-interest bias. For three of these first-handers the conflicts are obvious; John Bailey set the wheels in motion for the CAGE Syndicate and Company and, as Chairman, didn't take sufficient account of information that was available from Western Australia while soliciting money from Sydney investors. That's just before the Expedition set out; more was to follow with privileged communications and unjustified delays that may have contributed to Lasseter's death. Errol Coote was a booster from the beginning, more for himself than the Syndicate. He was not a professional pilot, was unlicensed at the time the Expedition was mooted, crashed two of the aircraft and, like Bailey, had side-deals on the go. Both of these men, who were in the AWU offices when Lasseter first walked in, had a lot riding on how they would be viewed by investors and history. Although he wouldn't have been concerned at the prospect of disgruntled investors, Albert Paul Johns – supposed dingo hunter and cameleer – also had reasons for caution about how his account was told; he had undeclared side deals, was the last European to see Lasseter alive and took a letter from him to the authorities in Alice Springs stating that Johns had tried to kill him, and there were rumours that he had.

The other five are, arguably, less compromised. Fred Blakeley was asked by Bailey to make a judgement about Lasseter and his story of finding a reef. After interviewing Lasseter on a number of occasions Blakeley remained suspicious of his mining and bush skills but, despite that, of Lasseter's account of stumbling on the reef three decades earlier, Blakeley recorded: *There were a lot of gaps in it but I felt that there might be something in the yarn.*[32] On that basis his judgement might be questioned. But from early in the Expedition his suspicions of Lasseter's inexperience and dishonesty mounted, and it was Blakeley who finally made the decision to call the Expedition off predicting, correctly as it turned out, that the CAGE Directors would blame him for the Expedition's failure. With the exception of Lasseter, Philip Taylor was admired for his energy and professionalism by all the members of the First CAGE Expedition and was onstage longest, from the opening scene to the penultimate act as Bob Buck set off to find Lasseter's body. For Blakiston-Houston the Expedition was a bit of fun; he left before it all began to fall apart and was soon far away, the section on the Expedition in his memoirs clearly coming through as a digression from his main military story, the title, *Australia, Lasseter's Last Ride*. obviously from Idriess. The last two, Friedrich Albrecht and Walter Smith – pastor and bushman – would also appear to have no conflicts of interest in how they presented their recollections of their involvement, albeit both relatively peripheral to the main action and decades afterwards.

Witnesses: reputation

In terms of credibility and trustworthiness, the concerns that might be raised about Pastor Albrecht and Walter Smith are mainly the vicissitudes of memory over the passage of decades, particularly in relation to events about which there were many accounts and opinions in the public domain. Albrecht, for instance, seems to have confused some dates and conflated the First and Second CAGE Expeditions that were a year apart. But the relevant points he makes are not about chronology but key players – Albert Paul Johns, Errol Coote and Bob Buck. For Walter Smith, in addition to accuracy of recall across half a century between the events and his conversations with Dick Kimber, by comparison to Pastor Albrecht his background wasn't squeaky-clean. By his own admission, in his early life he'd been involved in cattle duffing that, while not uncommon among bushmen of the time, was crossing a boundary in more than one sense, and his brief contact with Lasseter could have been construed as colluding in a deception. But he had nothing to gain from those admissions and was widely regarded, as was Albrecht, as a man of integrity.

Of the six men directly involved, three would seem to pass the pub test. Blakiston-Houston had been Aide-de-Camp to the Governor General and his distinguished military career continued; he served in the next War as a commander of the Southern Rhodesia Armoured Car Regiment before being appointed to public office in Ireland. Taylor's reputation before and during the Expedition has not been questioned and he went on to a career in international aviation. And what about Fred Blakeley... There is no evidence to suggest, then or since, that he was anything other than an honest man, a hard worker and an experienced bushman. He made a difficult call and was correct in his assessment that there was no gold reef, which was ignored by the CAGE Directors. As news that Bob Buck had found Lasseter's body was reaching Sydney, they were already busy organising the Second CAGE Expedition to find the reef that they still believed Lasseter had relocated. Also, Blakeley's restrictions on the material that was lodged with the Mitchell Library suggests that he was concerned that he might cause distress to the family of the very person who had led him on what he felt was a wild goose chase. For Blakeley the potential for more harm took precedence over getting his side of the story out, even though he had provided an account to the CAGE Directors immediately on return from Central Australia – which was disappeared lest it spook investors. Instead, he set out to write the story of his 1908 bicycle odyssey which was released in 1938 as **Hard Liberty**. While Fred Blakeley was convinced that Lasseter did not die in the desert, a view not shared by many, his integrity is not in question as a reason to challenge his version of the Expedition.[33] The same can't be said for the last three – Bailey, Coote and Johns.

On 22nd May 1930 Fred's brother, Minister Arthur Blakeley, received a letter announcing: *There has now been formed in Sydney a Gold Exploration Syndicate for the purpose of despatching an expedition from Sydney by aeroplane and portion of the party by motor truck from Alice Springs.*[34] The sender was the newly-installed Secretary of the Syndicate, Ernest Bailey, son of its just-appointed Chairman, John Bailey. When Lasseter walked into the Australian Workers Union, John Bailey was about to turn sixty and it had been four decades since he left the shearing sheds to fight his way up the ranks of the Labor Party and union movement. Pugnacious, divisive and a wily manipulator behind the scenes, he was elected to the New South Wales parliament in 1920 but promptly ran into problems, the result of which was a clinging sobriquet – *Ballot-box*

Bailey, As presented at the 1924 New South Wales ALP Conference, the ALP Executive had determined:

> *That a number of ballot boxes, each with a sliding panel had been made just prior to the 1920 Sydney Selection Ballot. (Most of these are now in the possession of the ALP Executive.)*
>
> *That they were made for the obvious purpose of fraudulently manipulating ballots for selections in the Labor Movement. …*
>
> *That John Bailey, MLA, was one of the principals responsible for the obtaining and construction of these faked ballot boxes.*

Other issues were raised including *conduct in connection with the issue of the faked delegates' badges for use at the ALP Conference, and the use of forged blocks for printing AWU tickets.* And lest there be uncertainty about the person in question, the Chairperson of the committee formed to investigate the allegations, A.C. Willis, concluded: *We do not pretend to have given an exhaustive account of Mr Bailey's misdeeds, or to have fathomed the depths of his infamy … The cumulative effect of the evidence has forced the Committee to express in definite terms its opinion that Mr Bailey, MLA, is a menace not only to the Labor Movement, but also to the body politic.*[35]

Some of the allegations raised against Bailey went back decades. Challenges to the charges rolled on and included a libel win against Willis for some £4,500 in December 1929. But in 1923 Bailey had been expelled from the party and didn't contest the Federal seat of Goulburn in 1925. Regardless, he remained a New South Wales Labor player, and whether branch-stacking experience influenced the CAGE Syndicate structure, mates and relatives seem to have taken precedence over experience. He was an organiser rather than a planner and, despite his position as Chairman, seemed less concerned with considered caution than boosting the prospects for profits, including gung-ho, cavalier statements to the press that bit back. Just a couple of weeks after Minister Arthur Blakeley received Ernest Bailey's importuning missive, Reverend W. Morley, Honorary Secretary of the Association for the Protection of Native Races, wrote: *Dear Sir, On behalf of the above named Association I beg to direct your attention to a statement in the **Sydney Morning Herald** of July 8th to the effect that an exploring party is going to Central Australia seeking* *for gold, and that Mr J. Bailey of the A.W.U. is also reported to have said* "*THE PARTY WAS TAKING NO RISKS AND WAS ARMED TO THE TEETH*".[36]

The next day Minister Blakeley responded, reassuring Morley that his brother, Fred Blakeley: *has had a long experience among the natives in Central and Northern Australia* and would *see that none of his party will interfere in any way with the aborigines*.[37] But, despite being Expedition leader, Fred Blakeley had no control of the CAGE Company Chairperson. Bailey withheld important information from others, was probably responsible for suppressing Blakeley's report as leader on his return to Sydney lest it dampen investor enthusiasm, and later initiated a storm of correspondence to the Western Australian and Commonwealth Governments (ironically to Minister Arthur Blakeley) to shore up the proposed Second CAGE Expedition. Fortunately for the Baileys a benefactor stepped in and, although the Second CAGE Expedition came up as empty-handed as the First Expedition, they had been bitten by the gold bug, or saw what its fever could do to loosen purse strings. In late 1932 the CAGE Company unsuccessfully sought funds for a Third Expedition and just a couple of years later, with a new Federal Government in office, an inquiry was launched into the float of the Arnhem Gold Development Company which appeared to involve fraudulent claims and salting of samples that had been presented for assay by Bailey. An article in *The West Australian* reported that it was raised in parliament that the: *prime mover in the company … was a Mr. John Bailey, who was notorious by his association with the sliding panel ballot box scandals of 1923*.[38] Bailey's account - *The History of Lasseter's Reef* – was written two decades later, just before he died, and concluded: *I write these comments for the benefit of students to protect them from bounding publicity agents that have not a scintilla of truth in their publicity*. It might be thought that he had been motivated by honest reflection in the face of imminent mortality; not so – he fell off a ladder in Stanmore.

With John and Ernest Bailey in the AWU offices when Lasseter first presented himself was Errol Coote, a journalist with the *Daily Pictorial*. Coote was 32, city-born and well-educated enough to have made it to

Sydney University during the War. The photographs of him taken around the time of the First CAGE Expedition show a slim, dapper man in calf-high boots and flying outfit that suggest a distinguished military bearing. But while he had the kit and had been in the military, it had been far from distinguished. Coote enlisted in August 1917 and embarked for Europe in December. Two years later he signed a statutory declaration at sea on *H.M.T. Raranga* on his way back home:

> *I, Errol Hampton Coote of the Australian General Base Depot, late of the 2nd Infantry Battalion, Australian Imperial Force, do hereby solemnly and sincerely declare as follows: 1) On enlistment, I stated that my full name was ERROL COOTE, that I was born in Vancouver, British Columbia in the year 1895 and that my age was twenty one years, eleven months. 2) On enlistment, my correct particulars were:- My full name was ERROL HAMPTON COOTE; I was born in Sydney, New South Wales, Australia in the year 1898 and my age was eighteen years, eleven months.*[39]

It's not known why Coote began his military service with a lie, but it didn't get better. Most of his two years in uniform were spent in hospital, *the glasshouse*, or jail. He only made it to France two months after the cessation of hostilities, as part of a deal to spring him following a conviction for stealing a civilian motorcycle. Back in Sydney he took up journalism and flying, and in 1928 was awarded a pilot licence although he failed to maintain its currency. That caught up with him after he crafted an image of himself as an aeronautical expert for the CAGE Expedition. On 21st June 1930 Coote wrote to a real military man and aviator – H.C. Brinsmead. The Director of Civil Aviation, Brinsmead had seen action at Gallipoli and Pozières before joining the Australian Flying Corps where he supervised the Australian Training Wing. Whether Brinsmead was aware of Coote's less-than-distinguished service record is unclear, but the Director's was well known to Coote. Under the freshly minted header of the *Central Australian Gold Exploration Syndicate*, the letter begins *Dear Colonel*:

> *In writing this letter to you I am asking for your blessing in connection with an enterprise I am about to embark upon. I admit that I have*

sadly neglected the regulations governing flying inasmuch as I have not applied for a renewal of my flying license, at the proper time, but I have always kept up my flying nevertheless, when my newspaper duties would permit, with the result that I have now nearly 80 hours solo to my credit.

After acknowledging that he was *heavily financially interested in the above Syndicate* Coote rambled on, throwing in irrelevant technical and social teasers before mentioning that: *[the] Minister for Home Affairs, and several Federal members are members of the Syndicate.* Then, below a flamboyant signature affirmed in type as *Errol. H. Coote* – two afterthoughts:

P.S. A fellow named Burlington is trying to butt in on this expedition, but several Federal members have warned us that his presence will not only be a handicap, but will be resented. He says he is a competent aircraftman, mechanic, and flying man. Could you let us know if this is not. Anyhow he is NOT going with us.

P.P.S. You will remember me as a member of the "Pictorial" staff, and my work for aviation there, especially in regard to the "Southern Cross".[40]

Brinsmead probably also knew about Burlington who, as well as having been an accomplished pilot was far from trying to butt in – he was a foundation member of the CAGE Syndicate. And although he did not know it then, Brinsmead would be in correspondence about the CAGE Expedition for over a year and his first letter was prescient. Two days after Coote's unctuous appeal, Brinsmead wrote to A.E. (Texas) Green, the Minister for Defence and Member for Kalgoorlie, who had been involved early in the Lasseter saga.[41] Having noted the political connections of the Syndicate, which would also not have been news to Texas Green, Brinsmead observed:

My informant is a Mr. Coote – a journalist on the staff of the Sydney "Pictorial" – who desires to be pilot of the "Moth" accompanying the expedition. As far as I know he is not qualified to make a satisfactory job of it, and it is essential that only the most expert of pilots should, in in the interests of the Syndicate, be allowed by them to handle their aeroplane in that very inhospitable neighbourhood. Coote was issued with an "A" Licence (Private flying) in June 1928 – it expired in June 1929 and has not been renewed. He states, however, that he has done a considerable amount of flying since. If so, then it has been in contravention of Air Navigation Regulations.[42]

In the end maybe politics prevailed over prudence and Coote was in – Chairman of Transport – but was only dissuaded from buying a totally inappropriate air-racer for the mission by Charles Ulm. Ulm was a veteran aviator who had completed the first crossing of the Pacific with Charles Kingsford Smith in 1928. A highly skilled navigator, he was present at a public meeting to jolly-up investors when Lasseter, who claimed to have been trained as a surveyor, presented coordinates for the reef with the rider that, as his watch was found to be out by around an hour, the readings could not be relied on. Ulm pointed out that that would not affect latitude and that an hour difference in measurement of longitude would place the reef in the Indian Ocean – Ulm didn't invest. Regardless, he found a sturdier plane for Coote, which may have saved his life.

Coote crashed *Golden Quest* and was lucky to be cut out alive. He returned in *Golden Quest II,* concealed important information from the leader – Fred Blakeley – who ultimately had had enough of him and sent him off. But Coote was reinstated by the Directors after Blakeley pulled the plug on the Expedition. He headed back out, stopping at Hermannsburg where Pastor Albrecht recalled that Coote's: *supplies of provisions for such an undertaking were anything but adequate.*[43] Albrecht was sufficiently concerned that he arranged that if Coote didn't overfly them in a few days they would organise a search party. Just as well; with typical poor planning and another dodgy landing which damaged the propellor after running low on fuel, he was stranded at Ayers Rock – *Hell's Airport.*

Ten days later he was found by Phil Taylor who repaired the damaged propeller, and Coote flew back to Alice Springs. At Ilbilba two months later, on 6th January 1931, Taylor wrote his report that was sent to

Colonel Brinsmead – the same person who had received Coote's obsequious letter asking for his blessing six months earlier. By the time Brinsmead received Taylor's report Coote had been called to Sydney and fired by the Company Directors. But they weren't giving up on the reef – or aeroplanes – and *Golden Quest II* was flown back to Alice Springs by Leslie Pittendrigh with a mining engineer, S.J. Hamre, as a passenger. But the CAGE aeronautical misadventures were far from over and they didn't make it to Ilbilba. After a forced landing near Haasts Bluff the two men were stranded for nearly three weeks until a rescue mission involving three RAAF aircraft and led by Flight-lieutenant Charles Eaton. Pittendrigh and Hamre were still missing when Taylor wrote: *Owing to the loss of Capt. Pittendrigh's machine in this area, I think that a full report on the part played by aircraft during the Central Australian Gold Exploration's expedition into this country may be of interest to your Dept.* What follows starts with a guarded endorsement of Coote as a pilot but moves quickly to questioning his judgement. Having jury-rigged a repair for the damaged propellor at Ayers Rock, Taylor noted in his report: *I entered in the log book that the prop. and petroflex were good for the return flight to civilisation and were NOT to be used beyond Alice Springs.* True to form, Coote ignored Taylor's warning and set out to fly to Adelaide. He may have avoided a third crash by being turned back soon after take-off because of engine problems.

Coote wasn't finished with Lasseter's Reef and was involved in a second air expedition in 1932 from Western Australia – which also brought up nothing. **Hell's Airport** was first published in 1934, three decades before Fred Blakeley's **Lasseter's Dream of Millions** was released. Blakeley's criticisms stirred Coote to revise his book but he died just a year later, in 1973. Completing that task fell to his *friend and business partner,* George Austin Stapleton, who republished it in 1981 along with a *companion book* – **Lasseter Did Not Lie!** – the need for which *stems from certain claims and statements contained in the posthumously published* **Dream Millions**.[44] In his reprint of **Hell's Airport** Stapleton retained the Foreword of a real aviator – Charles Kingsford Smith – but seems to have missed that when Smithy shifted from discussing aviation in remote and challenging environments, to mentioning Coote, he was choosing his words carefully:

An airman and a journalist, Lasseter's story was irresistible to him and he readily forsook the 'inky way' to soar forth into the unknown in search of the allegedly fabulously wealthy reef in the heart of the Continent. Stalked by tragedy, marooned and starved at Ayer's Rock in the heart of the desert, and dragged bleeding and battered from the wreck of a 'plane 200 miles from Alice Springs, he is still anxious to go out again to search for that thin gold line of reef. I do not necessarily agree with all of Errol Coote's somewhat trenchant criticisms, but it is hard for one who has not actually been on the spot to form an accurate judgement.

And finally there is Albert Paul Johns. Explaining that he was bounty-hunting dingos, Johns – *the dogger* – arrived at Ilbilba with two Aboriginal men from Hermannsburg on 31st August. This account begins: *A small camel team slowly making its way towards a waterhole in the Ehrenberg Ranges, the sinking sun throwing long shadows ahead of us making each step of the camel swing fifty feet ahead and swiftly back to the soft scrunch in the sand, the bodies of the beasts swaying, and the loadings creaking in rhythm with the moving shadows.* The lyrical style is Ernestine Hill not a German *dogger* but, even so, in what was published under his name, he was supposedly prospecting for gold near Lake MacDonald when lack of water forced him to head to Ilbilba. As they were getting close:

> *one of my boys pointed excitedly to the smoke of camp fires in the distance. "White fella longa kwatja!" – White man's fires at Ilbilba. I thought it absurd for we were three hundred miles out in the Never Never and the chances of meeting a white man were very remote. Kosumai insisted, however, and towards evening, on approaching the fires, were not only five white men engaged in the task of preparing a camp but a motor-lorry, and more amazing still, an aeroplane. So I met the ill-fated Lasseter expedition, the tragedy of which is not widely known, and the facts uncertain.*[45]

Johns agreed to remain close by Ilbilba while the Expedition set out on a final push south four days later. He reappeared soon after its return and on the 13th September 1930 a hand-written contract was drawn up. Witnessed by *LHB Lasseter* and *G Sutherland,* the parties signing off on this contract were *Fredrick Blakeley as leader of the expedition here*, representing the CAGE Company, and *Paul Johns, of the Hermannsburg Mission, Central Australia, on the other part.* The contract stipulated that: *Wherein the said Paul Johns agrees to place himself and team of five camels at the disposal of the said company for the period of two calendar months from date hereof and to work with and under the direction of Harry B Lasseter during the currency of this agreement for the sum of five pounds a week.*[46] Johns became an official member of the CAGE Expedition, albeit soon thinned out when Lasseter and Johns with five camels left Ilbilba to continue the Company's work while Blakeley and the rest of the Expedition team packed up and headed back to Alice Springs.

But this was no chance meeting *three hundred miles out in the Never Never.* Johns had been in the region for more than a year and Pastor Albrecht recalled their first meeting in 1929: *Whilst walking the streets of Alice Springs a young man approached us, asking whether we were connected with the Mission and if a job was available for him.* There was, but it didn't last long: *we had to terminate his agreement after less than twelve months, when he returned to Alice Springs.* Billy Marshall-Stoneking, who half a century later interviewed some of the Aboriginal men who were alive at the time of the Expedition explained that: *the missionaries had caught him making amoral advances toward some of the younger Aboriginal women and had chucked him out.*[47]

Johns didn't go far and in early 1930 was at Ilbilba with Bob Buck setting up the landing strip for the second Mackay Aerial Survey expedition.[48] And in July, while the First CAGE Expedition was making final preparations in Alice Springs to head to Ilbilba, he was in Alice Springs. Years later Walter Smith related to Dick Kimber:

> *Lasseter went on one of his solitary walks. He met Walter, swore him to secrecy and began talking. Walter got Lasseter to agree that Frank Sprigg be told of the discussion then, after talking with Frank, another secret meeting was held. Lasseter's initial concern was to obtain some*

gentle riding camels. He had already contacted a dogger, Paul Johns, who had his own small string of camels, but some more gentle riding camels were needed, and also some cash for supplies. Lasseter would ensure that part of the fabulous reef was pegged in the name of Walter Smith and Frank Sprigg if they provided the necessary assistance.[49]

Not long afterwards Johns was back in Hermannsburg – as Pastor Albrecht recalled: *In the winter of 1930 this same young man returned to the Mission in search of camels for hire or purchase.* According to Albrecht *the cameleer* gave information about a *Gold Exploration Company*, newly formed in Sydney, which was heading in an: *eight-wheel Thornycroft truck to Ilbilla in the Ehrenberg Ranges, thence across desert country to the Peterman ranges. ... "They can't do that." The young man argued, "as from Ilbilla they will need camels. I am going out there to meet the expedition, so that when they are stuck, they will hire me." And this is exactly what happened.*[50]

On 6th October 1930, just a few months later, Albrecht himself visited Ilbilba where a local Aboriginal man, Kamutu, showed him the supply depot set up before Lasseter and Johns set out: *"This is the property of Das Lasseter. Unless you are in want, don't touch it, as I depend on these supplies on my return from the Peterman Ranges. (Signed) Das Lasseter."* But not long after, at the end of October, Johns again arrived at Hermannsburg with a firearm he told Albrecht he had taken from Lasseter after a fight, and with letters from Lasseter that he had opened. One was to the authorities in Alice Springs describing that confrontation and recommending that: *his camelman be locked up for having threatened him with a firearm.* Johns proceeded to Alice Springs, arriving on 13th November where he showed the letter to Errol Coote – recently appointed leader of the rump Expedition. According to Coote: *its contents were surprising to say the least. Lasseter claimed he had found his reef, but it was not 'quite as rich as I thought it was'. He also reported the revolver incident. Then he told how he had pegged six leases on the reef, and wanted fresh camels and supplies.*[51] It was all on again and Coote and Johns were in the thick of it. But not for long, Coote was soon in

Sydney and dismissed as pilot, and while Johns remained involved in mopping up for a few months, it ended where it began, at Hermannsburg. Phil Taylor entered in his diary on 17th February 1931, that he: *had some conversation with Rev. Albrecht concerning Johns, and appear to have given him proofs of which he was not sure,* and for the next day recorded:

> *Johns was given twelve hours to get off the Mission ground this morning and owning to this and other reasons I have dismissed him; I have obtained from him all the information relative to Lasseter's location, and Buck should have no trouble finding him. I hear tonight that the natives are sleeping with their spears alongside in case he should return during the night. Also that in A.S. it is said that Johns has murdered Lasseter, this from an Afghan at the Mission. Mr. Heinrich tells me that Johns has threatened to shoot him also, this during a row at the Mission. Johns left this evening.*[52]

Trouble marked John's sojourn in Central Australia but was also his companion before and after. Born in Diesdorf in 1906, two decades later he stowed away on the SS *Viola* from Hamburg to London but, being refused entry, somehow gained passage to Australia on the SS *Halle*, arriving at Port Adelaide on 13th July 1926. The next few years were spent in South Australia where he sought but was refused naturalisation in 1929. Carl von Czarnecki, who spent time with Johns in Clare, recalled four decades later: *we knew Paul's ways pretty well. Paul could do anything like that out of spite. He was pretty resourceful and could tell fantastic lies. He was also, incidentally, an expert pickpocket, and could pick any lock. ... He had a terrific nerve. And what he didn't know, he made up. He also had a real Omar Khayyam philosophy, which may be interpreted in the words: Gather ye rose-buds while ye may.*[53] Although Johns left for *the outback,* they met again in Alice Springs and worked together at Hermannsburg and with Bob Buck setting up the strip for the Mackay Aerial expedition base at Ilbilba. They separated before Johns set off to meet the First CAGE Expedition and von Czarnecki's only other contact, several years later, involved Johns defrauding him of £15. In the meantime Johns had worked around Alice Springs and reapplied for naturalisation in September 1932, the letter for police clearance being sent by H.E. Jones, the Director of the Attorney-General's Department in Adelaide. V.G Carrington, the Government Resident and the person who would have received Lasseter's letters delivered by Johns two years earlier, forwarded the application which was eventually successful with naturalisation granted on 16th February 1933.

Whatever his beliefs about Lasseter and the reef, Johns remained in the game. In 1936 Sydney businessman Mark Foy was in furious correspondence regarding his own plans to prospect south of Lake Christopher, and on 16th March wrote to J.A. Carrodus at the Department of the Interior, noting: *I have my agent Paul Johns in Alice Springs now arranging for thirty Camels in charge of Old Bob Buck.*[54] Later that year Johns headed south and Kurt Gerhardt Johannsen, legendary bush mechanic who had spent part of his youth at Hermannsburg and who is credited with developing the first road train, travelled with him for a while. In his collated memoirs – **A Son of the Red Centre**[55] – Johannsen describes Johns' questionable activities on that journey in 1936, the year after which Johns was arrested in Brisbane and sentenced to six months in jail for car theft, following which he was deported. During the War he reapplied for entry to Australia – which was refused – the key issues of the intervening years captured in a letter from Major General V.G.W. Kell in London to Colonel H.E. Jones in Canberra – the same person who had sought information about him in 1932 in relation to his successful application for naturalisation. Johns had been reported by intelligence services to have been in Berlin in 1938 where he attended a *Nazi Instruction School* and to be *an active member of the German Secret Service*, Kell's letter continuing:

> He has apparently boasted of successful sabotage there, which he performed with the help of six members of the British Union of Fascists (Sir Oswald Mosley, who has since been arrested by the British authorities), who were engaged in some A.R.P. group. Johns stated that when he entered the Dolphin Square A.R.P. there were only two Mosley men but he enrolled four more. He is

believed to have stated that he joined the Mosley party shortly after his arrival in London because that gave him the best opportunities for finding conscious or unconscious – but active anyway – support for his activities in the interest of Hitler. ... I may add that most of the information was obtained from JOHNS himself by his fellow workers. It is of course possible that he was merely boasting and wished to appear as a more important and dangerous person than he actually is.[56]

Maybe Kell was right – Johns was just trying to *appear as a more important and dangerous person than he actually is.* A decade earlier Johns was swaggering about Central Australia and Blakeley recalled their second meeting, returning to Ilbilba after calling a halt to the Expedition: *Nobody heard him come and the first we knew of him was a sharp command to put up our hands while he played with a revolver. It lasted only a second and was his idea of humour but I gave him a piece of my mind that was not music to his ears.*[57] Johns was interned in England and remained there after the War and refusal of his application to return to Australia. He married locally and saw out his working life selling antiques in Kent.

Bailey, Coote and Johns – they are the only informants for particular parts of the story. But they were flawed characters whose self-interest was played out through scheming, silences and, ultimately, selective projection of blame on others. Bailey blamed Blakeley and, later, Coote, and took no responsibility for the disaster he had, himself, set in motion. Coote blamed Blakeley as well, but also Taylor, and framed his involvement around a triumph of the spirit and technology rather than acknowledging an aeronautical fiasco. And as for Johns, while he didn't say as much to Coote when they met up in Alice Springs in November, he called the air chaos for what it was, but was silent about his meeting with Lasseter in Alice Springs in July – and their conflict three months later that led to their separation. Witnesses – yes; reliable witnesses – no. So, what did happen…

John Bailey - CAGE Chairman.

Errol Coote - Pilot.

Fred Blakeley - Expedition Leader.

Paul Johns - The 'dogger'.

Phil Taylor - Engineer.

John Blakiston-Houston - 'Explorer'.

CHAPTER 3

The Expedition

For something that never existed it's amazing the volume of written material published on Lasseter's Reef. Most of it purely speculative as there is no reef to assay and no genuine map shows its location. But this persistent myth did have sound beginnings ... for a myth, in National Archives file 1930/512, usually referred to as the Gepp Report.

Robert Ross, Lasseteria.com.[58]

It is now known that in the late 1920s Lasseter was struggling financially but had lots of ideas. When those that spawned the First CAGE Expedition coalesced into a proposal is unknowable, but the paper trail goes back to October 1929 and a letter to Texas Green, Member for Kalgoorlie and Minister for Defence in the Scullin Government, which eventually resulted in what is now known as the *Gepp Report*.[59] Idriess didn't know about that when he was writing the first draft of **Lasseter's Last Ride** eighteen months later. For him and most of those directly involved who left accounts, there is a later starting point – when Lasseter first arrived at John Bailey's Sydney office.[60]

According to Bailey, Lasseter was unexpected, and it was probably the end of March or the beginning of April 1930, although Bailey recorded it as some time in 1929 in a 1936 *Daily Telegraph* article, and June 1930 in his 1947 documentation for the Mitchell Library. With him were several others including his son, Ernest, Errol Coote (according to Coote, not mentioned by Bailey) and Jack Jenkins, a union mate of Bailey's with mining experience. Lasseter claimed to have stumbled on a fabulous gold deposit in a quartz reef outcrop in the centre of the continent in 1897. He'd been working on coastal shipping, he said, and had come ashore in Cairns, deciding to head to Alice Springs because he'd heard about a ruby find which, when he got there, turned out to be garnets.[61] He continued west and, lost and with his horses dead, stumbled on the reef, which he estimated extended for nearly ten miles somewhere near the border with Western Australia. Despite his condition he collected nuggets, tried to identify landmarks and staggered on, eventually collapsing. Fortunately, he was found by an Afghan cameleer and taken to a camp where he met a surveyor, Harding, with whom he travelled to Carnarvon then on to the Western Australian goldfields where they worked for several years until they set out from Carnarvon with camels to relocate the reef. That they did, returning with samples that were later assayed at three ounces to the ton. With Harding a surveyor and Lasseter claiming to be similarly qualified, they had taken bearings but, back at the coast, they realised that their watches were more than an hour out. Lasseter told those in Bailey's office that, while he knew that rendered the coordinates useless, he was confident that he could use landmarks to locate the reef that he had found twice. He went on to explain that he and Harding tried to raise capital in London but were unsuccessful. Eventually Harding died and Lasseter's life took him elsewhere until, decades later and with the Depression gripping, he arrived at Bailey's office.

As the story was being told, back-of-envelope calculations by Jack Jenkins suggested staggering riches. Soon after, John Bailey wrote to the Minister for Home Affairs, Arthur Blakeley, who was already aware of the *Gepp Report*, with a suggestion: *I have been wondering if it would be possible to get your brother Fred to go with this chap. For years Fred has had an idea of prospecting in this part of the Territory and I think he would be just the man for the job.* Four days later, on 7th April, Minister Blakeley wrote to his brother, Fred:

Herewith enclosed please find a letter which I have received from Jack Bailey, together with one from a Mr Lassiter, [sic] which is self explanatory. Do you feel like taking on a jaunt into Central Australia? On approved cases we make sums available for prospecting and if you care to take it on I would be pleased to give the application sympathetic consideration. I will be in Sydney on the 12th and will call on Mother and yourself. With kind regards, I remain, your loving brother, Arthur Blakeley.[62]

Whether Bailey's intent was to draw on field experience or fraternal connections, Fred Blakeley had prospecting and bush skills, and was tasked to make a judgement about the credibility of Lasseter's story. They met on four occasions, Blakeley ultimately judging that the claims couldn't be dismissed despite obvious *gaps* that Lasseter covered by responding to Blakeley's probing with: *"If I told you that, you'd know as much as I do, and you wouldn't want me."* Blakeley reported back and the decision was made to find funding. In late April the Central Australian Gold Exploration Syndicate was set up with John Bailey as its Chairman, his son, Ernest, as the Secretary, and Errol Coote as the pilot. Shares were offered and funds started flowing in; and more than money – a special bush-bashing, six-wheeled truck was provided by the Thornycroft Company, support to get to Alice Springs from the New South Wales and Commonwealth governments, and other contributions in kind.

The Expedition was touted as high-tech and an appropriate aircraft was identified for Coote by Charles Ulm, who remained sceptical about Lasseter's story. He was not the only one, as emerged in correspondence between the Commonwealth and Western Australian Governments, including questions about the elusive Harding and doubts about the reef's supposed location being auriferous – the region in question was, for the time, reasonably well covered ground. The CAGE Syndicate leaders weren't without their own concerns about the unrelentingly evasive Lasseter, who agreed to deposit instructions as to how to find the reef in the Bank of Australasia in Martin Place. One set, for unfathomable reasons, was written in invisible ink, the envelope to remain unopened until his return or death, with instructions reading:

> *This envelope, with contents under seal, is only to be delivered to persons presenting an authority from me and signed as shown on the margin hereof. It contains a record which is as near as possible correct having regard to the unreliable nature of the scientific instruments used of a rich gold bearing reef known to exist in the interior of Australia. Prominent landmarks are described, and cross-bearings given and some Compass bearings undertaken by a compass which varied 27°E at Carnarvon in 1897 (signed) L.H.B. Lasseter* [63]

Regardless of the doubters and despite requests for Government financial support being declined, £5,000 was raised publicly. The spin machine was in overdrive and Lasseter was playing – or overplaying – his part. A leader in the *Forbes Advocate* from July read *GOLD REEF – Expedition to Central Australia – Lasseter the Leader*, the article starting: *A little man stepped out of the pages of Peter B Kyne into the "Post" office yesterday. He was Lewis Harold Bell Lasseter, leader of the expedition to Central Australia to rediscover a rich gold reef, said to be ten miles in length.* [64]

In short order the Expedition team was in place with, as Blakeley recorded: *myself as leader, Harry Lasseter as guide, George Sutherland, prospector and miner, Philip Taylor, engineer and driver, Errol Coote as pilot of the plane, and Captain Blakiston-Houston who was given the title of explorer.* Lasseter – *as guide* – received £10 a week with a £500 insurance policy on his life. Blakiston-Houston observed that: *Errol Coote, the pilot, was also a journalist and began selling the copyright of the story in advance.* The Englishman was also quick to identify planning problems: *None of them knew much about organising such an expedition. They had taken no steps to procure such maps as existed.* [65] Not quite; on 1st June 1930 Lasseter wrote to the Department of Home and Territories requesting information about the *reliability or otherwise of maps of Central Australia issued by Captain Kendrick* and making note of *the official map issued to me last January by your Dept.* [66] The letter in response, denying any knowledge of a *Captain Kendrick*, came from Assistant Secretary F.J. Quinlan who, four months before, wrote on behalf of Minister Arthur Blakeley that

The First CAGE
Expedition: (l – r)
Coote, Sutherland,
Blakiston-Houston,
Blakeley, Taylor;
(seated front)
Lasseter.

Packing the
Thornycroft:
Lasseter, with
head down,
with Blakeley,
Sutherland and
Coote watching
on.

Slow
Progress:
the
Thornycroft
and
Colson's
Chevrolet,
Sunrise.

Lasseter's applications for support from the Commonwealth had been rejected.

For Blakiston-Houston, maps were only one sign of slapdash preparation, which may have been because the pressure was on. With good reason – there were other players on the horizon. On 6th July Michael Terry, an experienced prospector and bushman who had been signed on as leader of the Endeavour prospecting party the day before, left Adelaide for Alice Springs, arriving on the 10th and was promptly *en route* to the Petermanns. By contrast, the CAGE team was struggling just getting to Alice Springs. But by 21st July, two weeks behind schedule, they were there, the Thornycroft by rail and Coote by air in *Golden Quest*. Once they had all arrived there was frenetic activity organising the six tons of supplies and fuel that would be needed. Blakeley soon realised that the Thornycroft, which was carrying petrol for the aeroplane, was ferociously thirsty, requiring another vehicle to transport fuel for the Thornycroft. A Chevrolet truck (nicknamed *Sunrise*) belonging to a respected mechanic with extensive experience in Central Australia – Fred Colson[67] – was sourced, and Colson hired to drive a third vehicle, his Chevrolet sedan. Colson's inclusion was over the objections of Lasseter, ostensibly because he wasn't a member of the Company, but probably because he knew the region well – too well for Lasseter. The high-tech Expedition was ready to roll – three vehicles and an aeroplane. Not a camel in sight.

During their stay in Alice Springs more concerns about Lasseter's story were expressed by locals who questioned his description of the settlement he had supposedly visited three decades earlier, and statements that were judged inconsistent with someone claiming the skills to have crossed the continent. It was a claim not lost on Blakiston-Houston who noted that, if true: *he was thus the first explorer to cross the continent from east to west.* Denied or rationalised, those observations didn't slow the momentum and on 24th July they set off but didn't get far – the Thornycroft bogged in the Charles River just out of town. It set the tone for the rest of the Expedition – slow, interrupted, lots of digging and repairing punctures, cheerful cooperation in overcoming problems giving way to irritation and squabbling as the weeks progressed. Heading west, on 25th

July they stopped at Redbank Station in the MacDonnell ranges where Archie Giles, whom Blakeley had met during his 1908 bicycle adventure, released one of his workers, Micky, to go with the Expedition as an Aboriginal guide. By increments they continued on to Oonah Springs, then Dashwood Creek and to Haasts Bluff at the end of July, Blakeley's alarm mounting with increasing evidence of Lasseter's lack of bush-craft, his odd behaviour commented on by Blakiston-Houston: *Lassiter [sic] appeared to be most suspicious of all of us and each night locked himself with all the firearms into the cab of the Thorneycroft [sic] to sleep, while we slept under the stars. ... We had begun to look upon him as a braggard and a bit of a liar.*[68]

Around that time they found that the state of the art radio which was to provide real-time connection with the world, and for which Lasseter had been trained, was missing a component and could only receive. This only added to the deteriorating relationship between Lasseter and Blakeley – whom he thereafter called *The Leader* – and between Lasseter and the others. Blakeley described having to take members of the team aside to head off confrontations: *I appealed to him to stop the slinging-off and try to behave as a grown-up man should. I said, "Try the other stunt and agree and say 'that's right', even if you don't agree. You can see that Harry is half-mad, and for the peace of the party try to fall in with the others."*

On 1st August Colson's truck stripped the differential attempting to negotiate the banks of Yaiyai Creek and camp was made. It was decided to prepare a bush airstrip there while Colson returned in his sedan to Alice Springs with Coote to pick up replacement parts for the truck and fly back to Yaiyai Creek. With them went Blakiston-Houston, whose time with the expedition was at an end – but not before a showdown over Lasseter's refusal to relinquish a navigation book lent by Blakiston-Houston. This was only resolved after Lasseter threatened not to go on, thus effectively aborting the Expedition, by Blakeley promising that he would make sure it was returned. On 3rd August *Golden Quest* arrived at Yaiyai Creek without incident, but there was a near miss on a landing the next day.

The aeroplane was left securely tied down at Yaiyai Creek while the Expedition continued in the Thornycroft and *Sunrise* to Mount Liebig and Mount Udor, arriving on 7th August at the strip built earlier in 1930 at Ilbilba in the Ehrenburg Range for the Mackay Aerial Survey expedition, which was the base for the rest of the First CAGE Expedition. By then Michael Terry with the Endeavour expedition had already arrived at the Petermanns. Once it was clear that the strip would suit, Colson drove Coote back to Yaiyai Creek to fly *Golden Quest* to Ilbilba. It didn't go well and on 9th August *Golden Quest* crashed on takeoff. Coote's life was saved by Colson who dragged him from the shattered plane and drove, overnight, to the hospital in Alice Springs. When no plane arrived, Blakeley, Sutherland and Taylor left Lasseter and Micky at Ilbilba and drove back to Yaiyai Creek, finding a note on the wreckage, the chaos of the moment probably explaining Fred Colson's confusion of Errol and Harrold: *Harrold badly shaken. I think fractured ribs. Will travel all night to Alice Springs for medical attention. Will return as quick as possible wait here until I return. Harrold said load plane & take to camp & repair but use your own discretion. Yours in Haste, Fred H Colson. ps Harrold not seriously hurt a miraculous escape.*[69]

While waiting for Colson to return, Blakeley wrote reports for the CAGE Directors begging *the Sydney crowd not to send another plane.* When Colson arrived he delivered letters from Sydney, and one from Coote in the Australian Inland Mission hospital in Alice Springs asking Blakeley to send a message to the Directors requesting another aircraft. Coote must not have been too incapacitated because also included was *Letter No. 2. (Confidential)*:

> *Dear Fred, While in hospital I obtained one of the latest Common-wealth Govt. maps & studied it very carefully with the result that I think I have located the whereabouts of Lasseter's reef & have marked it with a red circle. Now don't tell Lasseter this but just ask him if this is the right location. Tell him to be straight & not beat around the bush just to be cantankerous. Time is precious & if he starts his mamby pamby tricks just to be different from the map we will lose the reef. ALSO KEEP THIS UNDER YOUR HAT.*[70]

As a strategic afterthought Coote added: *Your brother is due here in a few days so I will be able to see him personally. I will tell him all is well.* Blakeley was probably unimpressed by both Coote's scheming and syco-phantic style, and certainly wasn't responsive to the call for more aircraft; he amended the reports he had already prepared to state the opposite and wrote specifically to Coote that he wanted camels not aircraft.

Colson headed back to Alice Springs, the remains of *Golden Quest* on the tray of his truck, and the others returned to Ilbilba. By then almost everything mechanical was failing and held together with jury-rigged solutions – the windows on the Thornycroft were gone, rough-cut branches tied across where the windscreen had been to shield the driver, boughs across the radiator for protection and to bash through mulga, mudguards removed for ground visibility, tyres more patch than original. When they finally arrived at Ilbilba they had their first close encounters with local Aboriginal tribes. They knew from early in the expedition that they were being watched and their progress communicated through smoke signals.[71] On 18th August, just as they were about to leave their Ilbilba base, they met a small family group including a man wearing only an old felt hat who, in **Lasseter's Last Ride**, George Sutherland christened *Rip Van Winkle* and who features, with photographs, in the book. Their progress from Ilbilba was agonisingly slow but eventually, on 24th August, they arrived at Mt Marjory (now Mt Leisler) in the Kintore Range. From Lasseter's original pronouncements and the Expedition's planning, this was close to where they expected to locate the reef.

Mt Marjory seems to have been a turning point but not quite the last straw for Blakeley, who on the second attempt made it to the summit with Lasseter. With the salt bed of Lake MacDonald in the foreground and the Petermann Ranges beyond the horizon. Lasseter applied himself to *his instruments*, followed up with *calculations*, and then pronounced to Blakeley that: *"I'm damned, if these figures are not the same as those left sealed in the vault of the bank in Sydney"*. Blakeley was confused and more so when Lasseter added that because his and Harding's watches had been out by more than an hour three decades earlier: *"I want to get a hundred and fifty miles further south"*. Blakeley didn't believe him and wasn't keen to head into country far from where Lasseter's original

Sutherland,
Blakeley and
Colson with
wreckage of
Golden Quest
at Yaiyai
Creek.

Rest stop:
Blakiston-Houston
and Mickey.

Spruiking the Second
Expedition: *On the
second page Bridge
is shown standing with
Bob Buck and John Bailey.*

*Three men connected with the Central Australia gold quest. Left to right: Mr. Bob
Buck, who is leading the Expedition; Mr. John Bailey, President of the Company;
Mr. Leslie G. Bridge, who organised the Expedition.
—Photo by courtesy Sydney "Sunday Guardian."*

story indicated. But he was in a bind, he knew that if he called the Expedition off he would be held responsible for its failure. Blakeley challenged Lasseter who, he recalled, played his standard, divisive, card:

He replied, "I have known for some time that you have doubted my story but I want you to play me fair. I have no complaints up to date of our treatment. We have had our differences and some exchanges, but you are like myself, quick to forget, and I beg of you not to go into a lengthy statement of my story. I do admit some things were said to mislead you. Why I did that was because another member of the party made me suspicious so I told little bits to mislead you, and I want you to trust me a little bit longer."

They returned to Ilbilba, Blakeley accumulating more reasons to doubt Lasseter. Rip Van Winkle and his family were still there. It was late August and while waiting for Fred Colson to return from Alice Springs they prepared to follow Lasseter's latest directions, which Blakeley agreed to in order to demonstrate that he had taken the Expedition as far as possible. Over the next days two important events occurred. The first, on 28th August, was that Blakeley noticed that Lasseter's trunk, which was usually securely locked, wasn't:

During the day I did the meanest thing I have ever done in my life – I opened Harry's tin trunk and went through all his papers, also the box with some gold specimens. I think there were seven stones in it all showing gold freely. I got out Phil's breast-drill and bored a hole in each and filled the hole up with white metal, concealing the hole with glue. I did this so that if ever the stones turned up again I could identify them.[72]

The following day Blakeley decided that they should retrace their steps to find Fred Colson who had not arrived back at Ilbilba. They got as far as Derwent Creek where, on 29th August, they met Colson heading the other way. The news he brought wasn't good; he'd been informed from Sydney that he was no longer needed. After letting the authorities know that he was going to return to the Expedition regardless, he did, also bringing a letter from Coote informing Blakeley that another aircraft – *Golden Quest II* – would fly to Ilbilba in a few days. Information having been exchanged, on 30th August Colson returned to Alice Springs, dropping off Micky on the way, and the Thornycroft was on the trail to Ilbilba – again.

On 31st August, soon after they arrived at Ilbilba, Rip Van Winkle and his family departed just as a new group of sandhill people appeared near the camp. On that day the second important event occurred – the first appearance of Albert Paul Johns, who emerged from the bush with camels and two Aboriginal men. Johns explained that they were after dingo scalps and that he had worked with Bob Buck preparing the strip for the Mackay expedition. There was no mention of meeting Lasseter in Alice Springs or having set out from Hermannsburg intent on finding the Expedition. Unaware of the collusion, over the next two days Blakeley opened up to Sutherland and Taylor about his suspicions of Lasseter: *I told George and Phil that was what I thought had happened to Lasseter. He had told his yarn so many times that he had come to believe it himself.* Then, on 2nd September, *Golden Quest II* arrived, piloted by Oliver Blythe (Pat) Hall with the still-recovering Coote on board. The next day Pat Hall flew Lasseter on a two-hour flight south in search of supposed landmarks, and then another flight with Taylor to scout the terrain for the Thornycroft.[73] Wanting to know whether Lasseter had recognised any features from his journeys three decades earlier, Coote quizzed him in confidence, Lasseter responding that he had: *and what's more I saw the reef, it's there as plain as a pike staff. We flew at only about 30 feet when we were near it. It is in the heart of mulga and timber country.*[74]

Coote had already sought Blakeley's confidence in an attempt to have the *cantankerous* Lasseter confirm the pilot's theory about the location of the reef. Now he was in cahoots with Lasseter to keep the new information from Blakeley. When Coote and Hall departed for Alice Springs on 4th September they carried with them reports from Blakeley and, unbeknownst to him and against his instructions that he should see all correspondence with the CAGE Directors, a message from Lasseter that the Directors should be wired and informed that he had located the reef. Within an hour of the departure of *Golden Quest II,* the Thornycroft was on the move as well, Johns agreeing to remain close to Ilbilba. Slowly climbing over the next three days, on 6th September they confronted: *the strangest sight of tumbled, tangled country. I knew when I looked over that we had come to the big breakaway, and knew that the truck would never look over into the valley.* Blakeley challenged Lasseter and pointed out that they were in the place Lasseter had indicated at Mount Marjory, that this was hundreds of miles south of where Lasseter's first descriptions in Sydney indicated, that the country further south had been visited by numerous prospecting expeditions, that the Petermann Ranges, where Lasseter now told Blakeley his *instinct* directed him, were across perilous country as the hot season was closing in – and that to get there would require a 500 mile detour. They were turning back, and Blakeley made it plain that the only remaining option Lasseter had – to save face rather than find the reef Blakeley no longer believed existed – was for Lasseter to go on from Ilbilba with Johns and his camels.

On 13th September, two days after they made it back to Ilbilba, Johns reappeared and a handwritten contract was signed,[75] a store dump prepared, and on the 15th Johns and Lasseter set off, without the two Aboriginal men who chose to return to Hermannsburg mission. The next day they ran into Fred Colson transporting more fuel for the Thornycroft who, at Ilbilba on 17th, told Blakeley that Lasseter had sent a message to the Directors via Coote that he had seen the reef from the air. That didn't shift Blakeley's opinion of Lasseter or the reef. On Sunday 28th September – some ten weeks after it had bogged on the way out of town, the battered, bush-bashing Thornycroft struggled back into Alice Springs. Blakeley arrived to discover that he had been relieved of the leadership of the Expedition in favour of Coote, who had just returned from Adelaide in *Golden Quest II*, now fitted with longer-range tanks. Coote soon set off for Hermannsburg and on to Ayers Rock where he planned to meet up with Taylor. Instead, he ended up stranded there from 28th October after the propeller damaged on landing. When he and Taylor finally connected on 6th November, Taylor jury-rigged a solution for the propeller and Coote returned to Alice Springs two days later, just in time for the Government Resident, Carrington, to rescind an order for the dispatch of two RAAF rescue planes from Melbourne to find him, piloted by Eaton and Durant. Just over a month later they were heading back to find the re-stranded CAGE aircraft. Coote was in Alice Springs when Paul Johns arrived on 13th November, approximately two months after he and Lasseter had set out from Ilbilba. In due course a new propeller arrived for *Golden Quest II*, but Coote was instructed by the Directors to fly to Sydney where he arrived on 20th November.

Despite being a founding shareholder of the CAGE Syndicate the Directors had had enough of Coote and replaced him with another pilot, Leslie Pittendrigh. There was still plenty of optimism about finding the reef and Pittendrigh was ordered to return to Alice Springs with a mining engineer, S.J. Hamre, who was also a founding member of the CAGE Syndicate, and then on to Ilbilba where Phil Taylor and Paul Johns had been tasked to transport more fuel and supplies by camel. Taylor and Johns duly left for Ilbilba on 27th November but, battling heavy storms, *Golden Quest II* only arrived at Alice Springs on 15th December. When Pittendrigh and Hamre finally set out for Ilbilba five days later they overflew it but landed safely near Haasts Bluff after running out of fuel. Stranded, they walked to Dashwood Creek where they found water and bunkered down. By 22nd December Taylor had correctly presumed a forced landing and on Christmas Day Johns set out for Hermannsburg to get a message to the Government Resident in Alice Springs, who was probably exasperated by the whole CAGE Expedition farce. Carrington, in turn, contacted Minister Arthur Blakeley – almost certainly similarly jaded – initiating the train of events that ultimately bought the two RAAF aircraft from Melbourne. When they eventually landed at Ilbilba on 10th January one sustained damage, requiring a replacement wing to be brought overland and yet another *'plane* dispatched from Melbourne. But they finally identified a marker made by the two lost men and after supplies were dropped by parachute the emaciated Pittendrigh and Hamre were found by Archie Giles, closely followed by Fred Colson and the Government Resident, Carrington, who returned with the aviators by vehicle to Alice Springs.

By that time Lasseter was known to have been on his own since Johns arrived back in Alice Springs in the middle of November, two months earlier. Although Idriess makes no mention of it, the Company's focus was on *'planes* and prospecting, not finding the lost prospector. And while the aeronautical misadventures aren't incidental to the saga they take up an inordinate amount of space in ***Lasseter's Last Ride***. It was only on 16th January 1931 that the RAAF pilots, who were retrieving their damaged aircraft from Ilbilba, delivered a request to Taylor from the CAGE Directors to locate Lasseter. Taylor was over it and declined. Instead, he returned to Alice Springs and set out again with Colson to bring back *Golden Quest II* from Dashwood Creek, arriving in Alice Springs on 26th January. And so it went on. On 17th February Taylor was at Hermannsburg; the decision had been made to bring Bob Buck in to find Lasseter. This is where Paul Johns ignominiously left the stage.

When Buck arrived, Taylor provided detailed written instructions for how to locate Lasseter as he understood it from discussions with Johns.[76] He also made sure that supplies were in place and then left for a final drive back to Alice Springs expecting that Buck would set out the next day. But, as Pastor Albrecht recalled, it ended up being more complicated:

> *There was but one snag. Bob was not prepared to go on such a hazardous journey without a case of brandy, and since this commodity was not stocked at the Mission Store, we had to wait until a supply was brought out from Alice Springs. It was in his favour that the Mission expected a truck with stores within a few days, so a wire was sent to Cloncurry and thence around the Australian coast to Alice Springs from Adelaide. The brandy arrived in due course. Unfortunately, this had caused a delay of about four days, by then Bob left, accompanied by two coloured men.*[77]

Bob Buck departed Hermannsburg on 24th February 1931 and on 24th April he was back. Two days later he travelled to Alice Springs in a car belonging to Walter Gill. Gill was a War veteran, wounded in 1918, who after discharge went to work in Fiji as an overseer in the sugar industry during the last days of indentured labour. A keen observer at a time and in a place when it was easy to ignore colonial injustice, his posthumously-published **Turn North-east at the Tombstone**, is an unflinching critique of that system.[78] After a financial windfall Gill returned to Australia and set out on a journey by motorcar around the country, stopping in Hermannsburg just before Buck arrived. In Alice Springs they delivered to the Government Resident the items that Buck had found with Lasseter's body near Shaw Creek between the Petermanns and the Olgas on 29th March 1931. Within a few weeks Buck would be back there with Walter Gill whose account – **Petermann Journey** – deploys the same colourful honesty as does his memoir of Fiji.[79] Buck was then on his way to Sydney to be feted as the man who found Lasseter.

Although Buck delivered nothing of substance to the CAGE Directors, hopes remained high. Dreams and desperation – the money had run out. Fortunately, they were thrown a lifeline by Leslie Bridge, a Sydney businessman bitten by the gold bug and stirred to action by rumours of duplicity and double-cross that were already circulating around the players of the First CAGE Expedition. Bridge provided the money for the Second CAGE Expedition and was duly acknowledged for having *organised the Expedition* in a flashy flyer, on the cover of which a slasher across a map of mainland Australia proclaims *God save Australia* above a discrete *Central Australian Gold Exploration Company* logo. Inside the cover *THE TEAM* is identified, starting with *BOB BUCK: Leader of the Expedition* and *FRANK GREEN: Assistant Bushman to Leader and Practical Miner* – and concluding with *22 CAMELS: The pick of Mr Buck's fine stock of fifty*. On the second page Bridge is shown standing with Bob Buck and John Bailey, and almost half of the pamphlet's twelve pages is taken up by what is titled: *Verbatim Broadcast Address by Mr. Leslie G. Bridge.* In the middle of it all he gets to the star attraction:

> *Now we come to Bob Buck, the bushman leader of the Expedition, who, with his friend, Frank Green, will have the care of the Expedition whilst it is on its long journeyings. It has been my very great pleasure to have Mr. Buck live with me during his two week's stay in Sydney – a memory I shall cherish. Take it from me, he is one of the finest and*

sturdiest, and, at the same time, one of the most lovable, characters it has been my pleasure to meet – like a Jack London type really. As some evidence of this, one evening I said to him: "Tell me, Bob, what will happen if the 'nigs' get nasty?" His answer was typical of the man, and simply given: "I will go ahead of the Expedition alone, and fix everything O.K."[80]

Bob Buck – the Fixer.[81] Bridge may have been the only person totally taken in by it all and the hype continues to a finale on the back cover that is dazzling in its hypocrisy:

The Federal character of this Expedition suggests the spirit which to-day is animating the Central Australian Gold Exploration Co. Ltd. This spirit can truthfully be denoted by the word – FEDERAL – Each letter of which has been given a signification, demoting the policy which the Company is determinedly putting into force in the interests of Australia:

F	*Faith*
E	*Enthusiasm*
D	*Determination*
E	*Energy*
R	*Right Thinking*
A	*All for Australia*
L	*Love of Australia*

With the money assured the Directors were gearing up for the Second CAGE Expedition that would leave from Alice Springs without vehicles or *'planes* in September; it was all on again. On 23rd November 1931 the Second CAGE Expedition was back in Alice Springs, empty handed save for a collection of papers that would soon be known as *The Diary*. By that time **Lasseter's Last Ride** was about to go into its fourth edition.

CHAPTER 4

Seven Hills

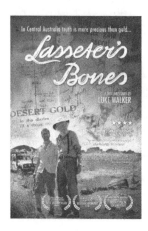

Take good care of Bobby, Betty & Joy please. I want Bobby to be a Civil Engineer try & educate him for that.

Harold Bell Lasseter, 1931.

November 2019

From Central Station the train journey westward tracks the expansion of a colony and the annexation of a continent. Through what was Rose Hill, across the plains on which Pemulwuy fought, to Toongabbie. Kings Langley is off in the distance; that was the sentimental nod that Mathew Pearce gave to his motherland birthplace for his land grant on the other side of Toongabbie Creek, and its rump is still there. But, as the nineteenth century began, Pearce's homestead became known for a nearby hill, the seventh on the track from what by that time was called Parramatta.

Looking north from the Seven Hills Station, packed carparks extend into the distance. In eight hours it will be emptying as commuters head homewards. Exiting to the south there are eateries from across the Levant and South Asia – and Pizza Hut. Outside the Dee-Licious Kebab shop I settle by an aluminium table and wait for coffee – I'm the only customer.

There's no rush; I'm early for a meeting with Bob Lasseter and I've been warned by his wife, Elsie, that Bob's health is not good: *He's 95, and there's been too many questions, too many people bothering him.* It took a week of calling to set up a meeting, and I've agreed to keep it short. Elsie always answers the phone and making it through to Bob is contingent on family, appointments, naps – age. While Elsie's voice conveys concern and, maybe, harassment, Bob's is slow, thoughtful and – it seems – interested.

I have mental images of both Bob and Elsie from several viewings of the 2012 documentary by Luke Walker.[82] The cover of the DVD is bisected by a tumulous horizon with the ochred scrub of desert flatlands below and a cloudless sky above. Written across the darkened top rim, *In Central Australia truth is more precious than gold...* leads into the title – **Lasseter's Bones** – behind which float spectral images of aged newspaper headlines, handwritten notes and one of the classic photos of Harold Lasseter. To the left there is a four-wheel-drive with a solitary figure in the foreground – Bob Lasseter dressed for work in boots, long trousers, braces, his shirtsleeves rolled up. Through glasses that are just discernible in the shade of a white cotton sunhat, he's looking into the distance to the left of the camera, his grey beard below a shaved top lip giving him a quaintly Amish appearance. There's a slight curvature to his stance but, for someone who was then in his eighties, he looks well-preserved.

In the opening scene of **Lasseter's Bones** Bob's bearded face is lit by the flitting back-glow of a projector. The panning camera moves from Bob to what seems like an enthralled audience and then to the screen that has their attention. Bob's paintings of his father's story, archival material and photos from his own expeditions to Central Australia flick over as he maintains a commentary. Jump-cut to the wide, cloudless sky of Central Australia into which an aluminium ladder hesitantly intrudes. Bob's head appears as he manhandles and locks an extension into place, then struggles a bit higher and fastens a safety tie around his back. The view slowly zooms out as Bob points a camera into the distance, his index finger trembling on the shutter button. That's when the viewer realises that the whole contraption is on the roof of a four-wheel-drive, the octogenarian perched twenty feet above the sparse scrub somewhere west of Alice Springs.

Lowell Thomas: *I would say this is Harold Bell Lasseter.*

*Lowell Thomas did the voiceover for **The Blond Captive: A Story of a White Woman Lost Among the Oldest Living Race!***

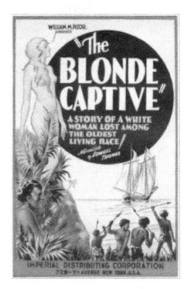

*... Frank Green, who found the documents that became known as **The Diary** ...*

Luke Walker got to know Bob and Elsie well and spent a lot of time at their home in Seven Hills. In the film there are many others interviewed – from true believers to committed sceptics – but the star is Bob Lasseter on a mission to vindicate his father. And the out-takes in the Extras section are as interesting as the film. One has a closeup of this aged man describing how, eighty years earlier, he'd been told that his father would not return. Behind his glasses there seem to be tears in his eyes as he recalls, as a child, crying. Perhaps to firmly locate himself in the memory, that recollection is repeated, then there's a hint of a smile as he adds that, *while it may have been a bit mercenary,* he was upset that he would not have the emu that his father had promised him before he left.[83]

Another scene opens with a wide angle of Bob and Elsie sinking into oversized chesterfields. Bob is in shorts and an open-necked, blue shirt, Elsie wearing beige slacks and a buttoned, floral top. There are books neatly arrayed in a case behind Elsie with framed photographs on a side-table next to Bob. It's not immediately obvious what Elsie is talking about, but she's angry. It then becomes clear that she's discussing the film crew that in 1957 located the rough grave where Bob Buck had buried Lasseter's body in 1931, exhuming the skeleton and taking it to Alice Springs to be re-interred, rationalising the desecration of the grave as ensuring Lasseter had a Christian burial. *Dug his remains up from a grave and carted him in a sugarbag into Alice Springs* – Elsie is looking past the camera to an unseen interviewer, Bob gazing across her lap and occasionally at her. She continues: *They had a photo of this big fellow in America, Lowell Thomas, who was going around the world making films of adventures. They had a picture of him in this film standing there with Bob's father's skull in his hands. That was awful, and that was when we first got into it.* Elsie hesitates, turns to Bob while reaching out to touch his elbow, suggesting gently that he pick up the story, which he does: *I just thought it was time I did my own research and investigated it for myself.*

Lowell Thomas was part of the American broadcasting scene for six decades and was probably an even more effective self-promoter than Idriess. His career was kick-started by filming T.E. Lawrence in Palestine towards the end of the First World War and he leveraged the publicity that came from the shows that followed to develop the genre of travel journalism and broadcasting. And he had form in using his reputation to sensationalise depictions of Aboriginal people; in the same year that Lasseter's body was first found, Lowell Thomas did the voiceover for *he Blond Captive: A Story of a White Woman Lost Among the Oldest Living Race!* Research film footage from Stanley Porteus' ethnopsychology expe-dition to northern Australia in 1928 was misappropriated and used as a backdrop of exotic primitivism to the story of the *Blond Captive*. In the film, first screened in New York in 1932, the wife of the captain of the *Douglas Mawson,* wrecked in a Gulf of Carpentaria cyclone in 1923,[84] is adopted by an Aboriginal tribe and eventually chooses to remain with her *Neanderthal husband* and their child. Raunchy stuff that stained Porteus' reputation[85] but probably didn't do too much harm to Thomas. I driess probably would have approved; it's the same setup as his fictionalised adaptation of the shipwrecked Barbara Thompson in the Torres Strait in *Isles of Despair* and *he Wild White Man of Badu*.

In the 1950s Lowell Thomas fronted a CBS series, *High Adventure*, with seven episodes produced in Australia by Lee Robinson, better remembered for much else including *Skippy the Bush Kangaroo*.[86] The Extras section of the *Lasseter's Bones* DVD contains segments from the *Australian Outback* episode that offended Elsie and mobilised Bob. Land Rovers slowly negotiate gnarled country, the desert tones emphasised by the deterioration of early colour film. Aboriginal and European men are seen holding tight as four vehicles cross washaways and battle through scrub. Thomas stands out; a white shirt buttoned at the wrist and loosely fastened by a bolo at the neck, neatly shaved with his trademark pencil-thin moustache, the effect finished off with dark glasses under a spotless fedora. In the penultimate scene – obviously staged – the dozen or so members of the expedition are moving in single file between boulders, the Aboriginal men holding spears, woomeras and boomerangs. They arrive in a clearing where one of the group, who had been at that place decades before, identifies where Lasseter's body is buried. After a bizarre exchange between the American and two traditional men, Thomas reflects on the remarkable abilities of *primitive man* – and the digging begins. Soon a skull is found and Thomas comments that its *racial type* and the absence of upper teeth should be enough for identification but defers to a doctor standing nearby. In shorts, open-necked shirt, battered hat and boots, he's indistinguishable from the other Europeans in the scene except for Thomas, and is seen re-articulating the mandible with two teeth attached, to a toothless maxilla and the rest of the skull as he softly intones: *I would say this is Harold Bell Lasseter.*

I would say this is Harold Bell Lasseter – in the background stand the two Pintubi men who led the film crew to the spot, one of whom, identified by Thomas as *Mick*, had guided Bob Buck to where the body of Lasseter was found in March 1931. The other is Nosepeg Tjupurrula, of whom Billy Marshall-Stoneking reported that, over four years in the early-1980s: *I spent hundreds of hours with Nosepeg, and much of this time was taken up talking about Lasseter.* Some of that, as I discovered in Adelaide, was about teeth which, from the 1958 *High Adventure* segment, seem to be almost completely absent. And as I found from Lasseter's military records, there weren't many left fifteen years before he died.[87] Nosepeg's recollections may have reflected the passage of time – nearly thirty years passed between his interactions with Thomas and Marshall-Stoneking.[88]

In the Lowell Thomas sequence Nosepeg is at ease with the white men and the camera, and laughs easily at clumsy attempts by Thomas to play on metaphors: *if not a wild goose chase, maybe a wild kangaroo chase.* The traditional man he's translating for and who makes the decision about exactly where to dig doesn't look at ease at all – this is Mick Kuruanyani.[89] In the final scene of the 1957 *High Adventure* episode, Mick Kuruanyani and Nosepeg Tjupurrula have played their part and are off-camera as the focus returns to the real subject – Lowell Thomas. He seems to be channelling the Bard as he turns the freshly disinterred skull toward himself and solemnises:

> *Alas Harry, I didn't know you well. However there is one thing I do know – you may have been a failure, a fake and a fraud, but to have lived and wandered alone as you did out here in this wilderness you must have been a great bushman. For twenty-eight years the mystery of*

Harold Bell Lasseter has shaken a continent. We may not have found Lasseter's Reef, but at any rate we have solved the mystery of what happened to Lasseter – the great mystery of the back of the beyond.[90]

No wonder Bob and Elsie were pissed off; that thought surfacing momentarily during the ten minutes in the Uber from the Dee-Licious Kebab shop to the Lasseter house. The bungalow is shadowed by gum trees and framed to the left by a towering bougainvillea gone rogue, engulfing a building or a tree that is lost behind a chaos of climbing colours. The land slopes down from the road with the drive winding through a spacious yard, disappearing between the house and sheds that are just visible as I turn towards the front patio and knock on the glass-panelled door precisely on ten o'clock; it's opened by Elsie, who doesn't seem entirely resigned to their peace being disturbed: *It's the doctor from Cairns, the one who was on the phone.* Elsie leads me down a hall and into a room I recognise from the film. She's just had a treatment for her eyes, she explains, leaving me to take in the view to the southeast where, in the distance, the dense verticals of Parramatta puncture the smudge of suburbia. The photographs that were behind Elsie in the out-takes of **Lasseter's Bones** sit on a shelf below one of Bob's paintings of his father's saga.

That was our seventieth anniversary – Bob Lasseter has quietly entered the room. Wearing a blue shirt buttoned at the wrists, with braces above beige trousers, his top lip is clean-shaved and he is immediately recognisable although his beard and hair have thinned since he was filmed by Luke Walker. His forehead seems more prominent without glasses, his brows slightly hooded and his eyes misty, but his gaze is direct. He's spotted me scrutinising a generation-spanning family photograph and immediately begins identifying everyone in the frame – 28 grandchildren and counting. Bob may be in his tenth decade but I would have guessed a lot less. He excuses himself to find his hearing aids and from the other end of the house I hear the shouted exchange of a couple with mutual hearing loss.

There are many stories and Bob is as interested in what I've found in my searches as I am in his recollections of the distant past. The conversation ricochets across time and space, starting with events ninety years ago, the emotions captured in Luke Walker's film, the six year old boy learning of his father's death. But there were also two daughters, Louise Betty who would have been four and Vera Joy who was a baby: *they're both alive, Betty lives in South Australia and Joy lives in Glen Innes.* Bob was not the only male in the house; for the duration of the Expedition his mother's brother was there: *Uncle Tom Lillywhite was the youngest of the family. A bit of a scallywag. But he came and stayed with us while my father went to Central Australia. He would have liked to have gone with him. But he missed out because they wanted him to look after my mother and us children while my father was away.*

Bob also had three half-brothers whose father was Frank Green, who found the documents that became known as *The Diary* and delivered them to Bob's mother, Irene, whom Green married in 1935. Both died during the Second World War. We don't mention Lillian Agnes or Beulah Ruth, the children of Bob's father's other wife, Florence Scott, whom he married in the United States in 1903 and brought back to Australia six years later. Lasseter researcher Murray Hubbard met Bob and Beulah and regretted that he couldn't organise for Bob to join Beulah in April 1992 for a commemoration of their father at the opening of an exhibit at the South Gippsland Historical Society featuring the refurbished *Victory*, the shallow-draught, broad beamed, dory-style workboat built by Lasseter to work the shallows of Corner Inlet just after the First World War.[91] Same father, different memories; there's a story attributed to Beulah's older sister, Lillian, from 1960, two years before she died, that describes the early arc of her life from the United States to northern New South Wales and Victoria, which was sundered by the War and her father's infidelities that, she claims, resulted in several pregnancies before he left to marry Bob's mother. Florence never got over it, as is obvious from Lillian's last poignant lines: *My mother died about 18 months after he did – her death was hastened by the grief over the way he suffered and died. She loved him all her life and forgave him for all the heart-ache and misery he caused her.*[92]

Eighteen months of heart-ache for Florence Elizabeth, but also a tough time for Irene. As Bob related to Murray Hubbard in the early

1990s, the CAGE Company refused to pay the £500 insurance policy taken out on Lasseter's life because: *the policy stated that if my father died of a heart attack the company would not pay up. No one could prove that he died of starvation, not heart attack, so they refused to pay it.*[93] Irene's plight seems to have been of little concern to John Bailey, who wrote in 1947:

> *The alleged Mrs Lasseter became very annoyed when the Company stopped payments on behalf of Lasseter. She went and made a statement to the "Truth" newspaper and a reporter from that paper came to my office … and informed me of what the intentions of the paper were. I asked him if he were sure he had been talking to Mrs Lasseter or the Alleged Mrs. Lasseter. I informed him that we had received a communication from the lawful wedded Mrs. Lasseter from a suburb of Melbourne and she had forwarded her [certificate of marriage] to Lasseter, so I thought he would be well advised to call on his informant and ask her to show him her marriage certificate. He then wrote the article, "Is this woman Mrs. Lasseter?" From then on we received no further request from that quarter.*[94]

That article appeared in May 1931 under the header: *Dead Gold-seeker Claimed as Husband by Two Women! Mystery of Missing Treasure-Plan New Aspect of Grim Wilderness Romance.* Clarifying as the article opened that *TWO women, each now claiming to be the wife of Lasseter – that is one romantic angle of the situation,* the writer seemed pretty keen to press the importance of his new angle: *Surely, this amazing double-sided claim to the dead man as a husband over-shadows even the circumstances associated with the hopeful expedition into the arid expanses of the heart of Australia.*[95]

Sensationalising Lasseter's private life was probably just an attempt to salvage a story, but it played well with the CAGE Directors and, given their priorities at that time which no longer relied on Lasseter as an investment, they probably didn't have much sympathy for Irene and the kids. But on the last page of the final financial balance sheets for the CAGE Company, signed off by the auditor on 31st October 1932, and listed with sundry expenses, are two items: *EXPENSES RE LASSETER ESTATE – £2,* and *DONATION. Mrs Lasseter – £25.* Just £25 – not a lot

– and as we continue to talk about the aftermath of the Expedition we get to another visitor to the family home – Ion Idriess. Bob can't remember whether he met Idriess nearly ninety years ago, but he told Murray Hubbard in the early 1990s that his mother was desperate for money when Idriess arrived on the doorstep, and wonders whether Idriess left with some of the letters that Bob believes went missing. But there's no uncertainty about *The Diary;* as Bob comments philosophically, Idriess bought that: *for £25. Angus & Robertson sold it to the Mitchell Library for $1,000.* That was much later and in between, Idriess insisted, nobody had access to it except for himself. Until, however, soon after Lowell Thomas exhumed a skeleton and removed it to Alice Springs in 1957.

...he did draw a plan for a single arch bridge across Sydney Harbour in about 1913 or 1914 and if you look up there...
Bob Lasseter, Seven Hills, November 2019.

That's what got Bob Lasseter fired up and launched him on a mission that would last more than half-a-century. In the Mitchell Library there is a correspondence trail dating to the year after, between Bob Lasseter and George Ferguson, the Director of Angus & Robertson from 1948 to 1971 and a major figure in Australian post-war publishing.[96] Frank Clune and Ion Idriess were the company's most successful authors and the first letter, written in January 1958, is to Bob from George Ferguson responding to a request from Clune that he forward Bob a copy of his recent book, **The Fortune Hunters**. Ferguson noted that Clune had mentioned: *some query about your father's diary.* In his reply written a month later, Bob thanked Ferguson for the book, noting:

> *I am obliged to Frank Clune for what he has done (ref. Truth 20 Feb 55) in attacking the vindictive "Hoax" and "Escape to America" yarns which have been rumoured from time to time over the years, but these additional paragraphs which he has added to his story and the theme of auto-suggestion which they present, belittles my father's mental make-up which according to other sources was of a high calibre. This theme is in fact the same as that which was included in Michael Terry's derogatory and distorted article in the S.M.H. of Feb 1st '58, and therefore these few paragraphs of Frank Clune's Book deserve the same criticism as Terry's article.*[97]

In the 1950s Michael Terry was known for magazine articles about remote Australia. In 1931 he had been on his way to the Petermanns with the Endeavour expedition while the First CAGE Expedition was packing and repacking in Alice Springs, and two years later he found Lasseter's westernmost traces at Lake Christopher. When it came to Central Australia he was no slouch; the Terry Range, a few hundred kilometres north-west of where Bob's father disappeared in 1931, was named after him just before Bob's correspondence with Ferguson, and an image of Terry with his camel – Dick – adorned the Bicentennial commemorative ten dollar note. Terry was a straight-shooter and called out both Lasseter's fantasies and Idriess' fictions. Whether or not Terry exchanged thoughts about Lasseter with Idriess' mate, Frank

Clune, they certainly read each other's work and, coincidence or not, Clune's last son was Terry Michael. After dismissing Terry, Bob's letter then tacks towards Idriess:

Referring now to my father's diary. The diary was purchased by Angus & Robertson, from my mother for £25 on the undertaking that it would be handed over to the Mitchell Library after you had used it to write the book ("Lasseter's Last Ride" by Ion L Idriess; one of the first copies of which was presented to my mother by the author and which I still have). As far as I can make out the undertaking has never been honoured. A few years ago I had the fancy to inspect my father's diary and went first to the Mitchell Librarian who said they didn't have it. I went to your shop in Castlereagh St and although the diary was apparently there, I was unable to see it. My feelings were mixed indignation and disappointment.

Three weeks later, in March 1958, Ferguson replied noting that the diary is: *here in our strongroom,* continuing: *The full circumstances of its actual purchase do not seem to be recorded here. Certainly Mr Cousins senior, who is now dead, bought it from your mother for £25. At the time he may possibly have remarked that some day it would find its way into the Mitchell Library but that I think should not be construed as meaning that we would present it to the Mitchell.*

The next exchange includes arrangements to see the diary and, in late May, Bob replies thanking Angus & Robertson for photographs of the diary, noting that: *Mr Idriess states that although the diary has only 29 pages remaining, the original book probably contained 100 pages. I wonder if there is any way of confirming this so that the number of missing pages can be deduced.* The last letter in the series, a week after Bob's question, is from Ferguson:

I think the best way to find out what there is to know about the Diary itself would be to have a discussion with Mr Idriess. He is really the only one that knows much about its history. All I know is that the Diary as it exists now is exactly how it was when we got it. As I explained to you, I took no part in the negotiations at the time of its purchase, and any story that may have gone with it would have been known only to Mr Idriess.

In relation to your last paragraph however, I can tell you definitely that no one has had access to the Diary except Mr Idriess from the day on which it came into our possession. Many people have wanted to see it, but you are the first who has actually seen it. Some portions of course were reproduced in Lasseter's Last Ride, and thus became common property. The remainder of it has been locked up in our strongroom all these years.

Although Bob couldn't remember meeting Idriess when he was a child, he does recall meeting him decades later: *He used to go to Angus & Robertson, he had a room there and he'd sit and write. There was a cardboard box in the corner and he said 'you can sit there'. I was in my twenties and at that stage he must have written sixty books or so. He said he couldn't remember much about my father's story.* Bob *didn't find out much at all* – from the person credited with kick-starting the Lasseter legend and whose career took off because of it… Before I have time to think that through Bob returns to Idriess in Kogarah, meeting Irene Lasseter: *He met her and he may have had a thing for her – at least that's what uncle Tom Lillywhite said.* A 37 year old woman who a few weeks earlier was caught up in a whirlwind of publicity and expectations of release from the financial vice of the Depression; by April 1931 she was a widow with three young children including a baby. Her hopes for some financial support in that time of need were dashed by businessmen from the big end of town, who were not above leaking to the media that she was not *the lawful wedded Mrs. Lasseter* to rid themselves of hassle and responsibility. Just £25 – whether it was a donation or payment for the papers, it was a pittance. Idriess could be a charmer and he probably used that to his advantage. He got *The Diary* and – according to him and George Ferguson – nobody else saw it for nearly thirty years. Except, perhaps, Frank Green.

Bob is silent for a moment as he readjusts his hearing aid: *Frank Green's mother was a Catholic and there was a big division. I don't know whether churchy was the right word but she was very Catholic, she didn't like my mother. Grandma Green we knew her as. The rest of the Green family were all a bit on her side whereas Frank had left the family and met my mother.* Through age-misted eyes he seems to be trying to focus on something in the distance as he continues about the man who became his stepfather: *I didn't get on with him at all, it would take too long telling you. When he first got with my mother he took me on a trip in a horse and sulky over the mountains and was going to show me how to pan gold. He'd been away on a second trip with Bob Buck after my father died. Frank Green was on the expedition as a prospector.* Among the papers of the CAGE Syndicate and Company is a contract dated 17th August 1931, signed by Frank Green and John Bailey, hiring Green for the Second CAGE Expedition. But Green and Bailey had history – they'd been involved in a dodgy deal in Sydney in the 1920s about which there had been a Royal Commission, and they went on to mining scams after the Second CAGE Expedition.[98] And before he set out as the *prospector* for the Second Expedition he was no stranger to Central Australia – he'd already spent time in jail in Alice Springs.

Talking about Frank has brought Bob back to Seven Hills: *He married my mum and then they had three boys – Frank, Bruce and Jim – my half-brothers. I got on well with Frank, the eldest. Frank became an electrician and he did all the wiring in this house. He died recently.* Our trajectory now shifts to a different history, a history of place – this place – and then to another home, the house that his real father built, one that had a name: *He called the house Harrene, made up of Harry and Irene, in Ramsgate. He also made a very nice box out of red cedar that had Harrene engraved into the lid. Elsie and I had five children and the first we called Harrene.*

Harrene; it sounds vaguely like Earani, which triggers connections to my recent Lasseter cyber-sleuthing and to science fiction writer Erle Cox, Earani's creator, who intimated that Bob's father had a thing for her. At least that's what Cox wrote in a 1948 letter about a meeting 21 years earlier while Lasseter was working on the construction of Parliament House in Canberra. Lasseter had been contributing to the *Canberra*

79

Community News as the *Gleaner* while he was living at the Russell Hill Settlement and, in March 1927, he wrote to the editor, J.H. Honeysett, about an upcoming visit by Cox, at that time a journalist for *The Argus,* to cover the opening. Lasseter was keen to offer local expertise and, as he put in his letter to Honeysett, there might be a possibility of having some of his own articles republished: *I am offering him all the assistance I can, even to the effect of allowing him to reprint the "Gleaner" articles. I feel sure you would not raise any objections to this & just fancy how surprised & pleased the readers of the "Argus" would be at the wonderful find of information contained therein.*[99]

Honeysett replied the next day agreeing to the request, adding: *By the way, can you let me have another "Gleaner" article in your usual inimitable style in the course of the next few days.* The writers for the *Canberra Community News* and *The Argus* subsequently met up and in his 1948 letter Cox recalled: *I first got in contact with him about 1926. He appears to have been extremely interested in a novel of mine "Out Of The Silence" that was published that year. I believe he named his daughter Earani after my heroine.*[100] Maybe not; Lasseter's children to his first, American, wife were born before *Out of the Silence*[101] was serialised in *The Argus* in 1919, and his daughters by Bob's mother, Betty and Joy, were born in 1926 and 1928. But Lasseter was probably familiar with Cox, journalist and novelist, who was syndicated around the country. Erle Cox was, in his day, a shaper[102] – *THE STORY SO FAR* from the graphic serialisation in the *West Australian* fifteen years after Earani first appeared captures the vibe:

> *"OUT OF THE SILENCE" – No. 75 (Earani Defies Gravity!). By ERLE COX.*
> *THE STORY SO FAR – Alan Dundas discovers in his vineyard a vast underground structure in which is a beautiful woman, Earani, who is restored from a state of suspended animation by his friend, Dr Barry. Earani, who possesses almost boundless scientific powers, recounts the history of her race. Against Alan's advice she breaks in on a social gathering at the township of Glen Cairn, and, after causing Dundas*

much trouble, disappears. Alan finds her waiting at his home. Earani accepts the love he offers her. Later she demonstrates her powers of invisibility.[103]

Whether or not Earani had a separate life in the Lasseter household, as Cox's letter goes on to detail, in 1927 he did meet Bob's father, in Canberra:

He was living in Canberra then and I had my only personal contact with him. … He gave me a walking stick cut from Victory oak that was part of the Speaker's chair which he told me had been taken off to make it fit the platform in Parliament house. Lasseter struck me as being a bit off-balance in the longest conversation I had with him which took place about midnight when I was dead weary … He walked with me – forsaking all other topics of conversation he tried to drive home to me for newspaper publication a theory of his that Australia should cut clear of Britain and ally herself with America against the Japs – he showed sense in his suspicion of the Japs.

An offcut from Nelson's flagship destined to support the workings of democracy a world away – maybe. But Lasseter was absolutely clear about the threat from Japan, he wrote about the failure to develop naval defence in the north and, as Bob reminds me: *my father wanted to write to the head of Japan and he asked somebody to give him the right way to address the letter to him.* He certainly tried. In documentation from the Embassy of Japan, seized during the Second World War, is a letter received on 3rd March 1930 sent from Lasseter *C/O WF Roberts, Terranora Bldgs, Reiby Place, Sydney,* and addressed to the *Consul General for Japan*: *Dear Sir – Will you please supply me with an envelope correctly addressed in your own language to the Chief of the General Staff of His Imperial Majesty The Emperor of Japan as I have some secret information of value for transmission to him.*[104]

At that time Reiby Place overlooked Circular Quay in Sydney and Lasseter's return addressee, W.F. Roberts, was a confidant of John Bailey and had a history in mining.[105] The request was made just a few months after Lasseter had put in train the process that would lead to the Expedition and his death with his letter to Texas Green. But between that letter and the formation of the CAGE Syndicate there was a storm of correspondence between Lasseter, representatives of the Western Australian and Commonwealth governments,[106] and an expanding coterie of investors infected with the fever and selectively inattentive to cautionary advice. Lasseter's letters from the end of 1929 to June 1930, including to the Consul General for Japan, Minister Blakeley and H.W. Gepp were written from "Harrene" Orient Rd Kogarah in Lasseter's neat hand on the back of blank invoice documents, Lasseter explaining to Gepp at the bottom of his letter of 6th November 1929 that: *P.S. I am running the Pottery mentioned on the reverse of this & seldom leave before 6.30 PM.*[107]

The address at the top of the invoices is *112 & 114 Walker Street, Redfern* and doesn't come up on searches, but those on either side – 110 and 116 – were the Disabled Soldiers Pottery set up during the War by the Red Cross, supported from around 1920 by donations and producing, among other items, Jenolan Pottery.[108] But that fades from the records by the middle of the decade, and by the time Lasseter was claiming to be *running the Pottery* he was also running from the bailiff as evidenced by *Sydney Morning Herald* advertisements in March 1930 to sell *Harrene.*[109] A few weeks later Harold and Irene thought they were out of trouble – but it was just beginning. Just six months on, in the middle of September, the rest of the Expedition watched as Lasseter left camp with five camels and Albert Paul Johns.

Paul Johns – Bob repeats that name and after a moment of silence, turning again to take in the view, continues: *Apparently he was in trouble in Central Australia from interfering with Aboriginal women.* The last European to see his father. I'm not surprised that Bob is reflective. But I am by what follows: *I talked to him on the phone once. He was in London at that stage and he had some sort of a shop selling second-hand furniture or something. I rang him, I was trying to do a bit of research into anything that would lead to the reef. I can't remember much of it at all now, the conversation didn't amount to much.* It would have been about thirty years or more since Johns and Bob's father separated – a generation, a war, a different hemisphere and a changed world – Johns would have been over sixty and probably more interested in recycling old objects than old stories.

We've been talking for an hour and although Bob seems happy to go with the flow of memories, I know I've overstayed and I don't need Elsie to tell me. As I prepare to leave I reach out and touch the copy of **Lasseter's Last Ride** that's on the table and am about to make a comment about Idriess when Bob cuts me off:

> *You might notice in the book he did not get on well with Blakeley, the leader of the expedition. Blakeley said, when my father talked about things, 'you've done everything' as if he was making it up. And one of the things he spoke about was that he had some work in connection with the Sydney Harbour Bridge. And, of course, the timing didn't work out in terms of the bridge. But, he did draw a plan for a single arch bridge across Sydney Harbour in about 1913 or 1914 and if you look up there…*

Bob lifts his arm slowly and points to an age-yellowed document in a polished wooden frame above the door into the sitting room. Against white backing its frayed edges and the vertical shadow-lines of repeated folds gives it the appearance of parchment. Now more than a century old, the image is familiar from my readings and Luke Walker's film. And from its striking likeness to *The Coathanger*. I shift my iphone from record to camera and get the shot. Standing framed by the door is an elderly man in blue shirt and braces, a biro ready in his breast pocket, his kindly, aged face surrounded by a penumbra of white hair and beard. He stares directly to the camera – as he has done for dozens, maybe hundreds, who have made the trip to Seven Hills chasing a legend. Now, of course, Bob is a legend.

CHAPTER 5

The Story

Jack delved into the occult over a long period of time. In 1931 after Lasseter's disappearance he and several of his friends had held the occasional seance in the hope of locating Lasseter. There is an undated letter from a gentleman in residence at Raraku in Mosman which contains a map drawn by a Mrs Scott while in a trance, showing the location of the reef. The writer notes that he 'weighed a rabbit's ectoplasm' at the exact time of the drawing. There is no statement of whether the drawing of the reef was dependent on the weight of the rabbit's ectoplasm or if each was an unconnected act. Obviously neither resulted in the finding of the lost reef.

Beverley Eley, 1995.[110]

Idriess moved to Sydney in February 1930 with one failed book behind him, **Madman's Island.** He was soon working on **Prospecting for Gold** which would be released in early 1931, and his wartime diaries published as **The Desert Column** the next year. In an interview four decades later he referred to himself during the period leading up to his first books as a *freelance journalist*[111] but he was a long way from making serious money from writing. Gold had been on his radar for years and

Lasseter from the middle of 1930; he knew that there was a story to be told but he needed a source. And he found it in the CAGE Company and its secretary, Ernest Bailey, who was probably keen, as 1931 rolled on and as investors were sought for the Second Expedition, for any publicity that would stir hearts and loosen purse strings.

In the National Archives there is a document that dates to May1930 that is headed *THE FOLLOWING HAVE EACH CONTRIBUTED £20 (1 SHARE) TO THE CENTRAL AUSTRALIAN GOLD EXPLORA-TION SYNDICATE,* [112] the list of 49 names including: J. Bailey, E. Bailey, E. Coote, E.C. Coote, Mrs E.C. Coote, S.J. Hamre, H.B. Lasseter, C. Burlington, F. Blakeley, G. Sutherland, several politicians – and one G. Warnecke. Glen William ("George") Warnecke's career in the early 1930s was in the ascendant – he became Editor-in-chief of Frank Packer's Australian Consolidated Press. Idriess had contributed to *World's News*, a paper run by Warnecke who approached Idriess in 1932 to write for its successor, the *Australian Women's Weekly.* [113] While Idriess declined, it's likely that Warnecke and Idriess knew each other. And another name on the list, sandwiched between *H.B. Lasseter* and *F. Blakeley* is *C. Burlington.* Charles Lexius-Burlington – known as *Lex* or *Burlington Bertie* [114] – hoped to be on the Expedition and was responsible for organizing the Thornycroft truck but was replaced by Phil Taylor when Lasseter and Coote objected. A pilot in the First War, he learned some lessons that he put to use flying on the New Guinea goldfields in the late 1920s. And more; after four prospectors were killed on the Nakanai Mountains in New Britain in 1927:

> *Burlington Bertie joined a punitive expedition of Rabaul volunteers who were signed on as special police and sent to seek out the offenders. He was an unpredictable sort of a chap and he had bombs made out of galvanised water piping to use if the group was attacked. He cut the piping into eighteen-inch lengths, filled them with dynamite, sealed them with a cap then put a fuse through it. When he got back Lex said the bombs were used to effect on the village where the attack took place. They certainly won him a kind of notoriety.* [115]

Notoriety... The senior officer on the *expedition*, Raphael Cilento, *described Burlington as a coward and attributed his throwing the bomb, which caused no injury, to "absolute funk". The man later had to be physically hauled away from the machine gun which he had been about to fire when alarmed by what he thought to be an ambush.*[116] Whether or not, Burlington Bertie got more than passing mentions in despatches to the Secretary of the Department of Home and Territories and made it into the press. Idriess certainly knew about it all and wrote a long article in 1932 describing the massacre and reprisals in detail – *Head Hunters Kill Prospectors: The Trouble at Nakanai. By Ion L. Idriess (Author of "Lasseter's Last Ride," "Flynn of the Inland," "Men of the Jungle." Etc).*[117] Maybe discretion was why he didn't mention Burlington by name, even though he could have been a character in an Idriess book. And soon he was; two years after **Lasseter's Last Ride** first appeared **Gold Dust and Ashes** was released, the last half of which celebrates the pluck of pilots and the potential of *'planes* in the mountain goldfields inland from Salamaua. At one point two pilots meet by chance: *Meanwhile for Parer in Rabaul, time just drifted by. One day when down in the dumps he ran into Burlington, a tall young Englishman with plenty of laugh and energy. Possessed of aviation experience, some bright ideas, and the gold-fever was Charles Lexius-Burlington.*[118]

A few pages later the pilots, having landed at a *'drome like a wee tennis-court among scrubby hills,* are welcomed by a malarial miner whose first words are: *"Hey! What ho, Burlington Bertie!"* Between the author and the aviator there was probably a fair amount of tit for tat; around the same time that Idriess was fawning over his frontier flying, Burlington Bertie was returning the favour by having **Lasseter's Last Ride** reviewed by a visiting American publisher.[119] His experience with the CAGE Company didn't dampen Lexius-Burlington's enthusiasm for gold mining; he was involved with several projects in New Guinea to the 1930s, and in Aus-tralia as a Director of British Mining Finance Pty. Ltd. which entered negotiations in 1934 with *a group represented by Sir Herbert Gepp* regard-ing Queensland mining leases[120] – the same Herbert Gepp who had been tasked by Texas Green to investigate a proposal he had received in October 1929 from Harold Lasseter.

Idriess knew he had to protect his sources and that access wasn't unconditional. For the first edition he was told not to include material that could give away the location of the reef. At that time the Directors still believed Lasseter had relocated it when he had a message sent to them after his flight from Ilbilba with Pat Hall in September 1930 and had reaffirmed in his letter that arrived in Alice Springs with Paul Johns in the middle of November. By the time the Second CAGE Expedition returned that had changed, the word was out – there was no gold except, perhaps, in gullible investors funding more expeditions.

As Idriess was writing the draft of *Lasseter's Last Ride* through the first half of 1931 the news of Lasseter's death was only just being circulated. The Second CAGE Expedition set out from Alice Springs in September 1931. That was a month before *The Diary* was unearthed by Frank Green in the middle of October, and by the time Green, Buck and the rest of the Expedition were back in Alice Springs it was late November and *Lasseter's Last Ride* was about to go into its fourth edition. Not long after that Frank Green was in Sydney and when he arrived in Kogarah to pass on *The Diary* to Irene Lasseter, Idriess wasn't far behind. Idriess knew what he was after and came with an offer – £25 – which may have been the £25 listed as a *donation to Mrs Lasseter* in the CAGE financial records. That material was incorporated into a new edition released in March 1932. Ion Idriess had the inside running on the story and seems to have had the imprimatur of the CAGE Directors. So it's all the more curious that when the Chairperson of the CAGE Company, John Bailey, lodged his account with the Mitchell Library in 1947 he noted on the first page: *I desire to transgress to make the following comments. It is regrettable that Ion L. Idriess should have misrepresented the facts in his book "Lasseter's Last Ride". I shall have more to say relative to this matter later on.* Maybe it slipped his mind, but on reviewing the document on 26th September 1947, Bailey added in longhand:

> *"Lasseter's Last Ride" by Ion L. Idriess is not based on fact. Idriess called on my office at 321 Pitt St. Sydney, he asked for information about the expedition dispatched to Central Australia. Idriess was given all the information available from the minutes of the Company books*

and from this he prepared his story. He had never met Lasseter or any members of the expedition before writing his book. It is regrettable that this man should deceive the public and posterity.[121]

Whatever happened to sour their relationship must have taken time to ferment. Sixteen years earlier, on 21st September 1931, as the first shipments of **Lasseter's Last Ride** were being dispatched by Angus & Robertson,[122] Walter Cousins wrote from the company headquarters on Castlereagh Street to Arthur Blakeley, who was still Minister for Home and Territories, though no longer for a separate Central Australia which had been disestablished just a few months before. There would soon be a change of government but at that moment Blakeley was it, albeit probably already bruised by his associations with the CAGE Company. Cousins' reason for writing was that in the next edition of **Lasseter's Last Ride** the publisher wanted to include a map in which a lake discovered during the Mackay Aerial Survey expedition would be included and named for Donald Mackay. The letter began: *Dear Sir, This is written at the suggestion of Mr John Bailey. We are publishing the second edition of "Lasseter's Last Ride" by Mr Ion L. Idriess ...*[123] Given Bailey's interest and advice, the relationship between the CAGE Company and Directors, with Idriess and his publisher, would seem to have been cosy in late 1931.

As it turned out the Second CAGE Expedition, like its predecessor, came up empty handed. Despite that Ernest Bailey, still Secretary of the Company in its agonal phase,[124] wrote to J.A. Perkins, the new Minister for Home and Territories, on 25th October 1932, following up a phone call that his father had made. Whatever John Bailey had said in that conversation regarding yet another CAGE Company venture, Ernest made an outrageous claim: *Our second expedition was in the Petermann Ranges last year and found a huge reef 70 feet wide and outcropping for a considerable distance. Samples of stone brought back and assayed at the Port Kembla works proved that this stone was definitely gold bearing.*[125] Whether a straight out lie or not – it only alludes to gold-bearing stone – the Baileys were still in the game; which makes it almost incomprehensible that just four years later John Bailey wrote in the *Daily Telegraph: I was the man to whom Lasseter came with his story of a rich gold reef in Central Australia. I introduced him to the group that put up the money for his expedition, and I put money into it myself. But I never really believed he had a reef.* [126]

Whether that 1936 assertion is to be believed or not, in the article Bailey deferred to Idriess' novel rather than relating Lasseter's explanation to Bailey and his coterie at the AWU offices in March 1930 as to how he stumbled on the reef three decades earlier: *His story, which is now well known through Ion Idriess' book, "Lasseter's Last Ride".* Well known and authoritative enough for Bailey it would seem. And well known it was; by that time **Lasseter's Last Ride** had gone through revision and eighteen editions – there were 34 thousand copies circulating. It had become the accepted, popular account. But when first released in September 1931 the final act had yet to begin – the Second CAGE Expedition that brought back *The Diary*. There's no suggestion of problems in the relationship between Idriess and Bailey senior, and his relationship with Ernest Bailey clearly ensured his privileged access to Company files. Even so, there wasn't a lot to go on to finish the story and complete the book. So – What did he know and how did he pull it together…

Sources, sections and sequences

On 25th April 1931, four months before **Lasseter's Last Ride** went to press, Robert Buck certified that he had found the body of Lasseter to H.A. Heinrick at Hermannsburg, and the news was radioed on to the Government Resident in Alice Springs, V.C. Carrington, who on the 27th telegraphed Canberra: *R BUCK REPORTS THAT ON 28th MARCH FOUND BODY LASSETER OF GOLD EXPLORATION COMPANY AT SHAW CREEK PETERMAN RANGES APPARENTLY PERISHED STOP BUCK HAS HANDED IN CERTAIN WRITINGS PROVING IDENTITY STOP LASSETER WRITES PEGGED REEF BUT THIS DISCREDITED GOVRES.* The word was out, and in one file in the National Archives are two streams of correspondence that followed. [127]

Four words, LASSETER WRITES PEGGED REEF precipitated one, a torrent of correspondence from the Directors of the CAGE Company lobbying the Government to support another expedition, regardless of Carrington's DISCREDITED qualifier. That may have been because he had spoken with members of the First CAGE Expedition who had returned to Alice Springs convinced that Lasseter was either deceiving them or himself. News of the prospector's death initiated the other, including correspondence from both of Lasseter's families. On 29th April 1931, Lillian Hodgetts wrote from Olinda, Victoria, to Carrington: *I read in yesterdays paper of the death of Mr LHB Lasseter while searching for gold in your locality.* She was referred on to Canberra, and on 18th May wrote in more detail to the Secretary of Home Affairs:

> *I am his eldest daughter, and, as I have been informed that there is a woman living in Kogarah who poses as his wife. I should like you to know that she is not and she is not entitled to any of his papers etc. as my mother is the one to receive them. This woman told a representative of "Truth" newspaper that she was his legal wife as she was married to him in 1924. My mother was married to him at Clifton Springs, U.S.A. on the 29th Dec 1903 so it seems as if she is his legal wife as they were never divorced …*
>
> *P.S. I have proofs to show that this woman in Kogarah has known for some years that my mother was still living and that there had never been a divorce.*

Between those letters Carrington had been busy. On 2nd May he had written to the Secretary of the Department of Home Affairs: *I am forwarding, herewith, the original writings for perusal but I consider that at least the one addressed to his wife should be transmitted to his wife.* The Mrs Lasseter referred to in that letter, Louise Irene, wrote on 5th May from Kogarah, New South Wales, to the Commissioner of Police in Canberra: *The body of my husband L.H.B. Lasseter was recently found in Central Australia by Mr Bob Bucks [sic], and I believe the papers etc. brought in by him to be in the hands of the police at Alice Springs. Kindly advise me how to obtain these.*

Carrington issued a death certificate on 9th May, the second, signed *RH Buck, Pastoralist, Middleton Ponds,* listing the cause of death as *Starvation* and the date of death as *January 30th, 1931.*[128] On 19th May the Acting Secretary, in the Department of Home Affairs, F.J. Quinlan, wrote to Ernest Bailey noting: *At the direction of the Minister for Home Affairs, I forward herewith four communications found on the body of the late Mr. H.L.B. Lasseter of your Syndicate, who recently perished in Central Australia.* Carrington went on to note that: *property, also found with the deceased, has been handed over to the Police.* That list did not include dentures. On the same day he wrote to Irene in Kogarah: *I forward here a communication addressed to you, which was amongst Mr. Lasseter's papers. All other papers related to the work Mr. Lasseter was performing on behalf of the Company, and have therefore, been sent to the Company's representative.* Four days later Quinlan responded to Lillian in Victoria in relation to the same materials: *One of the five papers was addressed to "Rene," and this has been forwarded to Mrs. Irene Lasseter ... The remaining four documents, which were general in nature, have been forwarded to the Secretary, Central Australian Gold Exploration Syndicate.*

Lillian Hodgetts didn't receive any of her father's papers and remained bitter about the treatment she and her mother had received after the man who had deserted his family had, for a moment, paced the national stage and then disappeared – again. Three decades later she gave her version of her father's life, concluding with comments about underhand *doings in Sydney,* both *a dubious crowd on the outer fringes of politics in N.S.W* – probably a reference to Bailey and his mates – and the other woman, *"Irene": There had been much underhand doings in Sydney and we have had to prise every bit of information out of them as their sympathies were entirely with the family he left in Sydney. As nothing came of the mine we felt that there was no need to embarrass those children who were growing up – and "Irene" married another man and subsequently died.*[129]

Once the CAGE Directors became aware that Irene was *the other Mrs Lasseter* it allowed them to rationalise ceasing payment of the missing prospector's wages to her, but she did get the note beginning *Rene Darling,* forwarded on 19th May:

Don't grieve for me. I've done my best & have pegged the reef, not strictly according to law as the blacks pinched my miner's right & I don't know the number but I photographed the datum post on the Quartz Blow the post is sticking in a water hole the photo faces north. I made the run in 5 days but the blacks have a sacred place nearby & will pull the peg up for sure.

I've taken the files & will plant them at Winter's Glen if I can get there the Blight has got me beat all because Jack Jenkins never put the Argerol in the medicine chest as I requested. He got boracic lotion instead which relieves the smart but does not cure.

Take good care of Bobby, Betty & Joy please. I want Bobby to be a Civil Engineer try & educate him for that. Darling I do love you so. I'm sorry I can't be with you at the last but God's will be done

Yours ever   X Harry XXX

The four items sent to the CAGE Company were part of the trove that, as Idriess wrote, *were kindy made available to me by the Secretary, Mr E.H. Bailey.* That's what Idriess had to go on in the middle of 1931 – vetted CAGE Company documents and photographs, the opinions of certain Directors, and the first tranche of communications from beyond the grave that had been found by Bob Buck, which Fred Blakeley saw in the CAGE office just after delivering his report to the Directors:

> *There were only three or four pages, telling how Lasseter's camels had bolted. He claimed that he had wandered about with a tribe of natives for days, then dysentery and sandy blight had set in. All but one native deserted him. He described this native as having a big wart or loose lump of skin hanging from his behind, and asked those who found him to be kind to old Warts. On another page he said that he had pegged his reef and gave a vague description of its position.*[130]

Even a *vague description of its position* was enough to maintain the frenzy, and Blakeley's voice of experience went unheard. To his amazement his formal report was ignored at the meeting of Directors of the CAGE Company:

It was one of the most remarkable scenes that ever happened in Australia's Gold History, that some 150 people could be bitten so hard by the gold bugs, that their judgement and sense of fairness could be so warped, that in their delirium of raging gold fever they would rather accept the soft whisperings of pretty story tellers of dingos who were steeped in vile, suspicion and distrust – that of the 150 people present who could have heard the true story not one of them asked a single question. … the poor, gold fever stricken people put up over twelve thousand pounds backing the pretty story teller against my cold statement that the Lasseter Reef was only a myth.[131]

Whether Idriess saw Fred Blakeley's formal report isn't known. If he had, he would have been told not to use it, as he had been with the instructions that the departing Phil Taylor, as the only remaining representative of the CAGE Company, had provided to Bob Buck before Buck left Hermannsburg on 24th February 1931 to find the lost prospector. Idriess prefaced it in the newly included Chapter XXXI in February 1932 with: *This letter of instruction was not inserted in the earlier editions of this book, as Mr E.H. Bailey, the Secretary of the Company, asked me to withhold it pending the result of the second expedition.* Through winter 1931, with hopes still high and competition hot, that information was commercial-in-confidence.

Although Idriess later denied it, there was a lot in the press for him to use from, at least, January 1931, including interviews with Irene Lasseter disclosing information that returned with Paul Johns to Alice Springs in November 1930.[132] But while that material identified the principals in the Expedition, Idriess knew little about their backstories – with one possible exception. Alec Chisholm, a friend of Idriess who was also published by Angus & Robertson, wrote an article in 1936, by which time Idriess was successful, describing how his friend did it. In the context of outlining Idriess' work routine at the Angus & Robertson offices in the period around 1930, Chisholm notes in passing: *Incidentally, it is an odd reflection that one of the staff-men then was Errol Coote, who became pilot of the Lasseter expedition, but who did not get his book, **Hell's Airport**, published until several years after Idriess, who was not with the expedition,* *had scored heavily with* **Lasseter's Last Ride.**[133]

Coote the journalist, present at the foundation meeting of what would become the CAGE Company, was almost certainly wary of his Angus & Robertson acquaintance who had inveigled his way to become the quasi-authorised teller of the tale. But after returning from Central Australia only to be dismissed by the Company, Coote had other things on his mind. He was convinced that Lasseter had identified the key landmarks to the reef on his flight from Ilbilba with Pat Hall. Despite agreeing to be party to deceiving Blakeley by remaining silent about Lasseter's disclosure that he had sighted the reef, Coote chose not to question Lasseter's intentions and honesty in relation to himself. What Coote thought was a shared secret cemented his status as a co-conspirator and true believer. As Idriess was revising the first edition of **Lasseter's Last Ride** Coote was with the West Centralian Gold Exploration Company's 1932 aerial expedition flying out of Warburton across the lands of Lasseter's last wanderings. Coote then set to writing, but by the time **Hell's Airport** was released more than 25 thousand copies of **Lasseter's Last Ride** had been sold.

In early 1931, around the time of Buck's discovery of Lasseter's remains and while Coote was gearing up for his second adventure, Idriess' working title was *Lasseter's Last Ride: The Tragic Story of the Central Australian Gold Exploration Coy. Ltd.*[134] That wasn't going to go down well with the CAGE Directors and by the time it was released in September 1931 the corporate *tragedy* had become an Australian *epic* – **Lasseter's Last Ride: An Epic of Central Australian Gold Discovery.** In 228 pages over 28 chapters were entwined three stories. The first and central is an account of the First CAGE Expedition drawn from three sources, the first and largest being documents and photographs from the Company files covering the period from the arrival of Lasseter at the AWU offices in March 1930 to the return of Blakeley, Taylor and Sutherland to Alice Springs in September, six months later, after Lasseter and Johns had left Ilbilba with five camels. The second source contained the later reports of Paul Johns and the letters that he delivered to Alice Springs in November when Lasseter was alone and still alive. The third source was Bob Buck's description of finding Lasseter's body at the end of March 1931, the four documents sent to the CAGE Directors, and the letter from Lasseter to Irene.

To be the first in print and to capitalise on the wave of public interest following the news of Lasseter's death and Buck's arrival in Sydney, Idriess wasted no time. But with the material at hand he couldn't spin an engaging story – he had virtually nothing to go on for the last months of the saga. To complete the tapestry he built on that fragmentary and incomplete warp with two other elements, the first being a speculative conclusion before he knew the details of the final act. The second element – the weft that held it all together – is woven around the facts of the Expedition in the first half of the book and is the fabric of the fictional finale. It might go by the column header under which he was published using various pseudonyms two decades earlier in the *Bulletin* – *Aboriginalities* – anecdotes of frontier life in which Aboriginal people were important elements of the scenes he conjured, but largely incidental to the tales. Not so with **Lasseter's Last Ride**; Idriess complements the wilderness backdrop to the main action with an extensive, quasi-ethnographic depiction of the native peoples of the region – reinforced with the imprimatur of Herbert Basedow's glowing foreword.

The third element of Idriess' weave, colourfully knotted into the second half of the book where source material was most sparse, is an incidental filler, and recounts what Phil Taylor called *the part played by aircraft during the Central Australian Gold Exploration's expedition*. Idriess was a believer in the potential of 'planes in the bush; within two years of **Lasseter's Last Ride** two other titles in his expanding oeuvre tracked the triumph of aerial technology over isolation and terrain – **Flynn of the Inland**[135] across the vast expanses of remote Australia, and **Gold Dust and Ashes** in the rugged and densely wooded highlands of New Guinea. And despite *the part played by aircraft* in the First CAGE Expedition being unimpressive, with crashes, strandings, near fatalities and, ultimately, four additional planes deployed in replacement, rescue and recovery, Idriess needed a story and this one – repurposed to exemplify pluck and persistence – fitted nicely. The tapestry was complete.

Flight risk

Of the three spliced strands the tale of the aviators was the least relevant but the easiest to tell. The main problem was that there was almost nothing to be said about its role in the Expedition other than stuff-ups and, while the *Golden Quest* appears reasonably often in the first chapters, the pilot is hardly mentioned, save an almost passing mention as the members are being described with Coote: *anxious for his job in the Golden Quest to begin.*[136] That job didn't last long and even the crash of the *Golden Quest* at Yaiyai Creek seems incidental to Idriess' description of the quick thinking of Fred Colson, who extracted the seriously injured Coote from the wreckage and drove him through the night *with all his nerve and speed* to Alice Springs.

Coote returned in *Golden Quest II* as a passenger in September with Pat Hall as pilot, whose brief stay at Ilbilba and flight with Lasseter are described in some detail. He and Coote quickly recognise that the new plane, like the previous one, was ill-suited to the job and needed extensive refit. Hall and Coote flew out, the latter only re-entering the story when it became known that Lasseter was alone in the desert: *The directors telegraphed instructions via Alice Springs that Coote and Taylor were to get in touch with Lasseter with all speed.* That didn't happen; Coote proposed a base at Ayers Rock, set out from Hermannsburg inadequately prepared and ended up stranded at what he melodramatically called *Hells Airport*. After he and Phil Taylor finally reconnected and Taylor jury-rigged a solution Coote flew out, exiting both the CAGE Company employ and ***Lasseter's Last Ride***.

That might have been the end of it, but of the last hundred pages some forty, in five chapters, tell the story of the forced landing of Pittendrigh and Hamre on their way to Ilbilba in *Golden Quest II* and their stranding at Dashwood Creek, the search for them by RAAF planes, and their eventual rescue after three weeks in the bush. It's a ripping yarn with dialogue so lively that it suggests Idriess interviewed the pair. Perhaps too ripping; as Pittendrigh and Hamre confront death from dehydration, Idriess has them stare fate in the face:

"Pitt," said Hamre seriously, "we both know how things are. Have you any suggestions to make, any scheme at all to pull through?"

"None whatsoever, old bean," admitted Pittendrigh cheerfully, "except one."

"What is that?" demanded Hamre hopefully.

"Let us die like gentlemen, in comfort." And Pittendrigh knelt clumsily to fix his ragged mosquito-net in the shade of a mulga tree.

Saved by a passing shower they stagger on, surviving on *milk tabloids* and little else, filling empty hours with fantasies of food – and notebook cricket. The chapter, *Christmas on the Desert Fringe,* includes a copy of the scoring card they used and has Pittendrigh describe the rules before play begins at a shilling a game: *In the long days that followed it helped pass many a forlorn hour.* Sterling stuff; with the new year there are sightings of search planes but time and hunger drag on until, alerted by the RAAF pilots who find them and drop temporising supplies, help arrives: *Horses and camels sounded crashing through the mulga as from the bushes the huge form of Archie Giles appeared, his face wreathed in smiles.*

The revived aviators were soon aware that the search for them and their rescue were national news with headlines transforming the ongoing CAGE Expedition air debacle at a trot. *Vivid Messages Tell of Rescue When Life Was Ebbing! 'PLANE SUCCOR FOR GOLD-SEEKERS. Pittendrigh and Hamre "Getting Weak" In the Arid Desert. Mystery of Fortitude* – that was just the header to the article in the *Daily Pictorial* on Monday 12th January 1931.[137] And lest readers be unappreciative of the heroic qualities of those involved in the search led by Charles Eaton, the last column began: *COLORFUL LIFE OF LT. EATON. ... Six feet tall, clean shaven and bronzed, war pilot, big game hunter, and all-round sportsman. These are the characteristics of Flight-Lieut. Eaton.*

Idriess knew that what sold newspapers worked for books. Even if *the part played by aircraft during the Central Australian Gold Exploration's expedition* was less than inspiring, he needed to weave it in, but gave the last hurrah to the lone prospector in the desert, conjuring a vision of the future as he trudged along next to his camels: *Lasseter gazed up at the clear*

blue sky. Out of it would come aeroplanes. That was where modern trans-
port would come into its own, when the pathfinder's job was done. Then
would come the rush, the opening up of a goldfield, the settlement of a new
State.

Saucing up the source material.

That was, of course, pure fiction. But all he had to go on for the story after Lasseter and Paul Johns parted ways were the letters that Johns brought back from Ilbilba, the reports of Bob Buck and the small cache of papers found near the corpse. For the rest of the book – accounting for more than half of the total and interspersed with the five chapters devoted to Pittendrigh and Hamre – Idriess lifted arresting elements from those thin and fragmented sources to crown the saga with drama and tragedy. It was a mix just sufficiently leavened with scraps of evidence so as to rise and be palatable to readers hungry for adventure and the exotic. It worked a charm.

The first half of the book is very different; there was a lot to go on, including photographs. Idriess was keen on photographs but in 1930 he wasn't a photographer.[138] Instead, he scoured archives and reports and maintained furious correspondence with anyone who had, or could get, the pictures he wanted. For **Lasseter's Last Ride** he struck a rich lode of images in the Company files, many of which had been taken by Phil Taylor, and ultimately found their way with the Company papers to the Mitchell Library.[139] Ironically, Lasseter appears in only a single full photograph opposite the title page – *Harold Bell Lasseter and Family*. Taken at the Russell Hill Settlement for construction workers building the nation's new capital in early 1927, Lasseter stands behind Irene who sits on a swing holding their two infant children. That photograph was not from the CAGE files and must have come from Irene. Idriess' biographer, Beverley Eley, gives a clue to how it was obtained:

> *George Ferguson, then scarcely in his twenties and the man who would eventually become a publishing director of Angus and Robertson, drove Jack, mid-1931, to the Lasseter home in Kogarah in NSW to buy from Mrs Lasseter the diary which was said to have been found with Lasseter's*

body. Ferguson recalled that there was a great air of excitement about the project and that the buying of the diary by Angus and Robertson was a 'hush-hush' affair.[140]

Eley is not the only person to confuse the fragments found near Lasseter's body by Buck on 29th March 1931, with the notebook unearthed by Frank Green during the Second CAGE Expedition on 16th October – seven months later. What Irene had in the middle of 1931 was the letter forwarded by Carrington to the Department of Home Affairs which was then sent to her, and family photographs – including from Canberra. On 12th August 1931, Idriess wrote to Walter Cousins at Angus & Robertson, commenting: *Re Lasseter's letters (or letter) which you wish to reproduce. Mrs Lasseter has loaned me a letter to her which Bucks [sic] found. ... also that photo you took a fancy to.*[141]

That *photo* is probably the image that faces the title page of the first edition. Of the other 32 photographs two simply show camels that may have been those that arrived with Paul Johns.[142] Of the remaining thirty, four show landscapes, six capture expedition-related activities, and six depict the *part played by planes*. That leaves fourteen that are of Aboriginal people. Of these, five are woven into the story and are of the same family. The remaining nine photographs seem to have been selected to represent what, in later editions, is titled *types of primitive men*. And there is one other image, Edgar Alfred Holloway's graphic dust jacket which shows it all – two fully-laden camels careering towards the viewer, the bearded prospector on his knees with a revolver pointed in the direction of the departing dromedaries. In the background are two Aboriginal warriors emerging from behind a grass tree, the shafts of half-a-dozen scapes and spears suggesting the blurring of natural and human dangers. And above it all is the perfect circle of a relentless sun in a desert-coloured sky with the spectral outline of a biplane passing over the scene and the title.

Idriess' account of the CAGE Expedition, up to the point where *Lasseter with two camels set off alone on his last ride,*[143] broadly fits with the accounts of the others who were there. But, even to that reasonably well documented point, much about what happened has been contested since. Even in 1931 there were tensions and unresolved claims that Idriess chose to gloss over, including Lasseter's backstory about finding the reef thirty years earlier which is covered at a gallop – in just two pages. Idriess knew that there were questions about Lasseter that were best only hinted at through allusions to an enigmatic personality:

> Lasseter was cheerful and reserved in turns. His determined face did not belie the nature of the man within. An unusual man in several ways. ... Highly educated men with whom he came in contact have expressed their surprise at his knowledge of unusual subjects, never suggested by the man's everyday talk. His mates on this expedition found him a good camp-mate, but liable to be impatient at even unavoidable delay. They had an idea, too, that though the finding of this reef occupied his mind, his ultimate object embraced something greater.

Enigma and determination; Idriess describes Lasseter's reaction to news received while the CAGE Expedition was still in Alice Springs that Michael Terry had already set out for the Petermann Ranges with the Endeavour expedition *presumably in search of the reef.* Suggesting Terry was likely the first of many, Idriess conjures a response from Lasseter as a statement of intent and character: *"Let them all come – if they can!" smiled Lasseter, grimly.* And as the Expedition gets under way the conflicts, chaos, malfunctions and mistrust that rapidly emerged go unmentioned in Idriess' confection of cheerful cooperation in the face of unrelenting obstacles. Like getting bogged, punctures, smashed windows and engine troubles – it was all a matter of right attitude, like in the trenches: *Taylor, with "Hurrah! Up and at 'em boys," would lift her into high gear and the big lorry would go lumbering through the mulga with the crew bawling – Sailing up the Clyde, sailing up the Clyde, Back to Bonnie Scotland where the old folks bide.* Maybe... Idriess drew on snatches from photos and correspondence to create cameos of the party. Within one page he has almost all of them:

> Blakeley was ... short, powerfully built, somewhat slow of speech, with clean-cut features, not so ready, perhaps, as the other members of the party to break into a laugh – his was the responsibility. ... Sutherland

was a sly humourist. A six-foot slab of a bushman, his weather-beaten
face never lacked its smile. … Colson, the bushman, proved a first-rate
worker; tireless and always cheery. … Taylor … was typical of the
engineer who could lose himself in a machine. … Coote was a young
fellow bubbling over with enthusiasm.

Idriess used the photographs in the CAGE files to add detail to his descriptions of the Expedition members and to draw the reader into their routines in ways that supported the credibility of the narrative and the narrator. Although the part he played was small, the aristocratic Blakiston-Houston was too good a subject to be missed. In one photograph in the archive but not included in the book he is sitting on the driver-side running board of Fred Colson's Chevrolet, the vehicle and the man dappled by shade from a tree just outside the frame. The brightest element in the photograph is knee-length, white shorts which on closer inspection are the Englishman's underwear, his lower legs still in his trousers which are bunched below his knees. He's looking toward the camera as if just caught by the intruding lens, his eyes drawn away from the task in front of him, his hands held carefully just below his face – he's threading a needle. Idriess has this mundane scene do serious work, underscoring the challenges and the character of the men who rise to them:

Said Houston, as he wiped the sweat from his noble brow, "If we've
done nothing else we've certainly made a road." And he retired to the
shade of a tree to mend his trousers. A regretful party said good-bye to
Houston. His capability and unfailing cheeriness had made him much
liked. "He's a damn good bushman gone to waste." Said Sutherland,
regretfully, as they watched the Chevrolet disappear through the bush.
"Him plurry white man!" voted Micky.

The only Aboriginal member of the team, Micky, one of Archie Giles' stockmen, serves various purposes for Idriess and he features in several photographs. In another not included in the book, he's standing in front of the driver side door of the Thornycroft, the logo of the expedition partly obscured by his shadow, as are his eyes in the darkness beneath the rim of a bush hat. He's wearing a shirt and collarless, oversized coat, trousers and boots, and dangling from his hands, which are held together at chest height is a white object that, only on careful scrutiny, resolves into an immature kangaroo – a joey – held by its tail:

> At this soak Taylor shot their first 'roo.' Roo-tail soup was a welcome addition to the bill of fare. Micky was in ecstasy; for this unfortunate 'roo carried a baby in its pouch. Micky, tenaciously gripping the baby, explained that this food was a delicacy, "taboo" to all the young men of his tribe. Only the old men were allowed to eat it. And now this luxury that he had expected to enjoy only in his crafty old age was in his hands. Micky cooked his stolen delight on a little fire away by himself.

Micky was a real person, an Aranda man with some schooling at Hermannsburg and basic English. But in **Lasseter's Last Ride** he's a device – *the "civilized" blackboy* – through which the author shifted gears from embellished narrative to sensationalised fiction. Micky stands as a transitional figure, sufficiently civilised to be part of the team, but liminal enough to exemplify childlike wonderment at technology, like the propeller of the 'plane: *As he stroked them with reverent hands he said: "By cri', good feller boomerang this one."* Perhaps to make sure the point isn't missed, on the same page Idriess has Micky's coerced introduction to radio:

> They put the ear-phones on Micky. Seated on a box he submitted with a grin, anticipating anything might happen. Something did. Statics! Micky bolted. When they caught him they held him down, patting him as they would a horse. They hung on until he got the music which "soothes the savage breast." The glare faded from his eyes; his breast heaved less riotously; the frightened gash that was his mouth expanded into a grin that spread from ear to ear; his eyes grew normal, then sparkled.

Micky is also an intermediary between worlds, and the distance to those untouched and untainted by civilisation is played out when a tribal group approaches: *He hardly understood a word of their "lingo"* and clung close to the whites, obviously afraid of these "Myall" countrymen of his. The wild men, however, treated their civilized brother with disdain. Civilized brother – the reader is left under no illusion that being so touched is anything other than superficial, and Idriess uses Micky to introduce the theme that is critical for the dramatic, fictional denouement of the Lasseter story – sorcery. A few days after another group of *desert nomads* arrives at Ilbilba, with goodwill supposedly assured through *the present of a few shattered pieces of glass*, Idriess describes a sudden change in Micky's behaviour – *frightened hostility* – the cause of which only becomes clear when Micky rushes into camp: *with his eyes nearly starting from his head: "Kaditcha!" he gasped. "Man in Kaditcha shoes he walk about! We go away quick feller!" Micky's veneer of civilization had vanished. He had slipped back into the stone age from which he had never really emerged.*

In **Lasseter's Last Ride** the *Kaditcha* story runs in two parts, the first introduced by Micky's horrified realisation. At that point the Expedition is still intact and through the first half of the book Idriess alternates chapters filtering in snippets of what was known about its progress, with five that develop the Aboriginal themes: *The Kaditcha, Stone Age Men, Mystery and Magic, What "The Stick" Meant,* and *The Hoodoo.* The central character behind *The Hoodoo* is the classic trickster hiding in plain sight, to all appearances an amiable buffoon discovered, too late, to be anything but – *Rip Van Winkle.*

Ngapatjukurrpa's country included Ilbilba, where the Donald Mackay Aerial Survey expedition had set up base three months before he met the members of the First CAGE Expedition on 18th August 1930. Idriess neatly creates the scene as he appears with his family, wearing the item received from the departing Mackay expedition that led to the name by which he's known to us: *The newcomer carried a firestick in his hand and an ingratiating smile on his wrinkled old face. He wore a moustache, a comical pointed beard, and an old felt hat! "Rip Van Winkle come to life again,"* drawled Sutherland. *"All dressed up and nowhere to go!"* It's a catchy handle. But despite attributing it to Sutherland, Idriess himself claimed responsibility for the name in a 1936 letter to *The Wide World Magazine* in response to an article by William Charnley[144] (Chapter 6). Whoever coined the name, it was an inspired descriptor and typical of the practices of the time. The year after this encounter and Sutherland's supposed whimsical naming of Ngapatjukurrpa, Walter Gill was with Bob Buck as he headed back to the Petermanns and commented on nicknames, or what he called *the Territory's questionable custom,* as Buck settled handles of convenience to two Aboriginal youngsters: *It is this lack of inventiveness on the part of the average white man which has been responsible for the horde of Lions, Tigers, Billys, Nuggets, Paddys, and Jackys – together with the host of poor devils with unprintable names – who litter the countryside. And now Buck has excelled himself; adding "Pig's Tit" and "Buggerlugs" to the tally.*[145] Writing **Petermann Journey** years later, Walter Gill chose his examples from experience. On the journey to where Buck had found Lasseter's body just a few months earlier they are accompanied by an Aboriginal man and his family who join Buck, Gill and two Aboriginal stockmen as they set out from Buck's property. Gill refers to that man as *Lion*:

> *a stockily built man, middle aged, with a beard of which he is extremely proud. He comes from the Petermann and he has no English. About to describe him as simple, I changed the word to primitive; a better description. He seems a happy soul, smiles when spoken to and looks very elegant in pants, shirt, and handkerchief à la Buck: they are the first garments he has ever possessed.*[146]

In **Petermann Journey** Lion figures prominently, and Gill came to understand that the man he had fleetingly thought of as simple was anything but. He was, rather, a tribal man of qualities and Gill got to know Lion and his family. By contrast, Idriess never met any of the Aboriginal cast in the Lasseter saga – what he knew of them was from photographs, including Rip Van Winkle/ Ngapatjukurrpa and his family, who appear in six of the fourteen images of Aboriginal people in the first edition of **Lasseter's Last Ride,** Ngapatjukurrpa himself in three. Among the others are his toddler son, *Bubbles* – Jimmy Tjungarrayi[147] – who half-a-century later shared his memories of meeting Expedition members with Billy Marshall-Stoneking.[148] In the first image Jimmy Tjungarrayi appears in profile with a bulging lower abdomen above a title –*"Bubbles" filled his tummy with water* – next to which he is mesmerised as he examines an object held just in front of his face, a mirror – *and failed to recognize himself.* The third image on that page is an Aboriginal man similarly entranced – *so did uncle.*

Two of the photographs of Ngapatjukurrpa that Idriess selected for the book are taken seconds apart, and in both Blakeley is on one side and Mickey on the other. The three men are kneeling and in conversation, the title to the first being *Blakeley questions Rip Van Winkle,* and to the second *Rip Van Winkle lies to guard the immemorial waterholes.* In the third image, titled *Rip Van Winkle introduces portion of his family,* Ngapatjukurrpa appears to the side of a group of seven women and children. Those photographs were taken at Ilbilba, probably by Phil Taylor in August 1930. In late May of the following year Walter Gill was travelling west with Bob Buck and Lion, and in **Petermann Journey** Gill includes photographs he took of Lion and his brother, and a family group – *Lion with his relations* – which looks remarkably similar to the image used by Idriess of Ngapatjukurrpa and his family – right down to the pointed hat.

The same man... Lion and Gill met close to Middleton Ponds, seventy kilometres from Hermannsburg. Ilbilba, where Ngapatjukurrpa and his family were photographed, is just under 300 kilometres north-west – a long way but entirely possible. And between the moments when those images were captured, on 6th October, three weeks after Lasseter and Johns left Ilbilba with five camels, Pastor Friedrich Albrecht arrived at Ilbilba where he found the supply dump set up for Lasseter by the departing CAGE Expedition three weeks earlier, and a small tribal group: *One of them, Kamutu, a leader of this group, greeted us with a pair of trousers he held in position with one hand, and a shirt, put on hastily with front to back.*[149]

Despite distance and terrain there was clearly traffic between the two sites. Two years later, in *The Brisbane Courier* for 15th September 1932, there is a boxed set of photographs relating to a visit to Hermannsburg by *Miss May Spinks, the first woman to visit Central Australia by aeroplane.* But one photograph is of an Aboriginal man with a copy of *The Brisbane Courier* held in front of him. Only his nose stands out from the dark shadow cast by his battered, pointed hat, the title above the image proclaiming *RIP VON WINKLE* and the explanation below: *Rip Von Winkle who figures in the book, "Lasseter's Last Ride," is shown here reading "The Brisbane Courier" of September 1, delivered by Pilot Alan Cameron at Hermannsberg [sic] Mission station on September 3.*[150]

Three years later another photograph taken at Hermannsburg shows Pastor Albrecht seated with camels and dogs to the left of the frame and a group of Aboriginal men and women sitting in the foreground with the most prominent wearing a battered felt hat. That photo was of *Albrecht visiting tribal people in the Haasts Bluff area* on the way to Ilbilba, and so aptly captured the spirit of the mission project that it was used as the chapter header throughout the biography of Albrecht. In the same book there is another powerful image, the title reading: *In October 1930, the elders of the Hermannsburg congregation decided with Albrecht to hold a Christian service to 'open' the traditionally sacred cave of Manangananga in the nearby hills.*[151] Gathered in what looks like a rugged natural amphitheatre, close to one hundred Aboriginal people, many in mission-days Sunday best, look to the camera as the important moment is caught. Probably half of the men are wearing battered, pointed hats.

Rip Van Winkle, Ngapatjukurrpa, Rip Von Winkle, Kamutu, Lion; one person – or more... One battered, pointed hat – or many... It's hardly surprising that from the dozens of images in the CAGE Company files Idriess selected those of a readily identifiable individual whose indistinct, shadowed visage perfectly accepted the projections of duplicity, intrigue and imputations of black magic that he needed to complete the story.

But there are eight other pictures of Aboriginal people in the first edition, with titles like: *This lass of fifteen sees her first white man; This desert Sheikh arrived in his best pants; Children of the sun,* and; *A desert brood.* They are interesting without being compelling – except for one, the last of all, which is of four naked young women standing in a row and facing away from the camera. With thickly plaited hair and each holding tufts of grass or brush, their backs are densely and intricately decorated above their waists. The photo is the lower of two, the other being a group of six adult men who appear to be grooming themselves and each other; the title: *Dressing up for the dance.* The reader should presume that both relate to traditional practices and lest the obvious sensuality in the image of these naked women be too obvious – which it is – the title attempts to be playfully suggestive with a caveat of ethnographic detachment: *"Back to nature" the patterns are symbolic.*

Two months after the first copies of **Lasseter's Last Ride** were being stacked for distribution, the same photograph appeared in *The Mail* in Adelaide under the header *Magic and Mystery in Central Wilds: Savage Tribes Still Live in World of Stone Age Sorcery and Barbarism* – the article commencing: *Stone Age sorcery and barbaric rites still linger in the wilds of Central Australia. Such was the experience of Harold Bell Lasseter, who died there while in search of a mineral field.* After briefly noting the probable near extinction of tribal populations, the anonymous author lurches into a heady description of male initiation: *Unprotesting, he is roughly gagged, their bestial faces breathe into his. The crowd sways as they break a lane through which comes a fearsome being under brilliant feathers and tufts of dyed grass. He carries the dreaded knife in his hand.* Below a graphic description of other aspects of this male ritual, the same incongruous photo of four naked young women appears, titled: *NEWLY INITIATED GIRLS, their backs patterned in symbolic designs. Most of these skin mutilations have totemic significance – and mark a curious mythical linkage of each aboriginal with legendary ancestors, half-animal, half-human.* [152]

There are other photographs on the page that also appear in the first edition of **Lasseter's Last Ride** and although Idriess is not credited as the author of that piece, he is of exactly the same article that appeared in Brisbane's *Sunday Mail* just weeks after the release of the book.[153] The title to the photograph of the four naked young women – *Newly-initiated girls* – is the same as the anonymous article that appeared later, and lest there be any doubts about the connection to Lasseter an accompanying column begins: *A highly civilized man, thrown suddenly back into the Stone Age, fighting for his life against weird superstitions, brute strength, and unprintable savageries – such was Harold Bell Lasseter, late of Kogarah.* Idriess clearly wanted to get the message out about **Lasseter's Last Ride** and the *Mystery and Magic* angle probably played well. Having photos that were in turn exotic and erotic wouldn't have hurt – except that the *newly initiated girls* were not – they were young men. This image also does not appear in any of the three files of CAGE Company photos in the Mitchell Library where the others in the book can be found. Idriess may have chosen it from another source to spice up his narrative – and got it wrong.

Just a few months after that article was published Idriess was back in Kogarah, at Irene Lasseter's doorstep, and left with the various items that Frank Green had brought back from Central Australia. But by that time there had been four editions of **Lasseter's Last Ride** and from September 1931, when it was a hot new item, the potential reading public had been titillated and primed to expect more than a simple Central Australian prospecting tragedy. There had been lots of those; this was about something far more interesting – sorcery. That theme was captured in Alan Wauchope's article in the *Leaves From a Booklover's Diary* section of *The Mail* (Adelaide) for 19th September 1931, which led with: *Was Lasseter "Hoodooed"? Theory in Book on Expedition.*[154] Just a few days earlier Idriess had reprised the Lasseter story and elaborated on treachery and sorcery in the *Sydney Mail.* In the last in a series of articles that itself was spread over two pages with photographs from the Expedition, there is an image in a rondelle at the top that is in the book, titled: *Blakeley and Micky questioning Rip Van Winkle. They know that when the nigger pointed water as being north it would actually be south; his object was to take them as far away from water as possible.*[155]

Ngapatjukurrpa – scripted as Rip Van Winkle to play a part involving

... the news of Lasseter's death was only just being circulated.

Micky was in ecstasy ...

Rip van Winkle with Blakeley and Mickey.

RIP VON WINKLE.

Rip Von Winkle, who figures in the book, "Lasseter's Last Ride," is shown here reading "The Brisbane Courier" of September 1, delivered by Pilot Alan Cameron at Hermannsberg Mission station on September 3.

Rip Von Winkle, The Brisbane Courier.

Blakiston-Houston: ... *he retired to the shade of a tree to mend his trousers.*

duplicity and dark rituals into which the First CAGE Expedition unwittingly fall, as Idriess reprised:

Meanwhile the truck party at Ilbilba were placed under a "hoodoo" by the natives on account of a stolen "sandhills god." This was a sacred Churinga stick, a totem on which was carved the history of a tribe from the time of its first man and woman. As vengeance in a tribal feud the stick was stolen and offered to the white men, who accepted it, quite unwitting at the time of the curse which was thus passed to them. On Lasseter, who touched the symbol first, the natives declared the curse would most heavily fall.

Idriess used sorcery – *the hoodoo* – as the plot device to resolve the unknowns for his story. Rip Van Winkle provided the ideal agent for the narrative task save for one inconvenient fact – neither Ngapatjukurrpa nor Lasseter were there for the critical event. In Blakeley's account, from numerous smoke signals it was clear that there were Aboriginal groups in the vicinity. On the evening of 12th September he left camp to send up a rocket trying to attract Johns' attention. Then: *When I got back about midnight the others told me that Rip and his family had cleared out just before handout time.*[156] The next day Johns reappeared and by that evening a contract of sorts had been written up to engage him as a CAGE Company employee to go on with Lasseter. On 15th September they left and it was a day or so later, Blakeley records, that a new group of sandhill people arrived and Phil Taylor, with some trepidation, went with the men to a waterhole, returning after sunset with: *a long board nearly twelve feet in length and about eight inches wide. It was an inch thick running to a flat, tapered point on each end, with lots of carving on it.* Blakeley, Sutherland, Taylor and Colson then witnessed a ceremony, after which the sandhill men disappeared, leaving the object with the puzzled Europeans.

In Blakeley's account, when the Expedition minus Lasseter was back in Alice Springs in early October 1931, Fred Colson brought a local Aboriginal man *to see the stick* – who explained that: *it was a sandhill native's god. The carving on the stick was the whole history of the tribe that it belonged to … He thought that very likely it belonged to Rip Van Winkle's*

110

tribe, and we later found out that it did. We told him we had it over three weeks and he said, "Well, it won't matter now because they are all dead by this, but you shouldn't have taken it." Blakeley states how ashamed he felt at having been complicit in removing the sacred object from traditional lands adding, with obvious reference to Idriess: *I may state here that Lasseter never saw this stick and had nothing to do with it. He had left the day before with Johns, so did not have the god-stick blessing or otherwise as many people believe.*

To make this morsel into a meal – to work as a central plot device – Idriess changed the timing of the event, the parties involved and the interpretation given by Colson's Aboriginal informant. An entire chapter – *Mystery and Magic* – is devoted to the task and is introduced with a paragraph that is cunningly constructed to encourage the reader to suspend disbelief:

> *Maybe this chapter does not directly concern the result of the expedition; perhaps it does. Maybe it could remain unwritten without affecting the story. However, I will write it, because the subject really interested the men concerned (they discuss it even more now) and because it may prove interesting to readers – especially those with a taste for uncanny things and anthropology. What is recorded here actually happened.*

Maybe it could remain unwritten without affecting the story... Maybe – but not the story Idriess was intent on telling. In his version the sandhill people arrive before the Expedition sets out on its last push to the south. They are there for several days and Idriess has Lasseter explain to Phil Taylor that Micky's mounting anxiety is about a *Kaditcha* whose actions seems to have ensorcelled the small group of sandhill natives. Lasseter recognises that for some reason they want Taylor to leave the camp with one of them and Lasseter encourages him. They return an hour later: *The native squatted by the fire, balancing upon his palms a flat hardwood stick some twelve feet in length, six inches wide and half an inch thick. Its edges tapered like a two-edged sword. The stick was remarkably carved from end to end.*

As described by Blakeley, the mysterious ceremony at Ilbilba occurred after Lasseter had already left with Johns. In **Lasseter's Last Ride,** however, Lasseter plays a central role and is selected by the elder in the group to *spread his hands on the broad stick.* Then:

Slowly, the warrior holding the stick began to withdraw his palms, as he did so signing Lasseter to place his palms underneath, finger-tip to finger-tip with the warrior. As his palms glided away so Lasseter's slid forward while his mates' finger-tips gripped the stick edges. As the warrior slid his hands away the stick was left resting on the palms of Lasseter. Instantly the chant ceased, and in the strained silence there went up a sigh of intense relief. As one man, the natives stealthily crept back, still facing the stick. On their finger-tips and toes they backed away into the night like giant baboons. Then the croon of the lubras ceased.

In the chapter *What "the Stick" Meant,* Idriess repurposes and rescripts the meeting in Alice Springs between the returned Expedition members and Fred Colson's Aboriginal informant. In this telling it's revealed that it was Ngapatjukurrpa – Rip Van Winkle – transformed by donning the *Kaditcha shoes,* who had terrified the sandhill people – and Micky. Supposedly, this was retribution for their theft of the sacred board some years earlier, a theft that had resulted in a curse on Ngapatjukurrpa's tribe. Now themselves doomed by sorcery there is only one way to escape the curse, as Idriess has Colson's Aboriginal informant explain: *"they did what no other sandhills, nor any other tribe, have been able to do under similar circumstances. They gave the stick to you and you took it willingly. No natives in Australia, probably in the whole world, would have taken, willingly, that stick, because in that way the curse passes on and the tribe who were circled by the Kaditcha shoes, go free."* As the Aboriginal man makes ready to leave he turns back to the four Europeans with one last question:

"Who actually laid his hands on the stick first?" he asked in a low voice.

"Lasseter," said Sutherland.

"He will never come back," said the man, and was gone.

Fictional finale

With this fanciful revision the elements of the hoodoo are in place; Lasseter is the unwitting recipient of a curse, the dramatic mechanism to take the story to what, at the time of writing, was understood as the final scene – Lasseter dead after having located the reef. The only constraint on the narrative arc was that it had to be consistent with the limited information that was in the public domain and that Idriess had access to – the documents found by Bob Buck and delivered to the Government Resident, Carrington, in Alice Springs. Fortunately, they were sent on to Arthur Blakeley at the Department of Home Affairs and were transcribed, like the letter that was addressed to Irene which was forwarded to her.[157]

The four notes found near Lasseter's body are short and one seems to have been written on the back of a letter Lasseter had received before leaving Sydney, informing him that goatskins he had ordered were ready to be picked up. One of the others was written on two sides of a folded sheet of paper so that the beginnings of each line on the left and the ends of lines on the right are indistinct. This is the only one that Idriess copies in the book and the sole fragment for which an original exists.[158] It reads:

> *... day the treacherous*   *they have made no ...*
> *... Wattee Mitta Mitta*   *to build me a ...*
> *... big revolver he should*   *anything for shade ...*
> *... a warning. If it were*   *78th day no food ...*
> *...in I could have got*   *I realize my end is ...*
> *...he is now dragging*   *I also realize ha...*
> *...ward some time*   *the appeal I s...*
> *...too weak to*   *blacks from (th)...*
> *...thout assistance*   *and nearly blind ...*
> *...his arm round me*   *about the body is (st)...*
> *...dragged me five*   *help with all speed ...*
> *...now lying in the*   *a pack horse or ridi...*
> *....(te sand) in the*   *might have got to ...*
> *...rek where they*   *but what hurts (most)...*
> *...e one old woman*   *is not to know why I ...*
> *...feed of ripe figs*   *abandoned thus. (I)...*
> *...(s) I'm done for*   *weak to stand & have*
>   *dysentery that will (fini)...*

The transcriptions of the three other notes that had been forwarded to the CAGE Directors in Sydney read:

27.12.30 Camels have bolted with water supply and spilled the rest. I'm walking on boot upper leather and terribly footsore will try & make it back to Winter's Glen & hold out till relieved, but ammunition is very scarce and blacks undeniably hostile. I tried to smoke them in & fired cannon crackers to draw their attention. I know they heard me but they have not come near so I expect treachery & have fitted treacle tin breast-plate across my stomach & loins, which is their favorite place to spear a man. I've got the blight bad again & no relief. If humanly possible I would like my wife to get anything you recover of mine. I'm planting things on this sand hill within a radius of 10 ft. from fire, expect the blacks are watching me, but can't help it.
Good luck to all   hope I get a chance to put up a fight. Lasseter.

I have been turned out of camp by Micky the headman. If this is handed to a white man by an old man with wart 6 inches long on his backside treat him kindly   if not do nothing for them. If you have brought my supplies from Ilbilla, give the blacks a dozen tins of beef & tell them another team is bringing them the rest LASSETER
I expect to die on the track and am very weak and have no tucker to start on

as soon as relief comes start a fire on the hill across the creek. If I am within sight I will start fire also & sit down and wait for you but please hurry. I will be Eastward if I deviate from camel pad will draw an arrow in the sand Lasseter.
(Across page) Could not make it and returned to Glen.

While the CAGE Expedition was still intact, and reports and first-hand accounts were available, Idriess used them to the extent they fit with his story. If they didn't, he improvised; the only absolute constraint was that he was careful to avoid saying anything negative about the CAGE Company and its Directors – his sources and benefactors. From the moment that Paul Johns left Lasseter at Ilbilba on 30th October 1930 and headed unhurriedly to Alice Springs where he arrived on 13th November, to Bob Buck being led to the body of Lasseter on 29th March 1931, the only sources for, and constraints on, Idriess' tale-telling were those four pieces of paper. He could fill in the dots between *the hoodoo* and its unwitting victim's inevitable demise as he saw fit – and he did.

The account of those months is spread over nine chapters, nearly sixty pages, in the second half of the book. The standout items from the fragments are incorporated: Lasseter's camels bolt, he engages with an Aboriginal group who give him food, despite that he feels threatened and is prepared to fight, his shoes give out, he leaves hidden messages, he is unwell and develops *dysentery* and eye problems – the *blight* – and he tries to leave *Winter's Glen* but is forced to return. Lasseter's notes identify three individuals, to two of whom he's given names. The most prominent is *Wattee Mitta Mitta,* with whom the word *treacherous* seems to be associated as does Lasseter's *revolver* as a *warning.* The second identified person is mentioned at a time when Lasseter appears to believe his end is close and being hastened by this powerful figure: *I have been turned out of camp by Micky the headman.* For the purpose of the story Idriess chose to make *Wattee Mitta Mitta* and *Micky the headman* one and the same person. For the last identified individual Lasseter provided no name – *an old man with wart 6 inches long on his backside* – but Idriess did, *Old Warts.*

On 10th June 1931, Walter Gill and Bob Buck visited the site where Lasseter had died, between the bushman's discovery of the body ten weeks before and his return with the Second CAGE Expedition some seven months later. Gill was present when Buck fulfilled the request in Lasseter's note: *Before leaving Putta Putta, we took ten minutes off to present "Warty Arse" with a bag of flour. Buck had named him … a tall, gangling, middle-aged native with a large wart-like callous on his buttock, a protuberance sufficiently eye catching to prod Bucks fertile imagination into branding him Warty Arse.*[159] His real name was

Kirrinytja, Marshall-Stoneking discovering fifty years later that he was a respected Pitjantjatjarra man.[160] Idriess did not know that but, like Ngapatjukurrpa and his battered hat, a credible link and an arresting visual feature meant that there was no way that he would not play a central role in the tale. And he did, Idriess adding for dramatic effect – but perversely, as photographs of Kirrinytja confirm Gill's description of him as *a tall, gangling, middle-aged native* – that he was *humpbacked*. A nice Gothic touch.

The drama is set up by the camels bolting after Lasseter had re-found the gold reef, leaving him not only alone but with limited provisions in a hostile environment. The arrival of an Aboriginal tribal group presents obvious threat but possible salvation, Lasseter's survival hanging on his cunning and supposed understanding of native lingo and ways – and a revolver. To carry the drama Idriess sets up three clichéd characters. *Wattee Mitta Mitta* – aka *Micky the headman* – is a young chief, a fired-up warrior and alpha male. *Old Warts* is, as the fragments suggest, a benign figure, whom Idriess has trying to protect the obviously vulnerable European. But this is scripted as a tragedy – Lasseter has to die. The mechanism is sorcery, the *hoodoo*, already set in play by Rip Van Winkle but ultimately executed by the last member of the dramatic triad, an Idriess confection – *the witch doctor*.

The three are introduced as soon as Lasseter is left alone. *Wattee Mitta Mitta* is hostile and intent on asserting himself, constrained by Lasseter who shows his revolver, spinning the chambers as a display of his power: *He patted the revolver, hissed "Kaditcha!" stared in the eyes of the chief, and rolled over for sleep".*[161] He also uses the limited food he has remaining to win over the group as a whole, promising that more will arrive by *'plane* and camel. While he is still taking stock of his situation he notices: *a wizened old man squatting a little apart from the rest. Around his neck hung a small, smoke blackened fibre bag.* Lasseter immediately recognises him as a major player in the tribe, which becomes clear in the chapter *The Witch-Doctor* as Lasseter watches the sorcerer slowly reveal the sources of his authority from the *smoke blackened fibre bag* – one item at a time until:

> Then came the culminating symbol of his power. With a snakelike movement the man's arm withdrew a thin package about ten inches long wrapped in tea-tree bark as thin as brown paper. Coiled around the bundle was a plaited cord of human hair. Then, for the first time, the eyes of the witchdoctor glared evilly towards Lasseter. He knew! That small package carried the Death-bone!
>
> Lasseter, with a knowing inclination of the head and an expressive stare, acknowledged this emblem of life and death. In sepulchral tones Lasseter turned to Old Warts and congratulated him and the tribe on their witch-doctor, who held greater Kaditcha than any other black doctor. It was only because he knew each of these Kaditcha so perfectly himself, and could control them, that he understood how powerful this witch-doctor really was.

Idriess needed names for the dramatis personae of the final act – the witch-doctor is thereafter *Bones* or *Old Bones* – and he summarises the motivation of the three Aboriginal principals: *Watta Mitta Mitta from the first day they met had urged the tribesmen to kill him. ... "Old Bones" regarded him as an outcast and a liar; but a desperately cunning one, a useful one, who had enhanced his own prestige with the tribe. Old Warts was Lasseter's one friend. He helped him right throughout.* While the central drama could be simply told, the conclusion of the tragedy in **Lasseter's Last Ride** is played out against an extended backdrop of tribal life. The author seems intent on consolidating credibility with detail, elaborating a fictional domestic cast in support of the doomed prospector: *This particular group comprised Old Warts and his lubra, Gadgadgery the Man-eater with Lerilla his wife and their brood, Thurragerra the Lousy-one with Miltijade his nagging wife and her brood, and Lasseter.*

Over several months the tribe moves across the country ending up close to where Lasseter's journey with them started, near *Winter's Glen.*

Within that frame Idriess crams in vivid descriptions of, well, just about everything. The wonders and perils of tribal life include accounts of hunting emu and kangaroo, using fire to trap rodents and lizards, gathering yams and honey ants, preparing food, and the techniques of fire-hardening wood for digging sticks and binding weapons with animal sinews. Idriess contrasts family cooperation and parental concern with seemingly gratuitous violence sufficiently offensive to Lasseter that he intervened to protect *Lerilla* from *Gadgadgery*, beating him senseless with a digging stick after which: *Lasseter flung the stick from him, trembling in every limb. Any blow would have killed a white man: the three had not killed this native. But he did not care, this was not a "thinking" enemy.*

The joys and celebrations of a good hunt and a full belly; the despair and harshness of dry waterholes and blighted bushfoods. In the face of the predictable dangers of hostile tribes Idriess recounts the strategic deployment of warriors in moving through country, and against the caprices of nature that demand the sacrifice of individuals to ensure the survival of the tribe, infanticide and the abandonment of encumbering elderly. And that's just the backdrop to the last scene which, for effect, is played out in two parts, in the first of which Lasseter, his reserves of cunning depleted and his ability to pretend possession of powerful *Kaditcha* exhausted, creeps up in the dark to investigate unusual noises and finds:

> *On a circle of grassy sward knelt Bones, Wattee Mittta Mitta and two old warriors of the tribe. The witch-doctor, crooning and swaying on his squatting haunches held a long sharp pointed bone in the direction of the cave. The other three men squatting at intervals behind him, held clear of the ground a twelve foot cord of human hair attached to the bone. The last man gingerly held a bone cylinder in which the end of the cord was fastened. Needle and cylinder had been carved from the shin bone of a man. The performers swayed to the movements of the witch-doctor and hissed to the croon of his song. They were "pointing the Bone," "singing" someone to death.*

To spin it out, Idriess has Lasseter understand the threat but mistake the target, assuming that the object of the sorcery is *Old Warts*. Over the next days he remains close to *his only friend* as the ambience in the tribe changes dramatically – the *Kaditcha silence* – which seems *directed towards the two men who sat a little apart*. Eventually, without it being said, he realises the awful truth: *It was the sorrowful look in Warts's eyes, that sad farewell from a man who cared, that told the truth. Lasseter stared at the bowed back of the old man as he walked away. The Bone had been pointed at Lasseter!*

Idriess knew the liberties he was taking in spinning a good yarn and maybe because of that he chose to finish this story on solid ground. The last mention of Lasseter alive has him writing lines found by Bob Buck: *"Could not make the Glen, too weak –."* The final pages are more or less from Buck and include the text of the folded-page fragment which, without evidence but for effect, Idriess records was: *Scrawled on the back of his small son's childish letters.* After which it's all over – save for a final fictional flourish: *Lasseter is dead. Two prospectors who set out on his tracks are dead. Old "Warts" is dead. A camel party brings word that he was "boned" after Lasseter's death. But Lasseter's dream lives. A big expedition has already been formed to carry on where he left off. This spirit will watch the dream come true.*

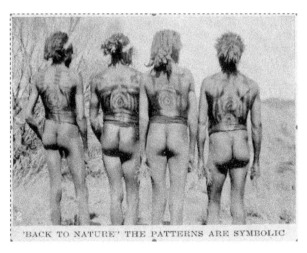

'BACK TO NATURE' THE PATTERNS ARE SYMBOLIC

...and got it wrong.

CHAPTER 6

Narrandera

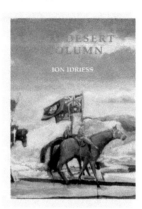

There was a bit of fun up at Quinn's Post a little while ago. The boys rigged up a good bulls-eye, and held it up above the trench. Each time the Turks got a bulls-eye the boys would mark a bull. For an outer, the boys marked an outer, for a miss they yelled derision. The Turks laughed loudly and blazed away like sports. After a while an officer came along and put a stop to the little joke.

Ion Idriess, 1915.[162]

December 2019

Narrandera – a few thousand souls comfortably settled on Wiradjuri land along the northern bank of the Murrumbidgee. Just south of the river is the meeting place of the Sturt and Newell Highways. An explorer and an engineer; a century apart, by river and road they brought time. Sturt came slowly and navigated the Murrumbidgee to the Murray and on to the sea. But he couldn't get through to the ocean and turned the whale-boat upstream all the way back to Narrandera. Soon there were other boats. And tracks, then the railway and roads. Newell built lots of them, all over the place. People, speed – time.

The only boats now are for weekend use on waterways drained by diversion and drought as distant lands burn. But with wildfires racing across northern New South Wales and southern Queensland, it's raining as I drive in. Narrandera railway station looks like an abandoned film set with pigeons rising off the road to circle the silent grain elevators as impatient road trains growl through the gears as they turn south along Cadell Street and on to the centre of town. A block away East Street is pumping, with sidewalk stalls and festive bunting. Nearby a stage stands empty as a loudspeaker drifts snatches of commentary across the street along which five unshorn sheep sporting festive red coats are led through the buzz of kids and their carers. It's just weeks to Christmas.

Next morning I head north out of town, past the race track, golf course and rodeo grounds, to a weatherboard house on acreage with a large, corrugated metal shed off in the distance. Unfastening a chain from the front gate rouses two dogs that need to be placated at the same time as dodging overlapping arcs of spray from a network of sprinklers that seem, at best, to be suppressing dust. Bonny's age-greyed muzzle and splay-legged walk signal her thirteen years, a Collie/Kelpie cross and open to attention of any kind. Saphie is much younger, her tall, lithe frame and wild, blow-away coat proclaiming Irish Wolfhound ancestry that, I'm told by Wendell, includes some Mastiff from the Singleton canine gene pool. A hunter by breed but not by name or nature, she slinks in the background, trembling and submissive. Wendell is distracted by one of her horses, a thoroughbred that could have been a contender but for a broken nose which reminds me of a bottle-nosed dolphin. Another mare muzzles up expecting to be fed, this one's face masked by perforated covers to protect her eyes from flies.

Twenty minutes later I'm with Bonny, Saphie and an old grey cat that hardly registers the dogs or the stranger in the living room of the house. A few steps away Wendell works on a pot of coffee in a kitchen that seems to be struggling to contain dishes, cutlery and more that cover every surface. The casual chaos continues from room to room under the dusted patina of a droughted land. Bonnie and Saphie have settled on a well-worn rug in the middle of the room as coffee and fruitcake appear.

There's no begging – these animals, like the rescue horses, are not neglected. Maybe before they were taken in by Wendell but not now, they're family. Her care for these creatures contrasts with apparent indifference to the inanimate world and, dressed for chores, she navigates around objects and animals with an efficiency that makes it clear she won't be distracted.

Wendell Peacock, grand-daughter of Eta Gibson, Ion Idriess's partner, is around sixty and has been in Narrandera for eighteen months. She was lucky to find acreage close to town that would accommodate her animals and included a shed-cum-barn to store feed for the horses and, as it turns out, the material remains of Ion Idriess' life. We make our way there flanked by Bonny and Saphie and shift the horses into an adjoining paddock – they tend to come into the barn and it's going to be confusing enough. Opening both doors, the interior gloaming is pierced by shards of light driving through holes in the corrugated iron walls and roof. Throughout are the accoutrements of horse-care – hay, saddles, bridles and more. Just inside the entrance, tarpaulins spread atop an irregular mass, part of which protrudes at floor level – the bases of wooden boxes and an old filing cabinet sitting on cracked concrete. As the tarps are pulled back the air is dense with cirrus strata of dust that drifts slowly across an exposed medley of containers that seem to have settled into a coincidental pile two by two metres and rising to shoulder height.

As the motes settle, the guts and bones of it – the dismembered anatomy of a life – begins to make sense. To one side are three leaning towers of wooden boxes across the top of each of which are ragged remnants of what look like old, black, bin liners. Nearby is a group of unsealed polystyrene containers layered over a base of black chests with yellow lids. Scattered throughout is an assortment of cardboard and plastic boxes and a wicker basket, and I can already make out markers of a journey. In my bag I have a photocopied document, the cover of which reads: *Valuation of MANUSCRIPTS, REFERENCE MATERIAL AND ABORIGINAL ARTIFACTS, AS INSPECTED AT 43 HILLCREST AVENUE, 2103*. That work was undertaken by J.D. Hathaway under instructions from Idriess Enterprises and concludes: *I have inspected the Manuscripts Reference Material and Aboriginal Artifacts and Estimate the Fair Market Value at (30,000) THIRTY THOUSAND DOLLARS at 20th October, 1977.*[163]

The valuation was completed at the residence of Idriess' daughter, Wendy, eighteen months before Ion Idriess died in a nearby nursing home. The two pages of this valuation list only draft manuscripts and artefacts. There is a much larger document which itemises the contents of seventeen boxes and a separate set of envelopes containing *letters of note and significance*. A handwritten comment on the cover addressed to *Tom* dated 11th August, 1995 is signed by Beverley Eley. It mentions conflicts with Wendell's mother, Judy, dating back to the 1980s, adding that the lists relate to:

> *seventeen boxes that have been rationalised over the years – several butter boxes that collapsed have been discarded and their contents placed in larger, foam, boxes for safer keeping. There is still the equivalent of 2 butter boxes to be categorised and listed along with other similar material, this includes Lasseter material and Caledon Bay material – this at the moment looms large as a project.*

The Lasseter material – the faded stencils on the remaining wooden butter boxes timestamp a different world. They may have been repurposed by Idriess himself. The now disintegrating polystyrene boxes appeared during Eley's research for her biography of Idriess that came out in 1995, published by Tom Thompson to whom the cover note was addressed. The collection remained with Eley until, after Wendy died, it passed to her sister, Judy, and was lodged in a container on a property at Murrurundi in rural New South Wales. Years later its journey started again, to Wendell in Singleton, and its final transfer eighteen months ago to this barn on the outskirts of Narrandera. Along the way other vessels appeared to carry the story – plastic bins, shopping bags – and where there may have been order the streams and stories have mixed and muddied. And as obvious as the stacks and layers, are spaces and gaps; I imagine a virtual inventory, the fragments of this narrative that have disappeared – too damaged or too valuable to continue on the journey.

The mausoleum of stories and secrets is crumbling and to get up close I have to remove smaller objects crowding the base, brought or thrown down by gravity or convenience. I'm surprised by the weight of the first butter box that I heft to one of the few uncluttered spaces in the barn. Decomposing tape tenuously holds black plastic to slatted sides and solid ends, on one of which is a blue, oval stencil proclaiming its provenance around the rim, *NORCO LIMITED, NEW SOUTH WALES AUSTRALIA*, and in the centre *PURE CREAMED BUTTER – NORCO – PASTEURISED.* Rather than books or documents, inside there's a collection of parcels, some wrapped in old newspaper, others in brown paper and tied with string. To one side is a manila envelope fastened by rusting paperclips across the back of which, written in blue biro is: *Hand grinding stone which handled vigorously by the woman ground the Nardoo seed into flour. The broken grain was thrown into the big stone dish then ground into flower [sic] by a vigorous swirling circular movement of the grind stone.*

An hour later and in large plastic trays, the brittle lids cracking with movement, dozens of foreign editions of Idriess' books appear, some in languages and scripts I don't recognise. In another are volumes that were part of his personal library; next to the **Rubaiyat of Omar Khayyam** is an aged and well-thumbed paperback with its spine reinforced by tape – Vivikenanda's **Raja Yoga.** On almost every page there are underlined sections and marginal comments. In an uneven hand that suggests that it might have been written on the move, maybe on a train or bus: *But this is the very thing that Yoga asks of the reader.* Opening the first of the poly-styrene containers reveals a jigsaw of parcels wrapped in brown paper and tied off neatly with string. On each there is handwriting that is not his, the first in view being: *IDRIESS: One Wet Season. Original MS + corrected typed copy. Pcl A Ch 1-18. One Wet Season.* There are thirty-nine chapters in the book so maybe the rest is in parcel B – somewhere, another piece of the jigsaw.

Other boxes; other rooms of his life. Spilling from split envelopes and files is mail from around the world celebrating his work, offering information or seeking something. The upper left corner of one sheaf of papers has been eaten away, removing the year from the date of a letter written on 22nd August by Charlie Uplin of the *Port Macquarie News* and sent to Idriess at Angus & Robertson: *Your kind and flattering remarks to my wife were something out of the humdrum of ordinary life for her and lightened the load of day's work. How about penning a few lines of your impressions of Port Macquarie and particularly welcome would be your views on the Old Cemetery. A word or two from you should have the desired effect.*

There are notebooks and diaries; he seems to have requisitioned anything at hand, his writing contracting with the size of the paper to an almost illegible micrographia, lines crossing and curling to fill space. Like floating embers, glowing bright before they disappear into the night with the smoke from a campfire, some sheets appear as an attempt to trap thoughts for later use – or not. I hold one with two entries separated by more than forty years: *Standing watching the great glass were the students of diseases. On it were shown the hospitals of the world, every medical institution, down to every individual labouring privately for the defeat of every disease known to the human body. Humanity plans its future, its hopes against the defeat of disease were laid bare on that great mirror.* Below is a date and comment – *March 14, 1959. The above and following pages were written way back in 1913, on Mt Fraser. Wish I'd kept the story going – whatever it was. I.L.I.*

Mt Fraser – in 1913 Idriess was in north Queensland waiting for his luck to change and collecting stories about the opening up of the hinterland. It may be a forgotten place now, embedded in the Mount Lewis National Park, but it was a marker for timber-cutters and miners then, and he wrote about it in **Back o' Cairns** which was published in 1958, the year of his reflection: *Behind Mount Molloy, beginning at Mount Fraser, a range runs north to the Mount Carbine wolfram field. In a future trip to the Tableland I was to work right along that range, for a time on a mixed tin-wolfram reef on Mount Spurgeon.*[164]

Idriess described *that trip* in detail in a book published a quarter-century earlier. **Men of the Jungle** was first released in September 1932 – one year after **Lasseter's Last Ride**. Other than **Madman's Island** it was the first of his books relating to north Queensland and went through ten editions before the decade was out. Idriess had been scratching for tin along the Bloomfield with a mate, Charlie, and they decided to try their luck further south. Passing through Mount Molloy they heard that there was a *bit of tin up on Mount Fraser, about six miles out*. They stocked up and spent the next couple of months just below a hidden camp that had been set up by George, *the old hatter*, a prospector-become-recluse who had drifted to that spot and remained, stranded in the jungle by choice, with a dense set of relationships to the wild:

> *Now, he was a being who counted, a real mate to all the funny little wild things of the bush. They seemed to understand him. With queerly modulated hissings he could coax a snake from out the scrub on the forest grass. According to different species he would vary his hissing to the slow, seductive movements of his hands and feet as his one eye stared at the snake. The big carpet snake that camped in the hut was almost part of him. He would look at it, twitch his eye, and the thing would glide along the humpy floor, climb over his knee and slowly drape itself around his neck, its big, flat head motionlessly resting on the coil upon his shoulder. The snake knew perfectly well it was not to eat Brownie the rat nor Greenie the frog. All the pets preserved a perfect, though armed neutrality while in the hut, the only boisterousness being caused by Spots the goanna who really seemed to think he owned the show. I've seen him in his greed and jealousy scatter the birds, chase the rat, send the frog hopping and threaten the snake with show of teeth, lashing of tail and violent hissing. The big snake would lie motionless, steadily regarding the would-be bully out of cold, glassy eyes until George kicked the spotted disturbance out of the hut. Never without a shindy, however. Spots would even threaten George himself, which roused the old chap to a temper of shouts and kicks. But in his heart I believe he loved the beast just a little more than the rest.*[165]

That was Idriess at his best; I try to visualise Jack back at his camp with Charlie, writing in what remained of the day's last light filtering through the rainforest canopy. Moments before he mused about a barely imaginable future of technology-mediated cooperation as *humanity plans its future, its hopes against the defeat of disease*, maybe he had tried to capture that space of inter-species *armed neutrality* under the watchful, one-eyed gaze of *the old hatter* – George. Switching between the wild and the world; the first cinema in the region opened in Cairns just the year before, and it would be decades before images appeared on primitive screens that evolved into television. And another half-century until the information management functions that Jack seems to be imagining displayed *on that great mirror* are with us in the digital age. I wish he'd *kept the story going* too.

His handwriting is familiar from searching the Angus & Robertson archives at the Mitchell Library. It's clear, without abbreviations, precisely punctuated, and tends to slope upwards to the right across the page. There might be thousands of letters in this collection, almost all written in pencil, and I imagine him receiving them back with a final typed draft in his room in the Angus & Robertson office in Sydney. He kept the drafts for his records. I pick up correspondence between Idriess and Walter Cousins, by 1933 the head at Angus & Robertson, with attached copies of letters between Angus & Robertson and Jonathan Cape in London about the Empire rights to **Lasseter's Last Ride.** The last three pages form another attachment, a letter dated 26th July 1935, from Deal Castle. General William Birdsell had composed an introduction for the non-Australasian market and notes of the author that: *During the Great War he served under me in the Near East as a trooper in the Fifth Australian Light Horse Regiment.* He doesn't mention that both he and Idriess were sighters for Billy Sing, the north Queensland, Chinese Australian who became Australia's crack sniper at Gallipoli, eventually credited with two hundred kills.[166] A tale of courage and tragedy in a harsh and hostile land on the brink of transformation by British enterprise and ingenuity – that seems to be how Birdsell read **Lasseter's Last Ride** but his introduction was perhaps a little too jingoistic for Cousin's taste as one paragraph, which had been struck-through and bracketed for deletion, reads: *Some day the great deserts of Central Australia will be opened up. Wells will be dug. Towns will spring up. Corn will wave and cattle will graze where now are only the endless miles of sand and mulga. The 'dead heart' of Australia will be dead no longer, but a flourishing state of a great Dominion which is destined to play an ever more important part in the history of the world.*

Corn will wave and cattle will graze... Idriess and Lasseter would have smiled. But through most of a day rummaging there's disappointingly little about **Lasseter's Last Ride**. That's not the case for **The Cattle King**; while the Lasseter story was opportunistic and rushed, Sidney Kidman was bush royalty and the company a powerful patron. Idriess knew he had to get it right; more than accurate, it had to be acceptable. There are notes from Kidman executives after Sir Sidney died the year before **The Cattle King** came out in 1936, with suggestions about how sensitive matters, such as the treatment of native workers, should be presented. Idriess was the anointed biographer and **The Cattle King** would be an authorised text.

In the late afternoon light Saphie and Bonny meander into the barn, settling near bales of hay to the side of the now-dismembered pile. My eyes are straining to make sense of pencil handwriting, some of which was written a century ago. Wendell has been on the periphery through the day, an audience to the commentary I've maintained about the people and places that appear on the papers before me, and the books and periods of Idriess's life that they relate to. I seem to be providing a metanarrative to her story of *Pop*. It's time to call it a day, Wendell has horses to attend to and dogs to feed, and I need to surface for air.

Two hours later I pick Wendell up and we head to the Charles Sturt Hotel on East Street for dinner. Saturday night – it's all happening at The Sturt. We settle into a corner table at a three-way intersection between the restaurant, the front bar and a room that, from the muffled chimes and clatter that pierce the background easy-listening playlist, is where pokies supplement the revenue stream without disturbing the hotel's family ambience. As our food arrives Wendell is talking about *Pop*, the elderly man who visited from Sydney when she was a child on a property at Cumnock out past Orange. She remembers him as frail, explaining: *When he was in Papua New Guinea he got malaria and that just kept recurring. He was a thin man anyway and he always had a bottle of Stone's Green Ginger Wine beside him. I'd get letters from him giving me advice on horsemanship and things like that – he would write nice letters.*

Wendell recalls particular conversations; one that she found incongruous given how famous he became: *he said that he only took up writing as a career because he couldn't get work on the docks in the Depression.* Idriess said much the same in a 1936 radio broadcast:

> *Four years ago Old Man Chance, after tossing me about for half a lifetime, dropped me in Sydney streets, friendless and nearly penniless. It was a case of Sydney or the Bush. Either carry the swag away outback again, or find work and see what city life was like. After a fairly unenviable experience of the cold shoulder when seeking certain navvy jobs I determined to turn, if possible, twenty years of wandering in strange places and among interesting people into good honest coin. I began to realise how intensely interesting those years really were and that city people might be interested enough to read those experiences and pay for the reading. If so, then I could pay my landlady for the little old room in Paddington.*[167]

The title of that talk was *Glimpses of Romance* and although he was using the term loosely, that was around the time when he had his first glimpse, at a dance, of Wendell's grandmother, Eta Gibson. Eta already had a son, Maurice, and Wendell's mother, Judy, was born in 1932. By the time Eta's third child, Wendy, was born in 1934, Idriess had amended his will so that *my friend MRS. ETA GIBSON* had become the major beneficiary.[168] An already complex relationship was compounded when Eta met a much younger man, Frank Lax, also at a dance and, eventually, moved in with him. Despite that she maintained

... the dismembered anatomy of a life ...

Wendy (r) and Judy (l) with their older brother Maurice Gibson, George Street Sydney, 1948.

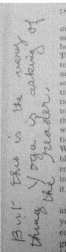

... But this is the very thing Yoga is asking of the reader ...

her relationship with Idriess and Beverley Eley's biography covers that period of his life in a chapter titled *Ménage a trois*. Wendell recalled: *she lived with this other guy in a house that was paid for by Pop. And she used to go back over to Kingsford Smith Street and still do all his household. Uncle Frank was a lot younger than her but very particular and he built the house. We would come down and stay at Sylvania Heights.*[169]

Idriess was more or less alone: *but when he got too old to look after himself he moved in with my aunt, Wendy, in Mona Vale.* That's where the valuation of the remains I've been grappling with was done two years before he died. I return the conversation to those materials, which remained with Beverley Eley after Wendy died in 1994 and were still there when Eley's biography of Idriess was published the next year – which introduces more family issues: *At the time the biography was being written Wendy was having issue with my mum. Whether Wendy told Beverley that mum wasn't his daughter, and whether she discouraged Beverley from speaking with mum... Even if she is not somebody's biological child, she spent her whole childhood growing up thinking of him as her father. So, she would be one of the key people you would want to interview...*

That thought also occurred to the publisher, Tom Thompson, who recalled: *I wrote to Judy a few times, I wanted Beverley to remake the book with the extras that Judy would like which would have been, in the main, corrections regarding the odd year, to place Judy in the story more.*[170] That didn't happen – but not because Judy was reluctant. On the title page of one copy of Eley's book is a note: *This copy was corrected by Judy Peacock, Idriess's daughter and delivered to the publishers for a future corrected edition. It is a one off and the only notation or correction that exists. Tom Thompson. ETT. 1996.* That provenance and assurance was for sales purposes and it found its way to the collection of Jim Bradly in Bolton Point (Chapter 15). The typed notes, each tagged to an issue on a specified page, are mostly corrections to times and places – except for one, which relates to page 334 and starts: *The fights between Mum and Dad were not regular nightly events, they depended on what he had been drinking and whether Mum stirred him or not.* Judy's note continues, qualifying that there was another side to his personality, and that they had: *many enjoyable evenings, together in the kitchen while he told us fascinating stories, or lectured us girls on the big bad wolf out there in the big bad world, or simply had his tea and went to bed.* But – grog was an issue:

> Yes, he was a drunk, he could be nasty, quick to change moods, sarcastically insulting and used the foulest language, spitting, dribbling and crying into his meal. But he was a bumbling, fumbling, frustrated drunk and for all the reasons stated in the book, was simply unable to demonstrate any personal or emotional feelings. But he never at any time struck any of us and we were never deprived of any of the comforts of life.[171]

Judy's memories are consistent with what broadcaster Tim Bowden found in 1975, three decades later, when he met with Idriess in Mona Vale: *On the small sink I noticed about 12 unwashed tumblers which seemed to have been there for some time. His favourite tipple, I discovered, was a mix of sweet sherry and milk, and I suppose he eventually must have had to wash some to keep going.*[172] Towards the end of that interview Idriess lamented the limitations of old age that, for him, had been compounded by the remnants of the War over fifty years earlier: *those little lumps is from Lone Pine – only tiny pin-heads of things now but they swell up now and I can't bloody well use it.* Bowden asked about a lump on the back of the old Digger's hand and Idriess replied: *Yes, that's ... a piece of dirty old shell in there, and I've got a bit in the hips because they ... said "if we cut that out it's so close to the ... artery you're going to bleed to death quick" I said "Well, leave the bloody thing there."*[173]

It's unlikely that the deeply embedded emotional shards that probably drove his drinking and sullen bitterness were understood in the same terms as the shrapnel that remained close to the surface. What is now understood as Post Traumatic Stress Disorder wasn't generally recognised, even in the 1970s, and was probably well masked in a veteran who had written more than a dozen books on military themes with an almost casual quality to the descriptions of his own experiences. Ironically, in his research for the stories that he wrote about the Torres Strait, particularly **Drums of Mer,** Idriess had read in depth the works of a group of men who had seen the psychological aftermath of the carnage of the First World War up close and went on to be the founders of the field now understood as traumatic stress studies.[174] Although in late-1914 all Idriess wanted to do was *to get to the bloody war* lest he *miss out*, by 1918 he'd had enough. He returned from the War but the War never left him. And Judy's reflections went no further; with tensions between author and publisher the revision was put on hold after the release of the biography and Judy died in 1999. But while she was alive, Wendell recalled: *Mum would do little presentations to the library.* So did Wendell, perhaps catching the incremental burden of years at the front on the adventure-seeking larrikin of 1915: *I was reading bits from* **The Desert Column** *– just taking snippets from the diary; it starts off all gung-ho – but doesn't end that way.*

From Wendy to Eley to Judy; Idriess' boxed materials continued their journey to the Murrurundi property of Wendell's sister Kym, who has since died, and from there to Wendell in Singleton where, in November 2013, she organised a launch of Jim Bradly's **Gouger of the Bulletin Part II** at the Singleton Library. An advertisement for the event in the *Singleton Argus – Life of Idriess comes to light at Library –* begins: *You could describe the life of Australia's most prolific published author Ion L. Idriess as being a life well lived – it was a mixture of Crocodile Dundee meets '007' author Ian Flemming [sic] and add touch of Banjo Paterson.* In a photograph on the *Singleton Argus* website Wendell sits surrounded by publicity flyers for various Idriess books from somewhere in one of the piles we have worked through today.[175] As Wendell continues to describe the archive's journey she drops another name in passing, one I've heard about from Tom Thompson – Idriess Enterprises: *Wendy and Mum were directors. [Wendy] was very concerned, she spent a lot of time trying to get copyright back, because I think Angus and Robertson had the copyright for the rest of them somehow, or they managed to get the copyright from him or not pay him because he certainly did not make a lot of money from his writing.*[176]

Sunday morning and back in the barn. Welcomed by Wendell, Bonny and Saphie – even the horses seem to recognise me. Today is about trying to shift the pile away from the porous corrugated iron walls to condense the load, ensure that missing covers are replaced, and cover it all with tarps. I've come prepared with black plastic bin liners and masking tape, but before resealing the tomb I continue to graze, looking for chance to throw up a connection to Lasseter. And finally, in one of the last containers, there's a letter written by Idriess on 14th August 1935 to Walter Cousins about *Gold Dust and Ashes*, which had been published in 1933. He was in Adelaide, probably dealing with preparations for the release of *The Cattle King* which would appear the next year. On the second page there's a digression:

> *Dr. Maddingan [sic] had a crack at Lasseter today, only a par. about a speech of his at some luncheon or other where he said any possibility of settling Central Australia was a myth as Lasseter's Reef was a myth. In several of my articles I have given Madigan praise and publicity, but apparently he is but another who seeks to climb to publicity by attacking a book. Madigan greeted me in very kindly fashion the only other time I saw him (in Eric Baume's company). However the book still lives and one by one those who have attacked it simply fade out. The queer thing about it is that I had a book on the Lake Eyre region in mind, and I had already planned how I would give recognition to Madigan in his trip flying over it, or his Simpson desert flight, and his recent drive out on [to] portion of the lake by motor.*

Cecil Thomas Madigan was not someone with whom Idriess would have tangled – explorer of extremes – the Antarctic with Mawson, and later the deserts of Sudan and Central Australia. Also a Rhodes Scholar, veteran of the Western Front, geologist and pioneer in aviation mapping. He knew how to find his way around Central Australia and was author of Crossing the Dead Heart – having done it. Idriess was prickly to criticism but sensible about who to take on. Just as with his self-promotion, his retorts and ripostes were often indirect, the pseudonymous author indignant at whatever perceived slight had been directed at Idriess.

A few moments later I'm holding another example that emerges from a stack of tanned papers each with the darkened perforations of rusted staples. The topmost four pages are a typed draft and, in pencil in his now familiar hand, on the front page is scrawled *Idriess draft of letter to Wide World Magazine – 19-3-36*. Below that, the first paragraph is a quotation that has come from an issue of that magazine: *"Long before Mr Idriess took up his pen the essential facts and main adventures of the Lasseter expedition had been widely exploited by the Australian newspapers and had become common knowledge and – according to my viewpoint – common property. I certainly knew the details long before Mr Idriess' book went to press."* Behind the four typed pages are another ten with the original handwritten draft containing various changes incorporated into the typed version. It's only on the second page that the identity of the author of the critical quote is revealed –*Mr Charnley*.

William Campbell Charnley was a prospector and prolific journalist who wrote as W.C. Charnley and various pen names in a range of magazines including the *Aboriginalities* page of *The Bulletin* – as did Idriess. Their subjects and styles were similar and, having lived from 1899 to 1916 in the Kalgoorlie-Boulder goldfields areas, he knew the players and places of Central Australian prospecting. Idriess must have respected him because his response is deliberate and detailed, and begins with a refutation of Charnley's quoted text, followed by emphasis on Idriess' privileged access to *The Diary* and his unique experiences and knowledge that allowed him to write the story. Along the way he hints at plagiarism – *Quite apart from all the above, in your Chapters on Lasseter there are a number of paragraphs practically word for word as in the book, especially of Lasseter's wanderings with the aboriginals* – concluding*:

> *However, although we felt somewhat hurt at the matter (it was first brought to our notice by telephone calls and letters from readers both of the Wide World and LASSETER'S LAST RIDE) we thank you for all the courtesy of your reply. As* <u>Lasseter's</u> *the book was just about to be published when your articles came out we were also afraid that the English publisher might have considered that we* <u>had</u> **might in some way have broken faith.** <u>We</u> **Had Mr Charnley only written us we would have advised him go right ahead if only Jonathan Cape, to whom we had submitted the book, had no objection.** *We are sorry too that an excellent series of articles as the "Dead Heart" are,*

* Deletions in the draft are <u>underlined</u>; additions and corrections are in **bold**.

*should have been, <u>in our opinion,</u> to our point of view somewhat marred by the **unacknowledged addition** of such a definite inclusion of the matter in question.*

Re your suggestion of mentioning the book and the English publisher in an early issue of the Wide World Magazine. We would be very pleased if you could manage this.

Idriess was clearly seriously pissed off and maybe the letter did the trick; in the July 1936 issue of *The Wide World Magazine* is a comment relating to Charnley's series – *The secret of the "Dead Heart"*[177] – that had been in published in the magazine through 1935:

In view of the widespread interest aroused by the publication of the above-named story in our issues for August, September and October, 1935, readers may like to know that a complete and authoritative account of the quest for "Lasseter's Reef," and the luckless prospector's fate, is given in the book "Lasseter's Last Ride," by Ion L. Idriess, published by Jonathan Cape.[178]

Sorting out the incongruities and inconsistencies is for another time. I can't absorb much more about Idriess but, before the ordering, stacking and covering begins, one last item declares itself. Near the bottom of a plastic container is a fifty page foolscap document, age-yellowed and stained: *SHOOTING SCRIPT of "LASSETER RODE WEST" The story of Lasseter's Lost Reef. Written and adapted by: RUPERT KATHNER. LOCATION: CENTRAL AUSTRALIA.* Below the name of the scriptwriter, in Idriess' undated handwriting: *Nothing came of this.*

Rupert Kathner was no stranger to the Lasseter story. He directed **Phantom Gold** (1937), coproduced with Stan Tolhurst who appears as Lasseter staggering through the bush. With footage from the 1936 expedition funded by Sydney businessman H.V. Foy, it included some of the players in the original drama including Bob Buck.[179] In that film the story is narrated with no synchronous dialogue and in this script there is. The opening scene: Sydney streets, a newspaper poster proclaiming *GOLD PRICES REACH RECORD* with *Roar of City behind music* as a man enters a building and steps into a lift, the indicator tracking its progress to the fourth floor where the operator directs him to the: *Third door on the left.* By the second page Lasseter has been introduced to John Bailey, and the tale begins. Forty-six pages later it finishes with Bob Buck talking to an Aboriginal boy:

> BUCK. "Dead, how long?" THE BOY. "Him bin dead, alonga cold. One, two!" Buck walks towards his camels. BUCK "Two days, eh? Just missed him! Anyhow, I was always unlucky!" Buck is completing the erection of a crude mulga railing. He is nailing a board to the rail. THE BOARD READS – LASSETER – R.I.P. Sunset – over a distant hill, Buck leading his camels are seen in silhouette. They disappear over the hill. MUSIC HEARD. Toward hill the sun sinks lower. A dingo slinks across the foreground. SOUND OF DISTANT HOWLING. FADE OUT.

Maybe lucky for everyone that *Nothing came of this.*

Wendell sits surrounded by publicity flyers ... Singleton Library, 2013.

CHAPTER 7

Revision

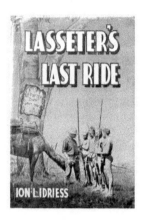

Awake! For Morning in the Bowl of Night
Has flung the Stone that puts the Stars to Flight:
And Lo! The Hunter of the East has caught
The Sultan's Turret in a Noose of Light.
Rubaiyat of Omar Khayyam, rendered by Edward Fitzgerald, 1859.

Twenty years before a third child was born to William and Agnes Lasseter in rural Victoria an anonymous pamphlet was published in Britain.
By the time Lewis Hubert Lasseter entered the world the author's name
was known – Edward Fitzgerald – and the **Rubaiyat of Omar Khayyam**
was on track to become one of the most influential works translated into
the English language. While later translators from the original Persian
suggested that Fitzgerald's work was *more in the nature of a fantasia than a*
translation,[180] it had enormous appeal that stemmed not only from *Fitz-*
gerald's poetic intuition but also his selective ordering of the original qua-
trains to suggest time – and a story.[181] Fitzgerald's rendition resonated with
Victorian and Edwardian audiences in ways that austere and non-narrative

translations could not. He created the **Rubaiyat** that was embraced by generations of readers and has come down to us a century-and-a-half later.[182] One of those readers was Ion Idriess – there were copies of the **Rubaiyat** among the personal effects of Idriess that made their way over half-a-century from Mona Vale to Narrandera.[183] With the arrival of new material after the first edition of **Lasseter's Last Ride** was published, he confronted some challenges that Fitzgerald would have understood. And, like Fitzgerald's masterful rendition of the Persian, Idriess' incorporation of Lasseter's last ramblings was *more in the nature of a fantasia.*

In February 1932 a new edition of **Lasseter's Last Ride** was released with additional chapters containing transcriptions from the notebook and other material that had been unearthed by Frank Green. Frank Theodore Green was but one of many flawed characters in the Lasseter saga and had a history of petty criminality, from his youth in rural New South Wales, through his army service, and after. And for a while he made a career of Lasseter; in addition to the Second CAGE Expedition of 1931, and with Bailey again in the Arnhem Gold Development Company, he was with the Scientific Gold Expedition of 1934, in the prospectus of which it was stated: *Mr. Frank. T. Green (friend of Ion Idriess and the late L.I. Lasseter, both well-known prospectors of the Inland) has been engaged in prospecting without interruption for upwards of 30 years, the last 16 of which have been spent in Central Australia.*[184] Hardly without interruption; Victor George Carrington – the Government Resident in Central Australia who signed the second death certificate for Lasseter – had this to say about the prospectus in a letter to the Secretary of the Department of the Interior in October 1934:

> *Attention is drawn to the portion "Prospectors Qualifications" particularly that referring to Mr. Frank T. Green. This person was imprisoned in Alice Springs for three months during the year 1929 on a conviction of "Unlawful Possession". He later accompanied the expedition led by Messrs. Talbot and Blatchford in search for the mythical reef claimed to be found by Lasseter and was again here with the party led by Tennant during this year. I think he has little pretentions to an expert knowledge of prospecting and that many of the statements contained in the prospectus are untrue.*[185]

Frank Green's claim to be a friend of Idriess and Lasseter was another lie, although it is possible that after he was released from jail he met Lasseter in Alice Springs while the First CAGE Expedition was preparing to set out. And if Idriess hadn't been told who Frank Green was during the frantic planning for the Second CAGE Expedition, he had certainly heard about him from at least October.[186] But, regardless of questionable subalterns, the leaders of the Second CAGE Expedition mentioned in Carrington's dismissal of Green's prospecting qualifications were both highly regarded Western Australian prospectors – Harry William Beamish (Bill) Talbot and Torrington Blatchford.[187] Talbot had been recommended for the Second Expedition by the Government Geological Advisor, W.G. Woolnough, who had been approached by Minister Arthur Blakeley, on behalf of John Bailey. The Second Expedition left Alice Springs on 2nd September and after travelling via Hermannsburg to Buck's station, Middleton Ponds, they set out on 22nd September 1931. Against his contractual obligations to the CAGE Company, Talbot's diary of the Expedition to the Petermann and Rawlinson Ranges was not given over to Bob Buck at the end of the Expedition. That document records that the Second CAGE Expedition was passing through the Petermann Range to its thirteenth camp after leaving Middleton Ponds on Friday 16th October 1931 when: *Just before we camped Buck noticed a tree on the bank of the Hull just below a cave. On the bark was cut "Dig on floor at back, attacked, Beaten off". After unloading Buck and Green dug up the floor of the cave and found a sealed note book and some other papers. Observed for Latitude 25°0'59".* Talbot's diary records that the next day: *Buck decided to remain here today to communicate with Sydney regarding the finding of Lasseter's papers. The wireless was erected last evening.*[188]

By the time the Second CAGE Expedition arrived back in Alice Springs on 23rd November the CAGE Directors already knew that the *sealed note book and some other papers* were the only real find. In his formal report to the CAGE Directors after returning to Perth, Blatchford concluded that: *we could find not the slightest evidence of the occurrence of gold and saw no geological features which would suggest the likelihood of the occurrence of gold or of other minerals of commercial value.*[189] With Talbot and Blatchford dismissing Lasseter's claims, the Directors probably had little interest in the dead prospector's last scribblings, and by the time that Frank Green arrived in Sydney with them Idriess may have already arranged to meet Irene at the Lasseter family house in Kogarah. Just a few months later and before the revised version of *Lasseter's Last Ride* was released, *Smiths Weekly* carried an article on Saturday 30th January 1932, which began:

GRIM DIARY OF DEATH IN WILDERNESS

L.H.B. Lasseter's Message From the Grave

"SMITH'S" EXCLUSIVE STORY

In the possession of Angus and Robertson, the Sydney publishers, is a roll of cracked and perished paper, containing the record of a sombre tragedy – the lonely death of L.H.B. Lasseter in the central wilds of Australia. Menaced by hostile blacks, against whom he had fired his last three revolver cartridges, Lasseter may have died from exhaustion, or he may have been speared. The last Diary of poor Lasseter was brought from Central Australia by Prospector Frank Green, who relates that he dug it from the ashes of a fire in the cave where Lasseter waited for death. Green gave it to Mrs. Lasseter, the "Darling Rene," to whom it was addressed. She entrusted it to Angus and Robertson, who in their turn will probably submit it to the Mitchell Library.[190]

The Diary did end up in the Mitchell Library – four decades after it was put into the vault at Angus & Robertson. But it was Idriess who was the intermediary between Irene and the vault. With six thousand copies already in circulation and other projects on the go he was probably keen to make sure that the new material didn't contradict the existing account that he'd insisted *actually happened* – which he'd been widely and successfully publicising. To do that he needed to get there first, secure the documents, extract what might not cause problems – and keep the rest out of sight. He succeeded; after getting what was necessary to ensure that his and his publisher's interests were not compromised, *The Diary* was effectively reburied. The first outsider to get a look, nearly three decades later, was Lasseter's son, Bob.

What Idriess found in that trove was disordered, undated, and in parts illegible. He set out to select elements and present them in a way that, as Fitzgerald had with his *Rubaiyat*, would resonate with a particular audience – one that Idriess knew was hungry for tales of exploration, exploits and the exotic – and would reinforce the story he had written in 1931. He used only the material he needed, about half of the total.[191] Idriess also chose to include the letter from Lasseter to Irene that had been found by Bob Buck some seven months earlier and which he'd seen when he visited Irene in mid-1931, but which he didn't use in the first edition.[192] Or, at least, he used most of it, the central paragraph as included in the penultimate chapter, *Deathless Pages,* in the revised **Lasseter's Last Ride** reading: *I've taken the films and will plant them at Winter's Glen if I can get there the Blight has got me beat.* That sentence, in the original, continued: *all because Jack Jenkins never put the Argerol in the medicine chest as I requested.*

What Lasseter was referring to was Argyrol, a treatment-of-the-time for trachoma; but that's not why Idriess edited out the remainder of the section. That was because of the mention of Jack Jenkins, who also appears twice more in the original of *The Diary* in the Mitchell library, but not in **Lasseter's Last Ride**. John (Jack) Jenkins was the Mining Secretary of the New South Wales Branch of the AWU. Not only was he a mate of John Bailey, he had been present with Bailey and Errol Coote when Lasseter first entered the AWU offices in 1930. As Coote wrote: *John Jenkins, the Mining Secretary of the A.W.U., had been one intent listener. He was an old goldminer, having been out on the western goldfields with Herbert Hoover, who afterwards became President of the United States of America. Jenkins was now an assayer and metallurgist, and the gold bug had bitten him deeply again.*[193] According to Coote, it was Jenkins who did the back-of-the-envelope calculation that valued the potential of the reef as described by Lasseter at that meeting at £66 million and, unsurprisingly, he was one of the original 49 subscribers who kicked in £20 each to set up the CAGE Syndicate – Idriess was playing safe.

With Idriess' selective inclusions and creative reconfiguration of *The Diary* any parallels with Fitzgerald might end – there's no poetry in **Lasseter's Last Ride**. But there was in the materials that Idriess received from Irene Lasseter. Ironically, its title was *Journey's End*:

On earth's red fields of war no glory dwells,
For flashing flags and rolling drums that boom

Herald the swift approach of Pain and Doom –
And loose the fiends of twice a million hells.
What glory lies in whirr of screaming shells.
Lo! On the night the ghosts of warriors loom,
Speaking to you from out the grassy tomb!
Hark! List to what each spirit whisper tells.
"O youth, sweet youth! A universal peace
Is that which we, your brothers, here implore!
Ring out Love's bells, my brothers, and release
The hate that springs from pallid-visaged war!
No flowers of glory bloom in mire and mud,
Watered by running tides of human blood."

Fred C. Biggers, 1931.[194]

Born in Lithgow, Frederick Charles Biggers was 22 years of age when he enlisted in May 1917. Like Lasseter he had defective eyesight and was assigned to *home service,* and in June 1919 was released from the military due to *reduction of establishment.* But of the two years that he was under the colours, more than five months was spent in medical care – including 135 days on Milson Island in the Hawkesbury which had been requisitioned by the military for the quarantine of soldiers with venereal diseases.[195] Again, like Lasseter, who after going AWOL from Seymour Barracks for nearly three days in early July 1916, during his first enlistment, spent nearly two months at Langwarrin Military Hospital on the Mornington Peninsula – also a military facility for the management of sexually transmitted infections.[196] They both lived to tell tales, but not those ones. In Biggers' discharge form he was listed as having been a *Concentration Camp Guard (L. Horse Section)* – maybe that was the stimulus for another poem, *The Lighthorseman,* which begins:

Galloping mad with delight,
Urged by the zest in the ride,
On with a whoop, sped the thundering troop,
Dashing with military pride.[197]

Like Idriess, who saw action as a Lighthorseman, Biggers went on to a career of words and was proprietor of the *Kingsford and District News* in the 1930s in what must have been a competitive environment; he was fined for assaulting Henry Norman Barrington of the *Randwick-Coogee Weekly* in 1932, settled out of court over libel claims with Albert James Donovan of *The Messenger* in 1938, and during the Second World War was named as a witness in a case of magazine fraud, in the report of which there is a photograph of him in a dashing Lighthorseman-stye slouch hat. And, also like Idriess, poetry was not his strong suit. Idriess admired those bushmen whose campfire-side skills included repartee and reciting *pomes* but, for good reason, he was spare with examples of his own, and may have regretted including in the chapter, *Poets of Nigger Creek*, a blokey ballad, *When Girlie Goes Looking for Nuts*, a play on reverse-evolutionary forces at work within the body feminine, which starts:

The doctors tell us that our bones
To them a tale unfold,
Of how we're degenerating
From the usual human mould.[198]

It doesn't get better. But while Idriess was no poet he might have appreciated Biggers' gung-ho depiction of Lighthorseman bravado. Lasseter probably wouldn't have – and he wrote verses too. Just months after leaving the military and before the end of hostilities in Europe, *Christian Warfare* appeared in the *Foster and Toora Mirror* on 4th April 1918. It begins:

'Twas the dawn of Armageddon,
And glorious and grand,
Methought I saw the hosts of earth
In battle order stand.

All was gay with panoply,
Loud martial music rolled;
And the breeze that swept across the plain
Stirred each proud banner's fold.[199]

Lasseter's poem runs to nine verses, the sentiments not dissimilar to those of *Journey's End* by Biggers that appeared in Sydney's *Evening News* on Monday 17th February 1930. At that time the sequence of events initiated by Lasseter's letter to Texas Green in October 1929 was winding to a close with negative responses from Western Australia and Canberra, and

Lasseter's approaches to Arthur Blakeley hadn't been encouraging. But within a month he would be at the offices of the AWU and the trajectory would change dramatically. But not in February 1930, as the Depression was biting for all Australians and he was expecting the Bailiff at the family home in Kogarah.

Kogarah is less than ten miles from where the *Kingsford and District News* circulated. Whether Harold Lasseter knew Frederick Charles Biggers or not, *Journey's End* had been carefully cut from page six of the *Evening News,* preserving a corded surround with snatches on the left edge of the border of the adjacent column. The top right corner is missing along a crease-line, with another slightly angled in the opposite direction in the bottom half of the cutting, both exactly mirrored across what was a pleat in the center – it had been folded carefully but not precisely.[200]

When Idriess set out for the Lasseter house in Kogarah, after he was told by the CAGE Directors that Frank Green had delivered the notebook and other materials found buried to Irene, he knew the way. And he understood that Irene was not only bereaved – she was broke. He had probably been told by the Baileys that they were no longer providing financial support for the family after discovering that Irene was Lasseter's bigamous wife. But Idriess didn't need to be told that either; soon after the first edition of **Lasseter's Last Ride** was released he had received a letter from Florence, signing herself off as *the **real** Mrs L.H. Lasseter,* in which she wrote: *In the Melbourne Herald I have just read an account of a book you have written about my late husband Lewis Herbert [sic] Lasseter. I do not know if you were aware of my existence or not, as I believe there is a woman in Sydney posing as Mrs Lasseter.*[201] Florence was aggrieved and clutching at straws. Within a year she was dead.[202]

By the time Idriess got back to work he not only had the four *fragments* found near Lasseter's body that had been sent to the CAGE Directors, which he had used in the first edition. He also had the letter to Irene that was with them which he had seen but not used, and the notebook from the Second Expedition that he referred to as *Lasseter's Diary* and photographs taken by Ernest Brandon-Cremer, the film-maker who went with the Second Expedition. And he was no longer constrained from using material from the First Expedition that he had been told by Ern Bailey to withhold from using earlier *pending the results of the second expedition* – Phil Taylor's detailed instructions, gleaned from Paul Johns, of where to find Lasseter. From December 1931 he was in a position not only to incorporate new material but also to correct inconsistencies with his account in the first edition. As it turned out very few changes were made to the text. On the last page a sentence was removed which had read: *Old "Warts" is dead. A camel party brings word that he was "boned" after Lasseter's death.* Kirrinytja was, of course, very much alive, and Idriess included a photograph titled *Old Warts, who befriended Lasseter* showing a fine-looking, straight-backed, Pitjantjatjara elder – although he didn't alter the description of him in the text as *humpbacked*. A change in tense from *Robert Buck had the reputation of being one of the finest bushmen in Centralia* to *has the reputation* was probably about Buck's publicity bankability. And one word in the last sentence which in the first edition read: *This spirit will watch the dream come true* was changed to – *His spirit will watch the dream come true.*

The image of *Old Warts* was not the only new photograph, in fact the number nearly doubled, and of the 32 in the first edition only two are not included in editions from March 1932.[203] One is irrelevant to the story, showing the distress sign that Pittendrigh and Hamre fashioned to attract attention while they were stranded after their forced landing. The other, though, is far from irrelevant; the photograph of Lasseter in the first and second editions of the book that were released in September 1931 – *Harold Bell Lasseter and Family* – which had been opposite the title page, was removed and replaced in the editions released in November and December 1931 by three landscape photographs – *Typical Lasseter Country.* From February 1932, starting with the fifth edition, these gave way to two images from the Second CAGE Expedition – *Bob Buck Questions the Natives* and *Lasseter's Cave.* In total there are 32 new pictures, of which two are of Buck and seven relate to the site of Lasseter's body and the cave where *The Diary* was found with one photograph of the documents laid out on the ground as if just unearthed: *Lasseter's Diary Dug up in the Cave.*[204] There are also four

Second CAGE Expedition. Blatchford and Buck on left, Talbot, Branden-Cramer (seated centre) and Green (leaning forward).

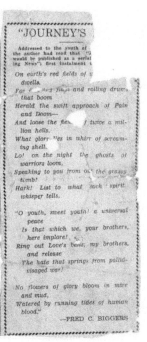
Journey's End.

On the bark was cut …

… Green dug up the floor of the cave and found a sealed note book …

of terrain and nineteen of Aboriginal people and activities, but none of Lasseter. The real Lasseter had disappeared from the face of the earth and, pretty much, from *Lasseter's Last Ride.*

With the text of the first edition essentially unchanged in the revision that was released in March 1932 and all subsequent editions, what was new was the addition of three chapters, *The Second Attempt*, *Deathless Pages* and *Fragments* – and it starts with more fiction:

> *Members of the second expedition that attempted to locate Lasseter's reef, on returning to civilization, report having failed by sixty miles to reach their objective.*
>
> *Apparently the hoodoo which pursued the first expedition was present here too, as although the party suffered no hardships, lack of food-stuffs forced them to return. Such lack cannot be laid to the Company's door, as an open cheque was given for the purchase of supplies.*[205]

As Idriess would have known, the only factual element in that statement was that the Company had not skimped in funding supplies. However, as Pastor Albrecht of Hermannsburg mission, through which the Second Expedition passed on the way out and back reported, the expectations of the members for amenities and comforts were unrealistic, the preparation was insufficient, and what was proposed as a six-month expedition lasted less than six weeks. Albrecht also recorded that he was told by technical men on the team that: *"It was absolutely the limit of what one was expected to put up with. There was no chef, and our fare was damper and rabbits, with some black tea for most of the time."* Albrecht knew Bob Buck well, including his legendary drinking, and put the issue of the £300 that had been supplied for provisions to the publican of Buck's favorite drinking hole in Alice Springs, The Stuart Arms, who replied: *"The cheque went over my counter, with the exception of about £80.*"[206] But like *Rip Van Winkle* and *Old Warts,* Bob Buck was too good a character not to use, particularly as he'd briefly been the darling of the Sydney press and Idriess was always keen to court publicity. By the end of the decade he was also on the cover of *Lasseter's Last Ride*. But in the three new sections included from 1932 on, only the six pages of the chapter, *The Second Attempt,* extends the story, and having led off with fantasy, it continues. There is a passing mention of the Expedition meeting a tribe who ran from them shrieking *"Kaditcha! Kaditcha!" (the devil! the devil!)*. But that's basically all in terms of Aboriginal content, a sharp contrast to the earlier text and maybe Idriess realised that in the Aboriginal story he'd conjured in the first edition he'd over-reached himself. And, of course, with the Second CAGE Expedition what he could write was constrained by witnesses.

The rest of the chapter is made up of mixed but suggestive geological speculations, descriptions of the *little red-covered* notebook and its contents, and rumor masquerading as fact, including a way of resolving the loose ends of Lasseter's repeated mention of a new character – Johannsen: *When he felt his "abandonment" most keenly, he never quite gave up hope that Johannsen would come – little knowing that the strange "hoodoo" had already marked out Johannsen and his mate to be speared by the blacks in the Rawlinson Range*. In the middle of December 1930 Lasseter had made it to Lake Christopher at the western extremity of the Rawlinson Range and at the beginning of November 1932 Michael Terry found a message there that Lasseter had scratched into the dry lakebed. Idriess didn't know that, or who Johannsen was (Chapter 18), or anything more than rumors about spearings in the Rawlinsons, but the added frisson of collateral *Kaditcha* casualties didn't hurt.[207]

The second last chapter of **Lasseter's Last Ride** – *Deathless Pages* – is, more or less, cut and paste from *The Diary*. There is no thread other than it starts with sections in which Lasseter claims to have found the reef and continues with his comments about his dealings with Aboriginal groups, almost all of which suggest a sequence – triumph of the find, then threat and treachery. The chapter concludes with agonal reflections and thoughts of his wife, the last being: *Good Bye Rene darling wife mine and don't grieve remember you must live for the children now dear, but it does seem cruel to die alone out here because I have always been good to blacks. my last prayer is "God be merciful to me as a sinner and be good to those I leave behind   XXX HARRY X*

The theme of tragedy is sustained by selections stressing struggle, survival in extremis, and stoic resignation. Idriess made sure it was unsullied by questionable language – there would be no mention of bottoms. Consistent with his relocation of *Warts'* skin appendage from his buttock to his back in the first edition, Idriess modifies Lasseter's statement which in *The Diary* reads – *Later an old chap with a wart 6 inches by 3 inches in the fold of his posterior took pity on me & brought 2 rabbits & some berries like cape gooseberries* – to read *a wart 6 inches by 3 inches on his back.* Perhaps just for consistency. But more obvious are the omissions of Lasseter's interactions with the Aboriginal group who had taken him in, including examples of Kirrinytja's help and kindliness, as Lasseter recorded: *previously mentioned with the long beard & wart took pity on me to the extent of carrying my things 5 miles up stream where more water was available & built me a bough shelter alongside ... The 5 mile walk was simply awful for me tho the old fellow carried the pack.* In *The Diary* there are also snatches of Lasseter interacting with children in a friendly way and three others in which he wrote that a *young buck* brought a *lubra* who he learned was named *Angola* to where he was camping, with some kind of exchange occurring – *I gave him this blanket camp sheet tommyhawk & sheath knife.* That episode appears to be repeated elsewhere in Lasseter's notes: *there is one here, a young headman, who understands a smattering of English. He posed as my friend and I gave him my remaining blanket & billy & sheath knife, and what remained of the ... then he introduced a young lubra into my camp and I put her out once but he brought her again so I gave her my watch & a clean handkerchief & cake of soap & sent her back to camp then ...*

While that section does not appear in the book, what immediately followed did: *he had 16 men with 2 spears each bar my path to a rabbit burrow up creek I took a risk & unloaded my revolver ostentatiously I had only 3 live cartridges in it anyway then folded my arms & walked right up & tro' the cordon then went & camped at his camp fire body touching body & slept the night thro Next morning I got up ...* While a manly face-off was OK, like any mention of Kirrinytja's posterior, an introduction with sexual intent was probably too suggestive for Idriess. But that's what it was and the girl, Yunutja Napaltjarri, was interviewed by Marshall-Stoneking as an old woman fifty years later at Papunya in 1981: *her father wanted her to 'marry' Lasseter 'because he might be a powerful man and he might give us lots of food.'*[208]

Those exclusions were probably about tact and narrative consistency but the other main set of issues disappeared from the inclusions relate to the CAGE Company and Directors: *why am I abandoned like this Paul Johns should have showed up with tucker 6 weeks ago. He gave me his word of honor. Blakeley assured me relief would be sent if I had not returned 1st November, it is now January but I have lost count of dates I think about 16th or 18th. 5 cwt tucker Ilbilla & me starving here. Why have not the people organized a relief ...* And elsewhere: *I leave my everlasting curse on Blakeley & Jenkins, Blakeley for not sending the relief as promised and Jenkins for omitting the Argerol ...* Also: *I've tried hard to forgive Jack Jenkins for his wilful neglect there I put it in writing & urged upon him the necessity of including an ounce or two in the medicine chest but he put ...* The most colorful accusations, reserved for Blakeley, were also left out:

> *if Fred Blakeley had been guided by me we could have got the ... truck in three ... damnable that man should be caricatured by the most satirical ... in Sydney ... His Ambition is to feed from a woman's breast. He wants six wetnurses each guaranteed to give a quart at a milking. I would suggest Smiths Weekly satirize him by drawing him surrounded by wetnurses ...ing him & fighting for the privilege of putting diapers on him. I would suggest that as personal equipment for him as leader of a gold seeking expedition he be furnished with 24 dozen diapers table cloth size and a guard of Wetnurses ...*

And where prudence dictated, Idriess was not averse to cuts that changed the meaning entirely. The book has a section that he deemed necessary because it includes finding the reef and also mentions both Johannsen and Lake Christopher, and which finishes with ellipses suggesting the original was illegible: *As I believe he also stumbled on this identical reef I had to go right out to Lake Christopher which is 100 miles across the W.A. border in order to get m ... bearings then I was g ... To go direct to the reef. The Company was ... Soften the tale of my sufferings...* But in the original there is no lack of clarity, that section continuing:

> *The Company was foolish mixing up politics with it all because A Blakeley was Minister for Home & Terr & Fred was Ambitious to have*

the road across Central Australia named "Blakeley Highway" the monstrous conceit of the man. He never did a thing to deserve such a memorial ... had not revised ... food supplies & cut all the fresh meat & fish I would have been able to get along nicely. I have 6 tins of corned beef now but I simply ... touch them. We had 750lbs corned beef 6 Hams (very salt) & 3 doz tins of kipper snacks (smallest size & also very salt) I wanted a case of sardines but Blakely cut it out. Curse the man. May he be fed on corned beef ...

Criticism of the Company was bad enough; taking on a Minister was another thing entirely – Idriess was certainly not going there. And for the fragments he did include he gives no commentary, appearing to let them speak for themselves – but only some of them. And there is another item in the Mitchell collection that does not appear in **Lasseter's Last Ride.** Written to fit a piece of paper that already had a corner missing and on the opposite side of which are childlike drawings of a camel and a truck – perhaps conjuring images of rescue – what were probably among his last written words: *This is cruel to die of starvation heartless of all who know I am out here when I didn't return by Xmas they knew there was something wrong. May God forgive them & [?strengthen] me in my last hour no food now for 2 days.*

The last chapter – *Fragments* – includes the previously embargoed letter from Phil Taylor and the line maps that were part of *The Diary* trove, which Idriess introduces with: *These sketches mark the partial finish of a remarkable story of courage, faith, and dogged perseverance to the last. The story proves that "Truth is stranger than fiction." The days of romance and thrilling adventure are with us still.* What follows are seven line maps that were redrawn from the originals, four of them compilations. There are maps in the original in the Mitchell Library that are not included in **Lasseter's Last Ride**, which is understandable given that their inclusion was for effect rather than as evidence. But there are also four maps in the book that are not in the Mitchell – which is a different matter. It raises the possibility that what eventually made it to the Mitchell Library after nearly fifty years in the vaults of Angus & Robertson was not everything that had passed from Frank Green to Rene Lasseter to Ion Idriess and on into the vault.

Idriess was certainly selective in how he used the material at hand to burnish a shine of credibility onto his tale and was probably responsible for *The Diary* being placed out of the public gaze despite it being in the public interest for it to be accessible. It's hard to imagine why Angus & Robertson would insist on that, except to protect the reputation of Idriess as a corporate asset. Doubts about Idriess and *The Diary* have long been raised, including by Fred Blakeley, who questioned the pristine condition of the notebook found by Green and the absence of any such item when he searched Lasseter's trunk early in the expedition.[209] And Robert Ross – webmaster of *Lasseteria* – raises the spectre of a forgery:

> *And it just may be that Lasseter never kept a diary or notebook, later to be found by the second expedition. Bear in mind that Bob Buck visited Sydney prior to setting out on the second expedition, and while there may have colluded with Idriess to arrange the finding of the record to add an evocative note to and further publicity for Lasseter's Last Ride. In a 1974 interview, "Mr. Idriess said the key to the mystery was a page missing from the diary found near Lasseter's body – Whether the missing page was inadvertently lost or deliberately torn out, I don't know he said". But matching Machiavellian plots with that "wily bushman" Idriess usually leads to confusion, excellent cover for the truth.*[210]

Collusion between Buck and Idriess in forgery seems unlikely; it's hardly plausible that they would go to the trouble of creating a document and include material that then needed to be excluded and for the notebook to be hidden away. A more likely explanation is that it was hibernated because it was an inconvenient truth; about the Company, the Expedition and Lasseter. And inconvenient for Idriess, who finished the last chapter of the new edition with a paragraph that begins: *So ended the attempt of a particularly determined man to open up that big area of new land which has defied many.* He then notes the sacrifice of lives and the commitment of others to follow in the footsteps of the *pathfinders* – his last sentence a reaffirmation of national spirit: *And we breed the men to answer the call.* And that should have been enough, but in the 1933 edition an index had been included giving a sense of academic legitimacy, and there was a new and more technical map on the page facing the back cover, showing *Lasseter's Area and the Livesey Range.* A note on the inside cover opposite reported on new hopes to find Lasseter's lost reef following recent discoveries to the south. It goes on to assert that *Lasseter's country is proved beyond all doubt to be auriferous,* that *syndicates have already been formed,* and that the most up-to-date technology is being brought to the task. This forward-looking addendum concludes that edition, but with a backwards glance: *If the combined efforts of these modern pioneers locate the goldfield that probably lies waiting there, Lasseter will not have died in vain.*

But there is another possibility relating to the provenance and possession of *The Diary,* and to its interment in the Angus & Robertson vault that may have involved collusion. Idriess was determined not only that his book would be the first in print, but that it would be the definitive account. He would not have wanted any material found by the Second CAGE Expedition to be used by someone like Errol Coote, or one of the other Expedition members, to claim authority. On 19th March 1936 Idriess corrected a draft letter to *The Wide World Magazine* in response to an article by Bill Charnley. The intent was that it would be sent by Angus & Robertson but Idriess wrote it and the message is clear[*]:

> *There was no story to Lasseter until after his death. And the only man who knew this story was Idriess. He is the only man who has ever read Lasseter's diary. This diary was* <u>nor even</u> **never** *ever read even by the Central* <u>Company</u> *Australian gold mining company. When the diary was dug up it was immediately claimed by Mr Green as personal property of Mrs Lasseter's (to whom it was personally addressed). On return to Sydney,* <u>he</u> **Green** *handed it to* <u>her</u> **Mrs Lasseter (now Mrs Green)** *intact. Neither* <u>Green nor she</u> **Mrs Lasseter nor Green** *read it, it required very careful handling before Idriess was able to unroll the* <u>frayed</u> **weather stained and fire cracked** *sheets and decipher them. The story of Lasseter's wanderings Idriess got from this diary,* <u>which neither other man or woman</u> **only he** *has read.* <u>Immediately that diary was dug up it was claimed and taken possession of by Green who since has married Mrs Lasseter. None of this diary was printed in the newspapers. ...</u>

* Elements deleted in the draft are <u>underlined</u>, additions are in **bold**.

Immediately he heard a whisper that a diary had been recovered he went straight to Mrs Lasseter and recovered obtained it. It was still wrapped As stated before, Idriess is the only man who has read the diary in its entirety, and it is this diary from which the book is written.[211]

Almost as an aside, the letter ends with a shot at another account that had been recently released: *As to Mr Errol Coote's book, this was not written until several years after the publication of LASSETER'S LAST RIDE. The author of HELL'S AIRPORT left the expedition and was in Sydney (2000 miles from the Lasseter country) long before Lasseter died even.* Of course, Idriess had never been near *Lasseter country* and the dismissal of his fellow journalist's first-hand account is telling as is his emphatic, and repeated, insistence that *[Idriess] is the only man who has ever read Lasseter's diary.* But it seems improbable that the finder and/or intended recipient of the last communications of a nationally publicised figure would not sneak a peak at its contents – unless they were already contractually constrained from doing so or talking about it. Idriess needed – at least – to be tipped off, and it was probably Bob Buck who did so. Whether the £25 that changed hands was from CAGE, Angus & Robertson or Idriess, Idriess was in control. And the amount should be put in context – Irene Lasseter was being paid her husband's wage of £10 a week by the CAGE Company before the fortuitous discovery of his bigamous marriage gave them the pretext to cease payment; and what he paid for *The Diary* was only five per cent of the £500 life insurance policy that had been taken out on Lasseter which she never received. When Idriess left Kogarah, the *weather stained and fire cracked sheets* were his means, through selective use, to protect his and the publisher's interests. When he had ensured that what by then would be referred to as *Lasseter's Diary* was rendered invisible, sealed in the Angus & Robertson vault, Ion Idriess was making sure that **Lasseter's Last Ride** was the definitive account – the urtext. And he succeeded.

CHAPTER 8

Victoria Park

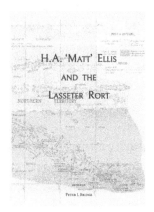

Despite [H.A. Ellis'] report the myth of the Reef lives on, with many futile expeditions and media beat-ups from infantilised journalists. Now we republish the report for a new generation of desert drongos as it nears a century since the first and final trip of the psychotic adventurer, now canonised by the tourism industry in the 'Lasseter Highway.'

The old appellation of the North West road would have been vastly more appropriate – Madman's Track.

Peter Bridge, 2020.[212]

February 2020

Driving past the East Perth police headquarters and over the Causeway linking Perth to the rest of Australia since the 1840s, the Canning Highway heads to Fremantle, the Albany Highway to the South-west, and the Great Eastern Highway past the airport to a continent and the world. Across the river where the paths diverge the first suburb is Victoria Park, an enclave of what was blue-collar residential, now cut off from gentrified riverside condos by freeways, commerce, and connectors to a casino and a corporate coliseum.

Not far from the now not-so-Great Eastern Highway and behind a limestone wall is a house with a history as a manse and more. The peeling painted cement of the veranda gives way beyond the front door to age-worn Jarrah, the floorboards perspective-lining a long corridor flanked by cabinets brimming with ordered chaos, and entries to book-filled rooms. There are collections of objects from the Middle East and Asia, shelves filled with ancient ceramics, and some less old and bearing the mark VOC – the Dutch East India Company. Above a door into another space of folios and files are two dark, incised boards that Idriess would have recognised as coming from the same world as that which returned with the First CAGE Expedition – *tjuringas*. Standing in the corner of a room in the centre of which is a table with a console and piles of projects in progress, next to a two metre high, polychrome Garuda and under framed Balinese silks, is a giant vase from which a dozen or so implements protrude, including two spears with fire-tempered, foot-long iron tips. One is a short assegai and the other long – *I was told they were from Rorke's Drift*. The Anglo-Zulu war, nearly a century-and-a-half ago and a year before Lewis Hubert Lasseter was born in Victoria – the State not the Park. On a nearby wall is a small painting in dark tones torn by wisped colours, a lonely female figure confronting a dark presence, a work by my host's daughter and, he tells me, inspired by William Blake – perhaps *The House of Death*. Nearby are artworks from different eras. Two are of the same person at different phases of life. One is a young, bearded man in bush-practical clothes, his eyes elsewhere – and serious. The eyes of the same man from a much later time are also serious but the face is reflective – a life of thinking, collecting and preserving. This is his house.

Peter Bridge knows a thing or two about minerals and prospecting. That's where his professional career started, slipping sideways from study through Leederville Technical College in Perth to work with the State Laboratories, and later from Curtin University to a position as a mineralogist and curator of the State Mineral Collection at the Government Chemical Laboratories. His interests were broad, including what today would be considered popular magazine journalism – to which he contributed, as he did through connections to CSIRO and the British Museum to the mainstream academic literature. Drawn to fieldwork, and the places, people and stories that came with it, he began collecting. Trinkets, treasures and tales. Pretty soon an interest became his vocation – to preserve the remote frontier and settlement history of Western Australia. Publishing began in 1969 with technical material for a niche prospecting market. It was the right time. But collecting continued, from further afield, and even with supplementing a modest government salary by selling imported curios, it was touch and go until the 1970s – and Charles Garrett.

Charles Lewis Garrett was born in 1932, the year after the first editions of *Lasseter's Last Ride* and *Prospecting for Gold* began to work their alchemy on the national soul. Texas-raised, he joined the Navy in time to be deployed to Korea. Trained as an electrician, he eventually graduated as an electrical engineer. His legacy rests on developing a device and an industry in the 1960s – Garrett Metal Detectors. Security and fossicking; it was the latter that brought him to the attention of Peter Bridge, and with Garrett's support Peter became the distributor of the leading metal detector in Australia at a time when the economy except for mining was tanking. Hesperian Detectors took off, including in its list of franchisees one Rob Lasseter in New South Wales. But the detectors were a means to an end, stories had his soul, and by the end of the decade Hesperian Press was rolling.

Rolling may be overstating it; Peter has particular interests which translate into a small market; stories about Western Australia and the Northern Territory that would otherwise disappear, either because they weren't written down or because they appeared in magazines and news-sheets that aren't prioritised for digital embalming. Tales of people on the edge of society and the wild; buccaneers and bastards, pioneers and pimps, explorers and exterminators – there are at least two sides to every good story. Most are small runs and I hear authors' names I've not come across and subjects I've never considered. The history of bicycles in the Australian outback – not something I'd thought about, but Jim Fitzpatrick's book covers it in detail. I flip through to find Fred Blakeley's bicycle journey from New South Wales to Darwin in 1908. Just over two decades later he even packed a bike on the Thornycroft before it headed out of

Blakeley: ... *he even packed a bicycle on the Thornycroft* ...

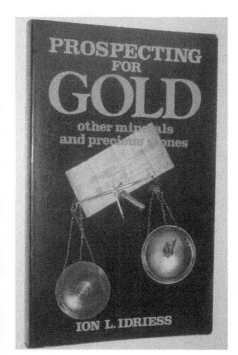

Prospecting for Gold – *we sold a lot or copies of that in the early 1980s.*

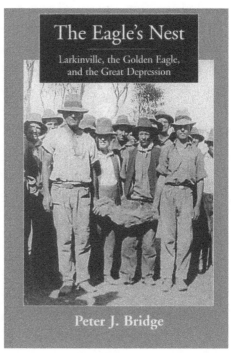

The Golden Eagle –
Idriess knew about that too ...

Alice Springs with Harold Lasseter on board. Lasseter and Idriess – each time I try to draw Peter to my reason for being here I can see the strain mounting until he snaps back to his natural hunting ground: *Idriess is remembered because he wrote books. In their day others were better known but they're forgotten now because they were journalists. John Drayton would get prospectors to write letters and used them in his gold-boosting articles. Bill Charnley was another, mainly published overseas – The Wide World Magazine. But in the long term it's books that survived.*

But Idriess was a prospector – and that's enough: *he knew the material, but so much of prospecting is luck. It's cyclical, the old prospectors of the '30s were scavenging around the workings of the 1890s prospectors.* Luck and a little knowhow; I'm curious how he sees Idriess' technical competency and raise the book that is the grail for collectors, **Cyaniding for Gold**: *it was too far ahead for the prospectors, that's when you get into big stuff. But* **Prospecting for Gold** *– we sold lots of copies of that in the early 1980s. The reason is that there was little else.* Mining and prospecting – related but different. Mining is a hard-headed calculation from survey and assay reports – how big does the hole have to be; how much dirt needs to be processed… It's a business and the less left to chance the better. Prospecting is all about chance, and patience, waiting: *for luck to unearth a little nest of those earthy-yellow, though often rusty-black, little eggs.*[213] That was Idriess, scratching for tin or wolfram in north Queensland, but gold was what really moved him and it was dreaming the big strike that drove him – as it did millions of others around the world – then and now.

Three hours later, next to the computer on the table dominating the room that has been our base as Peter and I traced down leads and digressions to books, reports, and objects throughout the labyrinth of this building, are three books that have surfaced as tying into my interests. As these slide into my bag and I make ready to leave, Peter casually asks: *You've checked out the Lasseter file…* The Lasseter file – through the afternoon Peter has made connections to historical and contemporary figures that relate, somehow, to Lasseter or Idriess. But almost always with a mantra-like disclaimer: *but it's not Western Australia, that's what*

I'm interested in. Even so there was enough but now, as I'm about to go, what's left on the table is a brown lever-arch file three inches thick – *the Lasseter file.*

Inside is a chaos of letters, email exchanges, reports, clippings and more. The efforts of Lasseterians to synthesise a story that Hesperian might take on. Only one seems to have made it; Peter published Bill Decarli's book ***A Dead Mans Dream: Lasseter's Reef Found*** – *an interesting theory* (Chapter 13). Slowly a rough order emerges that is, broadly, chronological, starting with paper clippings dating to before the Expedition. Under the header *CENTRAL AUSTRALIA – HUGE GOLD REEF – RICHER THAN THE GOLDEN MILE* there is a report in the *Irwin Index* for Saturday 24ᵗʰ May 1930, repeated exactly in the *Murchison Times*, which relates that *Federal and State Governments are shortly to be asked to assist an expedition …* the final paragraph proclaiming that *Mr. J. Bailey, president of the A.W.U., is a personal friend of Lasseter.* As if… Half-an-inch into the file the clippings shift to reports in national and regional papers of expeditions, new schemes and old dreams, reports of failure and fraud: the Second CAGE Expedition of 1932, Scientific Gold Exploration in 1933, Cutlack's 1936 Border Gold Reefs expedition, and on through others to Dick Smith in 1977 and Goldsearch in 1992. Among the letters to and from Peter I recognise now-familiar names – Bob Lasseter, Luke Walker, Dick Kimber and Austin Stapleton. And a curious letter from Peter himself to the Law Courts Library, Queen Street, Sydney, dated 11ᵗʰ June 1992: *We are preparing a biography of a well known 'character' of Australian history who committed bigamy in NSW in 1930. Your help in supplying details of the penalties for this offence under NSW law in 1930 would be greatly appreciated. Yours sincerely, P. Bridge.*

As I get towards the middle of this collection there are some of the earliest news reports of Lasseter's death. From the *West Australian* of 29ᵗʰ April 1931: *LOST PROSPECTOR – Remains Discovered. Canberra, April 28 – The Minister for Home Affairs (Mr. Blakeley) stated to-day that he had received advice from the Government Resident of Central Australia that the body of Mr. L. H. Lasseter was found at Shaw Creek in the Petermann Ranges on March 28 by Mr. R. Buck.* Just a few pages later is a near-full-page, glowing review in the same paper dated 3ʳᵈ October 1931 of

Lasseter's Last Ride by "*Telamon*". It reads very like Idriess. And immediately after is a review in the *Western Mail* for 19th November in the anonymous "*Just roamin' around*" section. Sprinkled through this trove and increasing as I mine deeper are the detractors, including Michael Terry, who was reported in the *Western Mail* on 1st February 1934 as insisting: *that it was impossible for Lasseter to have crossed Gibson's desert as he claimed to have done* – in 1897, at just seventeen years of age.

Just a few pages on is Terry's article in *Walkabout* magazine from 1936, around the time he got up Idriess' nose, precipitating correspondence with Walter Cousins at Angus & Robertson when Idriess thought Terry was being critical of *Lasseter's Last Ride.* This article is not about the book, it considers Lasseter's story and the expedition from the perspective of someone who knew the country first hand, with photos of Terry and his party with Lasseter's message etched into the lakebed at Lake Christopher. His concluding paragraph sums it up:

Now, perhaps you may be wondering why it is that I am taking upon myself to cast some doubt on this story of a lost reef. Well, it's simply this: The scout of the gold-mining industry – the prospector – is one worthy of support, for by his efforts are new mines discovered. Thus are Australia's resources developed. But support for the genuine prospector becomes increasingly difficult, for his suggestion to try out an area, because the right rocks are there for gold occurrences, sounds far too prosaic alongside a story of a mountain of gold already found and simply to be re-located. Those who have so far backed search for Lasseter's Reef have paid dearly, whereas, had they assisted to finance orthodox prospecting, their chance of return would have been infinitely less remote. To chase all over a countryside in search of a lost reef, more particularly having regard to the evidence on which its existence is based, is a very different proposition from that of combing the country systematically with pick and dolly-pot. For only by such trial will the area be thoroughly tested, and, if it carries payable gold at all, the fact will in time be established. Some day a bit of gold may be found out there; but, believe me, it won't be an El Dorado.[214]

A pity more people didn't listen to the voice of experience. Towards the bottom of the Lasseter file a four-page, fold-out brochure appears, the print and graphics in the dulled ochre tones of central Australia on sand-coloured, fine-quality paper. It's an advertisement for the *Lasseter's Reef Jubilee EXPEDITION*. To depart Sydney Airport on 2nd May 1981; at $1,279, the sixteen-day tour marketed by *Austrek* would cover the key stations in the saga in relative comfort and was to be: *Fully guided by members of the Lasseter family to all historic sights.* A picture of Harold Lasseter on the front, his rough-hewn grave site inside, on the last page the booking offices and display rooms are listed in George Street Sydney, Bondi Junction, Parramatta – and *Bob Lasseter's Explorers World, Penrith.*

Back across the Causeway and along St George's Terrace, a shadowed canyon of mining-company skyscrapers that testify to the foundations of this State's prosperity – for some anyway. I carry with me four Hesperian gifts. A bibliography of William Campbell Charnley and a collection of articles by John Drayton including stories of north Queensland that I'm only vaguely familiar with, but which Idriess knew well, like Christy Palmerston: *who never had a house, never nourished the ambition to own a shack in some suburb of a capital, who uncovered enormous values in gold, tin and other products of the underground – and died poor.*[215] Despite the flawed facets of Palmerston's frontier façade, like Lasseter he's remembered in the name of a highway, and died in Malaya in the same year as Lasseter's claimed continental traverse. Charnley and Drayton – preserved in Peter's pantheon of journalistic storytellers of the frontier. Both works compiled by Peter, as is the third item, **The Eagle's Nest: Larkinville, the Golden Eagle and the Great Depression**.[216] *The Golden Eagle* – Idriess knew all about that too, and in 1931 wanted to use the publicity of the national tour of the largest nugget found in Australia to leverage sales of **Prospecting for Gold**. The last item is an odd inclusion and handed to me as I walked out the door. **Anthropophagitism in the Antipodes or Cannibalism in Australia** has a curious dedication: *to the cloistered anthropologist whose categorical denial of the subject matter amongst our autochthones goaded the author to the endeavour, and, to the sometime rewriter of questionable aboriginal folklore whose* *forceful objections stirred the author's flagging spirits to the completion of the task.* The author is one James Cooke R.N. (Rtd.).

Since its publication in 1997 the whimsical double entendre of Peter's pseudonym is lost on almost all of those contributing to the online commentary, who seem to fall at the opposite poles of the culture and history wars. Lasseter is less contentious and perhaps my visit encouraged Peter out of his Western Australian comfort zone and back into Lasseter land. Whether or not, four months later **H.A. 'Matt' Ellis and the Lasseter Rort**[217] appeared in my mailbox. New Zealand born, Ellis was awarded the Military Cross in the First World War, was a Major in the Intelligence Service in the War that followed, and had a distinguished career as a geologist in Western Australia. In 1936 he had direct experience of an early Lasseter scammer, S.R. Hummerston of Border Gold Reefs, who was a sometime fellow traveller with the equally devious Morley Aubrey Hermann Cutlack (see Chapters 10 and 18).[218] Hummerston claimed to have located the reef in 1934 with the help of a map found in a bottle buried under the remains of a campfire,[219] which was enough to secure support to return in 1935 and again in 1936. He even flew his wife in to check it out, which piqued the interest of the *Australian Women's Weekly*.[220] One person not impressed was Ellis, who claimed that Hummerston tried to shoot him one night while they were camping nearby. Peter Bridge's reprint is of Ellis's technical report which appeared in the 1936 **Annual Report of the Geological Survey**. Following a comprehensive account of the geology of the region, the last section is *The Lasseter Myth*, concluding with comments that surely have the likes of Cutlack and Hummerston in mind:

> *It cannot be too strongly urged that "Lasseter's Reef" is likely to be held out as a bait to mining investors for many years to come, and it is necessary to urge just as strongly the necessity of extreme caution when contemplating any investment in a mining venture, the basis of which is a fabulously rich gold reef in Central Australia, which more than likely, the prospective investor will be informed is probably "Lasseter's Reef."* [221]

CHAPTER 9

Magnetic Island

The desert, as I have said, is a great obliterator; but while that is true, it is not the whole truth. The desert smooths away the remnants of death. It disposes of the husks of former life so that in a little while it is as though they had never come. This is because in the balanced economy of the desert, death is used to nourish new life with marvellous efficiency.

Michael Terry, 1974.[222]

January 2020

Murdering Point Road – the sign is barely visible until it's metres away, emerging through the monsoonal rainstorm. Even with wipers at top speed it's only just possible to make out the rear lights of the vehicle ahead. Turn left to Kurrimine, supposedly a *Djirbalngan* word for rising sun – and without the associations of history. Or turn right to Silkwood and on through Japoonvale to the Atherton Tablelands. It's familiar country from a quarter century living in Far North Queensland, familiar enough that I located a key element of the plot of **Vicarious Dreaming** near Silkwood. That involved a fictional character, Laszlo, whose obsession with Idriess drove the narrative. There are plenty of real people whose interests in Idriess are in the borderland of obsession and I'm heading to Magnetic Island to meet Garry Holmes, owner of the largest collection of Idriess first editions in Queensland.

Murdering Point to the left; Silkwood to the right – we continue straight on as the tempo of the rain on the roof increases and the sky ahead darkens with another bank of monsoonal storm clouds. In the driver's seat is Jon who, like Laszlo, is a central character of **Vicarious Dreaming**. But Jon is real and our stories of kayaking along the coast of Far North Queensland, before and after his spinal injury, are also in the book. His wheelchair is in the back and we pass through Townsville, straight to the car ferry for the eight kilometre ride. As we leave the harbour at the mouth of the Ross River, Magnetic Island rises sharply with the Palm Island group visible on the northern horizon. At five-hundred metres, Mount Cook is a feature no matter which way you approach – as did the *Great Navigator* on 6th June 1770. At midday the *Endeavour* passed from what Cook had called Bowling Green Bay that ended with a northern, sharp, rocky promontory, before another coastal indentation: *This bay which I named **Cleveland Bay** appeared to be about 5 or 6 miles in extent every way; the east point I named **Cape Cleveland** and the west **Magnetical Head** or **Isle** as it had much the appearance of an island and the compass would not travis [traverse] well when near it.*[223]

Cook was probably seen from the heights of *Yunbenun* by Wulguru-kaba people whose descendants are few on an island that is now a dormitory suburb and weekend getaway space for Townsville. Ultimately there was no resisting the European incursions, but as we drive across the island's spine to the northern shore we pass concrete reminders of threatened Japanese invasion. Emplacements for guns that were originally meant for Bataan before it fell. Completed after the Japanese air raids on Townsville in July 1942, these weapons were never fired in anger and the site now is for spotting koalas not foes. Then it's downhill towards Horse-shoe Bay and Garry's property.

We are expected; the font gate is opened by a middle-aged man dressed for another day on *Maggie* – shirt, shorts and sandals – and we drive into the shelter of a car port at the side of the house. Protection from the downpour is appreciated as I extract the wheelchair and Jon transfers from the driver's seat. There are steps to the front veranda – getting Jon up isn't going to happen and Garry and his wife, Neslea, transform the carport into a space for conversation. But I'm drawn up the steps by Bindi, a Jack Russell/wire-haired Terrier-cross, tethered on the deck. With assurances that we are dog people she's free and with us as if we've always been part of the pack. But just one glance through the front door and I've sighted glass fronted cases crammed with books that have exposed covers or spines that are familiar – Idriess. There are blocks of the same title lined neatly, probably with a subliminal secondary order, and behind those are more stacked books – all Idriess.

Garry is 72, Neslea a decade younger, from the Philippines. They met when Garry was based out of Singapore after serving two tours in Vietnam and a decade working around the world in marine surveying and were married in 1983. They have two children; their daughter Shannon is a teacher in Brisbane, and their son John lives on a rural block in southern Queensland. Like his father and grandfather, John went into the military and served in the Engineers in Afghanistan. Garry and Neslea returned to Australia to buy and run a caravan park at Flying Fish Point outside Innisfail, a venture extinguished by the perfect storm of the pilots' strike and cyclones. That initiated a decade on the move and in 1996 they arrived in Atherton, where Garry spent the next eight years working at the Department of Primary Industries research station until ill-health forced retirement. On the road again, they finally came to rest on Magnetic Island in 2013. But it was during their first year in Atherton that Garry went to Yungaburra and found Spencer and Murphy Second-hand Books on Eacham Road. And there on a shelf was an Idriess book, ***Men of the Jungle***: *I took a liking to his writing, it sounded more like fiction than fact. After that I got more and more and the collecting became an obsession. I loved his work – the history, romance, adventure of it.*

Neslea is bringing a feast to the table in the carport, more than we are ever going to finish. But she's listening to it all, smiling and nodding as the scale of his project becomes obvious. It wasn't enough to have a copy, it had to be a first edition, and not just one: *I've got some favourites –*

Headhunters of the Coral Sea, Madman's Island. I've got three of the first edition of Madman's Island. In the end I collected three complete sets of first editions. I gave one to each child, I told them one day they will be valuable. And if you look at Prospecting for Gold there are about twenty editions and I've got every one of them.

Once we are talking about finding individual works – the heavy lifting of obsessional collecting – names I've heard of tumble into the conversation. There are stories of support and exchange, complaints of misplaced intentions and skulduggery, warnings and advice. Competition among the cognoscenti: *Cyaniding for Gold is the golden fleece, a first edition is worth about $2,000 to $3,000. Once you get on the net there are people all over the world interested. It's very technical, I've never read it the whole way through. He could jump from there to The Cattle King, diamonds, or opal mining at Lightning Ridge.*

Another heavy shower, the crescendo on the carport roof tracking its passage. Neslea moves the chairs away from the exposed side, Bindi settling in next to Jon's wheelchair. Somehow the discussion has drifted to health issues and Jon is recirculating a well-travelled joke into a new setting – catheters. I've heard it before but Garry smiles. Whether it's the rain or mentions of liquids, the next stop is talking about bucket lists; Garry's is: *Escape River, I want to go where Kennedy was.* I've been close by, near the tip of Cape York, where Edmund Kennedy was speared in 1848 at the end of his third expedition, an overland journey from Rockingham Bay to the tip of Cape York that was a disaster from the start. Only Kennedy and Galmarra, an Aboriginal teenager from southern New South Wales who has ever since been known as Jackey Jackey, got close to where they hoped to rendezvous with the *Ariel* that was waiting in Newcastle Bay north of the mouth of the Escape River. Kennedy didn't make it; Jackey Jackey carried the body of his leader on and eventually covered it over in a place that he wasn't able to find when he returned with another party to search for survivors and retrieve remains. But Idriess reckoned he knew where: *he fell under the spears of the blacks – almost in sight of the relief ship. … Aborigines have pointed out to me the very spot where Kennedy fell. A dismal place to die alone, among the gaunt mangroves by that weird river mouth enclosed by those scrubby little hills, by those strange pitcher-plant swamps.*[224]

Maybe – but Garry has read more about it than the few pages by Idriess: *It's a fascinating tale, full of intrigue. Edgar Beale wrote the main story about Kennedy. Les Hiddens wrote a follow-up.* Hiddens published a facsimile edition of a survivor's account, and of the diaries of the Jardine brothers who led another expedition up Cape York nearly two decades later.[225] Idriess wrote about that too: *the epic of the two young Jardine boys, Frank and Alick, with the toughened bushmen Charlie Scrutton, Roy Binney, and Alf Cowderoy, and the laughing, recklessly brave, ever cheerful aboriginal youth Eulah, with Tracker Peter and Sambo, bringing their mob of cattle overland right to Somerset.*[226] What he didn't mention were the dead black-fellows along the way. Idriess got to know the Jardine descendants and one of his last trips to the Torres Strait was with Frank's grandson Bootles Jardine – a trip he lived to regret. The Jardines are long gone but the name remains – the Jardine River and the Jardine Hotel – only partly sanitised by the passage of time. But for Idriess, John Jardine and his kids were larger-than-life figures in an outpost on the edge of civilisation. They figure in several Idriess books; ***The Great Trek*** is a *Boy's-Own*-style rehabilitation of Frank and Alexander's gap year adventure.[227] Idriess and Les Hiddens also shared another interest – Lasseter,[228] which brings our conversation to ***Lasseter's Last Ride****: I heard about the lost reef and wondered if it existed. I saw **Lasseter's Last Ride**, so I picked up a copy, and then there was a first edition advertised and I grabbed that too. A terrific story, it got the imagination working – aeroplanes, search parties, people trying to go out there and find the reef.*

Half-an-hour later Garry and I head inside and stop at the glass-fronted bookcase stacked with Idriess first editions that I saw earlier, then on to a room set aside for Garry's *Aboriginal books*. This collection began while he was living in Darwin in the 1990s and intrigued by Aboriginal cultures of the Top End. He signed up for a university course but was disappointed by the readings and started finding his own. There are books that date back a century, authors and titles I know, many first editions and some in their original jackets. I recognise ***Aboriginal Health and History:***

Power and Prejudice in Remote Australia and sign it with my standard line: *an unappreciated classic.* Garry is not sure what to do with the collection; perhaps his daughter will take it, maybe he'll sell it. I can feel how difficult that thought is, each item forming part of a carefully assembled jigsaw – it all relates but just grows and grows. On the opposite wall are framed original posters for Charles Chauvel's film *Jedda* and, pointing to the buxom Aboriginal girl, Garry explains that in the original photograph Ngarla Kunoth's breasts weren't exposed. Whatever the market demands – in the UK the film was released as *Jedda the Uncivilized* and I suppose for mid-century Brits the primitive and the prurient were good for sales. Photoshopping 1950s style.[229]

Close by are paintings on bark by Mornington Island artist Dick Roughsey, Goobalathaldin, which introduces his friend and mentor Percy Trezise and from there back to where Idriess began his book *Madman's Island.* That was where my journey with *Vicarious Dreaming* took me – to Idriess' favourite Cooktown drinking spot in the years just before and after the First War – the West Coast Hotel. Like me, Garry has done the pilgrimage:

> *The front bar of the West Coast was covered in tiles that Percy Trezise painted of Cook's landing. There was a series of ten tiles half a metre square, from the moment he landed with a picture of the Endeavour. But someone decided to refurbish the hotel and chipped the tiles off. An entrepreneur got them together, put them in frames and they were up for sale in a craft shop in Manunda. I spoke to the lady and offered $20,000. She said that Percy Trezise was in a Redlynch nursing home and asked if I would like to meet him – so we went down and said hi. He was away with the fairies, but a lovely guy.*

An hour later I have half a dozen photographs of those tiles along with three pictures of the Split Rock traditional rock art gallery near Laura that Percy Trezise built one of his careers around – author, aviator, artist, environmentalist, advocate, publican, as well as rock art expert and conservator. For his time Trezise was a real bushman and had more experience of the country and Indigenous cultures of Cape York than his predecessor, Idriess, about whom he didn't mince words. Trezise was a careful observer – of wildlife as well as much else – and in relation to previous authors' accounts commented: *Popular writers such as Idriess were responsible for many of these misconceptions and wrote in the authoritative manner of men who were familiar with the bush and its creatures. They had been in the bush all right, but saw little and misconstrued much of what they did see. They handled the truth very carelessly ... Mundane facts were heavily embroidered with fiction for the sake of sensation.*[230]

My new Trezise ephemera are sealed in a plastic folder and sit on top of books that Garry has given me. Michael Terry's **War of the Warramullas**, an end-of-career book by someone who knew more about Central Australia in the third and fourth decades of the last century than either Idriess or Lasseter, and who found the furthermost point that Lasseter reached at Lake Christopher. Beneath that is the last book Idriess published, in 1969, **Challenge of the North: Wealth from Australia's Northern Shores**. Eighty years of age and still spruiking for northern development. The fly leaf of the dust jacket captures the vibe: *Houses under the Barrier Reef sea, a fish trap hundreds of miles wide across the Gulf of Carpentaria, power from our rugged, daunting Kimberley coast, sea-beef for the world's growing population – pipe dream ... or reality, dreamer ... or prophet? Who can say? But perhaps the reflections of Ion Idriess mirror an age, an era, to come, as they so often have in the past.*[231]

Perhaps... At the bottom of my loot is Gary's last gift. A first edition of **Lasseter's Last Ride** – the original. Except for two carefully restored elements. The cover is a facsimile and the picture that faces the title page is a replacement. It's of Irene Lasseter sitting on a swing holding two children, with Harold behind them grasping ropes that support the seat. Mother and father are smiling – the kids not so sure. In her right arm is a young boy in shorts and jumper with dark socks to mid-calf – Bob Lasseter. Garry has cut this page from a second edition and pasted it here – a careful act of respect to the edition and the author. Inside the cover is a name – *Evelyn M. Hughes* – and scrawled across the title page:

For Will and Evelyn a little Gift to You. Ion Idriess, 1932.

CHAPTER 10

Corroborators

But the Dead Heart keeps its own secrets. The motor-trucks could not climb the high dunes of clinging sand and the jagged escarpments of the broken sandstone country. The planes crashed in the arid bush and the pilots barely escaped with their lives. The expedition – the best equipped that had ever set out into the wastes of Centralia – failed. But Lasseter would not go back. He borrowed two camels from a chance-met dingo-hunter and pushed on into the desert alone, sure that his reef was waiting.

Ian Miller, 1941.[232]

The accounts of the *witnesses* – Bailey, Coote, Blakiston-Houston, Taylor, Blakeley, Johns, Albrecht and Smith – were influenced by Idriess' rendering of the First CAGE Expedition. In one way or another **Lasseter's Last Ride** is in all of them, as it is in the retellings and reconstructions that followed. The investments and motivations of these other voices – the *corroborators*, *sleuths*, *decoders* and *mythbusters* – are different from the witnesses and each other. While they share a common point of departure, Lasseter, over the nine decades since the release of **Lasseter's Last Ride** the focus has shifted from the mission to the man and, more recently, to the myth that has settled around the story. In so doing the frame has shifted from the troubled prospector to the text; from Lasseter to Idriess. But the categories are not tight and there is the occasional voice that sits out on its own – like Ian Miller.

On 31st July 1942 the Battle of Kokoda was just beginning and against Churchill's strident objections Curtin would pivot Australian's troops to the Pacific theatre. Just a week before, Axis troops had been halted in north Africa in the First Battle of El Alamein and two months later the Australian 9th Division fought in the Second Battle which Churchill declared: *is not even the beginning of the end, but it is, perhaps, the end of the beginning.* Stirring stuff to a wartime British population inured to serial bad news and struggling to maintain a semblance of normality – including the last day of the academic year at Hope Council School, Flintshire, in the northern borderlands of Wales. On that day the Education Committee awarded a prize to Peter Holroyd: *who made every possible attendance and displayed commendable industry in school work.* That's on the red-fringed plate pasted inside the cover of my copy of **The Lost Reef,** Ian Miller's book published the year before.

Facing the first page of the text is a map that is remarkably similar to that on the inside cover of the 1933 versions of **Lasseter's Last Ride.** The additions in **The Lost Reef** are a tree marked as *Lasseter's tree* in the Rawlinson Range, and three trees marked as *The Reef* in the Warburton Range. The title is *Map showing the route taken by Bill Meldrum* and there is a dashed line arrowed – as in the **Lasseter's Last Ride** map – to Laverton to the south-west. There is one other map in Miller's book that has similarities to the line drawings found with *The Diary* and included in the last chapter – *Fragments* – of the 1932 revised edition of Idriess' book. It shows the three trees in the Warburton Range with an arrow to an adjacent cross titled *REEF Glen with 3 ghost gums.* The map is quite detailed, the reef being some three camps from Possum Hill with an arrow to the Petermann Range to the north-east, and another path marked northwards through *Breakaway Country* to Lake Christopher, with the warning *4 days bad going no water,* bracketed below which is: *(They will meet me here).* The title to this second diagram is *Lasseter's Map.*

The Lost Reef makes no pretence to be anything other than fiction and reads like a sequel to ***Lasseter's Last Ride***. 'Mulga' Bill Meldrum is camping with his rough-haired terrier, *Bluey*, and three camels, *Daisy*, *Molly* and *Satan*, in the Rawlinson Range. Wary of the local *Wongaptichas* who might want *a little target practice with their spears* he's sighting his rifle on a mark on a tree which, on approach, he discovers is a blaze with a message:

2-3-31

FINISHED

DIG UNDER FIRE

LASSETER

Meldrum follows the instructions and finds a small tin with ore samples, a map, and a message that resembles the form and tone of Lasseter's *Diary*. He is about to head off when a young Aboriginal man, *Moorara*, appears with his dying partner who had been promised to an older man but was speared because of the wrong-way relationship with Moorara, with whom she managed to escape. Soon after she dies, featherfoot tracks of *Kaiditcha* men – *The Avengers* – are found. Moorara is resigned to his fate but agrees to go with Meldrum and saves him from death from thirst, after which they camp near a bora ground where Meldrum locates Lasseter's Reef. But local tribes are assembling for a corroboree and are joined by *The Avengers* in hot pursuit. Meldrum and Moorara make a run for it, heading west towards Laverton to avoid Moorara's country, with *The Avengers* not far behind. They both realise the country they are heading into is unforgiving: *Make one bad mistake and they were finished. That's what Lasseter did, losing his camels.* They are almost done for when they see smoke on the horizon and discover that a *'plane* has crashed on a salt-lake with two survivors, *Pat Kearney* and *Tom Dyson* of the *Central Goldfields Exploration Company,* who were out looking for Lasseter's Reef somewhere in the Livesey Range. One of them comments: *They say there's a hoodoo on Lasseter's Reef, and I'm believing it after this.*

It gets worse; the gathering tribes reappear with *The Avengers* and kill Meldrum's camels – they're all stranded. As for Moorara, *The Avengers* have him in their sights and *point the bone* – he's doomed whatever happens. But, they are able to jury-rig a fix for the *'plane*, climb aboard and, just in time, the heavily loaded aircraft accelerates towards the massed *Pitchenturras* – and *The Avengers*. As they take off: *A slight shock passed through the 'plane as they passed the fleeing men, and looking back, Meldrum saw one of them spread-eagled on the ground.* In fact there are two killed – *The Avengers* – thus breaking the spell on Moorara. And as they speed to safety: *Moorara craned back to look at the still shape. Visibly the slackness went out of his limbs, and the sparkle of intelligence came back to his eyes. 'Now Moorara need not die,' he said cheerfully. 'Your medicine is stronger than theirs.' He sat back and began to take a lively interest in the moving ground beneath.*

Safe and flying, Meldrum reveals to Kearney and Dyson that he had found the reef and together they start planning to set up a company, the last line of the book reading: *And steadily the battered D.H. 50 thrust the miles of desert and thirst behind it.* It's a line worthy of Idriess and the ***The Lost Reef*** channels ***Lasseter's Last Ride*** – the plot, maps, style and even the *Wongapitchas* prominently identified in the foreword by Herbert Basedow. In ***The Lost Reef*** there is a description of the Lasseter story that could be a precis for ***Lasseter's Last Ride***, the author even noting that: *No one knows the full story of his wanderings, though parts have been built up from odd pages of a pencilled diary and letters hidden near some of his camping places.* But there is no mention of that book or of Idriess, just a suggestion that this story self-propagates: *Every one has heard of Lasseter, that dreaming, half-legendary prospector about whom so many tales are told around the lonely camp fires of the Centre.*

Idriess could have written it and had a British publishing agent – Jonathan Cape.[233] But as the Second World War began he was busy; there were six books published in 1940 and 1941, and he was about to begin a series of nine military works that would be out before the War ended, it doesn't seem likely that he took time out for a sequel – Ion as Ian. But if the author really is Ian Miller he's elusive; the closest British writer with that name around that time was the author of ***School Tie***,[234] a 1935 tale set in an Edinburgh boarding school that was probably regarded as a somewhat risqué adolescent male sexual coming-of-age novella published by George Newnes Press. The by then deceased eponymous founder had set up a major magazine publishing house in Britain and among its titles was *The Wide World Magazine*, which Idriess contributed to in the same year as the First CAGE Expedition.[235] Idriess used lots of pseudonyms, but he wasn't the author of **School Tie** – that wasn't his subject or style. And it's not known whether that and **The Lost Reef** were written by one person or two, or whether either of them was really named Ian Miller. Whether or not, Idriess would have known about **The Lost Reef**, but although he was quick to respond when he thought other writers were straying into his territory, there is no evidence that he ever commented on this curious coda to his first successful book. While Idriess probably didn't write **The Lost Reef** it's possible that the author was someone close to Idriess – like Frank Clune, who had more than a passing interest in Lasseter.[236] *Lasseter's Ghost,* a chapter in Clune's **The Red Heart: Sagas of Centralia**, published in 1944, not long after **The Lost Reef**, starts by acknowledging Idriess before getting into the story: *Several years went by, but the Lasseter legend persisted, as prospectors and company-promoters kept on looking for his fabulous Lost Reef of gold! Then another legend arose, and was whispered by know-alls at many a camp-fire in Centralia.*[237]

The *Lost Reef ... camp-fires ...* The shared phrases of **The Lost Reef** and **The Red Heart** are probably coincidental. But between Clune and Idriess there was more in common than their writing styles and an interest in Lasseter. They'd both been at Gallipoli and were Angus & Robertson authors; there's a photograph in the Angus & Robertson papers at the Mitchell Library with the faces of six authors pasted on an old picture of men sitting outside a bar and holding tankards. A shard of paper with a signature is under each figure. Frank Clune is on the left, Ion Idriess in the middle, and between them Edward Vivian Timms who had also been at Gallipoli, and Colin Roderick. To the right are Colin Simpson and Alec Chisholm. Behind them is a window and one last figure – not identified but possibly George Ferguson – the boss. The image captures the high point of the firm's fortunes and probably of a long-past genre of Australian popular adventure writing – very much a boys' club.[238]

Corroborators

Frank Clune exemplifies the first set of voices other than Idriess and the *witnesses* that emerged as I began trying to make sense of the Lasseter literature – the *corroborators*. The works of this group of authors – Frank Clune, Lewis Charles (L.C.) Rodd and Austin Stapleton – responded to and were framed by existing texts, the accounts of Idriess, Blakeley and Coote respectively. And there's a curious fourth example, last written to vindicate the first storyteller, Lasseter, by Desmond Clacherty.

When Clune died in 1971 he had sold more books than any other Australian author with one exception, Ion Idriess, who died eight years later. Through the 1930s and '40s Idriess and Clune were the best-known authors of Australian exotica and adventure books, Clune making a transition as interest in that genre waned, to travel writing and other media.[239] Like Idriess, he cut his teeth writing about his experiences in the bush; he became a friend of Donald Mackay and in 1942 published ***Last of the Australian Explorers: The Story of Donald Mackay***. Mackay also had a long relationship with Bob Buck, who set up the strip at Ilbilba that Mackay used for his first Aerial Survey in early 1930, and which became the base for the First CAGE Expedition just a few months later.[240] Mackay was back in the western deserts in 1933, 1935 and 1937, with Bob Buck along on two expeditions.

In October 1939 Clune was in Alice Springs, a stop on a jeep journey from Sydney to Darwin, and he managed to join an expedition organised by Morley Aubrey Hermann Cutlack.[241] As Chris Clark discovered (Chapter 18) this Cutlack was cousin to Frederic Morley Cutlack who fought on the Western Front where he ended up as a war journalist with Charles Bean, returning to a distinguished writing career in Australia including ***Breaker Morant: A Horseman Who Made History***. Morley Aubrey was also a journalist but less reputable. He was involved in a number of Sydney-based companies including Centralia Holdings, formed to locate Lasseter's Reef, playing on and supplementing the legend to encourage investment in related ventures that all fell through. At the end of 1939 *Smith's Weekly* reported more spin:

EXCITING NARRATIVE OF GOLD SEEKERS

Morley Cutlack, just back from his eleventh attempt to locate Lasseter's Reef, is a Queenslander by birth, geologist, prospector, and has for many years hunted for gold in New Guinea and, more particularly, in Central Australia. His record there is five expeditions by air, three by truck, four by camel, totalling 35,000 miles by air, 16,000 by truck, 1,700 by camel, and over 300 on foot. Lasseter's Reef has taken some finding, assuming that it has now at last been located. Indications are impressive.[242]

Eleven attempts and counting… When that Cutlack expedition headed out of town towards Ayers Rock and Lake Amadeus they passed through Renner's Rock, where Bob Buck was living. Clune was obviously taken with meeting a living legend of the Centre and lubricated the exchange with a couple of beers, eventually raising with Buck the rumours that he had *got a share of Lasseter's insurance.* The reaction was predictable but ended with a summary dismissal from Buck that seems to have settled the matter: *"Lasseter's dead all right, old chap. The Luritchas led me to his burial place in the Petermanns, I dug up his body, souvenired his false teeth and diaries, and reburied him in whiteman fashion by the banks of Shaw Creek. He's out there where the dead men lie – I fenced him in – and why can't they let the poor flaming cow rest in peace?"*

Eventually the Cutlack expedition arrived by camel at Ayers Rock where a rough airstrip was prepared for a flight bringing in a geologist, after which Clune was: *left in camp to guard the stores while the prospectors rode away on the camels to look for Lasseter's Reef – or something like it – in the region of Lake Amadeus.*[243] But he wasn't alone, and over the next few days – *in a mixture of pidgin English and Luritcha, and demonstrated by many signs and gestures* – and referring to a handy *two hundred-word dictionary of the Luritcha prepared by Victor Dumas,* the expedition's camel-driver, he was well-entertained: *My companion was one of the Luritcha camel-boys, named Mulga Mick. … His proper name was Koorin-Jaminny and – this was a surprise – he was one of the tribe which succoured Harry Lasseter in the Petermann Ranges in 1931. When Bob Buck found Lasseter's body he adopted Koorin-Jaminny as a camel-boy. I had an eye-witness of Lasseter's death!*

Mulga Mick, Koorin-Jaminny – this is Mick Kuruanyani, the same person who two decades later with Nosepeg Tjupurrula directed Lowell Thomas to the site where Buck had buried the remains of the prospector in 1931. He appeared in the 1957 *High Adventure* episode that showed the disinterment of Lasseter's remains that so infuriated Bob and Elsie Lasseter (Chapter 4). In 1939, with the aid of Victor Dumas' *dictionary* Clune constructed an account that fitted well with that of Idriess, concluding: *So ended the eye-witness account of Lasseter's death. I was absolutely satisfied that the story was dinkum and that "old man Lasseter" really does lie buried "out where the dead men lie".*[244] For Clune it was settled, and ***Lasseter's Last Ride*** confirmed as an accurate account. With one exception; he raised the possibility that Lasseter was driven by a fantasy stoked in his fertile teenage mind by an 1898 serial story – *The Adventures of Louis de Rougemont as told by Himself* – published in the English "true-story" magazine, *The Wide World*.

Frank Clune was a prolific writer and became a household name. Lewis Charles Rodd was less well known but was an enthusiastic supporter of the writing and career of his wife, novelist Kylie Tennant.[245] Rodd's 1973 *Quadrant* article, *The mystery of Lasseter and his reef*, was written just before the release of Fred Blakeley's ***Dream Millions*** by Angus & Robertson and he had earlier been involved in editing Blakeley's original typescript written in the late-1930s. His regard for the down to earth bushman and his values is clear, as is his assessment of the urtext: *Thousands of Australians were prepared to accept as historical fact Ion L. Idriess's romantic but purely imaginary reconstruction in* ***Lasseter's Last Ride*** *of the heroic last days and death of the man who had given them hope.*[246]

Rodd reprises Blakeley's story of mounting suspicions about Lasseter's bush competence and the credibility of his backstory, and includes the text of a 1932 article in the *Aboriginalities* section of *The Bulletin* by *"Verax"* – an acquaintance of Lasseter from before and after the First World War. Whoever this author was, his impression of Lasseter and of the claims he made about Centralian gold were clear: *The yarn is hardly credible, but Lasseter wasn't a very reasonable being. I fear his reef was only one of* the many illusions and delusions that spattered his career.[247] As would later emerge, that assessment was spot on, and Rodd seemed to have shared it and accepted the view of Blakeley: *that Lasseter was in financial straits when he 'pitched his tale' and was after the £10 a week for as long as he could get it.* It was the money, and a modest amount to start with before greed swept what Blakeley called *the Sydney crowd* – and Lasseter – into spiralling fantasies of fame and fortune.

While the title of Rodd's *Quadrant* article was *The mystery of Lasseter and his reef,* it's really about Blakeley or, more specifically, Fred Blakeley and John Bailey. Rodd details Bailey's murky past, the inconsistencies in his account of events and his assiduous denial of responsibility: *With fine impartiality John Bailey allotted blame to everyone connected with the two expeditions except the chairman and his son, the secretary.* Despite rejecting Blakeley's Expedition report on his return to Sydney in October 1930, and not promptly acting on Phil Taylor's instructions for where to find Lasseter when there was still time to rescue him, in his 1947 account Bailey specifically blamed Blakeley for Lasseter's death.

Against the venal nature of the CAGE Company Chairman, Blakeley comes across as a man of sentiments and convictions, with deep connections to the landscape, fauna and flora of the Centre, and concern for the Aboriginal tribes of the region in the face of accelerating incursions. While Blakeley's account of the Expedition is credible, he was convinced that Lasseter somehow survived and made it to the United States. That belief gave ammunition to his detractors, including Ern Bailey, who in an interview with Billy Marshall-Stoneking in 1983 said Blakeley's account: *was an alibi for himself. He said Lasseter never died; he just went through to Western Australia, and caught a boat and went somewhere else. ... You see, Blakeley took this on himself and let this fellow get away. He was just a nincompoop! He certainly wasn't a good leader. It was only because his brother was a Federal minister and we thought this connection might be useful.*[248]

Ern Bailey's challenge to Blakeley's competence as a leader on the basis of his theory about Lasseter's life after the Expedition doesn't logically follow; Blakeley got it right while the CAGE Directors chose to keep on promoting the reef. The *alibi for himself* is a transparent projection for his own responsibility and was probably also motivated to support the reputation of his dad, which needed a lot of work. Blakeley wasn't similarly driven, and although his reasons for putting pen to paper were probably complex, on his first pencil manuscript written in 1936, five years after the events and the death of Florence Lasseter in Melbourne, but before Irene died in Sydney, he wrote: *Is it worth while as far as I can see if I tell the truth (or what I believe to be the truth). I will only injure a Woman and four little Australians, her load is great and anything I have to say only adds to that load, besides the two Books that have been written have given a lot of pleasure to the people of Australia.*[249]

Compared to the Baileys' disregard of the needs of the newly-widowed *other Mrs Lasseter*, Blakeley's concerns, which were repeated twelve years later in the version lodged with the Mitchell Library, appear sincere and suggest a degree of integrity uncommon in the saga. And then there is what seems an afterthought – *the two Books that have been written [that] have given a lot of pleasure to the people of Australia.* One, of course, was written by Idriess. The other, released in 1934, just a few years before Blakeley began writing, was **Hell's Airport: The Key to Lasseter's Lost Reef** by Errol Coote, the member of the Expedition that Blakeley had most difficulty with – more even than with Lasseter. Blakeley died in 1962 and his account was finally published a decade later, a year before Coote's death. **Lasseter Did Not Lie!** by Austin Stapleton was written in response: *The aim of this book is to re-examine the whole matter of Lasseter's claim, his competency and veracity and to restore, if possible, his former reputation. The need to do this stems from certain claims and statements contained in the posthumously published* **Dream Millions**.[250]

Austin Stapleton wrote a number of small books, including **Ayers Rock, the Olgas and Yulara,** and another historical piece published by Peter Bridge's Hesperian Press – **Willshire of Alice Springs**. William Willshire, Mounted Constable 1st Class, is an interesting choice of subject, being the first policeman in any Australian colony to stand trial for the murder of an Aboriginal person. Soon after arriving near Hermannsburg with a detachment of native troopers Willshire set up a station at Boggy Water.[251] Tensions with the missionaries resulted in an official Inquiry in

July 1890 into the shooting of Aboriginal prisoners at Glen Helen in 1885, allegations of *immorality* at Boggy Water, and reports of other abuses of tribal people. No Aboriginal witnesses were examined and ultimately Willshire was exonerated.

A few months later, in February 1891, Willshire was responsible for two killings at Tempe Downs, one of whom, Eraminta, an old adversary, had taken from Boggy Water a woman who in the past had been his partner – but was then with Willshire. Although discounted as being deaths in pursuit of cattle-killers, the Special Magistrate at Alice Springs, Frank Gillen, was tasked with taking evidence from witnesses. Willshire faced trial in Port Augusta in July 1891, his defence team headed by Sir John Downer, previously South Australia's Attorney-General. Irregularities included that Willshire cross-examined Aboriginal witnesses, providing translations of both questions and answers. While Willshire was found not guilty, it was the beginning of the end of his police career and a few years later, married with three children, he was a night-watchman at an abattoir. But he went on to represent himself as an expert on matters Aboriginal, writing four books with memorable lines including: *It's no use mincing matters, the Martini-Henry carbines at the critical moment were talking English in the silent majesty of these eternal rocks.*[252] And as for Frank Gillen and his role as Special Magistrate, Willshire later reflected: *In 1891 a forensic gentleman, notorious for his ignorance of magisterial duties, made a faux-pas by not taking my measure correctly. … He waxed vehement, boisterous, fierce, turbulent, angry, and frantic, and transported himself from place to place in a most unseemly fashion to interview a migratory clan of sore-eyed gins, and mobilize them all to give evidence against a "white man."*[253]

Although Gillen was Special Magistrate, his day job was as the telegraph station master in Alice Springs. He had served his apprenticeship in Adelaide where, sixteen years earlier, on 22nd February 1874, he had been on duty when a message was received from Barrow Creek, where the only Aboriginal attack ever mounted on a station of the Overland Telegraph was underway by a group of men from the *Kaititj* language group.[254] One man, John Franks, was dead and a young telegraphist mortally wounded, sustaining a perforated bowel and internal bleeding. While dying he made contact with Adelaide, his wife was called, and Frank Gillen was responsible for tapping out their final exchange, the last words received being: *GOD BLESS YOU AND THE CHILDREN.*[255] A decade later Gillen, who went on to be celebrated for his ethnographic work with Walter Baldwin Spencer, wrote: *Stapleton received a spear in the groin and lived a few brief hours knowing he was mortally wounded. ... and to me, as operator in the Adelaide office, fell the painful duty of conducting a telegraphic conversation between the dying man on the Barrow and his heart-broken wife in Adelaide.*[256]

In *Willshire of Alice Springs* there is a photograph of the author standing next to a memorial at Barrow Creek to John Lorenzo Stapleton and John Franks. If the two Stapletons were related it's not acknowledged, but Austin Stapleton did note his connection to the rogue policeman: *The author knew William Henry Willshire personally, and once boarded with him and his family for more than fourteen months. Association with his son in particular continued for another fifty years until he, too, passed to the great beyond.*[257] Regardless of Gillen's role in enabling telegraphist Stapleton to communicate with his wife in his last hours, Austin Stapleton is critical of his role in bringing about Willshire's prosecution, noting he: *had taken evidence only from Aborigines.* As Willshire was exonerated and dead, Austin Stapleton's book is about reputational rehabilitation, invoking the context and dangers of the frontier – *events and personal behaviours need to be expressed in the context of the standards of the times* – and the works he supposedly did on behalf of Aboriginal people. As more critical observers noted: *Stapleton defends Willshire in terms that Willshire defended himself: a frontier officer proudly protecting the advance of civilization in the wild Interior.*[258]

Austin Stapleton's loyalty to the memory of Willshire, whose books he read in childhood, might seem touching, were it not in the face of Willshire's own bloody admissions. Why Blakeley's *Dream Millions* should have stirred Stapleton to similar efforts becomes clear in the introduction to *Lasseter Did Not Lie!* Stapleton and Coote first met in the 1950s when both were working in public relations. Ultimately Stapleton: *established Pegasus Public Relations. When the latter began pub-*

lishing an internationally circulating shipping journal Errol Coote became its editor. Six years later both he and I were joint proprietor of a servicing enterprise, Media Sales Company.[259] Stapleton knew Coote, had as much assistance and access to resources as he needed from his widow, was in contact with descendants from both Mrs Lasseters, received information from Ern Bailey, and had guidance from Nick Deloraine of Winmalee who claimed to know where the reef was – having spent two decades unsuccessfully looking for it. Nick Deloraine was a true believer, undeterred by failure and facts. For different reasons, so was Austin Stapleton, his commitment to the task of defending his friend, Coote, in the face of Blakeley's **Dream Millions**, neatly captured by Lesley Synge (Chapter 16) who, with an insider's understanding of Lasseter-mania, commented: *Having given their faith to the myth of the hero/explorer, Believers become complicit in its growth.*[260]

Stapleton's problem was that to resurrect Coote's reputation he had to prove, as his book's title with emphasis claimed, that **Lasseter Did Not Lie!** However, in setting out the backgrounds to the *dramatis personae* of the First Expedition it's clear that someone was dissimulating, noting of Coote that: *In 1917 he enlisted in the First A.I.F. and saw active service with an infantry battalion in France until the armistice. Not discharged until 1919, he served two and one third years in all.* Not mentioned was that he saw no action, and his time in France was after the armistice to serve out a criminal sentence. And just as his military record is overstated, so is his role in the CAGE Company and Expedition: *In 1930, while with the Sydney **Sun**, he helped to form the Central Australian Gold Exploration company and was subsequently appointed its pilot and deputy leader of the expedition to locate Lasseter's reef. Later he was appointed by C.A.G.E. to organize and lead a search for Lasseter.* Stapleton's arguments about Lasseter are as credible as the representation of his old mate, Coote and, ironically, much of it hinges on the account of someone who wasn't there – Idriess: *Like most professional journalists he researches his subjects and deals with them authoritatively. His **Lasseter's Last Ride** is no exception, and being based on diaries and company information, it is still accepted for its accuracy, clarity and special interest. Probing and testing it readily confirms these desirable attributes.*

Suggesting a critical analysis of contested elements, Stapleton provides explanations that resolve minor and/or irrelevant problems with Lasseter's story rather than engaging with the big picture. Much is made of whether Lasseter was talking in terms of land or nautical miles to explain glaring distance inconsistencies, in the course of which Stapleton notes Lasseter's supposed past life at sea as a *master mariner*. Along the way Blakeley's leadership, bushcraft and integrity are repeatedly questioned. And despite noting early in the book that: *in all fairness it must be conceded that some of Lasseter's early behaviour during the expedition's progress did provide grounds for doubting some of his claims,* and having repeatedly emphasised his competencies, the failure to find any gold, then or later, is rationalised by suggesting that Lasseter had found a reef, but that it just didn't have any gold. In summing up, Stapleton is not shy about what he believes he achieved and what it says about the person he has defended – Lasseter – in order to vindicate his mate, Coote: *this work has for the first time provided a* **complete** *biography of Lasseter from his early youth at Stieglitz until his unfortunate death near Shaws Creek. In it he appears as a God fearing man, competent in his industrial pursuits and ever concerned for the welfare of his family.*

Quite a statement – **complete** is emphasised in the original. Stapleton thought he had the last word on Lasseter. It was not long before less partisan sleuths consigned **Lasseter Did Not Lie!** to its place alongside the rationalisations of **Willshire of Alice Springs.**[261] The last writer in this group met Austin Stapleton and draws on his suppositions to corroborate the backstory spun by Lasseter. In that process Coote and Blakeley are also cited, as is **Lasseter's Last Ride** and, coincidentally, there are connections between the author's family and Ion Idriess that go back more than a century and to my back yard – Far North Queensland.

In 1885 Pat Molloy discovered copper near Rifle Creek which runs through the northern Tablelands inland from Cairns, from just north of Mount Molloy near what is now Julatten. Idriess was there in 1913 and, on a tipoff, headed a few miles north to Mount Fraser where he did a bit of fossicking and writing (see Chapter 6). But he was no stranger in Mount Molloy which, by his account, was a happening place:

I would spend the week-end down in Molloy. ... As a rule, a little crowd would begin to roll up on Saturday afternoon; timber-getters freshly shaved in the luxury of a clean white shirt; lanky cattlemen in corduroys and leggings; a teamster or two from the dusty Carbine road. Perhaps a bush commercial traveller, certainly a few "tin scratchers." And maybe a "sheelite-chaser" with a wandering gold prospector to give colour to the discussion on minerals. There would always be a bush nomad or two – those chaps who float along the far-out bush-tracks doing goodness knows what.[262]

It wouldn't take long for the drinking to lead to wild shenanigans and cracked heads – it would all be on. And somewhere in the crowd was Robert Kirkpatrick Clacherty, a Scot who, a few years earlier, had been living in Stratford just north of Cairns where he ran a rice and timber mill next to the police paddocks on the banks of the Barron River. In the cyclone of January 1910 Robert, his wife Elizabeth and their young family, were marooned by floodwaters in the second storey of their home. When the inundation retreated they opted for safety in altitude and moved to Mount Molloy, the family eventually spreading through the area leaving traces – there are Clacherty Streets in Stratford and Mount Molloy, and Clacherty Road in Julatten. And a clutch of Clachertys in the Mount Molloy cemetery. Idriess probably met Robert Clacherty, who was active in local politics, and he would have admired the man known as *Hydro Bob* who, as a local Councillor for Barron Shire Council around the turn of the century, had promoted harnessing the Barron River's powerful flow from the Tablelands to the coastal plain to produce electricity. In 1935, the year Hydro Bob was buried in Mount Molloy Cemetery, Sir Leslie Orme Wilson, Governor General of Queensland, officially opened Barron Gorge Hydroelectric Station, the first in the State. And around four decades later Hydro Bob's youngest son, Alan, visited the ageing Ion Idriess in the nursing home in Mona Vale where, a few months later, he died.[263]

By the time Hydro Bob was laid to rest in Mount Molloy Lasseter was dead, the CAGE Company had been wound up and **Lasseter's Last Ride** was in its seventeenth edition. Lasseter was gone but the story was alive and well; there were already expeditions in the bush and more on the way. A half-century on, Hydro Bob's grandson, Dennis

Clacherty, after a career in radio frequency management during which he worked at sea, in military aviation and with the ABC, was far from north Queensland, finishing *On Lasseter's Trail* in Malvern, just south-east of downtown Melbourne. Clacherty brought his analytic and technical skills to the task of resolving the conflicting stories about Lasseter, acknowledging that legends of fabulous reserves of precious metals in the centre of the continent preceded Lasseter by decades and may have influenced him. For instance, the claims of a South Australian prospector of the 1890s, Earle, which were passed down through anecdotal reports, of finding a cave rich in gold somewhere near the Tomkinson Ranges around 1895, which sparked rumours that were repeated, or commented on, by Idriess, Herbert Basedow[264] and Michael Terry who, characteristically, called it for what it was – *a romantic story*.

In considering Earle – and other expeditions and reports including Lasseter's claims – Desmond Clacherty suggests objectivity by acknowledging controversy and critique, while at the same time encouraging the reader to suspend disbelief and simply consider *what if...* Credibility in the contested foreground of this account is reinforced by a backdrop of the extensively documented expeditions through the area – Warburton in 1873, Giles in 1875 and 1876, Forrest in 1874, Tietkens in 1889, Elder in 1891, Carnegie in 1896, and the ill-fated Calvert expedition of 1896-97. Accepting that there are grounds for Lasseter's claims to be challenged, Clacherty points out that the myth that accreted around Lasseter following his death was tainted by the vilification of the dead prospector that occurred after the Expedition in the press, particularly in *The Bulletin*. What he said that might be true was lost in the frenzy about who he was. And also by obfuscation and dissimulation for self-serving interests, including subsequent prospectors and local Aboriginal groups who, so this theory goes, know more than they are willing to tell. The argument that Clacherty lays out draws on a torrent of historical information supplemented by analysis of aerial maps from the 1980s and a flight over the region in 1986.

Framed by repeated conditionals and caveats, Clacherty deploys serial hypotheticals to suggest objectivity, with repeated emphasis on possibility rather than probability. His early comment – *The clues to the mystery of the lost reef of central Australia have been obscured by many factors, not the least of which has been deliberate attempts to disguise the truth*[265] – implies that *the truth* was as Lasseter related it before and during the CAGE Expedition. Additional sources are the accounts of Idriess, Coote and Blakeley, with some information from Marshall-Stoneking and Stapleton. Complicating this reconstruction, those sources record Lasseter's contradictions, omissions and evasions – hardly assuring reliability – which Clacherty explains as savvy wariness: *Lasseter was also cautious. He would have avoided giving sufficient detail to make his route easy to follow* – and – *Lasseter had no intention of providing sufficient details for others to find the reef without his help.*

Based on those sources and many assumptions the proposition is that, as he had claimed, Lasseter crossed the continent in 1897, and that in doing so he had access to a particular map that was, at that time, seventy years old and wildly inaccurate. It was, at best, an imagination, but serves Clacherty's purpose: *An early map drawn in 1827 showed the river system of northern New South Wales and western Queensland flowing westwards and combining to form the 'Great River of Desired Blessing' which entered the ocean near the present site of Derby in Western Australia.*

There is no explanation of how Lasseter found that document from seventy years before, or why it was preferred over more accurate maps which, even in the 1890s, were available. That is just one uncommented-on hindrance in the path of looped hypotheticals, despite which the backbone of the proposition is that in 1897 Lasseter followed the line of sandhills heading south-west from the MacDonnell Ranges that, as he would have understood from the 1827 map, went all the way to the Indian Ocean. In this scenario he crossed the border with Western Australia somewhere south of Lake Hopkins, near where he stumbled on the reef and to which he returned, successfully, from the west with Harding three years later. During the 1930 First CAGE Expedition, against Lasseter's insistence of travelling south of Haasts Bluff, Blakeley chose to pass to the north, the direction suggested by Lasseter's reports in Sydney and towards areas that were thought more likely to be auriferous. In Clacherty's world of possibilities that decision caused Lasseter to lose the markers that he may otherwise have recalled from 1897 and 1900. Later in the Expedition, Lasseter's flight with Pat Hall requires another caveat – that it was at maximum speed to gain sufficient distance. That, in conjunction with Lasseter's five-day land journey from Lake Christopher, allows the theory to accommodate a location somewhere near Lake Hopkins, just over the border in Western Australia. Incorporating Lasseter's comments in Sydney earlier in 1930 about a nearby body of water, and taking into account archival records of heavy rain before the time Lasseter claimed to be travelling, Clacherty used aerial photography from the 1980s to identify a dry lakebed south of Lake Hopkins which he calls *Lake Enigma* – a nice touch.

From the comments attributed to Lasseter about landmarks, speculation about topographic changes in the region in the decades since 1897, and the aerial photographs, Clacherty narrows down the possibilities to a set of features that, to him, are definitive:

> *every description given by Lasseter of the location of the reef, the landmarks in the area and the relationship between those landmarks and the reef are entirely consistent with the proposition that the line of surface anomalies marks the location of Lasseter's reef. The alignment of the line can be derived from Lasseter's description with awesome precision. The only possibility that could be more remarkable would be the discovery that the reef was not located in this position.*

Clacherty also invokes traditional Aboriginal practices in support of some of Lasseter's statements. For instance, the piles of stones among which Lasseter claimed he found samples of gold: *The Aborigines of central Australia are known to have made heaps of stones while clearing pathways through rocky creek beds and for ceremonial purposes.* And while on aerial photographs most remote parts of central Australia are scarred by camels pads, vehicles tracks and mining survey activities, those that he identifies close by the proposed location of the reef are: *consistent with the proposition that the Aborigines carry out inspections to ensure that all parts of the reef remain covered and invisible from the air* – and – *It is probable that the Aborigines ensure that all parts of the reef remain covered and that inspections are carried out periodically to this end.* These comments draw on Billy Marshall-Stoneking's comments from the 1980s that Pintupi men had revealed to him that the location of the reef was known and associated with a sacred site, and that when economic necessities demanded, the requisite resources in the form of nuggets would duly appear.[266]

It is 35 years since Marshall-Stoneking's stunning suggestion and its repetition doesn't make it any more plausible. But the hypotheticals and slippage from possibles to probables in Clacherty's theory are not the most obvious problem, which is that eight years after *On Lasseter's Trail* was released, Murray Hubbard's *The Search for Harold Lasseter* appeared (Chapters 13 and 20). Hubbard's careful research proved that, until he absconded in the middle of October 1897, Lewis Hubert Lasseter was in the Packenham Farm Reformatory for Protestant Boys. Harold Bell Lasseter's claim, more than three decades later, that he had crossed the continent in that year – a teenager on the run with no bush experience, and without funds or friends, the first person to do so across terrain in which many experienced bushmen had perished – was a lie. But flexible theories are just that – malleable enough to accommodate inconvenient facts. Desmond Clacherty maintained a website related to his book, and on it is a post that resolves the conflict:

> *The story begins with Lasseter's abscondment from the Reform School, the date of which is recorded as 14th October, 1897 … The first ship available that called at Cairns was the Changsha which sailed from Melbourne on 23rd November 1897, bound for Hong Kong. On 9th December the ship was in Townsville and scheduled to sail for Cooktown that day. However, the Cairns Port Authority record for December 1897 shows the Changsha listed without a date or any other details. The Cairns Post newspaper of 9th December 1897 reported "The Changsha for Hong Kong will leave port tonight." The likely reason for an unscheduled port call is to put a person ashore for crime or illness. It is reasonable to wonder if the law had caught up with Lasseter particularly since he had previously said that he had left the ship at Cairns. Another reason could have been illness, typhoid being prevalent at the time and a good reason for putting a person ashore. As Lasseter was apparently allowed to remain in Cairns, it suggests that*

the latter mentioned reason is more likely … He arrived in Cairns in December – summer – wet season. Good reason to wait for a change of season. Good reason to wait to make enough money to secure those horses and provisions. Two weeks pay as a cabin boy or deckhand could not do. It is likely that he set out for the MacDonnells in the middle months of 1898.[267]

Predictably, the weakest link in the chain of possibilities is Lasseter. When he was in Quorn in mid-July 1930, on the way to Alice Springs, he gave an interview to a journalist from the *Quorn Mercury* in the course of which he also related that he had set out for the Centre from Townsville.[268] That was also the story that he gave a little earlier on the journey, in Parkes, during which he described himself as the *leader of the expedition,* and that before leaving Townsville he had been *one of the hands on the coastal steamer Wodonga.*[269] Of course, multiplying possibilities doesn't assure probability – in fact, the opposite.

The Angus & Robertson stable: *… very much a boys' club.*

CHAPTER 11

Happy Valley

Contrary to the writings of Lasseter, Idriess and Coote and later recycled histories, the cave is not located at Winter's Glen, some twenty or more miles to the south east, where Lasseter perished in March 1931. Like the resurrection of Old Warts in later editions of Lasseter's Last Ride, Idriess blithely ignores the contradiction between the first three editions of his bestseller and subsequent editions regarding the location, indeed the existence, of the cave, and events that occurred there.

Rob Ross, *Lasseteria.com.*[270]

March 2020

The posters for the 1958 science fiction-horror movie – ***The Blob*** – starring a very young Steve McQueen, warn the viewer: *Indescribable… Indestuctible! Nothing can stop it!* It's been a bit like that for me with Lasseter, and Robert Ross probably understood early in our correspondence that it was just a matter of time until I was sliding and somersaulting into the vortex and void of Lasseter obsession – he made that pretty clear in an early email. It was mid-January 2020, the first diagnosed case of coronavirus in Australia was still more than a week away, and he threw back at me my own words: *Your opening line – "as you know my main interest is NOT Lasseter per se" – heh heh ... welcome to the club, fellow Lasseterian.*

A few months later it's a different world. Although we discussed meeting in person, with COVID I have to settle for a phone link to Happy Valley. *Happy Valley*; the associations sit somewhere between retirement village and pet cemetery. The original citizenry's graves and the rest of the village on the southern fringe of Adelaide are now underwater, submerged as the needs of the driest state in the driest continent on the planet were bolstered with another reservoir; completed in 1897 – the same year that Harold Bell Lasseter claimed to have crossed the continent and found a gold reef. The *Rapid Bay tribes* – the Kaurna peoples – were the original inhabitants of the Adelaide Plains, and despite assurances of protection were quickly dispossessed and displaced in the first half of the nineteenth century. What happened wasn't pretty, even close enough to hear the bells tolling in the *City of Churches*. Edward Burgess came up with the merry moniker. It worked for him – and for the South Australian Company which divvied-up the spoils for free-settlers. Robert Ross gives a different version*: It was a bit of a rogues' retreat in years gone by. It was the first wayside stop when you were travelling south of Adelaide and there was a rise, just past the university. Once you got your horses or oxen over that rise and down the other side your team was just about exhausted and there used to be a lot of shanties – hence the name Happy Valley.*

Six months ago I was in downtown Adelaide, not far from Happy Valley, and Robert Ross was on my radar as soon as I entered Lasseter into any internet search. Something from *Lasseteria: the Lasseter Encyclopedia* was invariably in the mix and although there was an associated email address – *bullion49@hotmail.com* – I had no idea who was behind the website. Eventually a response came, with a name – Rob Ross. But that was it, I couldn't seem to get any closer to whoever concocted the cryptic cyber-commentaries. I resorted to Google-sleuthing. Using the email hint – *bullion* – and common sense, I narrowed the possibilities down to the Padstow Coin Centre in Sydney, *one of Sydney's most respected coin, stamp and banknote establishments*, run by one Robert Ross. I tried – not my man. I also learned about the role of another Robert Ross in the Taranganba Gold swindle of the 1880s. And much else. And then there was an unlikely hit on a site which was an email archive, starting with one from Adam Meigs on 18th September 2003: *I'm an American student who is looking for a copy of the Iliad being read aloud in the original Homeric Greek. I would be willing to compensate you for a copy if you have one in the entirety. If you don't have one, a gentle nudge in the right direction would be greatly appreciated.* There were no clues as to whether Adam was nudged or not, but as I scrolled down (and back in time) the content of the messages was increasingly about Aboriginal Australia. And then, April Fools Day 2003, an email from my man – Robert Ross at *bullion49@hotmail.com*: *Dear Simon, thank you for yesterday's mail re the link to your site, I have amended the link as requested and it appears OK from my end but please check if satisfactory and let me know. Also thanks for the cross link. I am based in Adelaide and can be contacted on...* Bingo – I had it, a land line. Seventeen years old – but worth a try. I imagined the elusive cyberstacker's expression of dismay as, with one call, his cover was blown. Then, almost as I was punching in the numbers – it was the middle of March – another email from the *Lasseteria* webmaster arrived and, at the bottom, against my much earlier request for an interview: *Most certainly, When? Take care and cheers, R.* And he included his phone number – the same as in 2003. So much for the Lasseteria dark webmaster.

Robert Ross turns out to be quite chatty, in a cautious kind of way. If he doesn't have an answer, the question is taken on notice: *I've got that on the list, I'll get to it* – and he does. Gold is more than a vicarious interest, he's an occasional fossicker and his ancestors did well on the Victorian goldfields. One branch included a First Fleeter: *but not a convict, as I remind family and friends, we were in charge of the bastards. Peacocks – one was a third officer on the **Sirius**. It went to Norfolk Island on a relief mission and he was involved in putting it on the rocks. He was quietly warned not to return to England.* Peacocks; a colourful family – *several did runners to America.* The Ross roots were in Scotland, via Tasmania and coal mining. Rob is the South Australia pioneer, he arrived in 1972:

I started off as a cadet in the Commonwealth Public Service with the Department of Works. Eventually I thought the green machine would be more fun and I joined the army. I was an assault pioneer – combat engineer – in the Second Battalion, Royal Australian Regiment stationed in Townsville. In Vietnam for one tour, 1970 to '71. When I got out of the army I had my choice of where to go and I thought I'd head to Perth. The train trip was paid for with an overnight in Adelaide. When I stepped out of the station I thought that I might have found where I would set up camp. And I did – I phoned up work back in Melbourne and told them to get me a job in Adelaide; I was in building logistics.

Jobs in the building industry and maintaining a computer room back when it needed a room, and more – until he retired around two decades ago, which gave scope for emerging interests. Along the way he spent time at *amateur geologising*, making use of resources at Flinders University. He also had a gig delivering vehicles to Aboriginal communities, including Hermannsburg – all of which was moving him towards Lasseter. He met and made friends with Aboriginal elders, heard stories about Paul Johns, read Albrecht's Lasseter piece in the *Lutheran Almanac* – raising more and more questions: *I got curious so I decided to call the National Archives. Somebody must have been making enquiries about Paul Johns because the lady there had her hands on the file in ten minutes and sent me a copy. The story was definitely not what Idriess had written – Paul Johns was an absolute rogue. So, I started making enquiries, asking questions, and one thing led to another.*

Around that time he read Murray Hubbard's **On Lasseter's Trail** (Chapters 13 & 20) which he credits to the extent that his own research, he insists: *was on Murray's trail rather than on Lasseter's trail. He did a superb job.* But, as Rob was discovering, there are no edges to the Lasseter tapestry, it just keeps expanding. Around the millennium Rob was contacted by Lesley Synge (Chapter 16) who had married one of Lasseter's grandsons and was on a different journey in Lasseter-land in the course of which, Rob notes, she: *tidied up the details re Lasseter's American sojourn.* New sources, fresh insights – more complexity: *I decided to find out exactly what was going on. And then you start to pull up John Bailey, Ern Bailey – it all starts to unravel.* His problem was too much information rather than too little. Then, coincidentally: *There was a great course that* came up about how to build websites – which were new on the scene. I was thinking about an encyclopedia format and that's how I learned to do a website. I thought 'I can sort out each player in the game as I unravel it' – and the rest – well, it just grew.

The format for the collection came from Rob's soft science fiction interests and the **Dune Encyclopedia** that followed Frank Herbert's classic. And once it started it was as if it had a direction of its own: *one thing leads to another and you end up going down rabbit burrows. All interesting stuff but not germane to Lasseter.* Even figuring out what happened during the Expedition was a challenge, which led to *Sullivan's Diary*, just one of the sections on the site: *That part of Lasseteria is a day-to-day record of what all the characters were doing. I wrote down daily notes about where everybody was, what they were doing, when the truck broke down, when the plane crashed – all those sorts of things. It grew day by day. Two and a half years of data. Seven hundred and twenty entries – seven hundred and twenty days of work.*

How *Lasseteria* developed and operates is complicated enough; the objective is more-so. As Rob explains: *I'm trying to take apart two or three years of Australian history using the Lasseter saga as an example of fake history, to show how some of the things in texts and in the press are wrong. From that people can draw their own conclusion. How much else of Australian history is dodgy...* And this *two or three years* is more significant than Lasseter:

> There are a number of momentous events – the poor Scullin Government, within two or three days of coming into government Wall Street crashed. And there's the Baileys; after Lasseter they got themselves involved in another gold mine – Mount Arthur Gold – about the same time as Arnhem Land Gold, about the same time that the Second Expedition was winding up. And they were into another outfit called Scientific Films; they were going to flog Brandon-Cremer's film of the Second CAGE Expedition commercially but I understand the censors stepped in and put a stop to it.

Films – there have been more than a few about Lasseter. But like the dozens of books – and *Lasseteria* – getting it all in is impossible: *As Luke*

Walker found out you simply can't do it all in a documentary film in a span of time like two hours – it has to be done as a TV miniseries. But in the end it's more of a political thriller series than about Lasseter out there looking for a gold reef that didn't exist. He's a device to tell a story about a bigger picture.

A *device* – Idriess was a device for me while I was writing **Vicarious Dreaming**. But the device became a demon and I'm back travelling with him again. Maybe with a more critical eye; I'm interested in the person now, not just his tales. But even back then there were highlights and I ask Rob about his peak moments mining the Lasseter lode:

Getting hold of Blakiston-Houston's memoirs. The Military Archives in Britain didn't want to release it because I wasn't a registered researcher. So I got in touch with a lady in charge of research at the University and she took the whole thing under her wing – within ten days the memoirs turned up. He was one hell of a chap. It's probably an apocryphal story but he apparently took on an Italian fighter one morning in North Africa. One of those classy Italian fighters got in the habit of strafing the British camp each morning and everybody would disappear into the trenches. One day Blakiston-Houston was having a shave and was dumb-struck that nobody returned fire. That afternoon he trained them how to use their rifles as if they were duck shooting. So, the Italian turns up next morning and he was greeted with lead. He wrote in his diary that 'the enemy was last seen smoking and wobbling over the horizon'.

War stories – Idriess had more than a few and he kept mining them throughout his career – a whole series of books during the war that followed, while Blakiston-Houston was seeing off Italian fighters over desert sands. We're into the territory that most interests me, and Rob echoes my own thoughts about the origins of **Lasseter's Last Ride**:

*I reckon Idriess was on the lookout for a book to follow **Prospecting for Gold**. There was the Depression, the price of gold had gone up, there was a subsidy. And the Golden Eagle – what a good story. He didn't miss an opportunity; around May there were articles appearing in the press that mentioned Lasseter, Bailey, Gold Reef, Central Australia. Maybe he thought he'd keep an eye on the expedition and see* *what happened. And from Idriess' point of view the best thing happened – Lasseter didn't come back. But if he had returned with evidence of his gold reef then Idriess would have a story in that too. Whatever happened it had all the right elements – savage Aboriginals, Central Australia and gold.*

As the momentum of the interview with the *Lasseteria* webmaster wanes the track weaves back on itself, across a topography of names and places that, for me, was unexplored six months ago but is now familiar. As it is for more people than I'd care to guess at, in part because of a website: *I didn't bother to keep a webcount but it's had more than a million hits – it's read all over the world. One fellow has translated it into German; with Germans the interest is Hermannsburg and the German history of Central Australia. For some odd reason the Russians love it, but I don't think they understand it.* Like the whole Lasseter myth – how do you comprehend something that has as many interpretations as there are people to project them... Robert Ross believes the jury is well and truly back on Lasseter's reef – it did not and does not exist. He also understands that the quest – his quest – is for something different, which won't be sated by more entries on *Lasseteria*. Perhaps similar to trying to prove the *null hypothesis* or, as he explains it, alluding to Lasseter's ghostly desert saviour at the starting point of the myth: *It's a bit like the 'Harding effect' – how can you go searching and proving something that never happened...*

And there's the Baileys ... John Bailey: still in the game with
Arnhem Land Gold, 1933.

CHAPTER 12

Woollahra

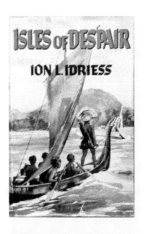

Jack was a heavy drinker, perhaps an alcoholic, who drank a bottle of whisky a day with beer chasers. His habit of drinking steadily from 1:30 each afternoon until 6 p.m. closing, the 'six o'clock swill', hadn't changed, it had actually accelerated. ... Each night Jack could be seen making his way home, literally sloshed to the eyeballs. Dressed in a blue suit and with deeply nicotine-stained fingers raising the grey felt hat he always wore to any ladies he passed on the street, he would wish them a gallant 'goodnight'. I suspect this was a larrikin gesture, not a truly chivalrous one.

Beverley Eley, 1995.[271]

July 2020

Idriess emerged from the chrysalis that had contained his alter ego – *Cyclone Jack* – when he moved from north Queensland to Sydney in 1930. West Street, Paddington, is directly behind St Vincent's Hospital and health was on his mind – he'd had a melanoma scare.[272] It was a short walk to the hospital, but also a half-hour stroll from 89 Castlereagh Street, the bookstore and offices for Angus & Robertson. Down Elizabeth Street with maybe a stop at the Hyde Park Hotel at the corner of

Bathurst Street, then across the park to Oxford Street – plenty more pubs on the way before he turned left onto West Street and home. But while he was working on **Lasseter's Last Ride** he would sometimes continue along Oxford Street, past Victoria Barracks and the Paddington Library on the corner of Oatley Road, to the Town Hall just around the corner. That was where he would go for *the Saturday night hop* – what he called his *safety valve*. And it was there on the dance-floor that he first saw Eta Gibson in what he referred to four decades later as *the year of tribulation.*[273]

By 1933 Idriess had moved to 42 Bayswater Road in Darlinghurst – about the same distance from Angus & Robertson and just as many places to stop. Just two years later and in a complicated triangular relationship, his base was 110 Cottenham Avenue in Kensington. That was more than a walk and he'd catch the tram or a bus, or take a taxi from the St James rank. But as he was preparing the draft and revision of **Lasseter's Last Ride** in 1931 and early 1932, West Street Paddington was home. But if he had continued along Oxford Street, past the Town Hall and towards Centennial Park, he would have arrived at Woollahra and could have cut across to Trelawney Street. Home now to many cultures, it's more than two centuries since Cadigal and Birrabirragal last moved freely across those low rolling hills with fleeting views down to the water where a few sailing ships may have been visible in what Arthur Phillip called *the finest harbour in the world*. Quickly dispersed, less than fifty years later Daniel Cooper's Point Piper Estate took in all the land from Woollahra to the water. He's credited for that name which he chose for his mansion – supposedly a word that he believed meant *lookout*. It certainly was that. And if Jack had strolled along Trelawney Street he would have passed country-estate mansions that have since given way to high rise developments and cosmopolitan café society – the Russian, Polish, Lebanese, Serbian and Turkish Consulates are all on the block and, close by, is where Clive English lives.

Probably appropriate for someone whose past life was as a foreign currency trader working out of London, Singapore, New York and Hong Kong before being lured by Macquarie Bank to Sydney in the early 1990s – heady days in *the millionaire factory*. Between COVID and kids that probably seems more than a lifetime away. High finance was likely never as busy. My path to Clive was not direct and bent through *idress. c om.au*, a website: *Dedicated to the Life and Works of Ion (Jack) Llewellyn Idriess*. That was a waystation in telling the stories that became **Vicarious Dreaming**, but I couldn't track down its creator. Then, as I was trying to tie the threads of my book together, I came across **The Truth about Charlie: the "madman" stranded on Howick Island with Ion Idriess** by Rob Coutts. At the bottom of the last page – *About the author* – I found:

> *His interest in Ion Idriess began sixty-four years ago when he was a paper-boy delivering newspapers in the Melbourne suburb of Ashburton. For his ninth birthday one of his customers gave him Idriess'* **In Crocodile Land.** *It was the imagery of "The Blood Hole" (where crocodiles waited at the gruesome blood drain of the meat works in Wyndham) that began a lifelong interest in Idriess' books. Rob still has that book as part of his collection. Rob administers the website: idriess.com.au.*[274]

The Blood Hole – it was in Cape York that Idriess had his crocodile moment. He'd decided to walk back to Cooktown from Ninian Bay, a hundred miles further north, where he'd been prospecting. It was around September 1914 and he was in a rush – hostilities had begun on what would become the Western Front and he was dead set to *get to the bloody war*. But he didn't get far; he had to cross a series of crocodile-infested rivers and ended up sleeping in a *wongai* tree for safety before turning back and waiting for Captain Dan on the *Spray* to pick him up on his return journey from Thursday Island. He didn't miss out on the War but it was another thirty years before he wrote **In Crocodile Land**[275] and another decade before *The Blood Hole* was making news. During the 1954 Wyndham races a tote was being run on the chances of an American ex-navy diver, Tom Snider, who was working on clearing the remaining wreckage of the *Koolama* which sank after damage by a Japanese fighter in 1942 alongside the Wyndham jetty – close by *The Blood Hole*. A journalist for *The West Australian* reported that local residents had the odds at: Sharks 8 to 1 and upwards; Groper 7 to 1; Crocodiles 6 to 1, and; Snider, even money. Snider survived.[276]

Rob administers the website: idriess.com.au; even with a name and a website I couldn't make contact with Rob Coutts and eventually gave up. Even so, **The Truth about Charlie** was woven into **Vicarious Dreaming** and I included a photo of the Cooktown grave of George Tritton – the real *Charlie*. That was just a few steps from the headstone for another Digger, Richard Albert Welsh, Jack Idriess' best friend and the subject of his later-life reminiscences of his Cape York days, **My Mate Dick**. Eventually I was able to track Rob to Summerholm between Ipswich and Toowoomba and we talked – but didn't meet. Age, retirement, other paths and interests, family – even passions lasting six decades eventually dim. And that's what had happened, the Idriess webmaster had passed on the flame – to Clive English.

Clive's first contact with Rob was transactional, an Idriess sale on ebay; they've never met. But he was already running his own website – *idriess.info* – which: *is different to Rob's site, which is about the man; mine is about the books.* Everything you need to know to be an effective Idriess broker and collector in one place, and currency trading came in handy:

> *It was hard-nosed experience from another market. You have to become immersed in it. And I became an expert on Idriess books. Which jackets you just can't get. The misprints in some of them. All the fine bits that you have to look out for that makes an item a rare example. I get booksellers calling me about a particular book; so I ask if on page 43 it says this word or that. He tells me, and I let him know what it's worth. That comes from attending old book auctions, finding how many people are interested in this and that. You need to find out where all the latent interest is.*

His approach and expertise landed him in the middle of a network of collectors and traders, and with another website to manage. For most of the others in that network to whom I've spoken, it's reading Idriess or some sentimental connection that sparks interest and triggers the searching. With Clive it was the metadata that led to his first purchase in 2003:

> *I'm a collector of all sorts of weird and wonderful things. I'm a nostalgic person and I remember old bookcases full of books at home. When I came to Australia I noticed this guy Idriess on ebay, there were always lots*

of his books. *I didn't know anything about him, but he seemed sought after, so I bought my first book. It cost me $30, not one of the better ones – **One Wet Season.** Then I found out that there were a few stand-out books you had to get and now I've got the full collection, mostly bought on ebay. I read* **Drums of Mer** *and* **Isles of Despair** *which was fantastic, a semi-true story about someone who gets shipwrecked and they think she's the daughter of a god.*

Clive repeats what I've heard from every collector – the grail is **Cyaniding for Gold**: *That's the one you have to have. I've got four of them at the moment; one with an original cover, one original with copy cover, one original with no cover, and the facsimile version which I bought because I thought I'd never get the real thing.* And like trading currency, the market never stays still: *There was a time you would see one and you wouldn't see another for five years, but If you go on ebay now there are three for sale; two with original jackets, one possibly. A while ago I tried to buy one advertised for $3,500 and I offered $3,100 – the guy said no way. Five years later I pick one up for one-and-a-half grand.*

Not much room for sentimentality – until I raise **Lasseter's Last Ride**. For this Londoner, whose lineage extends from Yorkshire Quaker ancestry, through generations in Devon and Cornwall, to his Australian son, it was enlightening. He'd moved to a city – Sydney – and Idriess gave a sense of the enormity of what lay beyond: *it taught me about how large and deserted Australia is. I had no idea about the size and harshness of it, the land and fauna. I was like a kid who reads his first book and gets lost in his imagination. An Australian may have been in the desert, been around mines, dealt with all these people. For me it was new, an eye-opener.* Our conversation is interrupted as Clive retrieves one of his copies of **Lasseter's Last Ride** in which he found a 1931 newspaper article about the search for Lasseter. He returns with an aged clipping with a photograph that's immediately familiar: *It's a tiny picture of a guy called Robert Buck. He has this huge moustache – like Dennis Lillee – and a very strange hat. I look at something like that and think about the owner, who read something in the paper and decided to put it in the book. I like that.*

As Clive talks on it seems that he's describing how his various collections have consolidated connections, and this one to Australia, his home. Not just to things, but to the people he's met on the journey: *There's a community of people that I'm part of now that have been another facet of making Australia home. I'm not trying to wax lyrical but it has cemented my Australian home for me.* Perhaps somewhat ironically, Clive recognises that what has been a connector for him doesn't work with younger generations: *They don't teach this guy at school. Whether they should or shouldn't, you won't get any youngsters involved, only people whose parents had a strong interest. It's history, you either want to go skateboarding or read about what Australia was like in the times your parents or grandparents lived. That's what fascinates me.* And where interest declines, there goes the market:

> *You could even argue that the whole Idriess thing petered out in the '90s and it was only the advent of the Internet that enabled people to go and source them from their armchair. When I came along in 2003 I could just go to ebay. You could say that was the top of the market. Ever since, I've seen a tapering off of prices, of interest, of email traffic. There was a time when a full first edition collection would be about $30,000. I think you can get it for $15,000 now. But that's OK, it's not about money, it never really was. We're just the custodians – of things and stories – and hopefully there will still be people interested enough to pass them on.*

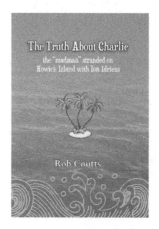 

The Truth about Idriess: George Tritton's grave in Cooktown

CHAPTER 13

Sleuths and Decoders

That he was ahead of his time there was no doubt. The proof is in his prolific writings, where in most cases he put down his ideas for a better Australia. His inability to take these ideas and transform them into reality was Lasseter's great failing which denied him what he sought – recognition.

Murray Hubbard, 1993.[277]

Lasseter had been dead for sixteen years when William Randolph Marshall was born into a military family in Florida, later appending the name Stoneking of a paternal great-grandfather. As with many military families, childhood was a series of moves and, after completing a liberal arts degree in California, Billy Marshall-Stoneking opted for a continental reset. In 1972 he arrived in rural Victoria where he taught for four years before another move – this one lifechanging – to Papunya, thirty kilometres north of Haasts Bluff. Marshall-Stoneking had heard about Lasseter as a child in the United States, but over the five years he lived in Lasseter-land his interest grew until it *finally reached proportions that are usually ascribed only to obsession.*[278] The results of Marshall-Stoneking's Lasseter obsession segued into a life of words – and poetry. His 1990 collection includes *A poem of Ayers Rock*, which opens with an aged Nosepeg Tjupurrula preparing to narrate a story:

Old Tjupurrula squeezes my arm
and puckers his lips, pointing –
Pintupi-style – towards the television set;
eyes fastened on the screen,
on dissolves of that sandstone monolith:
A montage of Uluru awash with rain;
water cascading, crashing down –
blackening the Rock…

Later in the poem are lines that might have applied to many of the strangers who entered those lands, including the man whose body Nosepeg helped Lowell Thomas locate in 1957:

It is like that other one –
The serpent in the Garden.
It turns knowledge into fear,
and fear into knowledge.
But, with the right fear,
you can protect yourself.
Be mindful of the Snake.
Take time to look, look again –
feel the land through your feet;
the Snake will not harm those
who show the proper respect.
Those who rush in must be strangers.
"It will attack strangers."[279]

Lasseter – The Making of a Legend is a curious book. Over more than a hundred pages the events of the First CAGE Expedition are reconstructed from the usual sources up to Lasseter's final, solitary journey. As for what happened after that he comments: *Of the white writers, Idriess' account of Lasseter's life with the Aborigines is the most complete. It is also, probably, the most fictionalised.* While Marshall-Stoneking doesn't specify who the other *white writers* were, and recognises Idriess' fictions, ***Lasseter's Last Ride*** and *The Diary* provide the scaffold for his reconstruction of Lasseter's time at Winter's Glen – *Karli Karru*, and the cave – *Tjuunti*. Marshall-Stoneking not only had Nosepeg Tjupurrula as an informant, he spoke with Pitjantjatjara people who, as children, had interacted with Lasseter. One of those men, Leslie Tjapanangka, was able to identify individuals described by Lasseter, such as the man Idriess labelled *Old Warts* – Kirrinytja – a man, as it turned out, of high regard. Marshall-Stoneking also clarified that Lasseter's nemesis in **Lasseter's Last Ride**: *was very near the bottom of the social ladder. The name itself – 'Watta Mitta Mitta' – means, literally, 'crazy man'. It is probably fair to say that he had some psychological or physical problem impairing his judgment that made him stand out from the rest of the tribe.*

Marshall-Stoneking's contribution is to have drawn on the accounts of Aboriginal witnesses to demonstrate that in the last weeks of Lasseter's life the Aboriginal people with whom Lasseter interacted and travelled weren't hostile – they supported the hapless intruder who was stranded in their country. That wasn't going to work for Idriess who, by the time the additional information from *The Diary* was at hand, had a story of sorcery-mediated skulduggery selling well, an account he had insisted was what had *actually happened*. Moreover, to make the tragic denouement of **Lasseter's Last Ride** in that original form work, he had to have Lasseter able to read the cultural signals, to understand and communicate with the tribal people that Idriess cast in the final scene, and to be a witting participant in his own death by sorcery. In all probability most of what passed across that cultural divide in those last weeks was mundane or mystifying. But Marshall Stoneking proved that Lasseter's end was not as Idriess scripted. It was still a tragedy – just a far greater and enduring catastrophe, to which Lasseter's demise and Idriess' fictions are but footnotes. **Lasseter – The Making of a Legend** does not really add much to an understanding of who Lasseter was or where he came from, just where he ended up. But as a poet and a dramatist, as his title suggested, it was the *legend* that fuelled Marshall-Stoneking's interest:

> *But the story of the reef is also a metaphor for a journey that is as old as religion and as complex as the human family. It is the wandering and the quest that takes people out of their own familiar circle of immediacy.*

And it is more. It is a story of expectations and their confrontation with realities – the difference between what one hopes is the case and what really is the case. The men who set out in search of the reef did, indeed, find something different from what they bargained for.

Sleuths

Billy-Marshall Stoneking was a poet. The sleuth who blew away the foundations of the myth by dismantling Lasseter's backstory finished his account with a poem – by Ted Harrington. An interesting choice; Harrington and Ion Idriess were both in the Light Horse in Palestine and at the battle of Beersheba in October 1917, Harrington in the attack with the 4th and Idriess in reserve with the 5th. Whether Harrington knew Idriess or not he had certainly read **Lasseter's Last Ride**, which was also the title of his poem that was set to music in 1940 by Peter Dawson. The last line of the stanza of Harrington's poem that Murray Hubbard selected to conclude **The Search for Harold Lasseter** is telling:

Lasseter rode from his camping-ground
As the sun sank low in the west,
But who can say what Lasseter found,
Or what was Lasseter's quest?
Others will go where the fierce winds blow.
And try as Lasseter tried,
But only God and the white stars know
The end of Lasseter's ride.[280]

Murray Hubbard has been a journalist, sports commentator, photographer and more (Chapter 20). Maybe it was his interest in people that drew him to trying to understand the person behind the legend rather than the Expedition around which the legend accreted. His book describes his own journey of incremental discovery nearly six decades after the events:

While others went in search of the reef, I decided to look for Lasseter. What HAD he done in the 49 years before he entered the AWU office? I had one clue to start with. There was an item about Lasseter in the **Australian Dictionary of Biography***, which stated that in a 1932 letter to the editor of the* **Bulletin** *there was a reference to the fact that*

*Lasseter lived in Tabulam, northern New South Wales, and wrote for a
local paper, one of his contributions being a bitter denunciation of World
War 1 in verse.*[281]

Hubbard's search took him around the country to meet relatives of
Lasseter from both his marriages, into libraries and archives, all the time
using a snowball strategy to uncover the next facet of an, until then,
undocumented life. The result is a book that ricochets across a half-
century, from Lasseter's Victorian beginnings to his death near Shaw
Creek. Among much that was not known before, Hubbard discovered
that Lasseter had been arrested in August 1896 at age sixteen for being
party to a theft that had been discovered by his guardian/employer after
the fact, as a result of which he ended up at the Pakenham Farm
Reformatory for Protestant Boys, from which he absconded in late 1897.
Even without all his other work, which resulted in an understanding of
the family Lasseter was born into and grew up in, his brief stints in the
military and his working life in Victoria, New South Wales and Canberra,
that was proof that Lasseter's account of having stumbled on the reef 32
years before appearing in the AWU offices, was fabricated. A teenage
runaway from rural Victoria could not have found a job on a ship, gotten
to Cairns, and then crossed the continent without friends or funds, finding
a fabulous gold reef on the way.

That could have been the end of it, but as the information accumulated, more glistening facets came into view. Lasseter was neither lunatic
nor loser; his humble beginnings and tragic losses early in life didn't
stifle his drive and, as I found when I first opened his military files on
my computer in Adelaide, ideas just tumbled out. Military strategies,
weapons modifications, hydroelectric schemes, boats, bridges, industries
– he thought about them, wrote it all down and pushed his plans to wary
bureaucrats. Sometimes he came close to recognition and appreciation,
but he never made it. Even so, he still had time to write articles for newspapers, compose poetry, build homes and raise two families. Hubbard's
view is sympathetic, Lasseter was a victim of dreams gone rogue – *I don't
believe he was a liar and a scoundrel. It was more likely he harboured delusions about his reef and did not question its existence* – but he wasn't crazy.
And a victim also of the greed of those whose appetites he whetted: *When*

Lewis Lasseter needed friends he was let down with tragic results. With gold reflected in greedy eyes 'friends' forgot the nuggety little man from Kogarah. Not all the recesses of Lasseter's early life were illuminated by Hubbard's sleuthing which continued a decade later when he was funded by Dick Smith and News Limited to go to upstate New York to learn more about *the American years* – 1902 to 1909.

Murray Hubbard's dismantling of Lasseter's backstory did little to deter the true believers, but his work focused the attention of kindred sleuths, including Lesley Synge and Robert Ross (later this chapter and Chapter 11). And Hubbard's almost-retired researcher was hired by film-maker Luke Walker (Chapter 17) who traced another set of connections to Lasseter that set up a family mystery for Chris Clark resulting in two more books (Chapter 18). But one of the challenges of the kind of jour-nalistic research that resulted in **The Search for Harold Lasseter** is that it involves cultivating relationships with people who are emotionally invested in the subject and the myth. Fred Blakeley was concerned enough that publishing his account might *injure a Woman and four little Australians* – that he didn't. In different ways many seeking to retell this story including Hubbard, Synge, Walker and myself have drawn on one of those *little Australians* – Bob Lasseter – as an informant. As was my experience in Seven Hills, that's tricky – who wants to taint the memories of a departing father/hero, never to be seen again, still sparkling in the misty eyes of a 95 year old man... Murray Hubbard's last word on Bob's father's story is clear: *Any suggestion that 'Lasseter's Lost Reef' exists in Central Australia can finally be dismissed with conclusive supporting evidence. There is no reef, there never was.* His resolution to the conflict of truth and trust was to dismantle the legend but preserve the person behind it, the nuggety battler: *For almost twenty years of ideas, dreams, plans, schemes and hopes there was little to show. Life had dealt him an ace – a sharp mind, above average intelligence, a good memory – but for much of his life the deck had been stacked against him.*

For film maker Luke Walker, Bob Lasseter was not only an inform-ant, he was also cast in the lead role of **Lasseter's Bones**. Walker's resolution involved foregrounding the reef rather than the backstory ending with a somewhat contrived, philosophical acceptance of uncertainty – we'll never know... But along the way Walker set out to seriously follow up long-voiced beliefs that preserved the reef while accepting that Lasseter had lied about finding it, proposing that, instead, he had heard about it from someone who had. The first of the two key suspects mentioned by Lasseter was *Harding*, who was part of his lie about having been rescued in the desert in 1897, but is repurposed as someone Lasseter met later on, with whom he shared his secret. The other is *Johannsen*, mentioned repeatedly in *The Diary* and in Lasseter's correspondence from Alice Springs to Irene and the Company.[282] Walker traced connections from the goldfields of Western Australia to an elderly woman, Ann Clark, in Benalla, Victoria, who had no memory of the father she believed had abandoned his wife and infant daughter in Adelaide in 1926. That lead didn't progress for Walker, but it set things rolling for Ann's son, Chris, whose grandfather was Olof Johanson.

Olof Johanson (1894-1955) was born in Sweden and arrived in Adelaide in 1914. Married to Grace Anwyl in 1923, they subsequently divorced and Olof lost access to his daughter, Avhild, later Ann, in 1926. Olof worked itinerantly through northern South Australia and the Kalgoorlie-Boulder area. He wrote to Lasseter after the first publicity about CAGE reached the Western Australian goldfields in May 1930, reporting that he had seen what he believed was the same reef while dingo hunting in the Rawlinson Ranges. Lasseter probably thought this would provide a way out of the hole he had dug for himself – someone actually knew where there was a reef in the region he had woven his tale around. Letters were exchanged and Lasseter expected to meet Johanson near Lake Christopher. It wasn't to be – Johanson's last letter didn't reach Lasseter. Ironically, Johanson ended up close by; he was financed by Joe Thorn, an American mining engineer and entrepreneur, to go to the area with John Jackson Smith. They set out from Alice Springs on 13th September 1930, just two days before Lasseter and Johns left Ilbilba. Out near the Olgas, when Lasseter was still alive, they left a message at Ayers Rock[283] and returned to Western Australia with much the same report as other expeditions to the area over the preceding forty years – there was no gold.

Olof Johanson was soon far away, in Melbourne. In 1939 he was injured in an accident and in 1948 returned to Sweden where he died in 1955. Fifty-seven years later, in Storvik, Chris Clark was presented with the suitcase that had accompanied Olof on his return, in which were photographs from Central Australia. Sitting on a white bedspread, that leather suitcase is on the cover of Clark's account of tracing his grandfather – *Olof's Suitcase: Lasseter's Reef mystery solved.*[284] In that contrived image the suitcase is open, a scatter of faded photographs on top of folded shirts to one side. On the left is a book with two camels racing across its cover through ochre skies – Edgar Holloway's cover of *Lasseter's Last Ride*.

There are two other works that fall into this category but neither adding more to the story. Like Murray Hubbard, Warren Brown's background was journalism and television. Also an avowed outback and military buff, he set out to review the extant material and to place it in the historical context of the Depression. The value of *Lasseter's Gold* is the emphasis he gives to the supporting cast: *The real treasure in Lasseter's tale is the coterie of self-serving and devious individuals who are there only to take advantage of the strange and inscrutable gold prospector.*[285] And on this *cabal of opportunists* he – rightly – doesn't let up, concluding: *Lasseter's story is in effect a morality tale. It has all the power and wrathful message of some fire-and-brimstone Old Testament parable. If you were to try to pinpoint precisely what Lasseter's story is about, it would come down to one word: greed.*

Chris Clark's second book on the subject, *The Truth About Lasseter: Why his elusive gold reef never existed,* was in part motivated by Brown's account and his response to *Olof's Suitcase* and followed up the story of his grandfather by focusing on Lasseter and placing Hubbard's and others' findings into chronological order, in the course of which he sets out to show that: *While other writers have previously disproved aspects of the life story that Lasseter claimed for himself, none has adopted the chronological biography approach which shows so sharply the pattern of behaviour that leaves no room for doubt: Lasseter was a compulsive delusionary liar, constantly demanding the attention of figures in authority for his own personal benefit.*[286] His conclusions about the venality of the support cast are much the same as Hubbard's and Brown's, and his thoughts about *Lasseter's*

Last Ride are clear: *Although Idriess's book was essentially romantic fiction dressed up as fact, it laid the basis for a whole new industry.* It sure did.

Decoders

Before a sleuth proved that the teenage Lasseter had never crossed the continent and that his claims to have found a gold reef were untrue, dozens of expeditions and prospectors headed into the bush to find it. Some were true believers but many, if not most, were true conmen. In 1939 Frank Clune ventured into Lasseter-land with Centralia Holdings' Morley Cutlack expedition. A decade later Max Cartwright was with yet another Centralia Holdings venture to the Petermanns with Cutlack, not long before his fraudulent ways were unmasked and he was replaced as Managing Director by the similarly devious ex-Lord Mayor of Sydney, Neville Harding. Max Cartwright had been living in the Northern Territory for forty years when, in the 1980s, he documented his participation in the 1949 and 1951 Cutlack charades[287] in **Ayers Rock to the Petermanns: Legend of Lasseter**. He knew that those making money were doing so by pushing the legend, and were happy to confect artefacts and clues to loosen investors' purses:

> *One early and prominent promoter of a company allegedly found a message in a pickle bottle buried by Lasseter giving the position of the reef. Another promoter found directions to the bonanza in a cave under a stone cairn built by Lasseter (the secret place). Yet another promoter had decoded the location of the reef from published fragments of Lasseter's diary. Other similar seekers just found messages under Lasseter's old camp-fires. Not many years ago one enterprising seeker found the golden reef by binocular survey.*[288]

After Cutlack, Cartwright worked with Neville Harding, including in the 1960s to support David Crocker filming elements of the story that eventually made it into the 1969 film **The Die-Hard: The Legend of Lasseter's Lost Reef.** That, of course, was not the first or last attempt to offset prospecting risks with entertainment gold; Ernest Gustav Brandon-Cremer was with the Second CAGE Expedition and produced a quasi-documentary, **Lasseter's Gold** (1931), Rupert Kathner and Stan

Tolhurst went with Hummerston on the 1936 Border Gold Reefs expedition funded by Sydney businessman H.V. Foy, the result of which was **Phantom Gold**. And, as I found among Idriess' documents in Narrandera, Idriess received a script from Kathner in the 1930s that was true to the text of **Lasseter's Last Ride** if not the reality of the Expedition and its aftermath, that didn't go anywhere (Chapter 6). But some did, and among the other layerings of the legend on screen are: Lowell Thomas' unearthing of Lasseter's remains in his *High Adventure* series directed by Lee Robinson (1957); Mike Willesee's 1979 documentary, also directed by Lee Robinson, **The Legend of Lasseter**; Les Hidden's 1996 *Bush Tucker Man* episode, **The Tragedy of Lasseter's Reef**, and; Luke Walker's 2012 production, **Lasseter's Bones**.

Bill Decarli credits Mike Willesee's documentary for the beginning of his *obsession* with Lasseter's reef. Like Marshall-Stoneking he was not born in Australia; Decarli came as a child from Italy to Melbourne in 1954, moving later to rural New South Wales. Like many of the informants that I've met or whose works I've read during this journey, Decarli was in the military and did a tour of Vietnam. In the book co-written with Angie Testa – **A Dead Mans Dream: Lasseter's Reef found** – Decarli reflects on the trauma of his return from Vietnam in the early 1970s, but of his time in uniform he's pragmatic, and grateful for what that provided to prepare him for life's challenges, as when he set out to find the reef: *In my mind the desert was like a predator. You could run from it all you liked, but eventually it would hunt you down and make the kill. My only defence against the predator was my military training.*[289]

Decarli's research included reading Murray Hubbard and accepting that Lasseter's account of finding the reef was implausible. But much earlier – around the beginning of his *obsession* in 1980 – he claims to have realised that *Lasseter had never actually seen the reef, merely heard about it from someone who had.* More than that, Decarli had a theory about who that was, why it had never been found, and where it was. It took another eleven years for him to test it. Critical to his theory is yet another Harding. This one is the third in the saga after surveyor Harding who Lasseter claimed rescued him in the desert in 1897 and returned with him to locate the reef a few years later, and Neville Harding who took over Centralia Holdings fifty years later. The third is Joseph Harding, who owned pubs in Oodnadatta and the gold mining town of Arltunga east of Alice Springs as the nineteenth century closed, returning to South Australia in the middle of the next decade. Joseph Harding died of nephritis in September 1922 and Decarli contends that he met Lasseter while they were both in hospital in Adelaide in 1917. This theory is that Harding talked about having found a gold deposit and gave Lasseter an indication of where it was, but with a catch that Decarli's military background helped him understand: *Right from the first moment that I watched that Mike Willesee documentary in 1980 the idea of a reversal of bearings, or mirror imaging, had occurred to me. It is an old prospector's trick, and one I learned in the army – to reverse a map to hide the location of something.*

As Lasseter told it in 1930, three years after originally stumbling on the reef, he relocated it by setting out from Carnarvon on the Indian Ocean coast with surveyor Harding.[290] With *mirror imaging* in mind and assuming that *if the reef existed it had to be within a 300-mile radius of Alice Springs*, Decarli: *checked a Shell road map and was astonished to find that there is a group of hills in Queensland called the Carnarvon Hills, right along the same latitude as the Western Australian Carnarvon.* Why Harding would share a secret, but with a cryptic catch, is unexplained, as is Decarli's assumption that Harding did not similarly disguise topographical clues – hills resembling *Three Sisters* and a *Quaker's Hat* reported by Lasseter. Regardless, he decided that if he found those features by reversing the original directions and distances, he would find the reef. And that's where he set out for in 1991.

By the time of writing Decarli had been to the area seven times. Convinced that he had located the *Three Sisters* and the *Quakers Hat,* and having pegged what he believes was the reef and entered into an agreement with a joint venture – Niche Exploration – his efforts foundered on other reefs and shoals, those of government bureaucracies and Aboriginal Land Council interests. But not before Les Hiddens closed his 1996 episode of the *Bush Tucker Man* – ***The Tragedy of Lasseter's Reef*** – with a trip to see it all with Decarli. In character, Hiddens was restrained but, in the same year, he wrote that when he first read ***Lasseter's Last Ride***:

I believed every word, not understanding that the book's author was a man who didn't let the facts get in the way of a good story.[291] Whether or not his later scepticism was shared off-screen, Decarli was philosophical: *I had no real interest in the gold itself, but in the finding of something that was so mysteriously lost, and so hunted for by so many people. It has altogether been a most wonderful adventure.*

And the adventure didn't stop there – as I discovered in the course of two phone calls in February 2020. I was in Perth to interview Peter Bridge at Hesperian Press, which published Decarli (Chapter 8). As I was scanning the contents of the *Lasseter file* that appeared as I was leaving, I noted a phone number on a subfolder crammed with photocopied articles, TROVE downloads, extracts from books and magazines, and more. Impressed mainly by volume, an hour later I was introducing myself to someone, who will remain anonymous, a continent away. That conversation and the longer one the next day was a little like sifting through the material in Peter's file – this Lasseterian had so much to say that successive waves broke over each other, the conversation churning around Lasseter, shifting from one side of the Northern Territory to the other. He talked about the mysterious Harding and a theory in which it was the explorer Ernest Giles who found the reef and told Harding, who later passed it on to Lasseter. It was Giles who named Lake Amadeus and much else in Lasseter-land during his expedition into the centre in 1873 and two crossings between South Australia and the coast of Western Australia in 1875 and 1876, which he documented in **Australia Twice Traversed** (1889). Working as a clerk in the Coolgardie goldfields, Giles died of pneumonia in 1897, the year Lasseter claimed to have crossed the continent and found the reef.

This enthusiastic informant described at length his own trips to the country Giles passed through and is convinced there is no reef there. As further proof he introduced William Harry Tietkens, who worked with Giles from the 1860s and was second-in-command to Giles in the first trip into the interior and the first successful crossing to the west coast. Tietkens was of interest because he took photographs – including the first of Ayers Rock: *I looked at the photos and I recognised the places, so I took the Land Rover out again, drove out there, walked ten kilometres across the sand dunes and took photographs to compare. Nothing there – there goes that theory.* Later on, he heard about Bill Decarli's theory: *I tracked him down in 2008 and we met up in Alice Springs and took a vehicle out to see the quartz show. I did the calculations and I could see that the mirror image went to that spot. I found the Quaker's Hat and those other features, it was all OK. Ten miles east of that is the reef and I went and found it.*

In the decade since, he'd been back several times: *In 2018 I went up to the reef and I walked everywhere. Up and out by eight and I'd walk the countryside on my own, take GPS coordinates and get samples. I had them assayed and there was a trace of gold. Bill came up with this investor mate, prepared to put in money to apply for the leases.* From there, probably as is often the way between prospectors and developers, things got complicated. And that was before they tried to factor in Native Title. Suddenly we were back in the original story – and gold: *nuggets, Lasseter had some, he used them to play with his daughters and Blakeley saw them. So where did he get them… From Joseph Harding, that's where. Before he meets Harding in 1917 he never mentions a reef. Then he's told how to find the reef but he goes west not east – that's how he loses out.* Of course, that doesn't explain how Joseph Harding knew that there was a reef east of Alice Springs, for which he had an answer: *He and his brother were stealing cattle and running them up to Cloncurry, and then they'd pinch some more and go back down to Alice. They knew where the waterholes were. So one day he was riding a horse and something catches his eye. I've been there and haven't picked anything up – but I'm going back up this year.*

With my cellphone signalling imminent battery failure the trajectory shifted to those who had dismantled the Lasseter backstory: *Murray Hubbard did one of the best jobs of the lot.* It got him thinking about how to analyse the information he was collecting: *I found when it came to dealing with Lasseter the only way I could make any sense of it was to break it down into segments and concentrate on one subject at a time – the description of country, of the reef and so on. You've got to deal with the facts and that takes time and money.* In the end he used up a lot of both chasing this story and he shared some of his findings, including Lasseter's lies and evasions about his early life. Much of this is recycled but I begin to realise that, like going and checking out the real landscapes through which the reef search progressed, he covered some fresh ground exploring Lasseter's backstory. Murray Hubbard provided the momentum but then: *I got a researcher in New York. I've got his birth certificate, death certificate, marriage to his first wife, birth of his daughters. On most of those it says what his occupation was and that was important. So when he comes back and says all those things about being a surveyor, a captain, other stuff – it doesn't show up.*

Again, those things are known but his researcher unearthed something that's new to me: *She found that when he arrived back in Australia and was in Tabulam he was writing letters to the editor in newspapers in the US. There's one where he's talking about being injured by an eight inch shell in the war. Another where he's sailing up the coast of Australia with millionaire mates.* Every informant brings something interesting – something new. I didn't know that Lasseter had his fantasies published in the United States. I was hoping to see the results of that research but our short relationship turned south and I now have a copy of my own book inscribed to a *Lasseterian* I never met.[292]

Kirrinytja - *Old Warts.*

CHAPTER 14

Oak Flats

"Mirror, mirror on the wall, who has the greatest Idriess collection of them all?"
"Jack and Leila Chapman."
I first heard of the existence of a private collection of 600 Idriess books about two years ago. I was scouting around the Southern Highlands of New South Wales, Moss Vale, Bowral, Mittagong, an area rich in secondhand bookshops.

Ronald Rowlands, 1995.[293]

June 2020

Leaving Wollongong heading south, the dystopian derangement of Port Kembla's heavy industry in agonal decay gives way to suburbia with glimpses of Lake Illawarra as the road crosses Mullet Creek. Moments later the Dapto Dogs is on the right, going since not long after Idriess wrote **Lasseter's Last Ride**. It's been tough times for the steel industry for decades and, more recently, not too good for greyhound racing in New South Wales. Another minute and more glimpses of the lake before the road squeezes between Shellharbour airport and the railway – then the turnoff to Oak Flats and the home of John Chapman: *in the early '60s they'd tell people if there was a burglary in Wollongong the police would* *go and take a look and then come out to Oak Flats and wait for them to come home and arrest them. It wasn't salubrious – a lot of people were poor and out of work.*

Long before the residential subdivisions and holiday townships, the coastal lagoons sustained Tharawal and Wadi Wadi peoples. Rich land and sought after – it was parcelled out from the second decade of the nineteenth century and that was that, much the same story right along the coast. An army officer, John Horsley, scored twelve hundred acres that became Oak Flats Run in the 1820s. With the twentieth century came coal, steel, then the Depression and a war – squatters were the norm in Oak Flats until it was developed for post-war migrant workers from the 1940s. A time of optimism and national pride; driving in I cross Barton, Deakin, Fisher, Parkes, Reid and Watson Streets. Chifley and Holt seem to have been runners up as Lanes. And John is on Fisher Street; William Fisher, the sixth Prime Minister – and the eighth and tenth to boot.

John's family were from Kempsie. Born in the year of Federation, his father was one of fifteen children and with two brothers set up a farm called *Holy Land*. His maternal grandfather was a fisherman in Ulladulla, 150 kilometres further south, and that's where John went to school, a time when a third of the kids were Italian, a third Aboriginal and the rest *Australian*. When he was around ten or eleven years old an uncle gave him **Drums of Mer**: *I thought it was fantastic. Then aunties and uncles bought me others for birthdays and Christmas. But I had this attitude that once you read a book it was worthless. So I promptly gave the books away to mates.* Even-tually he curbed his generosity, but serious collecting started much later – on Wednesday 22nd August 1979 to be precise: *On that day there was a headline in the **Daily Mirror** which read 'empty stomach turns bushman into a great author'. It was a historical feature and there was a subheading saying something about Idriess' 55 books. I didn't realise about all these other books. I set about finding them and not only did I collect each title, I set about to get every edition of every title.*

Before meeting John I had an image of him in a blue shirt and striped tie, sitting in a comfortable Chesterfield, reading.[294] That photograph is on the cover of *"Ion Idriess" – "A Comprehensive Collection" by John*

M Chapman, Including Dates of 1ˢᵗ Editions, Dates of Subsequent Editions, Associated Publications, Foreign Language Editions, Paperback Publications. Undated and self-published, it contains a listing of all of his Idriess books – including 38 editions of *Lasseter's Last Ride* not counting those in the 1939 and 1941 National Editions, three copies in the Australian Classics series, the leather-bound volumes released by Discovery Press, editions in Danish, Polish, German, and Swedish, ABC audio cassettes, and a scattering of later versions. And that's just *Lasseter's Last Ride*. Devoted to Idriess, the origins of the **Comprehensive Collection** were elsewhere:

> *I was in the building game and was working for a bloke when computers were just coming in and he got a mate to build a computer for me, a primitive one. I taught myself how to use it because I was writing a couple of books – poetry and recipes – and I started self-publishing. But the Idriess book was solely for my benefit, to know what I had and their condition. I needed a comprehensive listing of what was published. I found that there were duplicate first editions, or the first editions came out with the wrong dust jackets. Even the* **Guerrilla** *series – I think I've got at least three sets. Some of them were printed in America – at the time Australia looked to have an imminent take-over by Japanese forces through Darwin and the Australian government got on to Idriess and asked if he'd write some books about survival. Those books –* **Guerrilla Tactics, Lurking Death, Shoot to Kill, Sniping, Trapping the Jap** *and* **The Scout** *– were to be handed out to people in northern Australia.*

Sniping was Book 2 in *The Australian Guerrilla Series* published in 1942 and 1943 – the years of the Japanese raids on Darwin. The chapter titles tell the story: *The Real Sniper, The Cards of the Game, He Lives Longest Who Learns the Game Best, The Art of Hiding, The Art of Immobility: How Movement Betrays, The Art of "Freezing", The Art of Camouflage, Invisibility is Salvation, Form and Formlessness, Preparing for Action, The Sniper Fights, The Sniper is Adaptable*. I've never thought of that series as an attempt to upskill an outback Dad's Army to meet the sons of Nippon on home turf, and as I hold that thought I turn to the last line on the final page – *And now – good luck*.[295] With or without

Idriess' how to books, they would have needed a lot of it.

War stories; John moves on to two other Gallipoli veterans and Angus & Robertson authors in his collection – Frank Clune and Arthur Upfield. And, almost in the same breath, to an American – Zane Grey. Baseball player, traveller, sports angler, dentist – Zane Grey wrote about all of them except, perhaps unsurprisingly, dentistry. Idriess may have read him. Lasseter almost certainly did; he had a thing about adventure Westerns and **Riders of the Purple Sage** defined the genre. Zane Grey died in 1939, the year before Idriess' Cape York saga, **The Great Trek**, was released (see Chapter 9). To my surprise, John informs me that Zane Grey was as taken with the Jardines' adventures as Idriess. Before I can even form the question, John announces: *The Zane Grey books are in another room, I've run out of space down here.* A few minutes later he's back: *I found it,* **The Wilderness Trek: A Novel of Australia** *by Zane Grey.* It's not quite the Jardine story – but a kind of outback coming-of-age novella. Red Krehl and Sterling (Sterl) Hazleton, two young Texan cowboys, arrive in Australia to join *the greatest trek in Australian history. Seven or eight thousand cattle three thousand miles across the Never-Never.* If not inspired by the Jardines perhaps by the Durack trek; it's set across the Top to the Kimberley with everything from cannibals to crocodiles on the way, and ends with an impromptu marriage with a trusty blackfellow, *Friday,* in attendance:

"Come, Sterl and Leslie," boomed Dann "I require more practice. Here, before me, and join hands. Our bride and groom there may stand as witnesses." And almost before Sterl was sensible of anything except the shy and bedazzled girl beside him, clutching his hand, he was married!

Friday wrung Sterl's hand. No intelligence could have exaggerated what shone in his eyes. "Me stotum alonga you an' missy. Me be good black fella. No home, no fadder, no mudder, no brudder, no lubra. Imm stay alonga you, boss."

Sterl and Red walked by the river alone. "Pard, it's done," said Red. "We're Australians. Who would ever have thunk it? But it's great. All this for two no-good gunslingin' cowboys!"

"Red, it is almost too wonderful to be true!" It was as Stanley Dann had said of them all: "We have fought the good fight." In that moment Sterl saw

with marvellous clarity. It has taken a far country and an incomparable adventure with hardy souls to make men out of two wild cowboys. [296]

Lines worthy of Idriess – maybe he read them. But John has other connections closer to home: *Zane Grey also wrote a lot of books on fishing, I've got all the expensive first edition books –* **Tales of the Angler's Eldorado, New Zealand** *and* **Tales of Freshwater Fishing**. *When he came to Australia he landed in Melbourne and worked his way up the coast to Sydney. He called in at Ulladulla and went out deep sea fishing in my grandfather's boat.* As soon as Leo Berkelouw got **An American Angler in Australia** in at the Book Barn near Berrima John was there: *It's only 120 pages and I got my wife to drive the car; by the time we got to Berrima to have lunch I'd read the whole book and there wasn't one mention of my grandfather.*

In the way of such conversations, Zane Grey brings us back to Idriess and Lasseter. John doesn't think **Lasseter's Last Ride** is Idriess at his best, but its theme, and Lasseter's demise, resonates: *Ion Idriess had a knack of writing things that fit in with the Australian way of life. It was readable to Australians. There's a part in the book where Lasseter walked off to find the reef and got in with a mob of natives and he had to survive with them, and finally died after crawling into a cave and so on.* In the moment of silence that follows I imagine John visualising the dying prospector: *I think that touched a lot of Australians – dysentery, gnawing on old bones. Poor white man, the natives wanted to kill him. I think a lot of Australians felt sorry for Lasseter.* Or, rather, felt sorry for the Lasseter that Idriess created.

With the interview about to end I fumble in my bag for a copy of **Vicarious Dreaming** – a small gift that will probably be lost among the thousands of books that line nearly every room of the house. I'm about to write a note inside the front cover when he tells one last story:

I had a fetish once for buying books signed by Idriess. Booksellers would call me and tell me that they had one, maybe signed for a Prime Minister. Anyway, there was a time when I needed money and I had about one hundred signed books. I put them on ebay and sold them all. I ask people now if they've got any books by Idriess and if they say they've got a signed one I tell them I don't want it. He'd sign the Woman's Weekly if someone put it in front of him.

At the front door I hand it over – unsigned.

John Chapman:
*I set about to get
every edition
of every title.*

The
Battle
of the
Baloneys...

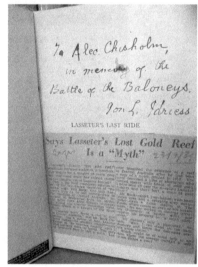

Jim Bradly:
*the **Drums of Mer**
drew him north …*

CHAPTER 15

Bolton Points

To "Cyclone Jack" whose books have become the most collected and collectable in Australia today, and whose stories stirred my imagination and set me on my own path of discovery.

Jim Bradly, 2008.[297]

March 2020

Built in Sydney in 1799, as the new century began the schooner, *Martha*, was trading along the coast and to Norfolk Island. It was despatched to secure a cargo of coal from a deposit first sighted near the mouth of Hunter's River in 1797. Captain William Reid headed north hugging the coast but turned to port too early, running aground in a body of water that turned out to be a saltwater inlet. He was in the wrong place – but there was coal there too. Even so it was almost two decades before free settlers began to arrive around the Hunter and the entrance to what was commonly referred to as *Reid's Mistake* was recognised to be an extensive saltwater lake and named for Lachlan Macquarie.[298]

In 1829 a mission, Ebenezer, was established on the western shore, but within a few decades that gave way to the irresistible forces of development

– the railway in the 1880s that transformed Newcastle into a BHP steel town from 1911. Where Ebenezer was is now Toronto, named in honour of Edward Hanlan, a world champion sculler who hailed from Ontario and visited Australia in 1884. And it was in and around Toronto and the Lake that Jim Bradly spent most of his life. Now, in his retirement, Jim lives across the bay at what from 1915 was the first residential subdivision in the area – Bolton Point. Leafy suburbia surrounded on three sides by calm waters and a constellation of moorings, the Point is crossed at its base by strands of bush bisected by a residential corridor – and that's where Jim lives.

While the coal that Captain Reid was looking for remains an economic driver, BHP is long gone. But for some seventy years it had its own shipping fleet and Jim's father was a chief steward, spending time on some of the ships built by BHP at Whyalla – also a thing of the past. He certainly had a lot of down time and was a reader, and that was Jim's introduction to Ion Idriess: *One of the books he brought home was* **Drums of Mer**. *My younger brother in Mackay has it now but when I was around ten to fourteen I got stuck into it, I got inspired. We were living in Toronto at that time. Our house was the original police station and we found old knuckle dusters and that sort of stuff there.*

Jim never strayed far: *I had several businesses, everything from running shops, a garage, a caravan park, post office, ship repair, working for Telecom. I was a night telegraphist with various little exchanges – they reckoned it wasn't safe for women on their own – just blokes. I drifted along and went with the flow, but always ended up on my feet.* Through his moves and occupations he never lost his interest and some forty years later the *Drums of Mer* drew him north: *I went on my own travelling through the Torres Strait and met some of the characters who were still alive – the oldest people remembered Idriess. Like Father Dave Passi, he was the Church of England minister on Mer – he was the one that told me about the caves on Mer that Idriess wrote about with the treasure in them. As a kid he'd seen the openings but he sure as hell wasn't going to tell me where they were.*[299]

Drums of Mer was the beginning for Jim and he's clear that it's the journey that's important: *it doesn't matter what you collect, it's the people* *you meet along the way. You and I – we're talking about a common subject; we have a common interest and I know what you're talking about, and you know what I'm talking about. It's the journey.* And there have been many fellow travellers along the way and some common themes on the slow build from curiosity to compulsion, and one particular book stands out – ***Cyaniding for Gold***:

> *When I started to get really interested and going to booksellers they would talk about **Cyaniding for Gold** – a phantom book – most of them had heard about it but hadn't seen it. Then there was one advertised and I grabbed it. It cost $1,200, a small fortune for a book. But against that, I had one of the phantom books. I took it to a book dealer up in Maitland and showed it to him and he held it in his hands and you'd think he'd found the Welcome Stranger – the gold nugget – the way he handled it. He couldn't believe it, he actually had in his hands an original **Cyaniding for Gold**. He said to me: 'you know the first thing that I'm going to do when I get home...' And I said: 'no, what...' And he said: 'I'm going to spruik to all my friends and tell them I held a genuine **Cyaniding for Gold** in my hands'. It made me feel good to hear him say it; it made him feel really good to be able to say it.*

Getting that book was special – there was only one edition, in 1939 – but the grail was more: *A jacket can virtually double the price of a book. A copy of **Cyaniding for Gold** may be $1,500; with a jacket in reasonable condition – $4,000. That's for a bit of paper that some bushmen used to rip off and light their fires with.* Collecting to compulsion; the difference is that, for the latter, completion doesn't bring satisfaction, it just ups the ante. A complete set of first editions of Idriess' books is an achievement but: *There's a few sets of firsts around. I think Duncan and I are the only two with full complete sets with original jackets. Some of them are a bit patched up but they are still first jackets. Someone told me recently that they bought one for $20, walked down the road and put it on the net and got some ridiculous price for it – it's all in the hunting, we're all doing our own prospecting.* And like prospecting for gold, it can easily get out of control. But a safety valve is trading and for Jim that began a year or two after his collecting took off. That meant some difficult choices; parting with hard-found items, but in pursuit of a more refined and valuable collection.

In the bookcases that line the walls of Jim's home, pride of place goes to jacketed Idriess first editions, all individually wrapped in plastic. Out of curiosity I ask him to open a copy of the first edition of **Lasseter's Last Ride**; not surprisingly it's signed by the author, but the dedication is to someone who is also familiar: *To Alex Chisholm in memory of the Battle of the Boloneys. Ion L. Idriess.* Alex Chisholm – the man who introduced Idriess to Angus & Robertson. Maybe the reference to *the Boloneys* was an insider joke, but it might relate to a cutting from a newspaper that is pasted just below. It's an image I've seen before and it conjures another player in the saga:

> *Says Lasseter's Lost Gold Reef is a "Myth"*
> *Lasseter's famous "Lost gold reef" which has intrigued explorers, prospectors and writers for a number of years, does not exist – and never has existed except in the imagination of Lasseter himself. This is the final considered opinion of one of the best-known identities of "the centre" – Mr. Bob Buck, who took Lasseter's body to its last resting place in the sandhills of Central Australia. He arrived at Melbourne from his station 150 miles from Alice Springs yesterday to attend the Central Australian Exhibition, which is a feature of the Royal Show.*[300]

Before the First CAGE Expedition Bob Buck was a struggling pastoralist. If there was anyone who struck it lucky through Lasseter – it was Buck. He played his cards close to his chest and was happy to help others lose money – as long as he was paid. Idriess was responsible for his moment of fame extending to a career of storytelling, which is probably what he did at the 1939 Melbourne Royal Show. Whether the inclusion alongside the dedication to Alex Chisholm was placed there by Idriess or not, it raises the question of who was playing whom. As I'm considering these two wily tale-tellers burnishing their bushman banter, Jim is reflective. Unlike some of the collectors I've spoken to, who don't seem to have read much of what lies between the covers of the books on their shelves, that's not the case for Jim. For him, Idriess' writing brings alive: *the stories of early Australia, stories of an Australia long gone – Idriess captures it. There are plenty of other writers, like Clune who seem to get it too. Clune said in one of his books that Idriess set him on his path writing his own books. So, I believe he captured early Australia and I don't think anyone since has done as well though a lot have tried.* For Jim, Idriess' voice is that of experience: *He talked to the early explorers and prospectors and the police and Aborigines in Western Australia, and he came across tribes that had never seen white men before – it's in* **Mantracks**. *Really interesting and wonderful reading; when you start you have to keep going.*

Jim Bradly is more than a collector and a reader – he's also a researcher and spent decades tracking down the newspaper and magazine articles that Idriess wrote from well before the First World War. Best known as *Gouger*, those anecdotes and descriptions of bush life appeared under various pseudonyms and Jim set himself the task of finding them. The results are compiled in two volumes that took years to reach print, with an effort that's ongoing – **Gouger of the Bulletin**. That material is different to Idriess' books:

> *Some are funny, some sad, some tragic. It's good reading, particularly if you've been there and realise how big the country is – I pity the poor buggers crossing the immensity of the outback. It captured a lot of those fellows – it's in their soul. Some of them have a thousand-mile stare, their brains are addled – the country has captured them. Some of them would have a lot of trouble living anywhere else. I've met characters like that.*

So have I; thirty years working as a psychiatrist in remote northern Australia – I've met lots of them and that's a central thread in **Vicarious Dreaming.** And as our conversation draws towards a close it loops back to where I began – finding **Madman's Island** in Cornstalk Bookshop on Glebe Point Road. I have the 1938 edition, rewritten as a factual account and I wrote the introduction to a recent republication.[301] But I've never held a copy of the 1927 version that Idriess was pressured to rewrite as adventure fiction with a romantic interest. It flopped; romance is not a genre Idriess ever mastered – in letters or in life. Jim hands me a copy with Edgar Holloway's original cover and tells the story of the find:

> *There was a lady whose grandfather had died and left thousands of books. I heard about it and had a look and came across a first edition '27 with*

jacket. I stopped and my heart missed a beat. So I asked 'how much do you want for that…', and they said '$20 will do you'. I couldn't get my money out quickly enough and afterwards clasped my hands together, looked to the sky and gave thanks. If she'd said $200 I would have jumped on it. But I bought a lot of stuff and they were happy.

On this journey of common interest I know Jim is more than a collector and is happy to share what he has and what he knows. And I'm not the only person to benefit from his generosity; in the *THANKS* section of the annotated Idriess bibliography, Paul Fein and Ellie Aroney give: *special thanks to Jim Bradly for being so generous with his knowledge, passion and collection of Idriess books, his jokes, his stories and the friendship found.*[302]

That might have been it, but two weeks after our conversation a parcel arrived. Buried in bubble-wrap were two books and an envelope. The enclosed letter ran to seven foolscap pages of closely spaced printing, two being of Jim's poems – *The Bushie's Last Wish* and *Clancy's Return*. On both there are prosodic markers, and errors have been corrected by pasting small oblongs of the same ruled paper over the offending sections with lines carefully matched. And there is a third poem – but not Jim's. He probably found it scouring through *The Bulletin* looking for traces of Idriess. It dates to February 1937 and is attributed to *Midford*. A little grazing through TROVE and other poems emerge that were probably written by Charles Whittens. The poem Jim has written out is *The Lost Reef*, and in its original location is next to a cartoon showing a camel at a gallop carrying a desert Sheik who is grasping in the slipstream a scantily-clad blond whose high heels form part of the trio's desert contrails – the legend reading: *"But, honest, Sheik, I'm not a bit of good at cooking!"* Before the first verse of the poem is a quote: *"The whole story of Lasseter's reef is a myth. I have covered every inch of ground twice and there is definitely nothing there."* Dr. Harris, geologist of the Cutlack Air Expedition. The attribution is presumably to Guy Harris who was involved with the Cutlack and Hummerston imbroglio of Border Gold Reefs Limited that sustained interest and investment in prospecting scams in Lasseter-land into the late-1930s:

Lasseter's reef! Lasseter's reef!
Its riches, 'twas hinted, would beggar belief.
Are there foreheads will wrinkle or hearts that will ache
To learn it's a fable, a fraud and a fake,
A ramp, in vernacular pungent and crisp,
A baseless elusion, a will-o'-the'wisp?
They're booked for misfortune and head for grief, The
chaps who go searching for Lasseter's reef.

Lasseter's reef! Lasseter's reef!
Of tales to beguile the unwary the chief,
You may traverse a desert, forbidding and bare,
But there's nothing remotely resembling it there.
It's the latest to add to the lengthening list
Of fictions and myths, for it doesn't exist.
The gold at the foot of the rainbow, in brief,
Is as real as the riches in Lasseter's reef.

Lasseter's reef! Lasseter's reef!
What a liar is Rumor and eke what a thief!
You may bung in your brass, if your fancy inclines, On
the wildest of cats in the matter of mines,
Or in hunts for the treasure reputedly hid
On desolate islets by Morgan or Kidd.
But don't, if you'd pay for your beer and your beef,
Don't take any tickets on Lasseter's reef.

Lasseter's reef! Lasseter's reef!
No hope of a harvest – not even a sheaf.
It's a traveller's tale, of Munchausen's own type,
A figment of fancy, a dream of a pipe.
It's as real as the fantoms a fellow may see,
Or reckon he does, at the end of a spree.
So let's merely record, with a sigh of relief,
That burst is the bubble of Lasseter's reef.

Midford.[303]

The two carefully wrapped books are Jim's compilations of Idriess' writings under various pseudonyms, the first in view with Idriess on the cover in his Light Horseman uniform is the most recent – ***Gouger of the Bulletin: Part 2***.[304] The other is the original ***Gouger of the Bulletin***, with a classic pen drawing of a down-at-the-heels swaggie cooking a goanna over a fire – probably from *The Bulletin*. As Jim has warned me there's a key typo with an errant e in his name – *Bradley*. Quickly scanning, there doesn't seem to be anything that relates to Lasseter – until the very last entry, dated 24th February 1932 and with attribution to *I.I.* – a piece written before the release of the revised version of ***Lasseter's Last Ride***:

> *There are mineral and pastoral possibilities in the no-man's land round about the Central W.A. border. According to the A.I.M. map, this country extends north, south, east and west 600 miles, permanently uninhabited by a single white man. Several geologists and a score of prospectors have penetrated it here and there. Frank Green, of the second Lasseter expedition, reports having gone over miles of granite, quartz and ironstone outcrops, which it would take years to prospect properly. Members of both the Lasseter expeditions found large areas of good grass country, especially the second expedition, which by trying a different route escaped the desert country. A number of waterholes of considerable extent was found, and the wild men of the region showed the party numerous locations in which water could be dug at a depth of several feet.*[305]

Frank Green – just three months after he arrived back in Alice Springs with Bob Buck.

CHAPTER 16

Mythbusters

Sudden wealth beckons most men with the same appeal, and in the Centre all men are, or have been, or will become, prospectors. Mines and mining are in the air. From the bar-tenders at the "pubs" on the line, to the farthest wanderer in the west, all men have felt the fever of gold and opal; and most will talk overpoweringly a jargon bristling with "lodes" and "dykes", "reefs" and "colours", and the astonishing results of yet more astonishing assays. Usually it is a passing, or at least an intermittent madness. There are those, however, who never recover, and they become the elite of the profession, the high priests of the cult. As the obsession grows, they lose all contact with the race of men, and brood alone in the outer solitudes.

H.H. Finlayson, 1935.[306]

During the years that mammologist Hedley Finlayson spent traversing the Centre his paths intersected those of prospectors often enough for him to be familiar with the rites and repartee of those who *brood alone in the outer solitudes*. Drawn by the light and warmth of campfires under chill desert heavens, he and they would struggle to fathom the other's principles and purposes. As he reflected in the

1930s: *As the night wears on, you draw closer together over the fire, the unwonted exercise of speech breaks down the barriers of caution. At length he tells you of that which gives a meaning to his existence. It is the "Lost Reef". And though you have heard that story up and down the country, till it has become a weariness, yet as you mark his fanatic earnestness, you half believe it yourself.* On 1ˢᵗ March 1935, Finlayson was in Lasseter country, a space he knew well – as he did the story and some of the players. Camping by a waterhole near a station homestead he heard about another prospecting party:

> *It is a Sydney crowd, and instigated by one Humerston [sic] who is now en route for the Petermann Corner by way of Ilbilla, with trucks galore. Funny if friend H gets in with them… Story goes that H Brown met Humerston out there, and they concocted a map and details of a reef purporting to be Lasseter's, and this year's lavish party is the sequel. Seems to be no end to the gullibility of the Sydney public.*[307]

Stan Hummerston was trading in gullibility and quite happy to materialise mementos to manifest the myth and encourage inflamed imaginations.[308] The *H* in question, who occupies much of the end of Finlayson's diary, had joined Finlayson at Tempe Downs on the recommendation of the station manager. Finlayson took *an immediate dislike*, describing him as: *about 5 ft 11 inches – rather spare, stoop shoulders black hair, green eyes, no teeth, deeply cleft nostril when seen from the side, and a prominent scar on the back of the right hand, encircling the base of the first finger. General aspect a very evil one.* His premonitions seem born out over the next weeks as the mysterious and unpredictable *H* – his identity is never revealed – incrementally adds to Finlayson's discomfort. At one point *H* confides that he wants to clear Lasseter's name, and soon afterwards a horseman, who has joined the group and for no reason was slandered by *H*, confides to Finlayson that he is: *thoroughly alarmed about the fellow, and is preparing to cut adrift altogether. He has heard that the two camels H calls his own are stolen, and has an idea not altogether impossible that the fellow is Lasseter.* When they are finally, and for Finlayson thankfully, going separate ways, Finlayson could only look back in horror and fascination: *H (an insult to the name) was himself a major discovery, and as a type of evil and beast-*

... brave bushmen and tricky savages ...
Bob Buck during the
Second CAGE Expedition.

... Mr Idriess, him gone home. Les Such,
Man Magazine, 1939.

... the triumph of technology ...
Errol Coote and the *Golden Quest*.

liness, a revelation to me, and certainly a theme of great interest, however repulsive. Over six decades later Nic Rothwell mused on Finlayson's encounter with *H* and his realisation:

> *that this bleak man, with all his understanding, his intimacy with the sand dunes and the secret, far-off ranges, is in fact none other than the lost, crazed, dead Harold Lasseter in some strange reincarnated form. A ghost; a devil; a mirror of some common darkness? He turns over his trip to his chosen country in his mind, and edges towards the realisation that it was H. he had been seeking in the desert, and had been forced to confront.*[309]

Lasseter as a reflection of a shadowed, shared recess – *a mirror of some common darkness* – the vector of myth. As early as 1935 scammers like Hummerston were trading on the legend and Finlayson, an experienced bushman and hard-nosed scientist, accreted intimations of malevolence around an impression of *the lost, crazed, dead Harold Lasseter.* Lasseter was already an idea to be mined and manipulated – the myth and magic were in place – and Idriess had cast the spell. But while Idriess may have set the myth in motion, it got a lot of help along the way. An example is Ivan Smith, who is remembered more for his radio productions, including *Dingo King* and *Death of a Wombat,* than for his collaboration with his wife, Jocelyn, in **The Die-Hard: The Legend of Lasseter's Lost Reef.** Produced by Don Philps and directed by David Crocker, with footage a spin-off from his trip to Lasseter country with a Centralia Holdings expedition of the 1960s, James Mason's narration added gravitas to a film that was soon forgotten. But at the time it won the Golden Reel award from the Australian Film Institute for the best Australian documentary of 1969, was the Australian entry to the Cannes Film Festival, and was adapted as an ABC radio broadcast in 1973 with music composed and conducted by John Sangster. And a decade after the film a limited edition of five-hundred copies of the prose poem **The Die-Hard**[310] was released, sumptuously illustrated by someone who knew more than a little about capturing the essence of tortured souls, a luminary of antipodean art aristocracy – Albert Tucker. And just to blur the distinction between fantasy and facts the foreword was by a historian who made a career of assembling the latter – Geoffrey Blainey.

In the author's introduction the Smiths decry the failure of this nation to recognise Lasseter as an *explorer*, noting that: *Lasseter twice penetrated to an area that no other white man has since seen, and he logged his journeys in a professional way. It is amazing that a young sailor could have learnt so much bushcraft so quickly.* Well, as we now know – not quite. True to his vocation, Tucker reflected in his preface on the journey to the interior as a metaphor: *man's never ending attempt to transcend himself. The tragedy of Lasseter embodies this process with terrifying clarity and evokes images which tell us more about who and what we are and about our own identity as Australians* – perhaps. At least the dealer in facts, Geoffrey Blainey, challenges a key element of the story noting in his foreword that the reef: *probably was itself a myth.* But, like Jason, this myth is more about the folly than the fleece – the journey and tragedy[311] – and Blainey considers the people and events that have become a *pivot for the imagination* for mid-century Australians They are all familiar:

> *The Eureka rebels, the explorers Burke and Wills, the bushranger Ned Kelly, and the soldiers of Gallipoli. They had much in common; they were brave, they battled against odds which proved higher than they had expected, they were in part the victims of poor timing or bad luck, and their end was an odd mosaic of conspicuous defeat and quiet victory...*
> *The paintings by Albert Tucker and the prose poem by Ivan and Jocelyn Smith show, in this fascinating book, that Lasseter's last journey also had these ingredients of legend.*

The prose poem includes extensive quotes from Lasseter's letters to Irene and *The Diary*. Intentionally or not, in the large-format presentation Tucker's warped and wounded images exaggerate the two-dimensionality of the text. Extending to more than four thousand words, perhaps the most that can be said is that the best was saved for last:

> *Robert Buck*
> *loaded his camels.*
> *He waited ten days*
> *for a case of brandy,*
> *and set a course for*
> *the Dead Heart*

with all his courage and skill.
He found Lasseter's
body, and buried it.
And he found a cave
where a dying man
had thought of a wife,
and had thought of a reef
in a region that no-one knows.

Even in his day Bob Buck's *reputation of being one of the finest bushmen in Centralia* was recognised for what it was by those who knew the Centre and the man. But it worked for Idriess, and the Smiths. And while there is no mention of **Lasseter's Last Ride** in **The Die-Hard**, that's what it's about. It wasn't until the principals had long exited the stage, decades after Idriess had died in Mona Vale, and following the systematic unpicking of the fabric of lies and exaggerations that Lasseter – and those who chose to believe or use him – had woven about his backstory, that the myth itself was systematically challenged. Lasseter, the Company, the Expedition, Buck, Idriess, Clune, Stapleton, Decarli … building and reinforcing the myth was a guy-thing; pulling it apart introduces the voices of women.

Mythbusters

Michelle (Mickey) Dewar moved to the Northern Territory in 1981 and, after supplementing her Melbourne undergraduate degree with a diploma in education, began teaching at Milingimbi. She went on to a richly diverse Top End life – research assistant to Nugget Coombs, senior adviser to the first female Chief Minister, Clare Martin, conservator, curator, librarian, historian and feminist. Her PhD thesis was reworked for publication in 1997 as **In Search of the Never-Never: Looking for Australia in Northern Territory Writing**, of which Chris O'brien noted in its republication following her death in 2017: **Never-Never** *reflects on stories about stories about the Northern Territory*.[312] Dewar's book identifies the ideas and images that recur across works written in particular historical periods, and tracks how these are repudiated or repurposed for later times.

Idriess was not a Territorian; his knowledge of bush life and ways was almost entirely from his early adulthood in New South Wales and fifteen years or so in Cape York and the Torres Strait before and after the First World War. By the time he wrote *Lasseter's Last Ride* he was living in Paddington, and Sydney would be his base for the rest of his life. Other than a tour through northern Western Australia and the Territory in 1934 which was the basis for a 1935 collection of frontier police stories – *Man Tracks* – his experience of the Territory was limited. Idriess used that trip for the 1941 story *Nemarluk* (the hero of which he met in Fannie Bay Gaol) and recycled elements decades later into *Our Living Stone Age* (1963) and *Our Stone Age Mystery* (1964) – but he was an old man by that time and long past tapping into, let alone informing, the national zeitgeist.[313]

When Dewar began her PhD research she: *discovered that people had come to the Territory because they believed it to be the place of legends and mythical Australian events.*[314] Until well after the Second World War the characters that carried those stories and, with a few exceptions such as Ernestine Hill, Mary Durack and Jeannie/Aeneas Gunn, the authors who created them were men. Over that period of some sixty years the focus for authors shifted – from attempts to depict an alien and threatening landscape at the end of the nineteenth century, to eulogising the non-Indigenous pioneers and *legendary bushmen* around the First World War, to tapping the veins of hope for buried riches, particularly gold, in the Depression and inter-war years, to more critical considerations of race relations in its aftermath, and on. While some things changed – the casual acceptance of interracial violence on the frontier and the emergence of European women from crinoline and lace to be active participants in the dramas of the Territory as examples – some themes didn't: *Dominating Territory writing this century prior to the Second World War were the seemingly contradictory notions of nationalistic celebration of the bush lifestyle and a desire to open up and civilise the outback through industry. ... This period of writing represents the flowering of the romantic notion of the bushman of the Northern Territory.*

Dewar demonstrates that the *romantic ideal of the noble white bushman* repeats across a range of authors including Clune and Idriess, representing the Territory as *the land of adventure, populated by brave bushmen and tricky savages.* Idriess was typical in contrasting tribal authenticity against a degraded alternative: *Idriess portrayed the 'myall' Aborigines graphically as at one with the landscape. ... In contrast he depicted Aborigines in close association with Europeans as comic objects of derision.* At one with a hostile landscape maybe, but *savages* none the less, and a ready device to contrast with pioneer sentiments and the simple dignity of European bushmen – even *in extremis.* Dewar shows Idriess exemplifying this trope with Lasseter rousing himself in his last days to a: *spirited and courtly defence of Lerilla from the savage wife beater, Gadgadgery.* And the more detail the better. Through the 1920s and '30s there was a national appetite for quasi-ethnographic depictions of exotic Aboriginal rites and rituals, that included: *the supernatural powers Aboriginal 'witchdoctors' exercised within their own community.* As Idriess exemplified, such *occult powers* were woven into plots in which: *Aboriginal power had overflowed into the non-Aboriginal domain.* Lasseter was the first to touch the sacred board. He was doomed before he set off alone and ultimately succumbed to sorcery.

Idriess' career took off and soared with another thirteen books after **Lasseter's Last Ride** before the Second World War broke out. By the last years of that decade his profile was consolidated by editing the *Australasiana* section of *Man Magazine.* He may have felt sufficiently confident by then to tolerate a humorous dig at his status; in 1939 a full-page cartoon by Les Such is included in which four Aboriginal men in ragged cast-offs sit about a campfire eyeing a fifth who stands wearing only a headband and the remnants of a shirt, the caption reading: *"Lets quit this plurry dressing for dinner; Mr. Idriess him gone home."*[315] Idriess' reputation as an expert on matters Aboriginal was reinforced as what he had to say was accessible and, more or less, acceptable given prevailing social and political attitudes in the 1930s and '40s. His opinion was respected and in some areas he bucked prevailing *laissez faire* government attitudes with recommendations that were decades ahead of service planners – for instance in his call for regionally-based, trained public health practitioners to address communicable diseases in remote Aboriginal populations.[316] Regardless, in Mickey Dewar's depiction of the inter-war period, Idriess fits the mould of writing about remote Australia – he neither made it nor broke it. In fact he probably ended up stuck in it. But in 1931 he knew from decades of writing for magazines and newspapers what that audience wanted and how to package it.

Around the time that Mickey Dewar was settling into life in the Northern Territory and refining her feminist lens, Lesley Singh (later Synge) was part of the women's movement in Brisbane and active in advocating for the civil liberties that Joh Bjelke-Petersen told Queenslanders they didn't need. Like Dewar, a teaching career led elsewhere. Having fallen in love with a young geologist in 1981, twelve years later she read Murray Hubbard's book and realised that there was a Lasseter family other than the Sydney one she had married into. It was her husband, Lasseter's geologist grandson, who suggested that she start writing the journal that kick-started her research into the women in Lasseter's life. That led to a Master of Arts degree in Creative Writing in 2001 in two parts, a novel – *Precious* – and a critical essay – *Men, Women and Gold: The Problem of Desire in the Writing of 'Precious'.*[317] A professional writer and mentor, she ranges across fiction and non-fiction, poetry and spiritualism, the non-fiction section of her website containing examples of her activism, and her personal trials.[318]

In *Precious*, Synge's travails and her unique vantage point are played out in displacement, it's an internal journey in Lasseter-land. While the driving force and the story are about Lasseters past and present, not about Idriess, **Lasseter's Last Ride** is essential. The central character in the fiction is Diana, born in Melbourne in 1966. The backstory is that her mother, Hilary, had married Lewis, a man whose grandmother, Scarlett Musgrove, was in a brief relationship with the already-married Lewis Lasseter in 1916 while he was in the army.[319] When Lasseter abandoned Scarlett she was pregnant, and quickly married a man who accepted and raised the child. Scarlett never saw Lasseter again but recognised him in newspaper photographs announcing his death fifteen years later. Four decades on, in 1972, a year before she died, the elderly Scarlett sent a letter to her grandson, also Lewis, who at that time was married to Hilary but leading a dissolute life. With the letter informing him of the identity of his real grandfather was a copy of **Lasseter's Last Ride**. Lewis took stock and straightened out, went to university to study geology, and told his teenage daughter, Diana, the story of his grandfather – Lasseter. But as much as discovering the link changed Lewis for the better, that didn't save the marriage and Lewis and Hilary separated – as was also the case with Lesley Synge and Lasseter's grandson. Traumatised by the marriage and breakup, Hilary began researching the Lasseter story in an attempt to make sense of the man she had loved and lost. As a friend says to Diana when they find the material Hilary had collected among her effects after her death in 1996: *"I think what motivated her research on Lasseter was trying to understand your father."*

Completing the journey falls to Diana, who discovers that her mother had attempted to fathom what happened with Lewis by assembling the accounts of all the principals in his grandfather's saga – Blakeley, Sutherland, Coote, Johns, Taylor, Buck, Bailey, Colson, Mickey... the whole cast. Most of what Synge incorporates is from the sources that I've foraged through, but also included is a contrived surfacing during the Second World War of the trunk that Lasseter took with him when he left with Johns, which was lost when his camels bolted and was never found. In the fiction – *Precious* – it resurfaces during the Second World War and Hilary was somehow able, decades later, to inspect it in Perth, finding notes from Lasseter, and also a copy of the **Rubaiyat of Omar Khayyam** inscribed to Lasseter from *Your darling Scarlett*.[320] With Hilary's 1946 edition of **Lasseter's Last Ride** in her own luggage, Diana undertakes to complete her mother's journey by going to Central Australia where she deposits the research – and tells the story – in Alice Springs. There are many twists and turns and a large supporting cast – with facing pages showing the fictional and actual Lasseter family trees. Just as well.

Hilary, Diana, Lesley – breaking silences. Silences are a significant theme that emerges in the essay that accompanies *Precious*, an explanation of how it evolved. Silences of the historical and contemporary Lasseter families. And silences form one of the categories of Lasseter literature that emerged for Synge, as they did for me when the first waves of books and articles arrived ten months ago. Hers are similar but different: *believers, agnostics, disbelievers* – and *silences*. The last includes women and Aboriginal players in the drama and its aftermath – but also Lasseter himself of whom, echoing Murray Hubbard, she notes: *that as a working-class man, Lasseter was destined to live a silenced life. That he rejected such a fate so zealously is a tribute to his ingenuity.*

As is clear from the way she positions *Lasseter's Last Ride* in *Precious*, in relation to Lasseter, Idriess *began the hero/explorer myth*, building on existing interests among Australian readers and mixing in sufficient facts to the fiction to sustain credulity. Synge points out that he avoids inconvenient facts, foremost among which, understandable given Synge's motivations and thesis, are his bigamous relationships and the abandonment of his family in Melbourne – which didn't fit well with the fallen hero trope. And, as Synge philosophically concluded, myths resist the assaults of research and reason because people want them, making it more important to listen to the voices of the silenced:

> *My fantasy about destroying the Lasseter myth was a conceit – it will somersault to its feet again, even without Lasseter and Ion Idriess to help. Some men will always want to keep it alive but other people will continue to challenge it – as they always have – with women and Aboriginal people having particular reasons for doing so. Their marginalised voices will add to the already existent but largely ignored, voices of honest men.*[321]

My fantasy about destroying the Lasseter myth… A myth can be forgotten, but not destroyed, and that's the case for the myth spawned by **Lasseter's Last Ride.** Other than some marginal tinkering when the Second CAGE Expedition returned with *The Diary*, Idriess chose to leave the text as it was rather than accommodate any revelations that emerged then or later. Most likely because he had enough to go on with, but probably also because it worked, it continued to sell well throughout his life. It sold as a book because it worked as a myth. Why it worked as a myth is the question Simon Ryan attempts to answer in **Lasseter's Last Ride** *and the Gothic narrative of failure.*[322]

Like Synge, Ryan studied at the University of Queensland where he was awarded a doctorate from the Department of English around the same time that Synge was beginning her studies. Ryan's career has remained firmly in the academy – Australian Catholic University in Canberra most recently – and myth has been on his mind throughout.

The Cartographic Eye: How Explorers Saw Australia was a 1990s book in which he examines how ways of seeing and representing – *the gaze* – supported the colonising project: *The privileged position of vision's role in knowledge generation should not disguise the fact that sight, and the discursive construction of sight, are mediated through a long history of repression and projection. The gaze of empire is ultimately narcissistic, as whatever it views is already a product of this gaze.*[323]

Perhaps inevitably, Ryan's *gaze* landed on the Lasseter myth and *Lasseter and the Mine with the Iron Door*[324] picks up on two knowns about Lasseter and weaves them together. The first is Lasseter's well documented appetite for reading, just about anything but with a penchant for science fiction and adventure. The second was his change of name; Lewis Hubert became Harold Bell Lasseter when he married for the second time in 1924, the same year in which a silent film was released – *The Mine with the Iron Door* – which was based on the book by the same name written by Harold Bell Wright which had been published the year before. Harold Bell Wright was, for the time, an enormously successful American writer who had made good from humble beginnings, segueing through sermonising to selling stories – science fiction and high-sierra adventures. He was well located to the task and spent the last three decades of his life in Arizona and California where, in 1936, a talkie version of *The Mine with the Iron Door* was made. By that time Lasseter was dead but Ryan contends that in the early 1920s Wright's fame and writing were influential in Lasseter's name change, and that it also reflected underlying identity conflicts and confusion. There was probably plenty of that, but he may just have been after a new start – a fresh name with a new family.

In *Lasseter's Last Ride and the Gothic narrative of failure* Ryan reviews the failings of the expedition in the light of its investment in the latest technologies.[325] With technology standing for colonialism and modernity – in contrast to Aboriginal inhabitants and presence in the saga – the *Gothic mode* allows Idriess: *a safety valve that excuses the failures of technology.* And *Lasseter's Last Ride* draws on all the devices of that *mode*: *Lasseter's Last Ride assembles an almost complete catalogue of Gothic topoi: a forbidding, haunted geography; dreams and visions; illegible manuscripts; stories within stories; a graveyard; humans reduced to a beast-like state; suf-*

fering and degradation; and, most importantly of all, a talismanic object that carries a curse.

And a hunchback to fill out the cast. Ryan notes some subtle differences between the 1931 and subsequent editions of the book which had to incorporate material from *The Diary*, regardless of which: *all identify a supernatural cause for Lasseter's death, which would both ennoble his end and insert it within the Gothic schema in a way that a simple death from privation would not.* Ryan concludes regarding the Expedition and the myth:

> *Lasseter's death was the result of a poorly organised expedition launched on the word of a confabulator who in all likelihood had never been to Central Australia. In order to build a heroic narrative upon a foundation of deceit and ineptitude, Idriess had to invent an oppositional force on which blame for failure could be placed. Departing from the rationalist machinery of the factual exploration journal, Idriess opted for a Gothic mode that provided a defence against the uneasiness that may have been produced by such a failure of technological modernity.*

Idriess made a myth out of a molehill – *a poorly organised expedition launched on the word of a confabulator who in all likelihood had never been to Central Australia.* For Micky Dewar it was a product of its time in terms of its subject matter and style and for Simon Ryan its dramatic conclusion was a way of resolving a narrative of failure into tragedy. But it will survive the mythbusters as Lesley Synge, the only insider to comment, came to believe: *it will somersault to its feet again, even without Lasseter and Ion Idriess to help.*

CHAPTER 17

Northcote

Walker was driven by a desire to understand a son's faith in the integrity of his late father. "I think Bob is sort of reaching back into the past and trying to mend his broken beginnings. Imagine still being compelled to go into the desert in your mid-80s, into the most hostile of environments and look in this enormous country for this missing seam of gold.

"It shows, I suppose, how the words that have been said about his father and himself have affected him in order to feel this extraordinary drive to vindicate the family name."

Victoria Hannaford, 2013.[326]

April 2020

Batmania – if only; but it wasn't to be and after only a couple of years, in 1837, it was renamed for a less contentious political patron – the Prime Minister, William Lamb, Viscount Melbourne. Just two years later John Batman died of syphilis, but by that time the grid for what would become a city was already laid out across lands he'd supposedly purchased from Wurundjeri elders. From bayside at St Kilda, Hoddle Street, named for the surveyor, defines a north-south axis passing through what, just a few years later, would be named after Stafford Henry Northcote. Originally a small number of comfortably large estates centred around William Rucker's spread; these started to give way to the clay pits and slaughter yards that fed the growth of the inexorably approaching city, which arrived at the doorstep with the housing boom of the 1880s. Absorbed within the City of Darebin a century later, gentrification has brought a cosmopolitan feel to what was a working class suburb that retains its left-leaning social inclinations despite carrying the name of an arch-conservative motherlander. Contradictions and cafés – a good place for a filmmaker.

Luke Walker's 2013 film, *Lasseter's Bones*, was on my radar within a few days of beginning my online search through Lasseter-land, and within a week I had a copy. From Birmingham and a brief stint in British soaps, Walker moved from acting to making films after relocating to Australia in 2004, including the award-winning 2008 documentary investigation into *Kenja*, a supposed self-empowerment technique focusing on *energy conversion*, founded in 1982 by Ken Dyers and his partner, Jan Hamilton – thus *Kenja*. Accusations, controversies and court actions were well in train when Walker and Melissa Maclean began their work on **Beyond our Ken**, just a few months before the release of which Ken Dyers killed himself. *Lasseter's Bones* also won awards and Walker took his time, the idea for the 2010 project germinating years before. And *PACmen,* released in 2017, followed the Republican presidential campaign of Ben Carson, Afro-American paediatric neurosurgeon and more, that crashed and burnt in the Super Tuesday primaries of 2016. Conservative, Seventh-Day Adventist – it was rumoured that Carson might even get a vice-presidential nod but, as things turned out, he had to settle for Secretary of Housing and Urban Development in the Trump Administration. Not bad from humble beginnings in Detroit, good enough for a 2009 miniseries starring Cuba Gooding Jr – **Gifted Hands.** Dyers, Lasseter, Carson – no shortage of self-confidence. Maybe it didn't end well for Dyers or Lasseter, but Carson did OK. The story of getting the go-ahead to get on board with the Carson campaign segues off a comment about Lasseter's optimism in the face of rejection:

Lasseter wrote hundreds of letters because he didn't see any reason why he shouldn't shoot for the stars. When you're working in documentary films you write a lot of Lasseter-type hopeful letters. I've written to people like Rupert Murdoch, and as soon as you write Dear Rupert at the top you realise that no matter what you write beneath, you're going to sound like a lunatic. I wrote to people on the presidential race four years ago and did get a bite – and found myself in the middle of a situation where I had to remind myself how I got there.

In the end Luke pulled that one off – for Lasseter it was very different: *He baited the hook by suggesting that he knew where there was a reef of gold. He managed to convince some people and then found himself out in the desert having to put one foot in front of the other trying to find it. He couldn't go back without any gold – to disgrace – he had to keep going.* A complicated story with a multi-generational cast; as a filmmaker he had to capture and condense the essence of the story – and the man:

People read the Lasseter story in different ways. I saw someone who was desperate to make something of himself; he didn't have anything – no money, no education, no right to try and be someone – but he didn't see any reason why that should stop him. And when you look at all the different times in his life when he tried to make something of himself it takes an enormous amount of resilience, determination and self-belief. And I found that quite inspiring.

But, however you read it, it ends up as tragedy. Not just for Lewis Hubert – or Harold Bell, or Das – Lasseter. I'm reminded of the sadness that Bob Lasseter expressed when he talked about his memories of his father before he left for Central Australia. Both Bob and his father lost their mothers early, Bob when he was eighteen and Lasseter senior at just eight. Ultimately Bob became the real subject of **Lasseter's Bones**, and Luke repeats his comment to reviewer Victoria Hannaford just after its release: *I feel his obsession with proving his dad wasn't a liar was about reaching back into the past and mending his broken beginnings.* With the idea germinating from soon after he arrived in Australia, it took four years to make: *When you don't have a lot of money to spend on something you spend what you've got – and that's time. Picking up and putting down the story – all on a shoestring..*

By the time the film was finished he felt he'd arrived at an understanding of Bob Lasseter and his father. But the interest that sustained him over those years started somewhere else. Luke Walker had family connections to Australia and had visited as a child. Even so, when he migrated in 2004 he was emotionally unprepared for the scale of his new home:

> When I became aware of the Lasseter story I tried to understand a country so big a seam of gold seven miles long could be lost in the centre of it – potentially worth a billion dollars. The Lasseter story means different things to different people – they see reflections of themselves in it. I've contributed to that. You get to the point where you've spent so much time going down rabbit holes that you realise you have to accept that that's it, I'm done. Although it was originally trying to get my head around the country I'd moved to, it became about deciphering a riddle – which can't be solved.

Making the film didn't solve the riddle but Luke opened up fresh burrows – lots of them over four years. Predictably, too many to be included in the film, though not forgotten, some of the most interesting leading into warrens and wild theories, idiosyncratic imaginings of some kind of alternative Lasseter universe. But it was the proponents that left their mark:

> They're interesting not necessarily because their theories have any validity, but often because of the 'Gollum' effect the reef has had on them. You see patterns in their thinking and behaviour that unifies them, despite all having disappeared down very different Lasseter rabbit holes. They've spent so long down these burrows they've often lost all perspective and can sometimes be comically suspicious that you're trying to steal their 'Precious'. One poor guy mortgaged his house to pay for expeditions and mining leases based on a theory that seemed quite delusional and was putting enormous pressure on his marriage. I felt very sorry for him and found myself trying to talk him out of pursuing it.

While most of those digressions didn't make the cut, one did – and led to a whole lot more digging. That was the Johanson connection that set his fellow Melbournian, Chris Clark, on his own burrowing. And to do that Luke capitalised on the work of a key predecessor:

> *I hired the researcher Murray Hubbard used. She helped me find out what had happened to Johanson and discovered that he'd put advertisements in newspapers trying to locate a daughter – Alvhild. That daughter was still alive, in her nineties, and I called her up and asked if I was speaking to Alvhild. She was confused because she didn't use that name and didn't know anything about his association to the Lasseter story. So when I told her about her father's advertisements she was, I think, enormously comforted, hearing that her dad had been trying to contact her – having been told her whole life that he didn't want anything to do with her. I ended up chatting to her son, Chris, and it sparked his curiosity.*

Sparking Chris' curiosity resulted in two more books for the Lasseter shelf. And Luke reckons that it all started with **Lasseter's Last Ride**: *If it wasn't for that book there would be no Lasseter obsession, he wouldn't have entered popular culture, he would have been in a few headlines and then forgotten.* Our conversation circles around his understanding of Idriess' strategy: *Lasseter wove a narrative into the diary and Idriess takes that unreliable narrative and turns it into his own version of events that doesn't have much value as a historical document, its value is cultural, as something that captured the public imagination.* And continues to, like Dick Smith who helped Luke to triangulate where the reef should be located based on Lasseter's reactions during his flight with Pat Hall from Ilbilba, and an informed estimate of how far Lasseter could have travelled by camel from where he camped with Paul Johns at Malagura Rockhole. And like the reef, even the Malagura Rockhole has taken on certain mythic qualities: *That rockhole has been taken off the maps, I haven't seen it on any map since the fifties, I didn't understand why that was until I found out that it was a sacred place. Or maybe they took it off the map because of the Lasseter story, too many people out there trying to find it.*

Our conversation turns to other films about Lasseter and a documentary interview with one of the few players in the original Expedition who commands respect – Phil Taylor. It was Taylor who ended up with what in **Lasseter's Last Ride** is called *The Stick ... one of the sandhill gods,* probably a *kupidji* or *churinga*, a sacred board that, in Idriess' rendition, is central to the Lasseter tragedy. That board existed and Blakeley, Taylor and Sutherland had its significance explained by a horrified Aboriginal man after they got back to Alice Springs from Ilbilba. The fiction that Idriess added to the reconstruction to sustain his plot was that they told him that Lasseter had been the first to touch it, to which he responds: *"He will never come back."* In Luke's recollection of the interview with Phil Taylor in the 1980s: *After he brought it home to England he put it above the mantlepiece for decoration and all sorts of things went wrong – people died, his fortunes turned for the worse – his wife became obsessed with the idea that it was due to the cursed totem board that he had brought. One night she pulled it off, chopped it into pieces and burnt it.*

That's similar but not quite the same as the account given by Billy Marshall-Stoneking in the 1980s, when Taylor was still alive and in Australia. In that account Taylor:

> *returned to England with his sacred board and married. Within a few months of his return, misfortune overtook his family with the deaths of several close relatives. Taylor, it is reported, fell into a state of depression and one night, while sitting in front of the fireplace, his eyes rested on the sacred board hanging over the mantlepiece. Standing up, he pulled the churinga down and then, taking an axe, chopped it into small bits, throwing the pieces on the fire.*[327]

Billy Marshall-Stoneking's informant in the 1980s was Bob Lasseter, who was Luke's window to the story thirty years later and who, with rheumy eyes still twinkling with conviction a decade on, for a few hours took me there too. As we are wrapping up I know we are both visualising Bob and Elsie's house in Seven Hills, the four-wheel-drive with its extraordinary ladder device on the roof which opens **Lasseter's Bones** still in the shed at the bottom of the garden. Well into his tenth decade, Bob won't be heading west in it again, but by being close by it probably helps him remain steadfast in his beliefs about a gold reef in the middle of the continent – and his father: *I think that he has a great capacity for faith; faith that his dad did not lie, and faith that the gold is out there. I think that Lasseter himself had faith in the fact that he would make something of himself. That's what drove him.*

CHAPTER 18

Docklands

*One of the many surprises to come from researching my recently completed documentary movie **The truth about Lasseter** was the number of well-known and significant people who became associated with expeditions to locate the mythical "lost" gold reef in Central Australia. … What really grabbed my attention, however, was coming across a group of photographs in the National Archives which portrayed an attempt that took place in late 1939, even as Australia entered the Second World War. Among the people participating in this venture was a United Australia Party senator from NSW (Adam Dein), the Northern Territory Director of Mines (W. A. Hughes), and popular writer of Australiana (Frank Clune). What particularly stood out were captions to these photographs which recorded that the expedition had been organised by a 'Mr. Morley Cutlack'.*

Chris Clark, September 7, 2018.[328]

April 2020

Chris Clark, the author of *The Encyclopedia of Australia's Battles*, was horrified to think that an esteemed predecessor might have been in the rogues gallery of charlatans and profiteers who fuelled the Lasseter myth for personal gain, as did Morley Aubrey Hermann Cutlack, some-time journalist and would be tycoon. While he too was a journalist, his namesake Frederic Morley Cutlack was a distinguished war correspondent and historian. But it was a close call – they were cousins (Chapter 10). Frauds, charlatans and rogues. As a military historian Chris Clark has thought about more than a few rogues and he was well trained. In the *Australian Dictionary of Biography* the entry for *Lasseter, Lewis Hubert (1890-1931)* lists occupation as: *impostor; prospector* – in that order. The entry, which dates to 1983, was written by G.P. (Gerry) Walsh, who was Chris Clark's mentor. Walsh was under no illusions about Lasseter – or about Idriess: *The myth of 'Lasseter's Lost Reef' has persisted and excited numerous further expeditions largely as a result of Ion Idriess's romantic novel Lasseter's Last Ride.*[329]

Chris Clark is speaking to me from the edge of the Melbourne CBD – Docklands. It's now more than half a century since containerisation sapped the economic lifeblood of Victoria Dock that had – in an Indigenous blink-of-the-eye – replaced the wetlands in which the Wurundjeri people harvested resources for millennia. Since the 1990s its pulse quickened again as heady, boomtime development brought investment and people – lots of them. But not now: *normally it's packed. I live right beside the Yarra and I overlook the river. There are a couple of bridges that would usually be full of people. Now I can see six people. As you said in your email – we live in the time of coronavirus.* My email – it's taken a while to get to this interview despite Chris being enthusiastic when I first made contact, and he reminds me of that while explaining the dangers of being blinded by detail, drawn too close by the siren call of Lasseter marginalia: *They're irrelevant if you focus on the man and find out what was in his head. Which was why I was so interested when you first contacted me and told me that you were approaching this as a psychiatrist. And I thought – bingo – you're in the perfect position to work out what was Lasseter's mental state.* Well, that's where I started, but not where the trail led.

For Chris, the task of disentangling Lasseter fact from fancy was grafted on to the rootstock of his professional career as a historian. From western Victoria, Chris graduated from Duntroon in 1972, moving from the late-1970s to the public service and, in 1991, gaining a doctorate from the Australian Defence Force Academy. His main interest was, and remains, military history; before retiring he headed the Office of Air Force History at the Air Power Development Centre in Canberra. What drew his attention to Lasseter was a brief telephone call in November 2010 to his mother, Ann: *from someone who asked if she was the daughter of Olof Johanson and what did she know about his involvement with gold exploration? She had taken down the man's name and phone number. He sounded well-educated, with an English tone of speaking ... He told her he was a film maker working on a documentary.*[330]

The caller was Luke Walker who was close to concluding research for **Lasseter's Bones.** Chris called him back and, although he had little additional information to offer, he was invited to the premiere of the film – which changed everything:

> *I was shocked when Luke said that there was a possibility that if Lasseter hadn't found the reef when he said he had, he was telling a story that he'd heard from somebody else – someone like Olof. And maybe he should have been looking for Johanson's Reef. That appalled me because of the possibility that Olof was the person peddling the fraud that the reef actually existed. I was interested in Olof from a family history point of view and I started researching the Lasseter story for* **Olof's Suitcase.** *I was trying to discover when and where Olof could have met up with Lasseter. It was suggested that they were in some sort of partnership together. But I looked at their two stories and I couldn't see any overlap and it was only from materials Luke came up with that were in Bob Lasseter's possession, that I realised that there were letters they'd exchanged.*

Alvhild Mathel Johanson – Ann Clark's birthname in 1924 – that had been the link for Luke Walker. Olof had been in the Western Australian goldfields in early 1930 when talk of the proposed CAGE Expedition was in the news. He made contact with Lasseter through the CAGE office in Sydney – and John Bailey. Although nobody, including Lasseter, knew who Johanson was, the name was in correspondence and being talked about, and Idriess embellished the scraps that he saw for his story. In the first edition of **Lasseter's Last Ride**, after describing *the fight in the desert* between Lasseter and Paul Johns, Idriess has Lasseter send Johns to Alice Springs with correspondence for the Government Resident and with instructions: *to return to Ilbilba with a bushman friend of Lasseter's named Jonahnnsen [sic] and remove the food dump to Lake Christopher over the West Australian border.*[331] A few pages later, while resting his camels at *Winter's Glen* Lasseter anticipates meeting *Johns and Johannsen at Lake Christopher, eighty miles west of the Glen*, and on the next page, having *found his reef*, Idriess depicts Lasseter making plans: *He would peg the reef, then return to the nearest soak he knew of, more than a day's travel away, then scout out towards Lake Christopher and wait for Johns and Johannsen with supplies.* Johannsen occurs once more in the first edition close to the end, as Lasseter is despairing: *Lasseter looked up at the skies; he was now always looking and listening. What on earth had happened to Johns and Johannsen, and the 'plane and everybody?* The differences in spelling were cleared up in subsequent editions and *Johannsen* is mentioned one more time in the versions from February 1932 that included the material he chose to incorporate from the Second CAGE Expedition, which in the case of the mention of Johannsen, is spiced with the wild speculation that *Johannsen and his mate* had been *speared by the blacks in the Rawlinson Range.*[332]

While the mention of Johannsen gave Idriess scope for invention, Luke Walker's comments set Chris Clark off on a tangent to his usual historical fare resulting in a book of family exploration and archival sleuthing – **Olof's Suitcase.**[333] During a moment of silence I imagine him looking out across empty streets and the Yarra. With bushfires followed by rain and pandemic shutdown the view is probably clearer than it's been for months. Clearing the air – that was part of the reason for **The Truth About Lasseter.**[334] Chris explains that what drives the historian – *getting to the nub of an issue* – forced him to look past the disputed claims and interpretations of people and events: *Once you examine the issues behind Lasseter's story you realise that it comes down to credibility – how truthful was he, what agenda was he running... The* *trouble was that when I was writing **Olof's Suitcase**, every time that I tried to go into the details, I found Lasseter taking over the story I really wanted to tell, which was about my grandfather.*

Perhaps another moment staring into the distance across a deserted cityscape – from a continent away how can you tell… Chris picks up the thread, his realisation that his project – figuring out and documenting the connection between his grandfather and Lasseter – was missed by most punters:

*Ultimately it was an unsatisfactory thing because the reaction that I got to **Olof's Suitcase** was: 'Yes all that's interesting, you solved the mystery of who Olof was and how he fitted in – but where's the gold…' They'd missed the point – the solution to understanding what drove Lasseter. From the correspondence he thought Olof had seen a reef a couple of years earlier, and he was going out to find it. That's what made me decide that I had to document what I knew about Lasseter.*

Chris is confident that he has solved the puzzle: *As far as I'm concerned I think I've got as close as anyone can get to what Lasseter was doing. If you look at his lifelong career of fantasising and lying and looking to people in authority for his own advantage – but not having much of anything to show for it – you realise he has tried to make use of his contact with Olof to reshape his expedition into Central Australia.* Another moment of silence – perhaps reviewing the logic trail, or maybe just another glance across deserted streets and bridges: *It's the only explanation for why – having initially told people that the reef lay off the western end of the MacDonnell Ranges – once he got out there he changed his story, saying that it was much further south. The only explanation for that is that Olof had told him.* What had gotten Lasseter that far – his font of hubris and happenstance – had run dry. All that was left was more of the same – lies:

The last letter that Lasseter wrote to his wife essentially said he'd found the reef and he was going to go out and peg it. That was his exit gambit; that's why he stayed out there with the Aborigines. He'd been caught out as not having a reef to show for the expedition and what he hoped was that they would come and find him and he could

continue the story – 'I've found it; it's out there and I've put pegs on it'.
He was hoping he would have another go, and to that end he needed to
make sure he was a figure of public sympathy. That's why he had to
create this story that he was being mistreated by the Aborigines, which is
totally fanciful; all the evidence is that they kept him alive. He was
timing all that – he stayed out there as long as he could – it was only
when he decided that he had pushed his luck that he decided to go in.

In Chris' pantheon of rogues Lasseter is up there and Idriess is not far
behind, recycling the false claims and devious obfuscations, carefully
selected and wrapped in outback fantasies. Idriess may have been the first
out of the blocks but there have been many since and I explain to Chris
the way I've tried to categorise the accounts and theories. As each name
is raised there's not a lot to say, for most authors their motivations and
credentials are obvious. Those whose work is more recent and have built
on others' research push a particular button for Chris – like Warren
Brown:

He's a frustration because he wrote as a journalist, he went through the
evidence and there's some original research on a couple of the figures. In
*the final section he got onto **Olof's Suitcase** – soon after it came out –*
but he only absorbed that I'd figured out who Olof was. He
didn't understand the impact of Olof's connection to Lasseter and what
it did to the rest of the story that Lasseter had been peddling. And
*what infuriated me with **Lasseter's Gold** [335] is that it is just*
repeddling and repackaging the myth. The clue is on the cover, the
slasher – 'It's out there somewhere'. No – it's not!

Maybe Chris has too much faith in the power of evidence and reason
to shift beliefs and behaviours. And some people can listen to the evidence and accept it while, at the same time, remaining true to what it
disproves. That's Chris' take on Warren Brown – marshalling the
evidence of fraud and fabrication but encouraging the fantasy – *It's out*
there somewhere. Chris continues on the theme of contradictory beliefs
resting easily alongside: *You're dealing with the same sort of reaction that*
you would have got from Lasseter himself. He returns to where we started
– his hope for some kind of understanding of Lasseter's state of mind.

He's thought about it a lot and is convinced that: *Lasseter wasn't mad or delusional, but he had a weird, strange personality.* In his chronological synthesis of Lasseter research Chris has been drawn to the impact of early traumas – the death of his mother, the loss of his home, his father's heavy drinking and abusive behaviour, and a censorious aunt/caretaker: *The tendency that Lewis exhibited throughout his adult life towards blurring the distinction between fact and fantasy, largely as a way or escaping the harsh realities of his circumstances, can most probably be traced back to his formative years at Bamganie and Meredith.*[336] Ultimately what we get with Lasseter, though, is a *weird, strange personality.* And drawing on the evidence of Lasseter's early years Chris believes that was evident early:

> *The descriptive variants that most closely seem to apply to him would be 'neurotic narcissist', where an individual exhibits low self-esteem rather than a monstrous ego – often as a result of an abusive childhood, such as Lewis suffered – and seeks recognition and validation by constantly inventing grandiose stories in which they are the central figure; and 'unprincipled narcissist', which refers to an antisocial, charlatan, fraudulent, exploitative, deceptive and unscrupulous type.*

Docklands; a continent away in the time of coronavirus. Probably like here, in Cairns, a lot of time to think. Our conversation lasted much longer than either of us expected – but it's at an end. And for Chris it's the end of the Lasseter journey: *To a certain extent the reason I said* **The Truth About Lasseter** *was my last word on the matter is that, having decided that Lasseter was a conman and a fraud, I don't think he is worth any more of my time, I'd much rather go on to other things.*

Olof
Johanson,
1918.

Adl. 20. Aug 18

CHAPTER 19

One More River to Cross

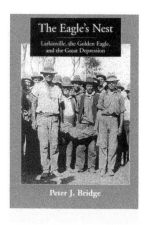

I knew Ion Idriess' "Lasseter's Last Ride" and read it years ago. Knowing the area covered very well through many expeditions during many years I was amazed with the 49 major factual mistakes which I listed. Ion when he wrote was essentially an east coast man out of his depth in The Centre. That book has persuaded folk that the reef was fact not FANCY…

Sincerely Michael Terry F.R.G.S.

P.S. we of The Centre & especially prospectors call it "Lasseter's Last Lie"

Michael Terry, January 1979.[337]

On 2nd November 1930 Lasseter was alone – Johns had left him at Ilbilba two days earlier and was making his way slowly to Hermannsburg. Errol Coote was stranded at Ayers Rock. And on that day, several hundred kilometres south, Louis Bailey extracted a troubling upper molar that had belonged to Edmund Colson, cameleer and brother to Fred Colson of the CAGE saga. Louis and Edmund were part of Michael Terry's Endeavour prospecting party which had been heading to the Petermanns while the First CAGE Expedition was packing and repacking the Thornycroft and Fred Colson's Chevrolet in Alice Springs. Exactly two years later Michael Terry was back in Lasseterland with Ben Nicker and other members of the Emu Mining team and found a message scrawled onto the dry bed of Lake Christopher at the western edge of the Rawlinson Range. Terry's find marked the westernmost extent of Lasseter's journey, where – perhaps – he waited in vain for Olof Johanson. Terry found virtually nothing else – but others did. The legend was kept alive not only in the retelling but in the refinding – things, maps, connections – anything with even the faintest hint of authenticity was enough to get money flowing – just like in 1930. Authentic or fabricated, turning up by coincidence or design, things found buried or on ebay have fired greed or curiosity. Five months after Michael Terry wrote his letter from Glebe Point Road, Ion Llewellyn Idriess died just twenty kilometres north, in a Mona Vale nursing home. Two years later Michael Terry was gone as well.

Fifty years earlier, on 15th April 1932, as the revised edition of **Lasseter's Last Ride** was being arranged for display in the Angus & Robertson bookstore, Idriess wrote from West Street Paddington to Australia's tenth Prime Minister – Joseph Lyons – with a copy of **Prospecting for Gold** which, he noted: *if you were seriously considering gold prospecting as a possible help to Australia at this time, the contents of the book would give you a practical insight on the subject.*[338] Lyons had been Prime Minister for only a few months, heading the United Australia Party that had split the Labor Party the year before. At that time he had been Minister for Works and Railways in the Scullin government – he would have heard more than a little about prospecting for gold in Central Australia. But he must have been interested because two weeks later V.C. Bagot, the Private Secretary to the Treasurer, wrote to Idriess to let him know that *Mr. Lyons has been daily expecting the arrival of your book, but it has not yet come to hand* – and requesting that another copy be dispatched.

Just a few months later the Prime Minister received a letter from Theodore Price in London, spruiking the British Australian Prospecting Company and its plans for air and land exploration of the country just to the west of where Lasseter had disappeared. Idriess knew about it and included a description, verbatim from the prospectus, inside the back cover of the 1933 editions of *Lasseter's Last Ride: A London company is including in the equipment of its expedition a three-engined aeroplane, two scout planes, three six-wheeled tractors, and a light boring machine; and with an efficient staff is prepared to prospect an area of fifteen thousand square miles of unknown country.* Price's letter to the Prime Minister begins: *Dear Sir, knowing how interested you are in anything that will be of assistance to Australia, especially at this critical period, I enclose herewith particulars of an expedition.* And before concluding, an afterthought teaser: *the British International Film Co. ... is sending camera men to make special pictures.*[339] He'd heard it all before.

The promise of solving economic woes with mining magic was – and still is – a perennial winner. And a crisis is an opportunity. Lyons died in office in April 1939 in the leadup to another and his successor, Earle Page, lasted just nineteen days. Six months later, on 13th August with the country again at war, a letter was sent by Walter Cousins at Angus & Robertson to Prime Minister Robert Menzies with an offer:

> *Three of Australia's ablest writers; Ion L. Idriess, Frank Clune, and E.V. Timms, have expressed their desire to put their talents at the service of your government. All three men are successful Australian writers whose names are very well known throughout the Common-wealth and beyond it. They are men with wide practical knowledge of Australia and each in his way is able to weild [sic] the pen vividly and accurately. All are Diggers.*[340]

Idriess had a busy war – sixteen books with ten on military matters. While his most popular works were behind him he kept up the output for another two decades – Idriess was a household name. But in March 1930 it was a very different matter. Idriess was just able to pay his way as a magazine writer and had only one poorly-received book to his credit – *Madman's Island.* The second Idriess book to be released, in February 1931, seven months before *Lasseter's Last Ride,* was *Prospecting for Gold.* Written within a few weeks, it was dropped into a Depression-primed audience hungry for any scrap of hope, be it prospects of a Central Australian find that would rival the rush forty years earlier, sparked by Paddy Hannan and Tom Flanagan near what

... the westernmost extent of Lasseter's journey ...
Michael Terry at Lake Christopher.

That's where Lasseter crossed the river...
Lasseter's Grave near Shaw Creek.

Russell Hill workers camp c. 1926: Lasseter second from right, top row.

would become Kalgoorlie – or a self-help manual for the man in the street to get a slice of the action. In August 1931 *The Talk of Sydney* column in *The Daily Telegraph* had two juxtaposed snatches by *The Gossip* set against an image of a youthful and thoughtful *Mr I. L. Idriess*. Under the header, *The Gold Trail*, the first alerted the reader: *Few would have suggested before the world tasted Depression that a book entitled "Prospecting for Gold" would ever prove to be a best-seller. And yet, a book by that title, written by the young Sydney naturalist and traveller, I.L. Idriess, is being eagerly bought up in the thousands.* And in case *Sydney naturalist and traveller* were not sufficient credentials, it continues just below under the header *Lasseter's Biographer*:

> *This fact, of course, is a commentary on the times, and your prospector today might easily prove to be an ex-professional man grappling hope-fully with the very old opponent, Circumstance. Idriess, who has received flattering notices from abroad, is also the author of "Madman's Island" and, I was told yesterday, has been specially commissioned to write "Lasseter's Last Ride," a novel version of that recent undoubted epic of lonely striving and daring in Central Australia.*[341]

Both pieces were probably written by Idriess, a bit of cross publicity that even provided an opportunity to kindle some interest in **Madman's Island**. Idriess was also likely to have been *Warrigal*, the pseudonymous author of a column in *The Land* which appeared just a month later under the title UNFINISHED EPIC OF "DAS" LASSETER: *Twentieth Century Treasure-Hunt on Australia's Farthest Frontier – A Gripping Story*:

> *From Lasseter's letters, from the company's records, from the experiences of the survivors of the party, and from his own knowledge of the country, Mr. Idriess has compiled a gripping story, a bush epic that will command attention throughout the English-speaking world. "Lasseter's Last Ride," with its appearance of fiction and its unimpeachable adherence to fact, is a unique tale of actual happenings in the heart of Australia, a hitherto virgin field for the writers of the world.*[342]

When that article was published in September 1931 the first copies of **Lasseter's Last Ride** were in the stores and on the jacket was an advertisement: *Second Edition, Revised and Enlarged. With 15 illustrations*

– Price 5/- PROSPECTING FOR GOLD. From the Dish to the Hydraulic Plant. By ION L. IDRIESS. With Introduction by F.S. MANCE, Under-Secretary for Mines, N.S.W. Below that are three *APPRECIATIONS*, the first attributed to *The Bulletin* and probably crafted by Idriess to suggest demand and drive sales that, till then, were slow: *'Prospecting for Gold' has struck an eager market. It has been only a few weeks on the bookstalls and already a second edition has been called for … Idriess yarns away, as one prospector to another, in language that nobody from the rawest newchum to Judge Curlewis, should find beyond him.*

The first printing run of **Lasseter's Last Ride** was 1,500 books; there were three more that year and another seven by the end of 1932, totalling 18,000 copies in circulation in Australia. But in mid-1931 Idriess was looking for a marketing strategy. Bob Buck was news but had not made it to Sydney; after reporting in Hermannsburg in April that he had found Lasseter's body he had travelled with Walter Gill to Alice Springs and then back to the gravesite in the Petermanns. But soon after they returned to Alice Springs Buck was heading to Sydney, where a confected reputation had preceded him. On 12th July, barely six weeks after Lasseter's death was announced, Idriess wrote to Walter Cousins at Angus & Robertson:

> *Bob Bucks [sic] owner of Tempe Downs Station and allegedly the best bushman in Australia, the man who found Lasseter's body & was also the bushman for the Mackay expedition, is due in Sydney in a fortnight. He is to be, I believe, leader of the expedition which is to go out again and search for Lasseter's reef. He has photos of the grave & all that sort of thing. His arrival will help further publicity. Also, it will make stronger the weakest chapter in the book for I have only the barest details as to his final tracking of Lasseter.*[343]

Later in that letter Idriess discusses placing articles in various newspapers: *at a time when I am convinced a gold boom is again pending.* He goes on, noting that: *Big Westralian men are exhibiting that nugget at Canberra simply to interest Federal Politicians. Well, if the suggested article appears in the Herald, it would attract the notice of those Westralian men, then when the nugget comes in Sydney we would have a lever to work on and possibly would be allowed to exhibit the book with the specimen.* The next day Cousins responded asking Idriess to call into the Angus & Robertson offices to discuss a *par.* in the *Herald* which might also be used in country papers, adding: *particularly if we link your name with the new book. Suppose we hold the copy back until the arrival of Bob Bucks [sic]. He is sure to get some publicity, and we could pack our publicity of both books at the same time.*[344] Cousins didn't comment on the *Big Westralian men,* but he would have known exactly what Idriess was talking about even though the Golden Eagle only made it to Canberra and Melbourne, where the power and the money was.

Just over a year earlier, in June 1930, south of Coolgardie and not far from Widgiemooltha in Western Australia, Micky Larkin found a nugget in an area thereafter known as Larkinville. Within a couple of months there were some 200 prospectors on the field but, despite finds, only about a dozen claims were returning. Then, on 15th January 1931 Jim Larcombe, aged seventeen and who claimed not to know much about prospecting but had a *feeling* that there was gold in his father's claim, struck a nugget which, with his dad's help, was unearthed and weighed in at 78 pounds. Named the Golden Eagle for its shape it put Larkinville on the map – as exemplified by the last stanza of the poem – *Come along to Larkinville* by *"Dryblower" Murphy* in the *Sunday Times* just three days after the find:

> *There's a waterbag and swag-strap, there's a dolly and a drill,*
> *What though eventide is nearing,*
> *Life's lugubrious clouds are clearing,*
> *For our inmost hearts are hearing – "Come Along to Larkinville!"*[345]

Within a month the nugget was sold to the Western Australian Government and a cheque presented to Jim and his dad for more than £5,000 by John – Jack – Scaddan – a man who knew the goldfields and had been Labor leader and Premier. He'd also been with the National and Country parties before leaving parliament in 1924, returning in March 1930 when he became Minister for Railways, Mines, Police, Forests and Industry in the Mitchell Labor government. Not long after that he was briefed by Michael Calanchini of the Mines Department about correspondence regarding Lasseter's claims and a request for financial support from Ern Bailey. Noting that several prospecting parties had been to the area, in June 1930 Scaddan informed Bailey that the Western Australian Government would not assist.[346] Just months after Jim's find, the Golden Eagle, by then the property of the Western Australian Government, was toured through the Eastern States, Jack Scaddan presided over *a Private Exhibition of the "Golden Eagle" Nugget recently discovered at Larkinville, near Coolgardie* held at the Reception Room of the Melbourne Town Hall on Monday 29th June 1931. Four months later, on 28th October, two weeks after *The Diary* was unearthed by the Second CAGE Expedition, the Golden Eagle was melted down at the Perth Mint.

Soon after the Golden Eagle tour, in September 1931, Bob Buck was carousing in Alice Springs before setting out on the Second CAGE Expedition to locate the reef. At that time the first copies of *Lasseter's Last Ride* were being sold and on the front flap of the jacket, below the header *Gold! Gold! In Centralia* the first and last paragraphs of a generously flattering description that Idriess probably crafted concluded: *No man in Australia is better qualified than Mr Idriess to write the story. His own experiences, as a wanderer for years with just such a tribe as that which dragged Lasseter to his death, peculiarly fit him to piece together from scraps of letters found buried beneath old camp fires, the tragic story of the ill-fated prospector's last days.*

Peculiarly fit him... Ion Idriess had never been *a wanderer for years with just such a tribe.* And he knew already that the story would change, the final paragraph on the flap anticipating that there was more to come: *Another expedition has set out to succeed where the last one failed. Readers of "Lasseter's Last Ride" will be able to follow its fortunes with an interest, an understanding and a sympathy they could not otherwise have.* And other expeditions did set out – lots of them. None generated the interest of the CAGE Expeditions, then or since, and Idriess is responsible for that. But not by a towering literary achievement, an antipodean mythopoeic masterpiece. *Lasseter's Last Ride* is, in fact, quite ordinary, not much better than the entirely fictitious *The Lost Reef.* Nor is it Idriess' best work. Its success stemmed from how Idriess and his publishers managed three processes – writing it, revising it and selling it.

Writing it

Idriess was in the right place at the right time. Not Central Australia or the outback but settled in Sydney as the Depression took hold. Eighteen months earlier he had gone against the demographic press of the times, moving from north Queensland with premature debts due on his body from War injuries, two decades of frontier life in the tropics and his heavy smoking and drinking. He had a project on the go, revising his wartime diaries into what would be published as *The Desert Column* – but he was struggling financially. Nearly four decades later, on being congratulated for having been made an Officer in the Order of the British Empire, Idriess wrote to Aubrey Cousins, son of his old boss, George Cousins, noting of what must have been a critical point in his career: *I never thought of "Honors" etc when writing Lasseter's Last Ride. All I was battling for then was a Ride for myself, and a crust.*[347]

Battling – probably – but Idriess had form living on his wits and had experience. From his youth in Broken Hill, prospecting days in north Queensland, and years as a journalist, he knew enough about mining and what the public read to string together an informed and good *yarn*. *Prospecting for Gold* had his attention and then another story appeared on the horizon. Through contacts – maybe Coote, Warnecke or Burlington – he soon had the inside running. He knew he had to work fast to cross-promote the Lasseter book and *Prospecting for Gold*, and to make sure he was first out of the blocks ahead of his fellow journalist – Coote. To assure as close to in-real-time information as possible his relationship with Ern Bailey was probably assiduously cultivated and to that end he was careful to make sure that nothing was written that would compromise the Company or embarrass its Directors.

With the known story to the middle of 1931 relatively uninspiring – infighting, no gold, the failures of technology to master the challenges of the bush – he chose to leaven the dull grind of what was known with accounts of pluck and courage, and descriptions of cultural exotica. That was entirely consistent with what was being written about remote Australia at the time. His biggest challenge was how to finish what was, in essence, a story of failure and, fortunately for Idriess, that was resolved by

Lasseter's death. Through his CAGE Company contacts he had privileged access to the information that was sent to Sydney after Buck found the body and, by that time, Coote was *persona-non-grata* with the Company and the gold bug had taken him elsewhere. They also provided access to Lasseter's wife, Irene, and Idriess and George Ferguson visited her in Kogarah in the middle of 1931 to secure material. With nothing but a few names on the scraps of paper found near Lasseter's body, Idriess chose to frame the whole story as a tragedy. He utilised the relative silence of the months after Lasseter and Johns separated to give free rein to a tale of sorcery that, in moving slowly to a conclusion that had been anticipated by Idriess' creative repurposing of the *sacred board* episodes, also allowed him to infill with quasi-ethnographic vignettes of Aboriginal tribal life. It was pure fiction and Gothic horror to boot. It worked a charm.

Revising it

Revising it was a very different matter – he had created a winning narrative and he had to make changes while preserving it. Idriess finished the first edition with a short paragraph that invited a sequel: *But Lasseter's dream lives. A big expedition has already been formed to carry on where he left off. This spirit will watch the dream come true.* He'd finished with Lasseter so what would have worked well was for the Second CAGE Expedition to come up with the goods – the fabulous reef. What he got was no gold and more Lasseter. That was a problem; **Lasseter's Last Ride** was selling well and the last thing he wanted was to undo the fictional device that held the story together, particularly as he had been at pains to emphasise – *its unimpeachable adherence to fact.*

The solution was to secure any material that was relevant to the story, frame elements in ways that would support the existing text, ensure that nothing was included that could embarrass his sources and benefactors, and make certain nobody else had an opportunity to examine it. With or without an arrangement with Bob Buck or Frank Green, he pulled it off. If Green or Irene read the material in what came to be called *The Diary,* they never said. Regardless of who paid Irene – Idriess, the CAGE Directors or Angus & Robertson – advantage was taken of Lasseter's destitute widow. And whether all the material brought back by Green made it to the vaults of Angus & Robertson and, over three decades later, to the Mitchell Library – it was not seen by anyone until Bob Lasseter in 1958. The revised version of **Lasseter's Last Ride** kept the text intact with just a few cosmetic changes, and three new chapters added nothing but some carefully selected quotes and a few line maps.

Selling it

Two factors were critical to selling the story. The first was Idriess himself – self-promoter *extraordinaire*. With two decades behind him of writing for magazines and newspapers under a number of pseudonyms, and his contacts through Angus & Robertson, he knew how to get flattering mentions in the right places, much of which he wrote himself. He also ensured that those pseudo-reviews emphasised his supposed credentials, in turn reinforced with the imprimatur of forewords penned by distinguished public figures – Herbert Basedow in Australia and General William Birdsell for the Empire market. In 1937 Walter Cousins even tried to organise a similar contribution from Herbert Hoover to charge up American sales.[348] The second critical factor was luck. With *Lasseter's Last Ride* and *Prospecting for Gold* he fell on his feet – a tale of riches and a manual to find them as the country slipped further into the Depression, and just as the largest nugget found in Australia was unearthed and being exhibited across the country. His style was right for the times and resonated with public attitudes and appetites. It was a story that sold – and a failed prospector and a journeyman journalist became household names.

One more river to cross

Idriess and Lasseter were men of their time and had much in common. They were born in the same decade and lost their mothers early. Both were bright but not favoured by family or fate to an easy young adulthood. Despite that, they were optimists, unrelenting boosters of developing national resources and, along the way, partisan promoters of an Australian identity, and wrote opinion pieces on issues of the day as the *Gouger* and the *Gleaner*. But there were also significant differences; the teetotal Lasseter would probably not have socialised easily with the heavy-drinking Idriess. And despite being bigamously married Lasseter was, at heart, a family man. Idriess never sorted out that part of his life. Idriess was famous in his lifetime as Australia's largest-selling author but has been largely forgotten since his death. Lasseter is known to us only because he died – and because of Ion Idriess. In October 1926 that was all in the future when Lasseter penned several pieces for the *Canberra Community News*.[349] In the section *Camp Notes*, the *Gleaner* lightly recounted goings-on in the capital followed by *"Gleaner's" Dream* as a letter to the editor:

> I dreamt I swam the Styx the other night and applied to St. Peter for admission to Paradise. "Hm! Hm! You're a pretty dilapidated specimen to want to come in here; what have you done to entitle you to admission?" Well, I felt very small and mean, and couldn't think of much to recommend me, but at last a bright idea struck me, and I said, "Well, dear St. Peter, I haven't done much good in the world, it is true, but I've tried to make the lives of the children a bit brighter by building playgrounds for them," St. Peter considered awhile and then said, "Well, you've got a pretty bad record, but that last evens up the score, so I'll let you in, so peel off and swim for it." Then I saw that there was another river flowing 'twixt me and him, and I thought of the old song, "One more river to cross," so in I went, and was just getting out on the other side where St. Peter was opening the gate for me, when a motor car came by and said, "Honk! Honk!" and I woke up. Now, Mr. Editor, I want to know if I shouldn't sue that motor driver for 00 dollars, as just think of the chance I missed. I might have been in Heaven now![350]

One more river to cross – Lasseter was a religious man, that river was the Jordan:

> One more river to cross
> I pray, good Lord, shall I be the one?
> One more river to cross.
> Oh, wasn't that a wide river
> River of Jordan, Lord
> Wide river
> There's one more river to cross.

When they flow, which is not often, Shaw and Irving Creeks run off the Petermann range. That's where Lasseter *crossed the river*. A few weeks before and just over the border, somewhere around Lake Christopher, Lasseter must have understood that it was all coming unstuck, whatever it was. And all that is left is a story that became a myth, told and retold, to become a kind of truth.

THE GOLDEN EAGLE NUGGET.

Two interesting snapshots of the Golden Eagle Nugget taken at Kalgoorlie. The top picture shows the Premier with his hand on the nugget. The bottom picture was taken in the Commonwealth Bank with a number of officials grouped round the nugget, including Sir James Mitchell, Mr. Scaddan, Mr. Larcombe (senr.), the Mayor of Kalgoorlie, and Mr. Claude de Bernales.

Block by courtesy of "The Cat" and "The Mirror."

Big Westralian men ... The Golden Eagle Nugget – *Mullewa Mail*, Saturday 14th February 1931.

CHAPTER 20

Manunda

That one word 'recognition' slipped like an oiled eel through Lasseter's powerful fingers. He craved, yearned, begged and probably died for recognition. But it never came to him.

Murray Hubbard, 1993.[351]

August 2020.

Wallaby Walk – Koala Court to the west and Ibis Avenue to the east, and just beyond that is Lily Creek and the railway line to Kuranda. In service up the Macalister Range from 1891, it took fifteen years to build and a major rockfall put it out of operation in 1910 – probably caused by the same wet season deluge that flooded Hydro Bob Clacherty's home and business on the banks of the Barron River. He headed for higher ground and settled in Mount Molloy, and a few years later Jack Idriess was there as well. Hydro Bob's grandson, Desmond, published **On Lasseter's Trail** in 1989 and had to incorporate a major revision after **The Search for Harold Lasseter** came out in 1993 (Chapter 10). And the author of that book, the key sleuth in this story, is in Cairns on his way to the Tablelands.

His next stop will be the Feathers 'n' Friends Cottage in Julatten – on Clacherty Road.

It's the end of August and I'm in the NRMA Caravan Park in Manunda just fifteen kilometres from my home. Right next to Manunda is Manoora, and it would be nice to think that the suburbs were named with the original inhabitants in mind – Djabugay towards the Tablelands, Yirrganydji to the north, and Yidinji and Gunggandji to the south. Aboriginal names for sure but nothing local – both suburbs were named after ships that had been launched in Glasgow in 1935, and as the *The Courier-Mail* explained:

> *It is interesting to note that Manunda, the name of the Adelaide Steam-ship Company's first modern inter-State motor passenger liner, is an aboriginal word, meaning "a place in the vicinity of water." Manoora is the name of a township in South Australia. It is an aboriginal word, meaning "a spring," and was chosen as the name of the new vessel for its euphonious sound and because it conforms with the company's policy of giving its motor ships names beginning with "M" and ending with "A."* [352]

The Courier-Mail – born of a merger and in the Murdoch stable for nearly a century, and I'm in the caravan park's communal dining area talking to someone who worked for what eventually became another News Corp masthead, the *Townsville Bulletin*. But that was back in the 1970s after he'd cut his teeth with the *Melbourne Sun* and *The Age*. Melbourne-born, Murray Hubbard is a Queenslander now and what has drawn him from the Gold Coast as COVID alerts are flashing through those communities – is birds. Or, more specifically, photographing them, and the highlight was just a kilometre away at Centenary Lakes – *Nectarinia jugularis*, an olive backed sunbird: *I waited about half an hour and sure enough a female sunbird turned up and posed on the end of these highly colourful flowers. Then she took off and I kept on snapping and I have a ballerina pose of this little bird standing on a pink-purple flower.*

Wildlife photography turns out to be a recent passion. But cameras have been part of his stock-in-trade since he began his career as a journalist, which landed him in Townsville in the 1970s, after which he started his own PR company and moved to the Gold Coast. And another career – co-host of *Grandstand* on the 7 Network that drew on his passion for AFL from growing up as a St Kilda tragic, and almost ended up with him being crowned as KFC Hubbard – or, more precisely, KTC:

> *On grand final day 1985 we arrived at the studio to do our last Grand-stand of the year and there's an esky full of beer. My co-compère Mike Murray said 'Fosters are looking after us'. So we had a couple of beers and introduced the show, then passed off to Peter Landy and Lou Richards to compare the game – and had another beer. Quarter time comes along – another beer. At half time Mike said 'we'd better thank the sponsors – I'll throw to you and you just do it'. Back live on air, no delays, Mike's on cue, 'I think we should thank our sponsors for support-ing the show through the '85 season'. So I came in with 'that's a good idea Mike and I'd like to thank Fosters firstly – a great supporter of our show, and secondly Kenfucky Tried Chicken'.*

Live-to-air on grand final day – Murray tells the story with a smile. He's a good raconteur and I can imagine him as a broadcaster, but at heart he's a journalist and along the way he was Queensland Country Press Journalist and a finalist for a Walkley award – three times each. Investigative journalism is in his bones and is responsible for his approach to Lasseter, although that doesn't explain how that story ended up on his radar:

> *People used to say that today's newspaper is tomorrow's fish and chip wrapper. I wanted to leave a mark so that when I'm gone there would be something left. That was the motivation. One day I was at home watching* **The Man from Snowy River.** *The credits rolled over and included almost the whole Lovick family. They were friends of ours, we used to go horse-riding in the mountains when we were kids. Jack was the overall consultant, Charlie was the master of horse, John was an extra. I thought how great it would be to have your name on something like that. Within ten minutes I had the idea – Lasseter. I knew nothing except the name, but then I started to read and I realised I wanted to know who the bloke was. I began researching and the first break was the Tenterfield library. That was like catching your first fish – gets you in*

for life – you're hooked. I wasn't remotely interested in the gold aspect, it was the man – who was he, where did he come from, what did he do…

Tenterfield – where Idriess spent his first years, but he was long gone by the time Lasseter was contributing Tabulam Tinklings to the *Tenterfield Star* just before the War. Soon after Murray began his research the information started to stack up and he was on the road, tracing a life that had ended more than half a century before. He met Bob and Beulah, children from both of Lasseter's wives, visited the sites of his early life and began to write it as a novel. He soon realised that wasn't going to flow and restructured it to follow the search itself rather than just to tell a Lasseter story: *the reason that it wasn't written chronologically was that it lost the excitement of the search.* In the end **The Search for Harold Lasseter** contains two stories, the search itself and Murray's attempt to let Lasseter speak. To that end his experience as a journalist was critical: *As a journalist in my era you quoted people in a story but you didn't have an opinion. The book allowed me to link documents that hadn't seen the light of day before, so that the reader could follow the trail. That fulfilled what I wanted to do – to let Lasseter have a voice. In the final chapter I got to have my say on the basis of what I'd discovered.* And in the end, through that voice, Murray developed sympathy for his subject: *Lasseter left a wife and three kids with no money. He was a real man, he wasn't just a bloke in the outback; he had a life back in Sydney – before the desert. He tried his hardest; he failed at lots of things. But he had great ideas and that was what I wanted him to be remembered for – that there was more to this guy than a bullshit artist.*

Murray's journey with Lasseter began when the name entered his consciousness as he was thinking of a project. He's clear that the reason it was there at all was because of Idriess. He hadn't read any of his books at that stage and remembers his first find: *I went to a fete at my daughter's school on the Gold Coast and I saw a tattered book, I think the second edition of* **Lasseter's Last Ride**. *The cover was almost falling off and as I was thumbing through I saw it was signed by Jack Idriess. I've still got it.* The power of the writing, for Murray, is that Idriess knew how to tell a tale and wasn't shy of what it took to make it work: *Storytellers invariably weave some fiction with the facts so that they can hold everything together. And Idriess was a great storyteller. So if he had an inkling he would try to* *check it and then be flexible so as to string it all together. You have to have a thread to connect the story.* That resulted in a good book, *albeit romanticised,* but also a legend: *Idriess started it, he took Lasseter out of the newspapers and into the libraries. Jack created the legend through* **Lasseter's Last Ride***. Simple as that.* And Murray is clear about why the legend lives on:

> *I've had people say 'I hope you don't solve it because, if you do, then that's the end of Lasseter'. The key part of my book was the discovery that he was incarcerated in a boys home at the time that he said he was crossing Australia. He couldn't have done it. But people love legends and don't want to destroy the mystery; when you take that away, what's left…*

Murray pulled it off, he wrote something that will end up more than *tomorrow's fish and chip wrapper.* A decade later he was in New York on a follow-up trip funded by Dick Smith to try and find out more about the *American years,* and found a copy of **The Search for Harold Lasseter** in the New York Public Library: *That made my trip.* And the search probably had collateral outcomes. Not long after the book was released Murray was contacted by Ray Connor, at that time the Liberal Party member for Nerang in the Queensland Legislative Assembly. Ray had read it and wanted to discuss another project. Together they researched and Murray wrote the manuscript for **The Day of the Roses** about the 1977 Granville train disaster: *It was an attempt to understand post-traumatic stress.* Whether it was influenced by his immersion in the Lasseter saga or not, it worked as well. Directed by Peter Fisk, the two-part 1998 dramatisation won the 1999 AACTA award for Best Telefeature, Mini-series or Short Run Series.

It's near midday and other campers are arriving to use the facilities and between the nearby caravans Murray spots his wife on approach. Their caravan is hitched and they have a check-out deadline. Certified members of Grey Nomads Australia – even in coronavirus times the journey goes on. They're heading north to Idriess country – and Clacherty Road.

*...a ballerina pose of this little bird
standing on a pink-purple flower:*
Nectarinia jugularis.

Lewis and Florence Lasseter with Lillian,
United States, c. 1907.

*... there was more to this guy
than a bullshit artist.*

Harold and Irene Lasseter
with Bobby and Betty, Canberra 1924.

CHAPTER 21

The Promised Land

Everybody regarded him as Happy Jack; but I knew the other side from Wendy – he wasn't Happy Jack.

Beverley Eley, 2007.[353]

July 2020

Angel Gabriel Modernises Promised Land.[354] It was 1938, and the power behind the change was electricity. And the celestial being in question was Angel Gabriel Capararo, ninth of thirteen children from near Muswellbrook, who had survived much in his 43 years, four of which were on the Western Front. Within two years of returning to Australia he'd married a local girl from Gleniffer and they eventually settled in The Seven Mile, in The Promised Land. So called, Beverley Eley tells me, because when Angel Gabriel arrived in this valley surrounded by forested slopes he found grasslands, ready for grazing. Grasslands; maybe country fire-managed by Gumbaynggirr across the long time before – but more likely cleared by cedar-getters and the other timber-cutters that followed the first European penetration along the Nambucca and Bellinger Rivers in the 1840s. Soon after, farmers were pushing inland from the coast around Corindi and, with thoughts of a Scottish home that was probably never seen again, a settlement was named Gleniffer on the banks of Never Never Creek – *Oscar and Lucinda* country. The Promised Land – Gumbaynggirr probably weren't part of that divine calculus and would have been inclined to keep out of the way after the Red Rock massacre just to the north in the 1880s. But The Promised Land it was for Angel Gabriel and Promised Land Road, which tracks Never Never Creek, is where Beverley Eley has been living for over three decades.

Beverley Eley knows more than anyone about the life of Ion Llewellyn Idriess, who even spent a bit of time just twenty miles south, scraping together some money to get back up north after hitting Sydney with a *shammy of gold* not long after after the First War: *so I went to the upper Nambucca, up the river from Coffs Harbour there, and there was quite a bit of gold, enough to get me back to Queensland.*[355] An aged Idriess was spinning yarns for Tim Bowden in the early 1970s in the house he shared with his daughter, Wendy, in Mona Vale. Idriess was chatty but time had taken its toll: *stupid throat, sometimes it sort of closes up; no damned teeth you see, and so I don't talk distinctly.* Around eighty years old, time and events had conspired to close his writing: *I woke up one morning with paralysis and about that same time these disastrous take-overs was the fashion, there was the two take-overs in Angus & Robertson and things got mixed up and I was lost and had to get rid of this bloody paralysis which I did finally get rid of, and I lost touch with everything.*

By the time of the interview Angus & Robertson, as Idriess knew it, was gone, torn apart through efficiencies and mergers during the 1960s, the flagship office and store at 89 Castlereagh Street where Idriess sat and wrote day after day, and where he met with Bob Lasseter around 1960, sold off. And the managing director and Idriess' close friend, George Ferguson, had bowed to the inevitable in 1971 – the publishing world had moved on.[356] But before that happened Beverley Eley briefly worked for the firm, then for eight years at Collier Macmillan and on to be Marketing Manager at the Australian Consumers' Association where she met Idriess' daughter, Wendy. And a few months after he died: *She asked me if I would write his biography. She gave me all his papers – twenty-three butter-boxes plus cardboard cartons that he'd carted around all his life. As I found stuff I had to preserve it – it was all falling apart. I wanted to give it to the Mitchell because it was only going to go rotten and disappear.* The inventory of the contents of those butter-boxes that I took to Narrandera was done in Wendy's house in Mona Vale where Tim Bowden's interview with Idriess was recorded a few years before he died. Kylie Tenant interviewed him around the same time: *he was dressed in glossy and immaculate brown with a knitted seaman's cap, and an eye-shade giving a beaked effect to his lean face and piercing eye.* Idriess was 86 and still yarning away:

> *'I've lived through the last of the dark ages', he said. 'Always in wild places – and there were plenty of wild places when I started out. I'd have a horse and camel maybe. I might be out from Perth, overland; come by the northern route with my own horses up to the Kimberleys. Just red ranges and men red with dust. I'd go along one valley and the Aborigines would be waving their spears from the top of the cliffs. "Kiss my arse", they'd cry. "Taste my spear", making gestures of contempt, smacking their backsides. I knew they couldn't throw a spear at that extreme range. I'd fire my revolver at the rocks at their feet. And come on water in the next valley. The Aborigines knew it was there.'* [357]

Unlikely – but a colourful yarn. A decade later Eley was trying to weave a credible narrative around the relics of his life. At that time she had a job and three children; sifting through what I found the remains of in a Nerrandera barn in December 2019 couldn't have been easy. But by the time the biography – ***Ion Idriess***[358] – was finished, she felt she had a handle on Jack's personality. She uses the name of his bush *alter ego* as if that is closer to the person she got to know, rather than Ion, the polished-for-publicity image he, and the company, presented to the reading world. Steeped in the backwash of his life, she feels that she eventually understood his traits and tricks: *He was a cunning bugger – writing that book I got to know him better than my own father. I'd be coming up on something and I'd think: I know what's coming next, he's going to twist this. I knew how he was going to play things right to the end.* He certainly was *a cunning bugger,* even when the chips were down. After his first book, ***Madman's Island,*** flopped in 1927, George Robertson told him to give up writing but he got another shot with

Prospecting for Gold, which also wasn't selling: *So he writes a letter to the Herald saying how frustrating it was that thousands of people weren't able to get copies of* **Prospecting for Gold**. *Suddenly the whole thing turns around. Before you know it there are three or four editions being published.*

His next project was already on the go; he was working on the First CAGE Expedition story and there were reports in the press that Lasseter had been lost and some documents had been found. Idriess went into action: *He and Cousins got really steamed up and it was a race between publishers to get hold of it. A physical race, driving madly to get it.* Driving out to see Irene – more than once.[359] And soon after ***Lasseter's Last Ride*** was in print he received a letter from Florence Lasseter in Melbourne, Beverley found it in his correspondence: *She was complaining bitterly that he'd written a book about her husband without her permission. She didn't know if you could do that sort of thing, thinking that perhaps it was libel. She died soon after.* By that time the story had been revised with the material from the Second CAGE Expedition – it had become the standard version. Beverley has several copies including one that had been in Idriess' effects but had originally belonged to someone else: *It was marked up through the whole book with annotations, question marks here and there, things underlined. He didn't sign anything but has his initials as MSS – someone who was on the committee that was trying to raise money.*

MSS – that was Malcolm Stanley, who was one of the original members of the CAGE Syndicate and who, a few years later with other expeditions on the way, encouraged Fred Blakeley to write his account. On the first page of ***Lasseter's Dream of Millions*** Blakeley records that, against his own reservations: *Stanley persisted, saying, "I think it would be a great mistake to let the deception go on. This mythical reef has already cost hundreds of thousands of pounds, sickening disappointment, and the loss of lives. It is not 'past history'. It is up to you to tell the story as you believe it to be correct."*[360] Stanley was a War veteran and an engineer and, as Beverley interpreted from his marginalia, regretted his involvement: *MSS pulled out early, he said he disliked Lasseter – or Bell – didn't trust him. As far as he was concerned the whole thing was a con. Seemed to be somebody who had a conscience and a clear view of what he believed was right – he got out* *because he couldn't trust Lasseter. And stuck in the back was an article from the Sydney Mail, written by Paul Johns.*

Stanley probably picked Johns as another con-man. What Idriess made of Stanley's annotated copy of **Lasseter's Last Ride**, or how he got it, isn't known. He'd written a story that he knew was largely fiction, but he believed that the reef existed. Beverley got to know Idriess' namesake nephew, Ion Morrison, a medico in Brisbane, and interviewed him for her book: *At the beginning of the War they were getting set to go out and look for the reef but their fuel was confiscated. He said he was only going along because his uncle was getting on and might need a doctor. He said Idriess had all sorts of theories, like if the wind was blowing from the south or the west the reef would be covered.*

Earlier in the year that the Second World War broke out Idriess received a letter from Mr. H.G. Melville of Parkes who had written seeking guidance: *I intend to go by Motor truck as far as possible and then by Camel team & only intend to take experienced bushmen with me not city men like poor Lassitter [sic] had.* In his reply dated 15th March 1939, Idriess echoed Mr Melville's sentiments about the inexperienced: *Parties of "Pitt Street miners" have also gone out, had a good holiday by a waterhole, and returned to say that the whole business was a stunt.* But Idriess continued: *To the best of my belief Lasseter's story was true. It is all taken from his own diary.* Idriess, of course, knew more about *The Diary* than anyone else, albeit clarifying for Mr Melville that: *A portion of the diary is missing but what happened to it no one seems to know.*[361] And if Idriess didn't know – nobody did.

Three decades later Idriess still believed the reef existed; he told Tim Bowden – with a qualifier: *I think it did. But my idea was much more north to where they've been looking for it.* Idriess' interview with Bowden reads like the early Idriess of the *Gouger* articles. Writing anonymously of life in the bush between 1911 and the early 1930s, the younger Idriess is liberal with what he probably thought of as down-to-earth language, particularly in describing Aboriginal and Torres Strait Islander people and practices; with some exceptions he cleaned up his act in his books even though the attitudes remained. Perhaps the disinhibition of advanced years and a lot of alcohol explains the language recorded in

Getting started:
the *journeyman journalist.*

The
established
tale teller...

The last gate. *Notice on the last station fence far across the Nullarbor Plain, before entry into Norseman, West Australia.*

Mona Vale days (1970s)
... he was a cunning bugger.

the 1970s.[362] And maybe some of the grandiosity. He told Bowden that: *It was through the book that ... years afterwards that the last big goldfield in Australia was found – Tennant Creek*. If only Lasseter had read *Lasseter's Last Ride*:

> *Lasseter could have found that you see, right in his line of travel, but to the north in gold country. I think that it's very likely that that was what he found and then wandering when he went sick and that sort of thing and lost his sight while the natives would still have him, God knows where he wandered to, well, they found him by this little cave because he had to follow while the natives would lead him, he couldn't direct them to go anywhere he just had to go where they went hunting for their tucker, see. That's what I think had happened. And he went with them until they left him to die – you see, that's what they do with their own people, they generally leave them a drop of water and a kangaroo bone ... they couldn't have weak and sick people on their hands in that dry arid country, especially if it's in a drought time.*

The elderly Idriess made no mention of sorcery but went on to tell Bowden how Lasseter hid messages in tins buried under camp-fires, and how he came to write the book – *a fluke book*. In the octogenarian's reconstruction: *It was from the police at Alice Springs ... they sent down to Sydney, said they found the body of a prospector out by this little cave thing ... I was down here from the bush with the usual shammy of gold ... I thought 'There's a story in that'.* What follows is a confused mish-mash of his transformation of that *story*. The Baileys are no longer father and son but brothers, and in the newspaper business – *The World* – but with Labor Party connections. Then he's back on surer ground – Ion Idriess:

> *... when the police sent them down the diary and that, my publishers then, they looked at me as something they couldn't understand ... I had only written three or four books but they'd each been best-sellers, and this bloody wild man from Borneo – from the bush. Of course they didn't believe in me at all, they reckoned it's not possible ... that Australian people actually bought Australian books.*

But buy them they did, and sales of **Lasseter's Last Ride** took off. As he told oral historian Hazel de Berg in 1974, it was his most popular book until it was overtaken by a slower starter released a year later – **Flynn of the Inland**: *The time came when book by book, sale by sale, it was gradually overtaking Lasseter ... at last with a photo finish with both books out at the extreme limits,* **Flynn** *passed the post with the shortest of half-heads ahead of* **Lasseter's Last Ride**.[363] By that time he was an established author with a lot on the go and **Lasseter** could take care of itself. *He was a cunning bugger* – that was Jack of much earlier times and perhaps it's fortunate that Beverley Eley came to write the biography after he'd passed. The final chapters track his Mona Vale decline, which coincided with Australia's transformation to a globalised, multicultural society. In his last years Idriess was happy to keep talking – telling his tales of past times. But that world – and the audience for which he wrote – were long gone. Which doesn't diminish the achievements, they are just time-stamped. **Lasseter's Last Ride** and most of the rest of his books are frontier *Whitefellow dreaming.* Jack Idriess should be remembered for telling us who we were. He was good at that, he just wasn't too sharp at telling us exactly what happened *– he was a cunning bugger.*

Cheerio. Jon L. Idriess

CHAPTER 22

Visions of Soul's Future Gold

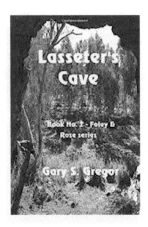

For twenty-five years Australians argued about where the reef of gold was to be found, so vivid was Idriess's recreation of Lasseter's wanderings with an Aboriginal tribe, a legend which owed much to Idriess's own knowledge of the inland. The official geologists might declare there was no gold-bearing country in the region, but the average Australian preferred Idriess's dramatic version, which sold edition after edition.

Kylie Tennant, 1976.[364]

Tastes change but myths, or fragments of them, live on – often grafted for effect. And so it is with Lasseter, written into a Northern Territory noir detective genre by Vietnam Vet and retired police officer Gary Gregor. The cover of the second in the *Foley & Rose Series* – **Lasseter's Cave** – seems to be framed by an insider's view of the shadowed jawline of a bellowing beast. In the lighted world beyond there's a stand of bush with a bifurcating gum to the left of a droughted but water-eroded foreground. Photographs from 1933 capture the elusive erosive agent – the Hull River. But that's not what Gregor had Russell and Sam find as they approach the cave. In the twenty-teens it was dry, as it was in January 1931:

It's hot, remote, desolate and dangerous; and about as deep into the infa-
mous Australian outback as anyone would dare to venture. An eminent
neurosurgeon, his loving wife and two adorable children, on the holiday
of a lifetime, are shot dead, their shattered bodies left to the ravages of the
desert sun and carrion-eating wildlife. Detective Inspector Russell Foley,
and his best friend and fellow Northern Territory cop, Detective
Sergeant Sam Rose, are sent into the heart of the legendary Harold
Lasseter, "Lost Reef of Gold" country to investigate the brutal murders. Is
it Gold Fever, or simply the twisted mind of a deranged killer protecting
that which he believes is his? [365]

Gregor's Centralian coppers would have had no confusion about where
they were; they would have walked along the tourist path and through a
gate with a bright-red lintel proclaiming *TJUNTI – Lasseter's Cave.* Crossing the river's powdered imprint, a plinthed primer of the
prospector's premature demise explains:

Kulpi Tjuntinya
Lewis Harold Bell Lasseter sheltered in this cave for approximately 25
days during January 1931. He was stranded without food after his
camels bolted at a point 15 Km. east of here. Although weak from
starvation he set out about 25th January to walk the 140 Km. to Mount
Olga, hoping to meet up with his relief party. Carrying 1.7 litres of
water and assisted by a friendly Aboriginal family he reached Irving
Creek in the Pottoyu Hills a distance of 55 Km. where he died about
28th January 1931.
                    Erected by Docker River Social Club Inc for Mr. R. Lasseter,
                                                        26th April 1974[366]

For Mr. R. Lasseter – erected 43 years after Bob's father died around
thirty kilometres distant, where the dry beds of Shaw and Irving Creeks
course through the fractured and fragmented granites of the Pottoyu
Hills. That's where, on 1st June 1931, Walter Gill carved the first
memorial to Lasseter into a blaze on the trunk of a salmon gum, the
only sizeable tree near *the weather-worn mound of red earth* where Bob
Buck had buried the body he found nearby three months earlier.[367] The
tree is long gone but Gill's misspelling of the dead man's name, *Lassiter,*
lives on in the photograph taken when Bob Buck returned with the

Second CAGE Expedition five months later – and that made it into the revised version of *Lasseter's Last Ride*.

That's where Mick Kuruanyani met Bob Buck in 1931, and where he and Nosepeg Tjupurrula directed Lowell Thomas a quarter-century later to find a skeleton that is now in the Memorial Cemetery in Alice Springs. In 1958 the cemetery was red earth and not much more, with the Mac-Donnell Range rising in the background. Surrounded by residential sub-divisions on three sides now, there are a few white cedars, European olives, kurrajongs and the occasional oleanders along the hashtag dividing paths separating the residents of the cemetery's nine sections – Lasseter is with the Anglicans. And with the Catholics not too far away is Bob Buck, who was interred there just two years after the man he had originally buried three decades earlier. Both graves are capped by sandstone, Buck's by an eroded boulder with a small, recessed, brass plaque bearing *BOB BUCK BUSHMAN 1880-1960*. It may have been for the symmetry of decades or of a birth year shared with Lasseter, or perhaps to reflect the looseness with facts for which he was renown, but Robert Henry Buck was born on 2nd July 1881 in Alberton, South Australia. As Walter Gill, Pastor Albrecht, Frank Clune and probably many others discovered, Buck could be diffi-cult to pin down on particular subjects and he's difficult to approach now, the ground about his memorial densely carpeted with three-cornered Jack – *Amex australis*.

Not so the well-trodden, pebbled surrounds of the memorial to Lasse-ter, a rough-hewn block that seems to have settled over time into a rotund, hirsute hobbit, who might be poking his thumb into a pie but which, with a few clues, resolves into a prospector panning for gold. Perhaps appropriately ambiguous, even the journey here was not straightforward. In one scene from Luke Walker's film – *Lasseter's Bones* – Elsie and Bob Lasseter's pained indignation is plain as they describe how, in 1958, Lowell Thomas: *dug his remains up from a grave and carted him in a sugar-bag into Alice Spring.* That was the beginning of another saga, and in the National Archives there is a file from the Northern Territory Administration in Alice Springs with correspondence that spans two decades – *Burial L.H.B. Lasseter.*[368]

288

It commences with a letter dated 10th February 1958 from Bob Lasseter who has just become aware from reports in the Sydney press that two men (Lee Robinson and Alton Frazer, both of whom were with Lowell Thomas) had been: *charged in connection with disturbing a grave suggested to be that of my dead father L.H.B. Lasseter.* As letters went back and forth between Seven Hills and Alice Springs, Bob's father's bones remained *in the custody of the Police Court, Alice Springs* – awaiting definitive identification. On 4th March Bob wrote to The Secretary of the Department of the Interior in Canberra noting: *Having examined the depositions together with photographs of the grave and surrounding area I am now of the opinion that the skeleton is that of my father, L.H.B. Lasseter, who died while prospecting for gold about 28th January 1931 and about whom the book "Lasseter's Last Ride" by Ion L. Idriess has been written.* At the end of March the Territory Administrator responded that: *From medical reports that were obtained at the time, and from other evidence adduced, it appears to be almost certain that the remains were those of your father.* By the beginning of June 1958 the correspondence has shifted to arrangements for reburial, the (Sydney) Lasseter family's wishes – and costs. Lasseter was reinterred at 2:30pm on 27th June, Archdeacon W. Rogers officiating, and a *Debit Note … in the sum of £25 – covering burial fees in respect of L.H.B. Lasseter* forwarded to his son, Bob, in Sydney.

There is a gap in correspondence of twelve years before a 1970 letter to the Director of Local Government and Community Services in Darwin from the Alice Springs District Office regarding a report relating to *directional signs at the Alice Springs Cemetery* to graves *of interest to tourists* – there being two: Albert Namatjira and *L.H.B. (Das) Lasseter of the famous expedition.* The letter goes on to note: *Negotiations are current between Mr. David Fish, a stone worker, and the son of the late Mr. Lasseter for the erection of a headstone.* The circle of correspondents extended in late 1970 to include Eddie Connellan, pastoralist and Territorian aerial-entrepreneur. On 4th July Bob Lasseter wrote to Connellan asking him *to convey my appreciation to Mr Lowell Thomas for his generous offer to erect a memorial to my father.* Bob Lasseter proceeds to suggest a simple natural granite boulder and plaque – *not too ornate or extravagant* – but went on to con-

*... settled over time
into a rotund and
densely-bearded hobbit
...*

*... Gill's misspelling of
the dead man's name – Lassiter –
lives on ...*

*The battered Thornycroft ...
seems to be channelling
Marlow's vessel ...*

sider that: *It could embody something symbolic of the earlier prospector – pick, knapping hammer or pan.* Negotiations must have been protracted, but by November 1971 it was settled and Eddie Connellan wrote to the Lord Mayor of Alice Springs confirming *the arrangement for Lowell Thomas to pay for a monument.*

It was probably Connellan who commissioned David Fish (later working under the name Bardius Goldberg), an eccentric artist who thought big; he is rumoured to have had plans for a geoglyph somewhere near Hermannsburg that would be visible from space and is widely suspected as being responsible for Marree Man. His Lasseter creation originally had a simple plaque at the front which read: *HAROLD LEWIS BELL LASSETER. Died in the Petermann Ranges on January 30th 1931 his grave was located on December 14th 1957 by an expedition led by Lowell Thomas and Lee Robinson. This is his final resting place.*

Final resting place perhaps – but not without changes. In 1976 Lee Robinson returned to the scene of the crime, where he had been arrested for desecration of Lasseter's bush grave. He had assembled a Lasseter cast with some old and new figures – Bob Buck and Phil Taylor from the Expeditions, Nosepeg Tjupurrula who had been with Lowell Thomas, and Bob Lasseter and Mike Willesee – that would result in the 1979 television movie *The Legend of Lasseter*.[369] While in Alice Springs they assembled on Sunday 29th August with Bob's son and daughter, Rob and Lucy, for a graveside memorial service conducted by Reverend Southey.[370] Maye it was penance on the part of Lee Robinson but the original plaque was shifted to the side, its replacement striking a different note:

> *"It is not the critic who counts, or how the strong man stumbled and fell or where the doer of deeds could have done better. The credit belongs to the man who is actually in the arena, who knows the great enthusiasms, the great devotion, and spends himself in a worthy cause. If he fails, at least he fails while daring greatly so that he will never be one of those cold and timid souls who knows neither victory or defeat."*
>
> *Theodore Roosevelt*[371]

Teddy Roosevelt; explorer, roughrider, conservationist – and President of the United States of America. Plenty of guts and gravitas but the full quote wouldn't fit and what was lost is more apt than the pared-down grab on the plaque; *the man who is actually in the arena* is followed in the original by: *whose face is marred by dust and sweat and blood; who strives valiantly; who errs, who comes short again and again, because there is no effort without error and shortcoming; but who does actually strive to do the deeds.* Plenty of *error and shortcoming* in the Lasseter saga even if it didn't make the cut for the budget tourist trail. And for the adventurous, Lasseter's Cave – *Kulpi Tjuntinya* – is probably more appealing than the other stations on his last journey – Ilbilba, Mount Marjory, Lasseter's Lookout, Lake Amadeus, Lake Christopher – or where he died, somewhere near Shaw Creek. The reason Lasseter's Cave works for tourists and as a setting for detectives on the trail of an outback murderer is the same, it channels the Gothic narrative of ***Lasseter's Last Ride***.

Ion Llewellyn Idriess is not memorialised in stone; he was cremated on 13th September 1979, and a banksia in the Northern Suburbs Memorial Gardens in North Ryde marks where his ashes were returned to the soil. When I started this journey I already felt that I was over Idriess – his Queensland writings were enough. Then I tripped into a parallel universe that his first best seller spawned. It was 2019 – pre-COVID – and the plan was to finish this project in the Centre, to process through those stations. That didn't happen. I didn't make it to Lasseter-land. But neither did Idriess, although he stopped by the Stuart Arms Hotel, Bob Buck's favourite drinking hole, when he was passing through Alice Springs after his tour of the Kimberley and the Top End in 1934 – three years and six books after ***Lasseter's Last Ride***. The result of that trip – ***Man Tracks*** – was another Idriess classic that was reprinted 21 times over the next two decades.

Idriess may have put Lasseter-land on the map, but even though he was close by, he didn't go the extra miles. That may have invited comment and Idriess was already aware of criticism, including from writers with real experience in Central Australia, like Michael Terry, Cecil Madigan and Bill Charnley. Maybe he was cautious because he was sensitive about not having been there before he raced to create a fiction to hold together a flimsy storyline of a poorly planned and executed prospecting expedition.

He didn't want awkward questions and to that end he not only made sure that *The Diary* wouldn't surface, he also avoided discussions that would raise uncomfortable questions – including with Fred Blakeley and Lasseter's son, Bob.

My journey into Lasseter-land started with a conversation and a comment about his mental health. Almost immediately I was drawn away, but it could be argued that Lasseter was manic around 1917 – extra-marital relationships, wild projects, discharged from the military with a *presumptive diagnosis* of *neurotic disorder with hallucinations*, and observations of him including *has an odd manner & is constantly talking*. And he'd had a head injury – it's possible. Perhaps he did experience *delusions and overvalued* ideas as John Cawte suggested, and it's hard to argue with Robert Kaplan's conclusion that he was a *pathological liar* and *fabulist*. Chris Clark would agree, but in pursuit of nailing down a specific diagnosis opted for *narcissistic personality disorder*. Chris Clark sought the causes and explanations for that condition in Lasseter's early childhood and, without trying to impose a label, so did Murray Hubbard and Luke Walker. They were trying to understand the person behind the story and were sympathetic to the pluck and persistence of the *nuggety little man from Kogarah* in the face of the serial hardships and disappointments that dogged his life.

As a psychiatrist, I understand the strengths and limitations of categorising mental states and mental disorders. That's what I did for four decades. I know how important getting the diagnosis *right* is, but its power is predictive not explanatory; it may expedite the prescription of medicines but, without critically engaging with context, runs the risk of denying ultimate causes, trivialising treatment and, too often, rationalising its failures by blaming the patient. In relation to Lasseter, the mystery is not whether the man born in Bamganie, Victoria, in 1880 as Lewis Hubert Lasseter, who died in Central Australia in 1931 as Harold Lewis Bell Lasseter, was duplicitous or deranged. Whether he was or was not is to miss the point – rather like trying to explain such religious figures as Caitanya or Teresa of Avila with a summary diagnosis is to miss why their enactments of raving or rapture proved meaningful for millions of followers who were able to decode them. The mystery isn't the man – it's the myth.

Without Idriess there would be no legend and the question of the state of mind of a man without mining or bush experience or expertise, who perished in a hopeless outback gamble, wouldn't be raised. *Lasseter's Last Ride* was being written as the shambolic events of the First CAGE Expedition were ongoing – the book is as much an event as the Expedition or Lasseter's demise. But while it claims authenticity, it's not the story of Harold Bell Lasseter, or even an accurate account of his last year. It's fiction – and it went on to become the *urtext* of a legend. Explaining that is the challenge; what it is about Idriess' fanciful story that resulted in continuing sales, imitation, appropriation, and adaptation to poetry, painting and film – there's even a version for children with notes for teachers.[372] Another guide for teachers accompanied the 2006-2007 capital cities tour of the exhibition *National Treasures from Australia's Great Libraries.* Among the six items in the section titled *Hope and Hardship,* was *Harold Lasseter's diary: An elusive reef of gold,* with the last lines of the display note reading: *Was this Australia's wildest goose chase? The answer still lies out there.*[373] Treasure was the driver of the CAGE Expeditions and those that followed, but the only *treasure* – albeit presented as a *national treasure* three-quarters of a century later – is the document unearthed by Frank Green – convicted felon, conman and failed prospector. And the alchemy that transmuted the last misadventures and missives of another conman and failed prospector to myth was wrought by Idriess' book.

Lasseter's Last Ride was responsible for loosing the legend on the Australian imagination; it was necessary – but not sufficient – for the legend to take hold. The other necessary ingredient was fertile ground and a receptive audience. And with the Depression casting long shadows as the new nation entered its fourth decade, Idriess hit the right note with an audience he'd come to know well through his journeyman journalism days. Adventure, exotica, tragedy, hope and hype; it was written *in language that nobody from the rawest newchum to Judge Curlewis, should find beyond him* – and with just enough facts to suspend disbelief. But that note – Idriess' style – was time-stamped and the legend has continued while *Lasseter's Last Ride* is now, for younger generations of Australians, a dimly recognised phrase that may or may not be associated with a book.

And Ion Idriess, for decades Australia's most popular author, has gone the same way. So, the enthusiastic readership of the early 1930s doesn't explain why the core elements of the Lasseter story continued to self-propagate from Idriess' original planting – over what is now nearly a century of changing times and tastes.

The legend – or the myth – lives on, as Albert Tucker suggested in the introduction to *The Die Hard*,[374] because the story is transcending: *The tragedy of Lasseter embodies this process with terrifying clarity and evokes images which tell us more about who and what we are and about our own identity as Australians.* It resonates with *who and what we are* as tragedy in a generic sense but, as probably drew Tucker to working on the project with Ivan and Jocelyn Smith, it's *about our own identity as Australians.* That's specific. The sustenance provided and riches relinquished to the settler societies of this country for over two centuries are buried in a tragedy – the dispossession, and what was anticipated as the disappearance, of Aboriginal Australians. They are central to the tale Idriess told about Lasseter and also to his larger writing project in which even Aboriginal resistance fighters – in *Nemarluk* and *Outlaws of the Leopolds* – are doomed, tragic figures. In *Lasseter's Last Ride* the Aboriginal presence is critical; it is the darkness in the heart into which the First CAGE Expedition clumsily intrudes, the heart of the continent and the heart of a shadowland collective soul. The battered Thornycroft, crawling through the bush with rough-hewn branches of mulga tied across the radiator and windscreen seems to be channelling Marlow's vessel: *Hugging the bank against the stream, crept the little begrimed steamboat, like a sluggish beetle crawling on the floor of a lofty portico. It made you feel very small, very lost...*

Joseph Conrad knew the coast of Australia well. He was first in Australian waters in 1879 as able seaman on the *Duke of Sutherland,* again in 1880 as third mate on the *Loch Etive* and in 1887 on the *Otago* when he had command after the death of the captain on the outward journey. His last visit was in 1892-93 as chief mate on the *Torrens,* his final voyage working at sea.[375] In 1924 Conrad told an Australian correspondent that he had: *acquired a great affection for that Young Continent which will endure as long as my faculty of memory itself endures.*[376] He never ventured into its heart as he did the Congo in the 1890s, and died before Idriess' first book, *Madman's Island*, was released. Conrad couldn't have read Idriess – but Idriess probably read *Heart of Darkness*. It's unlikely that there was any intent to imitate, but *Lasseter's Last Ride* worked because of mechanisms that it shares with Conrad's psychological masterpiece. The crews of the Thornycroft and the steamboat are cut off, their progress tracked by unseen eyes. Both are driven by the same motive force – rapacious greed – which is thinly disguised through the off-stage presence of missionaries in both books, as a civilising project. But what is brought into the heart is degeneration and death, and the native populations stand witness. In both books they are the support cast, but neither story would work without them. In both there is a sense of the native domain as powerful and threatening, which becomes a central plot device for Idriess through sorcery which, as Mickey Dewar commented, is an example of how *Aboriginal power had overflowed into the non-Aboriginal domain*. It all ends with Lasseter and Kurtz consumed by their obsessions, crazed and alone. Lasseter died because he had unwittingly transgressed and perhaps the myth's enduring potency hangs on the awareness that we, as a nation, are participants. Remote Central Australia stands for the Aboriginal domain and mining magically materialises value from the violent renting of the fabric of country. And a cave… Well, it works as a Gothic horror device and carries powerful associations – predators, paleolithic people, darkness and death.

But across the continent prehistoric cave sites have other meanings hidden from sight. Stratified below the surface are stories, the time-spans of which, as Marlow reflected thinking of the steamboat's progress against the enormity of the continent beyond the riverbank's jungle fast-ness, makes *you feel very small, very lost*. And however one construes the sacred, the numinous in that scale is unavoidable. As my writing draws to a close that is all brought home when on 23rd May 2020 a site with estimates of human presence for over forty-thousand years is destroyed. The dynamiting of the rock-shelter cave at Juukan Gorge in the Brock-man Range in the Pilbara on the Sunday before National Reconciliation Week – to expand Rio Tinto's already vast iron ore mine – collapses myth to grim reality. There are explanations, rationalisations, an apology, an enquiry, trivial financial penalties, strategic executive reshuffling and, for a moment, national outrage – as the profits continue. Noel Pearson is but one to question the company's lame rationalisations for discounting the incalculable cultural value of the site, noting the only plausible alternative: *the company was determined to exercise its rights to extract $135m of value from the Juukan Gorge area notwithstanding these [traditional] values.*[377]

Hype, hubris and greed – Rio Tinto and the Central Australian Gold Exploration Company share more than caves and tragedy. But corporations are not the stuff of myth. Myths persist in the retelling because they make sense culturally – and personally. They adhere to flesh – flawed flesh – that we recognise as ourselves: *Myth is a form of recycling. The stories it tells are often circular, in keeping with natural law. ... The mythological circles or cycles are almost always vicious, penalizing us for our casual vices.*[378] Harold Lasseter's story reverberates across the decades because readers recognise transgression, be it the big lie or existential trespass. It is more than its creator – while Idriess is responsible for transmuting mundane misadventure to myth he was probably surprised at the success of ***Lasseter's Last Ride*** and unaware of what made it work. What he did know is that it did and, in the years after, he chose not to tamper with it or to talk to those who could challenge the narrative.

In 1931 Idriess' starting point was tragedy, the working title was *Lasseter's Last Ride. The Tragic Story of the Central Australian Gold Exploration Coy. Ltd.* While that *Tragic Story* became an *Epic* by the time of publication, tragedy became a feature of his later writing, particularly in his Aboriginal tales. But with the Lasseter story it had already been so framed. In May 1931, just one month after the news that Lasseter's body had been found by Bob Buck was reported in the Sydney press, and four months before ***Lasseter's Last Ride*** was first published, a poem appeared in *The Daily Telegraph*. The title, *How Lasseter Died*, is followed by a preface: *Three or four tattered slips of scrawled-on paper, found on the body of Harold Lasseter, told how he died on a sandy ridge in Central Australia, while searching for gold.* And then the poem – perhaps a requiem:

He followed the trail by the mark of the camel's pad,
An arrow cut in a trunk with a broken knife,
He dared the desert to break him body and soul;
Lasseter stood – and so looked back at life.
With only the dingo's bark in the empty night,
The shadow of scrub to shelter the ranging black,
And the cold moon not so far as the hand of a friend –
So Lasseter came at last to the end of the track.
And one who followed the gloom for thirty years
Knew blindness over his eyes, and a failing breath,
With the gilt stars over his head, and gold at his feet,
Lasseter laughed – and so lay down with death.[379]

Originally from New Zealand, Betty Riddell was just twenty-one and had been in Australia for only three years, where she went on to a distinguished career as a journalist and poet. Whether Idriess and Riddell ever met isn't known and maybe he was wary of the young, talented, female writer. But he read that poem and kept it – a clipping of which was among Idriess *ephemera* auctioned in February 2021. The Lasseter tragedy starts with poetry and maybe the myth does too. Poetry is the natural language of tragedy, epic and myth. As this book demonstrates, there have been lots of verses written about Lasseter and perhaps it's appropriate that the most enigmatic poetic incorporation of the Lasseter legend into a mythic landscape comes from Western Australia, where the unshakeable belief in mining as the foundation of solvency, sovereignty and social order, at whatever cost, is least contested.

John Kinsella grew up in Perth and the bush in the 1960s and '70s as mining was again causing fevered imaginations to run wild through the corridors of the then modest office blocks of St George's Terrace. As Peter Bridge of Hesperian Press pointed out when I spoke to him just a few kilometres away, there was a brief surge then in sales of Idriess' *how-to* manual for the sole operator, **Prospecting for Gold**, forty years after he promoted it to Prime Minister Joseph Lyons as a Depression-era nostrum. When Kinsella applied himself to the Lasseter saga it had been a half-century from Riddell's forgotten poem and Idriess' first big-seller –

Lasseter's Last Ride. By that time Idriess had died and sales of his books had, more or less, flatlined. But enough of the three million or so of his books that had been sold were still lying around in homes and on outback hotel bookshelves that there was brand-name recognition. Within a few more decades the remains had settled into second-hand bookstores and specialist collections; for Kinsella's generation and after, mention of Idriess is more likely to be met with perplexity than passion.

Meanwhile, across Western Australia's boomtime cycles – gold, nickel, iron ore, diamonds, gold and iron ore again – the alchemy that elevates base greed to noble enterprise, and transforms sun-singed terrain into intoxicating visions of Haulpacs and excavators continues. In his day, Idriess was moved by the same magic and wrote about it. While he may be forgotten his creation, Lasseter, is not. Nearly a century after he died his name is linked, consciously or in some liminal network of connections, with delusions or dreams, and deserts and death. And whether John Kinsella knew much about Idriess, he was certainly familiar with *Lasseter's Last Ride*. Landscape is a recurring theme through his work and in *Night Parrots*[380] it's the desert that's the backdrop to a suite of 21 poems that, rather like *The Rubaiyat* – or *The Diary* – can be read in series or separately. The desert landscape in *Night Parrots* might stand for many things – for judgement or redemption – maybe for Kinsella's earlier-life desert-days. But in this telling it's the realm of the sun, of Nebuchadnezzar, destroyer of the Temple and architect of Exile, and into it strays the transgressor – Lasseter. He's in search of gold – but what is gold… Is it the sun… Is it Nebuchadnezzar… Is it fire… Is it fate… Maybe all of the above, maybe not. Like all myths, it's in the reading, which might be the whole poem or just a snatch, such as, *Lasseter Laments His Fall to the Wits of the Ignorant*:

> *He had tried to ignore*
> *the obviousness of his fate —*
> *misunderstood by the ignorant, judged by*
> *the ignorant, who in their need to shoulder*
> *or create guilt would look for circumstance*
> *best suited to this end.*

And yet
his sight had grown clearer.
And his faith in the Nebuchadnezzar
(who only knew in the brilliance
of his extinguished soul's fire),
grew in their praise of the reef's empty sun.

Were they too 'victims of circumstance'?
Nebuchadnezzar grew unsure.

Lasseter grew unsure.
His morality was born of thirst, theirs
of greed. He'd learnt to despise
the sanctimonious, those who felt secure in
reconciling this tainted view
with visions of soul's future gold.

Hunter and Collector: at a Lasseter Tree in Canberra. Ernest Hunter (left) with Duncan Quarterman.

EPILOGUE

Ultimo

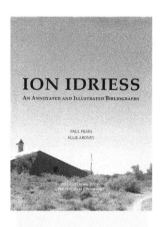

If I could find the inclination I could easily write another 50 books out of the notebooks that I've got over there. And upstairs I've got boxes and boxes the daughter has gone and put away in some place, out of the road somewhere. I've got boxes and boxes of notes. I kept things like that starting from a boy with the Bulletin and I'd write things like that down so you didn't have to trust the memory or think things up. Cripes, I've got enough memories and things in those notebooks to write for a hundred years.

Ion Idriess, 1975.[381]

December 12, 2020

Neptune, Surprize and *Scarborough* were among the six transports of the Second Fleet that set out from England in January 1790. Of over one thousand convicts boarded on those three vessels of horror just under 750 were off-loaded in June, half of the survivors diseased and/or disabled. On the *Scarborough* was a young lieutenant who had transferred with his wife from the *Neptune* after a dispute with the captain. John Macarthur went on to a career in quarrels and much more in the colony of New South Wales. Two days before they disembarked, the *Surprize* had arrived, and on it was a 36 year old, Anglo-Irish surgeon, John Harris. Harris was with the New South Wales Corps through the heady days of the Rum Corps and the Rebellion, and went on to a distinguished colonial career as a landowner and director of the Bank of New South Wales. In 1803 Harris was rewarded by Governor Phillip Gidley King – for support in trying to curb the Corps' excesses – with a land grant, a tract of some 34 acres between the Glebe and Cockle Bay. Having recently been acquitted of charges on the basis of a technicality involving the fortuitous misuse of a term in court papers, he chose to name his new estate for that loose use of Latin legalese – *Ultimo*.

John Harris's name is preserved in the street bisecting Ultimo from north to south which, at its midpoint, intersects that named for his fellow second-fleeter, Macarthur Street. And just to the west, on the corner of Macarthur and Wattle Streets, is a remnant of the Macarthurs' merino legacy, the seven-storied, Federation-style, *Farmers & Graziers* woolstore. Repurposed for changed times, an arched, street-level doorway now leads to the premises of Sydney Rare Book Auctions. And that's where Paul Feain has been based since 2011 when he moved from Cornstalks on Glebe Point Road. A quarter-century earlier I walked out of that antiquarian bookstore with my first Idriess – **Madman's Island** – the setting for the opening chapter of **Vicarious Dreaming** and, I suppose, the beginning of the journey that concludes with **Reef Madness**.

I'm here for an auction – *Important Australian firsts, the Idriess Estate & other intriguing items*. The *Idriess Estate* – a fraction of the material I surface-grazed in a barn on the outskirts of Narrandera almost exactly a year ago – but it's the same stuff. After that trip I contacted various people who understood its importance, including Henry Reynolds and Peter Sutton. On their recommendation I spoke with the Australian National Library, but also with the Mitchell Library[382] and James Cook University. Whether because of Idriess' out-of-cultural-favour status, or distrust of intermediaries' hidden agendas, the furthest it progressed was that the Australian National Library made contact with the custodian. But then my relationship with Wendell turned south and COVID-19 put everything on hold. And now it has taken a different course and what for half-a-century has been tenuously intact but in physical jeopardy will probably find disintegrated security.

I can imagine the strategy; identify and put aside the big-ticket items – the hand-written drafts of his books and key correspondence – and prepare the market with a sampling that has enough treasure among trifles to generate interest. And from my Narrandera browsing there are plenty of trifles that might be listed as they are or collected as sweepings of the appraisal room floor and bundled together as lucky dip *ephemera*. So it was no surprise that that's what I found in the online catalogue, with the first tranche of Idriess-related items accounting for around twenty percent of the thousand items up for grabs. From samplings of his racing tickets to copies of his books in translation – French, Croatian, Swedish – something for everyone. As I explored the catalogue some items stood out:

Lot 32: FRANK CLUNE – ION IDRIESS: Murders on Maunga-Tapu by Frank Clune Sydney Angus & Robertson 1959 Very good in dust-wrapper. Inscribed "For my cobber Jack Idriess, who loves a nice juicy murder with his Scotch here it is. Yours Sincerely Frank Clune 14/9/59" How much more Australiana can you get?

Lot 125: WHITLAM TO IDRIESS 1965: A Christmas card from the Whitlams to Ion Idriess "Thank you so much for your very kind gesture with your latest book Margaret Whitlam. We are enjoying it very much". They both knew everyone.

Lot 142: IDRIESS 6 NORCO BUTTER BOXES: 6 NORCO wooden butter boxes from the Ion Idriess Estate. NORCO was a dairy company established in the North Coast of New South Wales in 1925. The boxes were made from Hoop Pine by Munro & Lever Sawmill circa mid to late 1920s. Hoop Pine was said not to change the taste or smell of the butter. This butter was exported to places as far away as England. The boxes originally came with lids, but these are missing. The boxes are held tightly together with nails, but there is a distinct ambience to the wood as if they have been sitting in a farm shed since the 1920s. Each box is approximately 35 x 34 x 31cm and weighs 2.8kgs. Ion Idriess hand written manuscripts were stored in these boxes.

*Nemarluk
and
Beatrix Potter...*

*Idriess
Six
Norco
Butterboxes.*

Auction wizards
Sydney Rare Book
Auctions.

Lot 1000: LASSETER IDRIESS ORIGINAL PHOTOS: Seventeen original photographs all used in the book Lasseter's Last Ride by Ion Idriess. The photos are original prints and mounted on board. They measure 29 x 39 cm. Images are sharp, clean and clear. Most of the mounts are grubby and stained. The photos are by Bill Davis. These photos were wrapped in tatty brown paper some of which has been saved and this has notes by Idriess and someone else.

On the web-catalogue Lot 1000 appears with a photograph of a traditional Aboriginal man staring directly to the camera, mounted on backing with the title *A Warrior Bold*. It is the same photograph that appears in a set of four in Chapter 1 of the revised version of **Lasseter's Last Ride** which incorporated photographs from the Second CAGE Expedition. The image titled *Old Warts, Lasseter's Only Friend* appears in the book as *Old Warts, Who Befriended Lasseter*. Kirrinytja's eyes are shadowed by his high forehead, the bottom half of his face hidden behind a beard that falls in matted coils across his chest. He looks – as we know he was – a confident and respected man. A man of qualities, but known to history for a trivial blemish that is hidden from the camera's gaze. Although Bob Buck didn't resile from locational accuracy – *Warty Arse* – Idriess accommodated his audience's presumed sensitivities and relocated the ungainly growth.[383]

Entering off Wattle Street, the auction room has a dozen chairs at COVID-safe distance facing a monitor and terminals where the business of the day will be conducted. The walls are lined with books tagged individually and in groups, boxes piled in the centre and Idriess-related material scatted throughout. As I progress through the room there are locked glass display cabinets, one with a set of seven Beatrix Potter ceramic figurines in front of which are two beaded bands and another that looks like it is woven string or canvas – it's marked as Lot 911 and below, in handwriting that I recognise: *Headbands, fashioned for me by Nemarluk out of beads and an old discarded singlet, when he was a prisoner in Fanny [sic] Bay Gaol, Darwin, after the native and Japanese killings on the beche-de-mer luggers.* From the catalogue I know that somewhere in the chaos of displays there's another Nemarluk item:

Lot 985: Nemarluk Charge Sheet
Prisoners' Register Convict Department Large page folded comes in an
envelope with this note in the hand of Ion Idriess. Nemarluk's Charge
Sheet. Torn out of a charge book in Darwin jail by an Aussie soldier
during the big Japanese air raid.

Towards the back of the room I pass two stacks of NORCO butter
boxes, the same that I found in the barn in Narrandera and tried to
reseal – but empty now and ready for a collector's home. And that's where
the master of ceremonies bursts into view; Paul Feain is dressed in pink
trousers that might just pass on a tropical golf course, orange runners, a
shirt emblazoned with Christmas cheer and a red felt fedora. Nearby and
manning one of the computers is the co-author of the Idriess bibliography,[384] Ellie Aroney, and in the background three other women preparing
for a long day.

Just before the auction there are a dozen people scattered about the
room and as I stand to take a photograph one man in the audience,
seated in what seems strategic solitude behind a column, quickly lifts a
file to cover his face. Which begs the question… And then, promptly on
10:30am it begins, Paul settling behind a computer console and camera
that is also beaming the proceedings into cyberspace. Without introduc-
tions he's into it: *We are going to start today with Lot number 1, the book*
presented to Ion Idriess by Welsby, the Queensland fishing person. An internet
bid, we have $180 online … All the bids for the first lot are online, Paul
encouraging the flow: *don't be shy here … what a scarce book and a beautiful*
copy with dustwrapper, I've sold it for more than this in the past … Within a
minute the bid has nearly doubled then: *fair warning, fair warning. Sold*
for 350, that's better than 180. The first of a thousand lots, Paul wastes no
time: *Lot 2 is the book by Bill Harney inscribed to Ion Idriess,* **North of 23**,
can we have $180…

And so it goes, Ellie is managing the internet bids, Paul puts in his own
bids and those of his customers, and two women on mobiles relay offers.
Roles are changed as the auctioneer is spelled but the process doesn't
stop. A few items, like the Whitlams' Christmas card to Idriess, are
passed in – but not many. Paul has the banter and comments on just
about every item and then, an hour in, it's something I've handled:

Lot 142 is the six NORCO butter boxes, these come from the estate of Ion Idriess. His manuscripts were stored in these boxes. One or two didn't make it because they were eaten by white ants. But these are six good ones, can we have $180 with me, $180 for the six NORCO butter boxes, we have 190, 200 with me, come on we can't wait all day, online 225, 250 with me, fair warning, if you want it press your button now, 250, it's sold to my buyer, the architect. I don't know why he wants it – ratty old things.

I was tempted, but I'm not a collector and I don't need more stuff. *Stuff*, Paul seems to bait the punters by suggesting an equivalence between trash and treasure; with each box of ephemera or orphan item he seems to caricature collecting: *it's good stuff, we all need more stuff, how much am I offered…* Maybe it's also a personal insight, but he's in the business and in control: *I have 100 with me, and now 150 online, 175 in the room, 200 on the phone, do I hear…* During a spell from the console Paul circulates with biscuits – sugar hits to sustain bidders in the room who, to me, don't look like they are flagging at all. But by mid-afternoon – five hours after it all began – I'm over it. The rest of the Idriess items seem to have been positioned near the end of the proceedings. Three hours later I re-join through the website – and realise that I am one of more than 350 online participants still hanging in. It's now 7:30pm and an obviously weary Ellie Aroney passes off for the final set to a still colourful but clearly waning Paul Feain. In the last hour the *Nemarluk headbands* go for $1,200, the *Nemarluk Charge Sheet* for $2,300, *Original Artwork* for various covers from $500, with the *Artwork **Isles of Despair**: An original Oil colour by Quinton Davis* for $1,700 and *Artwork **Yellow Joss*** for $2,000. Then, finally, the only items directly related to ***Lasseter's Last Ride***, Lot 1000 – *Lasseter Idriess Original Photos* – listed with a low estimate of $4,000, it goes for $8,100. And that's it, a minute later, at 7:45pm, after nearly nine hours, the connection closes. As far as the *Idriess Estate* goes, this is just the beginning, there will be more hype and more auctions. But for me – it's over.

REFERENCES

Albrecht, F. (1964). On Lasseter's Trail. *Lutheran Almanac*, 34-50.

Albrecht, F. (1967, Sunday April 1). Lasseter: here is the truth. *Sunday Mail (Adelaide)*, p. 3.

Anonymous. (1894: Saturday August 25). New Gold Washer. *Australian Town and Country Journal*, p. 24; https://trove.nla.gov.au/newspaper/article/71263150.

Anonymous. (1920, Monday July 5). Missing Friends. *Kalgoorlie Miner*, p. 2; https://trove.nla.gov.au/newspaper/article/96133800.

Anonymous. (1926, Monday October 11). "Gleaner's" Dream. *Canberra Community News*, p. 7; https://trove.nla.gov.au/newspaper/article/66060466.

Anonymous. (1930, Friday July 18a). The Lure of Gold. Central Australian Exploration Co., Limited. Leaves Quorn for MacDonnell Range. *Quorn Mercury*, pp. 4; http://nla.gov.au/nla.news-article213014164.

Anonymous. (1930, Friday July 18b). The Lure of Gold. Expedition to Central Aust. Lasseter, the Leader. *Forbes Advocate*, p. 8; https://trove.nla. gov.au/newspaper/article/218358219.

Anonymous. (1931). *God save Australia: Advertising pamphlet for the Central Australian Gold Exploration Company Limited*. Central Australian Gold Exploration (CAGE) Company Limited records, 1930-1934. State Library of New South Wales: Mitchell Library. MLMSS10108.

Anonymous. (1931-1938). *Central Australian Gold Exploration Synd. Assistance to Prospect*. National Archives of Australia; NAS: A431. 1948/1143. Barcode 68988. https://recordsearch.naa.gov.au/SearchNRe-trieve/Interface/ViewImage.aspx? B=68988&S=1&R=0.

Anonymous. (1931, Friday December 11). Cave of Gold. Central Australia. *The Kyogle Examiner and Upper Richmond Advocate*, p. 6; https://trove.nla.gov.au/newspaper/article/234725095.

Anonymous. (1931, Friday February 20). Loneliest man in Australia sits and waits. Gold lured "Daddy" far away. His Sydney home. *Northern Standard*, 3; https://trove.nla.gov.au/newspaper/article/48056957.

Anonymous. (1931, January 26). Loneliest man in the whole of Aust. just sits and waits. Gold lured "Daddy" away. *The Evening News*, p. 3; https://trove.nla.gov.au/newspaper/article/201502904.

Anonymous. (1931, Monday January 12). Vivid Messages Tell of Rescue When Life Was Ebbing! 'PLANE SUCCOR FOR GOLD-SEEKERS. Pittendrigh and Hamre "Getting Weak" In the Arid Desert. Mystery of Fortitude. *Daily Pictorial*, p. 3; https://trove.nla.gov.au/news-paper/article/246421607.

Anonymous. (1931, Saturday November 21). Magic and Mystery in Central Wilds. *The Mail (Adelaide)*, p. 15; https://trove.nla.gov.au/news-paper/page/5306540.

Anonymous. (1931, Sunday August 16). Gold Seekers for Central Australia. *The Sunday Times*, p. 1; https://trove.nla.gov.au/newspaper/article/58684113.

Anonymous. (1931, Sunday May 10). Dead Gold-seeker Claimed as Husband by Two Women! Mystery of Missing Treasure-Plan New Aspect of Grim Wilderness Romance. *Truth (Sydney)*, p. 15; https://trove.nla.gov. au/newspaper/article/169129993.

Anonymous. (1932, Thursday September 15). Rip Von Winkle. *The Brisbane Courier*, p. 16; https://trove.nla.gov.au/newspaper/article/22001442.

Anonymous. (1934). *Prospectus for Scientific Gold Explorations Limited*. Central Australian Gold Exploration Synd. Assistance to Prospect. National Archives of Australia; NAA: A431, 1948/1143.

Anonymous. (1934, Monday May 14). Company News. *The Herald (Melbourne)*, p. 21; https://trove.nla.gov.au/newspaper/article/243250237.

Anonymous. (1934, Saturday December 15). Mining Men to Test Gold Story; On track of Lasseter; Money raised. *The Mail (Adelaide)*, p. 1; https://trove.nla.gov.au/newspaper/article/58857169.

Anonymous. (1934, Saturday January 30). Grim Diary of Death in Wilderness. L.H.B. Lasseter's Message From the Grave. *Smith's Weekly*, p. 3; https://trove.nla.gov.au/newspaper/article/234567954.

Anonymous. (1935, Friday March 15). Arnhem Land Gold. A Company Attacked. Commonwealth Making Inquiries. *The West Australian*, p. 19; https://trove.nla.gov.au/newspaper/article/32841191.

Anonymous. (1935, Saturday October 26). Has Lasseter's Reef been Found? Gold Explorers Return Secretly with Amazing Specimens. *The Australian Women's Weekly*, p. 4; https://trove.nla.gov.au/newspaper/article/47499437.

Anonymous. (1935, Tuesday March 26). Manunda and Manoora: Motor Ships for Queensland. *The Courier-Mail*, p. 6; https://trove.nla. gov.au/newspaper/article/35886219.

Anonymous. (1936). The secrets of the "Dead Heart". *The Wide World Magazine*, p. 296.

Anonymous. (1936, Tuesday June 23). Attack by Natives. "Exaggerated" Reports. Cutlack Expedition Returns. *Sydney Morning Herald*, p. 11; https://trove.nla.gov.au/newspaper/article/17245227.

Anonymous. (1938, Thursday September 29). Angel Gabriel Modernises Promised Land. *The Courier Mail* (Brisbane), p. 7; https://trove. nla.gov.au/newspaper/article/38729726.

Anonymous. (1939, Saturday December 9). Secrets of Lasseter's Reef. *Smith's Weekly*, pp. 1,5; https://trove.nla.gov.au/newspaper/article/234600061/225345152.

Anonymous. (1939, Saturday September 23). Says Lasseter's Lost Gold Reef is a "Myth". *The Argus* (Melbourne), p. 7; https://trove.nla.gov.au/newspaper/article/11248778.

Anonymous. (1954, Monday August 16). Even-money Snider wins life stakes. *The West Australian,* p. 5; https://trove.nla.gov.au/newspaper/article/49874385.

Anonymous. (1958, Saturday June 21). Burial 28yr after death. *The Sun (Sydney).*

Anonymous. (1976, Sunday September 5). Lasseter remembered at cemetery service. *The Star (Darwin),* p. 5 (Entertainment).

Anonymous. (2011). Chapter 8: Australian Labor Party, New South Wales Branch Annual Conference, 18-26 April, 1924. In M. Hogan (Ed.), *Labor Pains. Early Conference and Executive Reports of the Labor Party of NSW. Volume 4 (1918-25) (pp. 419-510;* https://ses.library.usyd.edu.au/handle/2123/7880).

Anonymous. (2013, November 5). Life of Idriess comes to light at Library. *Singleton Argus,* https://www.singletonargus.com.au/story/1885652/life-of-idriess-comes-to-light-at-library/ (accessed 6 November 2019).

Anonymous. (n.d.). Letter to Fred Blakeley. Letters to Fred Blakeley concerning Lasseter expedition, 14 June 1930-18 Feb. 1940. State Library of New South Wales: Mitchell Library. MLMSS8043. Item 8.

Anonymous ("Verax"). (1932, March 2). Untitled. *The Bulletin,* pp. 21; https://nla.gov.au/nla.obj-603948708.

Anonymous ("The Gossip"). (1931, Wednesday August 12). The Gold Trail. *The Daily Telegraph,* p. 6; https://trove.nla.gov.au/newspaper/article/246704820.

Anonymous ("Warrigal"). (1931, Friday September 18). The Unfinished Epic Of "Das" Lasseter: Twentieth Century Treasure-Hunt On Australia's Farthest Frontier. *The Land,* p. 2.

Australian Military Forces. (1917). *Lasseter, Lewis Hubert: Service Number - 23636: Place of Birth - Meredith VIC: Place of Enlistment - Melbourne VIC: Next of Kin - (Wife) Lasseter Florence Elizabeth.* National Archives of Australia. NAA: B2455; Control Symbol: Lasseter Lewis Hubert; Barcode 8334260; https://recordsearch.naa.gov.au/SearchNRe-trieve/Interface/ViewImage.aspx?B=8334260.

Australian Military Forces. (1919). *Coote, E H: Service Number 7699: Place of Birth - Vancouver British Columbia. Place of Enlistment Sydney NSW: Next of Kin F Coote Edward Charles.* National Archives of Australia. NAA: B2455; Control Symbol: Coote EH; Barcode 3415152.

Australian Military Forces. (1920a). *Biggers, Frederick Charles: Service Number 1861: Place of Birth - Lithgow NSW: Place of Enlistment - Sydney NSW.* National Archives of Australia. NAA: B2455; Control Symbol Biggers FC; Barcode 3082497.

Australian Military Forces. (1920b). *Lewis H Lasseter - Obtaining assistance in connection with land.* National Archives of Australia. NAA: A2489; Control Symbol: 1920/1492; Barcode: 514862.

Avery, P., & Heath-Stubbs (translators), J. (1981 (1979)). *The Ruba'iyat of Omar Khayyam.* Harmondsworth: Penguin.

Bailey, E. (1930, May 22). *Letter to Hon. Arthur Blakeley, Minister for Home and Territories.* Central Australian Gold Exploration Synd. Assistance to Prospect. National Archives of Australia; NAA: A431, 1948/1143.

Bailey, E. (1932, October 25). *Letter to Mr J.A. Perkins M.H.R., Minister for Home and Territories.* Central Australian Gold Exploration Synd. Assistance to Prospect. National Archives of Australia; NAA: A431, 1948/1143, p. 170; https://recordsearch.naa.gov.au/SearchNRetrieve/Interface/ViewImage.aspx?B=68988.

Bailey, J. (1936, Friday July 10). I Never Believed in Lasseter's Reef. *Daily Telegraph*, p. 6; https://trove.nla.gov.au/newspaper/article/247066572.

Bailey, J. (1947). *The History of Lasseter's Reef: And an explanation of the two Expeditions despatched to the Central Australia of where the reef was alleged to be.* State Library of New South Wales, Mitchell Library. A2753; .

Barry, P. (2014). The Tywerrenge as an Artefact of Rule: The (Post) Colonial Life of a Secret/Sacred Aboriginal Object. *History and Anthropology, 25*, 296-311.

Bell, L., & Shadbolt, G. H. (2002). *New Guinea Engineer: Startling stories of peace and war in Queensland, Papua, New Guinea, New Britain, New Ireland and the Sqally Islands.* Dural: Rosenberg Publishing.

Biggers, F. C. (1930, Monday February 17). "Journey's End". *Evening News*, p. 6; https://trove.nla.gov.au/newspaper/article/125971136.

Biggers, F. C. (n.d.). *A Song of Australia and other verses.* National Library of Australia; https://catalogue.nla.gov.au/Record/2330146.

Blackford, R., Ikin, V., & McMullen, S. (1999). *Strange Constellations: A History of Australian Science Fiction.* Westport: Greenwood Press.

Blakeley, A. (1930, July 11). *Letter to Rev. W. Morley, Honorary Secretary, Association for the Protection of Native Races.* Central Australian Gold Exploration Synd. Assistance to Prospect. National Archives of Australia; NAA: A431, 1948/1143.

Blakeley, F. (1930, September 13). *Memorandum of Agreement between the Central Australian Gold Exploration Company Limited and Paul Johns.* Central Australian Gold Exploration Company Ltd. Papers 1930-32. State Library of New South Wales, Mitchell Library; ML A3043, Item 1. CY Reel 1147.

Blakeley, F. (1948). *Statement concerning Lewis Harold Bell Lasseter, 1948, given to the then Mitchell Librarian, Phyllis Mander Jones. In the hand of Miss Mander Jones.* State Library of New South Wales: Mitchell Library. MLMDOC 3480.

Blakeley, F. (1984 (1972)). *Lasseter's Dream of Millions: New Light on the Lost Gold Reef.* (F. Wheelhouse & M. Mansfield Eds.). Sydney: Transpareon Press.

Blakeley, F. (n.d.-a). *Dream Millions: An account of the expedition in search of Lasseter's Reef, 1930. Volume 1.* State Library of New South Wales: Mitchell Library. MLA6962. CY1147.

Blakeley, F. (n.d.-b). *Dream Millions: An account of the expedition in search of Lasseter's Reef, 1930. Volume 2.* State Library of New South Wales: Mitchell Library. MLA6963. CY1147.

Blakiston-Houston, J. M. (1947). *I'd live it again.* Liddell Hart Military Archives, Kings College, London. GB 0099 KCLMA Blakiston-Houston.

Blatchford, T. (1932, February 18). *Letter to The Chairman, Central Australian Gold Exploration Co. Lt.* John Bailey - History of Lasseter's Reef, and an explanation of the two expeditions despatched to the Cenral Australia of where the reef was alleged to be, 26 Sept., 1947. State Library of New South Wales, Mitchell Library. Reference Code 457526. Call Number A 2753.

Bowden, T. (2020 (1975)). *Ion Idriess: The Last Interview.* Sydney: ETT Imprint.

Boyack, N. A. (2020). *More than Lust in the Dust: M.C. William Willshire's writings and frontier journey as a demonstration of traditional culture. MA Thesis.* (MA). Victoria University, Melbourne.

Bradly, J. (Ed.) (2008). *Gouger of the Bulletin: Paragraphs by Ion L. Idriess.* Uralla: Idriess Enterprises.

Bradly, J. (Ed.) (2013). *Gouger of The Bulletin: Part II: More Paragraphs & Short Stories by Ion L. Idriess.* Singleton: Idriess Enterprises.

Bridge, P. (1999). *The Eagle's nest: Larkinville, the Golden Eagle and the Great Depression.* Perth: Hesperian Press.

Bridge, P. J. (Ed.) (2020). H.A. *'Matt' Ellis and the Lasseter Rort.* Perth: Hesperian Press.

Brinsmead, H. C. (1930). *Letter to Hon. A.E. Green, Minister for Defence: June 23, 1930. Use of aircraft during expedition by Central Australian Gold Exploration Company.* National Archives of Australia: NAA: A705, 153/1/637.

Brown, W. (2015). *Lasseter's Gold.* Sydney: Hachette.

Byerley, F. J. (1994 (1867)). *Narrative of the overland expedition of the Messrs. Jardine, from Rockhampton to Cape York Northern Queensland.* Brisbane: J.W. Buxton (fascimile edition, Corkwood Press).

Cahill, R. (1990). *More than a footnote: a biographical portrait of L.C. Rodd.* The Hummer, 23-January/April, 1-4.

Carrington, V. C. (1934. October 28). *Letter to The Secretary, Department of the Interior. Scientific Gold Explorations Limited - Mineral Oil License and Exclusive Prospecting Licence.* National Library of Australia: Series number A659; Control symbol 1942/1/7/186; Barcode 80761.

Carron, W. (1996 (1849)). *Narrative of an expedition, undertaken under the direction of the late Mr Assistant Surveyor E.B. Kennedy, for the exploration of the country lying between Rockingham Bay and Cape York.* In L. Hiddins (Ed.), *William Carron's narrative of Kennedy's Cape York expedition* (fascimile edition) (pp. 1-79). Bundaberg: Corkwood Press.

Cartwright, M. (1991). *Ayers Rock to the Petermanns: Legend of Lasseter.* Alice Springs: Max Cartwright.

Cawte, J. (1998). *The Last of the Lunatics.* Melbourne: Melbourne University Press.

Central Australian Gold Exploration Syndicate. (1930). *Contributors to the Central Australian Gold Exploration Syndicate.* Central Australian Gold Exploration Synd. Assistance to Prospect. National Archives of Australia; NAA: A431, 1948/1143.

Charnley, W. C. (1935; 1936). The secret of the dead heart. *The Wide World Magazine,* 75 & 76, 390-400, 464-475; 034-044.

Chisholm, A. H. (1936, May 6). The Red Page: Making of a Best-seller. *The Bulletin*, 57 (2934)(2934), 2. https://nla.gov.au/nla.obj-558326442.

Chisholm, A. (1979). Barrett, Charles Leslie (1879-1959). In *Australian Dictionary of Biography*. Canberra: National Centre of Biography, Australian National University, http://adb.anu.edu.au/biography/barrett-charles-leslie-5142/text8607, published first in hardcopy 1979, (accessed 11 January 2021).

Clacherty, D. R. (1989). *On Lasseter's Trail.* Malvern: Malvern Press.

Clark, C. (2015). *Olof's Suitcase: Lasseter's Reef mystery solved.* Melbourne: Echo.

Clark, C. (2018). War historian F.M. Cutlack involved in Lasseter fraud? Author's website, uploaded September 7, 2018: http://chrisclarkhistorian.com.au/war-historian-f-m-cutlack-involved-in-lasseter-fraud/ (accessed 8 April 2020).

Clark, C. (2019). *The Truth About Lasseter: Why his elusive gold reef never existed.* Melbourne: Echo.

Clouten, K. H. (1988 (1967)). *Reid's Mistake: The Story of Lake Macquarie from its Discovery until 1890.* Lake Macquarie: Lake Macquarie Shire Council.

Clune, F. (1939, Saturday December 2). Lure of Lasseter's Reef: Desert journey by plane, truck and camel. *Smith's Weekly*, p. 1; https://trove.nla. gov.au/ newspaper/article/234599309.

Clune, F. (1944). *The Red Heart: Stories of Centralia.* Melbourne: The Hawthorne Press.

Clune, F. (1957). Chapter Five. In *The Fortune Hunters: An Atomic Odyssey in Australia's Wild West, and Things Seen and Heard by the Way in a Jeep Jaunt* (pp. 45-56). Sydney: Angus & Robertson.

Commonwealth of Australia: Home Affairs Department. (1929-1930). *L.H.B. Lasseter Auriferous areas Central Australia.* National Archives of Australia Series A1, 1930/512. Series number A1; Control symbol: 11930/512; Barcode 44813.

Conrad, P. (2017). *Mythomania: Tales of Our Times from Apple to ISIS.* London: Thames & Hudson.

Coote, E. (1930, August 27). *Letter to Fred Blakeley.* Letters to Fred Blakeley concern-ing Lasseter expedition, 14 June 1930-18 Feb. 1940. State Library of New South Wales: Mitchell Library. MLMSS8043. Item 4.

Coote, E. (1930, June 21). *Letter to Colonel Brinsmeand, Director of Civil Aviation.* National Archives of Australia; NAA: A705, 153/1/637. pp 39-40; https:// recordsearch.naa.gov.au/SearchNRetrieve/Interface/ViewImage.aspx?B=533697.

Coote, E. (1981 (1934)). Hell's Airport and Lasseters Lost Legacy (Third Edition) (G A. Stapleton Ed.). Adelaide: Investigator Press.

Cousins, W. (1931, September 21). *Letter to the Hon. Arthur Blakeley, Minister for Home and Territories.* National Archives of Australia. Series A431, Control symbol 1847/1640, Barcode 68609. Page 234. https://recordsearch.naa.gov.au/SearchNRetrieve/ Interface/ViewImage.aspx-?B=68609&S=2&R=0.

Cousins, W. G. (1939, October 13). *Letter to The Right Hon. R.G. Menzies, M.H.R., Prime Minister of Australia.* National Archives of Australia; NAA; A1608, Control Symbol 16/1/517, p. 4; https://recordsearch. naa.gov.au/SearchNRetrieve/Interface/ ViewImage.aspx?B=204515.

Coutts, R. (2013). *The Truth About Charlie: the "madman" stranded on Howick Island with Ion Idriess*. Brisbane: Boolarong Press.

Cox, E. ((1925). *Out of the Silence*: Project Guttenberg of Australia, eBook No.: 0604821h.html (first posted 2006).

Cox, E. (1934, Tuesday October 30). Out of the Silence, pp. 21, https://trove.nla.gov.au/newspaper/article/32819907.

Cox, E. (1948). *Harry Chaplin - letter received from Erle Cox concerning Harold Lasseter*. State Library of New South Wales, Mitchell Library. MLMSS 6397.

de Berg, H. (1991). Ion Idriess. In D. Foster (Ed.), *Self Portraits* (pp. 73-81). Canberra: National Library of Australia; https://www.nla.gov.au/sites/default/files/selfportraits.pdf.

Dewar, M. (2019 (1997)). In Search of the 'Never-Never'. In A. McGrath (Ed.), *In Search of the Never-Never. Micky Dewar: Champion of history across many genres.* (pp. 45-265). Canberra: Australian National University Press.

Drayton, J. (2013). Tribute unto Christy. In P. Bridge & G. Dreezens (Eds.), *There's gold there - look for it: 60 true tales of real finds and lost mines from Queensland to the Kimberley* (pp. 102-104). Perth: Hesperian Press.

Eley, B. (1995). Ion Idriess. Sydney: ETT Imprint.

Eley, B.(2007, Saturday February 10) *Jack: Beverley Eley in interview with Gretchen Miller/Interviewer: G. Miller.* Radio Eye, ABC Radio National (www.abc.net.au/radionational/programs/radioeye/jack/3388842).

Ellis, H. A. (1937). Report on some observations made on a journey from Alice Springs, N.T., to the country north of the Rawlinson Ranges in W.A., via the Musgrave and Petermann Ranges in 1936. In Under Secretary for Mines (Ed.), *Annual Progress Report of the Geological Survey for the year 1936* (pp. 16-31). Perth: Government Printer; https://geodocs.dmirs.wa.gov.au/Web/documentlist/3/Combined/NAA36.

Feain, P., & Aroney, E. (2016). *Ion Idriess: An Annotated and Illustrated Bibliography.* Sydney: Cornstalk Bookshop.

Ferguson, G., & Lasseter, R. (1958). *Correspondence between George Ferguson and Robert Lasseter, 24 January to 26 May, 1958.* State Library of New South Wales, Mitchell Library. Angus & Robertson Collection 3. Series 2 Correspondence, MLMSS3269. Vols 380-384.

Finlayson, H. H. (1946 (1935)). *The Red Centre: Man and Beast in the Heart of Australia.* Sydney: Angus & Robertson.

Foskett, A. (2008). *The Campbell Community: the history of the Canberra suburb of Campbell 1957-2008 (and before).* Canberra: Alan Foskett.

Foy, H., V. (1936, March 16). *Letter to J.A. Carrodus, Department of the Interior; March 16 1936.* National Archives of Australia; NAA: A1, 1936/2723. Barcode 46023. pp 5-6; https://recordsearch.naa.gov.au/SearchNRetrieve/Gallery151/dist/JGalleryViewer.aspx?B=46023.

Fuary, M. (1997). *A novel approach to tradition: Torres Strait Islanders and Ion Idriess.* The Australian Journal of Anthropology, 8(3), 247-258.

Gepp, H. W. (1929, December 2). *Memorandum for the Minister: Senator J.J Daly*. National Archives of Australia; NAS: A461. Control Symbol Q373/1/5 Part 1. Barcode 96408, pp. 74-78, https://recordsearch. naa.gov.au/SearchNRetrieve/Interface/ ViewImage.aspx?B=96408.

Gibson, C. G. (1930, May 4). *Letter to M.J. Calanchini, Secretary for Mines, Perth (received May 12)*. State Records Office, Western Australia; Series 20. Consignment 964. Central Australian Gold Exploration Syndicate. Item, 1 930/754.

Gill, W. (1968). *Petermann Journey*. Sydney: Rigby.

Gillen, R. S. (2019, 1995). Preface. In *F.J. Gillen's First Diary, 1875*. Adelaide: Wakefield Press.

Graham, M. (1988). Desirable Disabled Potters On. *Australiana, 10*(2), 52-54.

Gray, G. (2006). Looking for Neanderthal Man, Finding a Captive White Woman: The Story of a Documentary Film. *Health & History, 8*, 69-90.

Greeves, R. (1979). *The administration of justice and the European residents of Rabaul and the Mandated Territory of New Guinea, 1921-1942*. (Master of Arts Thesis). Australian National University, Canberra.

Gregor, G. S. (2016). *Lasseter's Cave*. ebook: Solstice Publishing.

Griffen-Foley, B. (2016). Digging up the past: Frank Clune, Australian historian and media personality. *History Australia, 8*(1), 127-152.

Hamilton, J. (2008). *Gallipoli Sniper: The Life of Billy Sing*. Sydney: Pan Macmillan.

Hannaford, V. (2013, Thursday October 31). Lasseter's Bones revives an outback enigma. *The Daily Telegraph*. Online at: https://www.dailytelegraph.com.au/ entertainment/arts/lasseters-bones-revives-an-outback-enigma/news-story/ a77d17978ee92c6028ff26811ac05e4d.

Haynes, R. D. (1998). *Seeking the Centre: the Australian desert in literature, art and film*. Cambridge: Cambridge University Press.

Henson, B. (1994). *A Straight-out Man: F.W. Albrecht and Central Australian Aborigines*. Melbourne: Melbourne University Press.

Herle, A., & Rouse, S. (Eds.). (1998). *Cambridge and the Torres Strait: Centenary essays on the 1898 Anthropological Expedition*. Cambridge: Cambridge University Press.

Hiddens, L. (1996). Lasseter's Gold. In L. Hiddens (Ed.), *Bush Tucker Man: Stories of Exploration and Survival* (pp. 167-187). Sydney: ABC Books.

Hill, E. (1933, November 18). *Letter to Ion Idriess (item in auction of Idriess estate, February 13, 2021)*. Sydney Rare Book Auctions, https://www.invaluable.com/ catalog/4eex0dvfr2 (accessed 7 February 2021).

Hill, E. (1951). *The Territory*. Sydney: Angus & Robertson.

Hodgetts (nee Lasseter), L. A. (1960). Story of Lewis Hubert Lasseter.

Hogan, E. (2021). *Into the Loneliness: The unholy alliance of Ernestine Hill and Daisy Bates*. Sydney: NewSouth.

Holmes, K. (1983). Excavations at Arltunga, Northern Territory. *Australian Historical Archaeology, 1*(January), 78-87.

Hubbard, M. (2017, 1993). *The Search for Harold Lasseter*. Sydney: ETT Imprint.

Idriess, I. L. (1915-1916). *Diary of Ion Llewellyn Idriess, 1915-1916.* RCDIG0000448, https://www.awm.gov.au/collection/C1357925?image=7.

Idriess, I. L. (1917). *Diary of Ion Llewellyn Idriess, 1917.* RCDIG0000453, (https://www.awm.gov.au/collection/C1357946).

Idriess, I. L. (1917-1918). *Diary of Ion Llewellyn Idriess, 1917-1918.* RCDIG0000454, (https://www.awm.gov.au/collection/C1358584).

Idriess, I. L. (1930). The Moonshiners. *The Wide World Magazine, 66 (November)* (391).

Idriess, I. L. (1931). *Lasseter's Last Ride: An Epic of Central Australian Gold Discovery.* Sydney: Angus & Robertson.

Idriess, I. L. (1931, October 4). Magic and Mystery in Central Wilds. *The Sunday Mail (Brisbane),* p. 20; https://trove.nla.gov.au/newspaper/page/10203186.

Idriess, I. L. (1931, Wednesday September 16). The Gold Quest: Lasseter's Romance and Tragedy. *Sydney Mail,* p. 10; https://trove.nla.gov.au/newspaper/article/159794235.

Idriess, I. L. (1932, April 15). *Letter to The Right Hon. J.A. Lyons, M.H.R.* National Archives of Australia; NAA: CP103/19, Control Symbol 51, Barcode 362134.

Idriess, I. L. (1932, Wednesday December 14). Head Hunters Kill Prospectors: The Trouble at Nakanai. *The World's News,* p. 20; https://trove.nla.gov.au/newspaper/article/131481029/114778673.

Idriess, I. L. (1933 (1931)). *Lasseter's Last Ride: An Epic of Central Australian Gold Discovery (thirteenth edition).* Sydney: Angus & Robertson.

Idriess, I. L. (1934 (1932)). *Men of the Jungle.* Sydney: Angus & Robertson.

Idriess, I. L. (1946). *In Crocodile Land: Wandering in Northern Australia.* Sydney: Angus & Robertson.

Idriess, I. L. (1947 (1933)). *Gold-Dust and Ashes: The Romantic Story of the New Guinea Goldfields.* Sydney: Angus & Robertson.

Idriess, I. L. (1957). *Coral Sea Calling.* Sydney: Angus & Robertson.

Idriess, I. L. (1959). *The Tin Scratchers.* Sydney: Angus & Robertson.

Idriess, I. L. (1969). *Challenge of the North: Wealth from Australia's Northern Shores.* Sydney: Angus & Robertson.

Idriess, I. L. (1974, November 25) *Ion Idriess interviewed by Hazel deBerg.* Hazel de Berg Collection, National Library of Australia; http://nla.gov.au/nla.obj-220875255.

Idriess, I. L. (1975) *Unedited transcript of Ion Idriess in interview with broadcaster Tim Bowden, in the early 1970s./Interviewer: T. Bowden.* Sydney http://www.abc.net.au/rn/legacy/programs/radioeye/documents/idriess.pdf (accessed 9 May 2016).

Idriess, I. L. (1979 (1958)). *Back o' Cairns.* Sydney: Angus & Robertson.

Idriess, I. L. (2019 (1932)). *Flynn of the Inland.* Sydney: ETT Imprint.

Idriess, I. L. (2019 (1942)). *Sniping.* Sydney: ETT Imprint

Idriess, I. L. (2020 (1938)). *Madman's Island.* Sydney: ETT Imprint.

Idriess, I. L. (2020 (1975)). *Ion Idriess: The Last Interview (interviewed by and with preface by Tim Bowden).* Sydney: ETT Imprint.

James, N. (1999). 'The Fountainhead': George Ferguson and Angus & Robertson. *Publishing Studies, 7,* 6-16.

Johannsen, K. G., & Palmer, D. (1992). *A Son of the Red Centre: Memoirs and anecdotes of the life of road train pioneer and bush inventor of the Northern Territory of Australia.* Morphetville: K.G. Johannsen.

Johns, A. P. (1932). *Typescript of 'Lasseter's Reef'. Statement given to Ernestine Hill.* Mitchell Library. MLMSS8444, Sydney.

Johns, A. P. (1934, Sunday December 9). Last Days with Lasseter....*The Sun*, p. 19; https://trove.nla.gov.au/newspaper/article/230157203.

Johns, A. P. (1935, Wednesday August 7). Lasseter's reef. *The Sydney Mail*, pp. 10-11; https://trove.nla.gov.au/newspaper/article/160499868.

Kaplan, R. M. (2019). Harold Lasseter: Flying too close to the sun. In R.M. Kaplan (Ed.), *Dark Tales of Illness, Medicine, and Madness: The King who Strangled his Psychiatrist* (pp. 13-21). Newcastle upon Tyne: Cambridge Scholars Publishing.

Keesing, N. (Ed.) (1967). *Gold Fever*. Sydney: Angus & Robertson.

Kell, V. G. W. (1940, March 20). *Letter from Major General Sir V.G.W. Kell to Colonel H.E. Jones.* National Archives of Australia; Series No. A367; Control symbol C75655, Barcode 771241.

Kevin, C. (2020). *Dispossession and the Making of Jedda: Hollywood in Ngunnawal Country.* London: Anthem.

Kimber, R. G. (1982). Walawurru, the giant eaglehawk: Aboriginal reminiscences of aircraft in Central Australia 1921-1931. *Aboriginal History, 6*(1), 49-60.

Kimber, R. G. (1986). *Man from Arltunga: Walter Smith Australian Bushman.* Perth: Hesperian Press.

Kinsella, J. (1989). *Night Parrots.* Fremantle: Fremantle Arts Centre Press; https://www.poetrylibrary.edu.au/poems-book/night-parrots-0400000.

Lasseter. (1986 (1930-31)). *Lasseter's Diary* (fascimile edition). Sydney: Angus & Robertson.

Lasseter, H. B. (1930-ca.1931). *Sub-series 3: Harold Lasseter diary with fragments, 1930-ca.1931.* State Library of New South Wales: Mitchell Library. MLMSS3269 (Safe 2/10). http://archival.sl.nsw.gov.au/Details/archive/110322067.

Lasseter, H. B. (1931). *Material relating to Lewis Harold Bell Lasseter, including a letter, an envelope and a telegram, 1931.* State Library of New South Wales, Mitchell Library. Reference Code 1382674. http://archival.sl.nsw.gov.au/Details/archive/110375638.

Lasseter, L. H. B. (1927, March 28). *Letter to the Editor of the Canberra Community News, J.H. Honeysett.* Canberra Community News. National Archives of Australia: NAA: CP698/9, 12.6. Barcode 262385, p.71: https://recordsearch.naa.gov.au/SearchNRetrieve/Gallery151/dist/JGalleryViewer.aspx?B=262385&S.

Lasseter, L. H. B. (1929, November 6). *Letter to H.W. Gepp.* National Archives of Australia Series A786, C64/7, p. 84: https://recordsearch.naa.gov.au/SearchNRetrieve/Interface/ViewImage.aspx?B=168885.

Lasseter, L. H. B. (1930). *Letter to the Consul General for Japan.* National Archives of Australia. Series C443. Item: J 244 (accessed 15 December 2019); on Lasseteria website: http://www.lasseteria.com/CYCLOPEDIA/134.htm (accessed 21 December, 2019).

Lasseter, L. H. B. (1930, June 1). *Letter to Information Bureau, Dept of Home & Territories.* L.H.B. Lasseter Auriferous areas Central Australia. National Archives of Australia; NAS A1 Control Symbol C1930-512. Item ID 44813, p.3, https://recordsearch.naa.gov.au/SearchNRetrieve/Interface/ViewImage.aspx?B=44813.

Lasseter, L. H. B. (1930, May 20). *Letter to Hon. Mr Gepp (received 21 May).* Mines and Mining Not Elsewhere included A-L Central Austra-lia. National Archives of Australia; NAS A786. Control Symbol C64/7. Barcode. 168885, p. 21; https://recordsearch.naa.gov.au/SearchNRe-trieve/Interface/ViewImage.aspx?B=168885.

Lasseter, L. H. B. (1930, September 14). *Letter to Chief of Police, Alice Springs.* Letters to Fred Blakeley concerning Lasseter expedition, 14 June 1930-18 Feb. 1940. State Library of New South Wales: Mitchell Library. MLMSS8043. Item 3.

Lawton, L. (2007). Conrad in Australia. *Signals* (81, Dec 2007-Feb 2008), 8-12.

Marshall-Stoneking, B. (1985). *Lasseter: The Making of a Legend.* Sydney: Allen & Unwin.

McKennna, M. (2021). *Return to Uluru.* Carlton: Black Inc.

Midford. (1937, February 10). The Lost Reef. *The Bulletin. Vol 58,* No. 2974, 58(2974), 15. https://nla.gov.au/nla.obj-562585667.

Miller, I. (1935). *School Tie.* London: George Newnes.

Miller, I. (1940). *The Lost Reef.* Oxford: Oxford University Press.

Morley, W. (1930, July 10). *Letter to Hon. Arthur Blakeley, Minister for Home and Territories.* Central Australian Gold Exploration Synd. Assistance to Prospect. National Archives of Australia; NAA: A431, 1948/1143; p.169; https://recordsearch.naa.gov.au/SearchNRetrieve/Interface/View-Image.aspx?B=68988.

Mulvaney, D. J. (1990). Willshire, William Henry (1852-1925). In *Australian Dictionary of Biography.* Australian National University, http://adb.anu.edu.au/biography/willshire-william-henry-9128/text16101, published first in hardcopy 1990 (Melbourne University Press) (accessed online 23 June 2020).

Nandan, S. (2000). The Other Side of Paradise: From Erotica to Exotica in Exile. In "New" Exoticisms: Changing Patters in the Constructions of Otherness (*Postmodern Studies 29*) (pp. 79-88). Amsterdam: Rodopi.

National Library of Australia. (2005). *National Treasures from Australia's Great Libraries.* Canberra: National Library of Australia. https://webarchive.nla.gov.au/awa/20060820071554/ and http://nationaltreasures.nla.gov.au/index/Treasures/item/nla.int-ex6-s53.

Nettlebeck, A., & Foster, R. (2007). *In the Name of the Law: William Willshire and the Policing of the Australian Frontier.* Adelaide: Wakefield Press.

O'Brien, C. (2019). Re-reading the Never-Never. In A. McGrath (Ed.), In *Search of the Never-Never. Micky Dewar: Champion of history across many genres.* (pp. 19-44). Canberra: Australian National University Press.

Osborne, P. L.-A. (2014). *"Offensively Australian:" Walkabout and Middlebrow Writers, 1927-1969.* (PhD). Thesis submitted for PhD, University of Tasmania, Hobart.

Parkin, R. (2003 (second edition)). *H.M. Bark Endeavour: her place in Australian history: with an account of her construction, crew and equipment and a narrative of her voyage on the east coast of New Holland in the year 1770.* Melbourne: Miegunyah.

Pearson, N. (2020, September 5-6). Rio's poor excuse on Juukan. *The Weekend Australian (Inquirer),* p. 16.

Price, H. T. (1932, August 11). *Letter to The Hon. J.A. Lyons, Prime Minister.* National Archives of Australia: CP103/19. Control Symbol 72, Barcode 780597, pp. 159-160; https://recordsearch.naa.gov.au/SearchN-Retrieve/Interface/ViewImage.aspx?B=780597.

Reed, B. (1929, Saturday March 23). Joseph Conrad. His Visits to Australia. *The Sydney Morning Herald,* p. 13; https://trove.nla.gov.au/newspaper/article/16540359-

Reid, F. (1954). Chapter Six: White women among savages. In *The Romance of the Great Barrier Reef.* Sydney: Angus & Robertson.

Richardson, R. D. (2016). *Nearer the Heart's Desire. Poets of the Rubaiyat: A Dual Biography of Omar Kayyam and Edward Fitzgerald.* New York: Bloomsbury.

Riddell, B. (1931, Thursday May 28). How Lasseter Died. *The Daily Telegraph* (Sydney), p. 6; https://trove.nla.gov.au/newspaper/article/246257423.

Rodd, L. C. (1973). The mystery of Lasseter and his reef. *Quadrant, 17*(1), 65-77.

Roderick, C. (1949). Introduction. In I. Idriess (Ed.), *Gems from Ion Idriess* (pp. vii-xi). Sydney: Angus & Robertson.

Rothwell, N. (2009). *The Red Highway.* Melbourne: Black Inc.

Rowlands, R. (1995). The Best Idriess Collection. *Australian Book Collector, 67* (October), 16-17.

Ryan, S. (1996). *The Cartographic Eye: How Explorers Saw Australia.* Melbourne: Cambridge University Press.

Ryan, S. (2013). Lasseter and the Mine with the Iron Door. *International Journal of Literary Humanities, 10* (15-22). doi: https://doi. org/10.18848/2327-7912/CGP/v10i04/58291.

Ryan, S. (2015). *Lasseter's Last Ride* and the Gothic narrative of failure. *Journal of Australian Studies,* 39(3), 381-395. doi:10.1080/1444 3058.2015.1051084

Scherer, P. A. (1994). *Camel Treks in the Outback.* Tanunda: P.A. Scherer.

Scherer, P. A. (1996). *Lasseter Demystefied & Two German Rouseabouts.* P.A.Scherer. Tanunda.

Sharp, M. (2021, August 14). Lasseter Looks for a "Missing Friend": Pearl Bell by Chris Clark. *Outback Family History*; https://www.outbackfamilyhistoryblog.com/lasseter-looks-for-a-missing-friend/ (accessed September 26, 2021).

Sharp, M. (2021, September 25). Another link in the Lasseter Story: William and Vera Bryant of Piesse Street, Boulder, by Chris Clark. *Outback Family History*; https://www.outbackfamilyhistoryblog.com/another-link-in-the-lasseter-story (accessed September 26, 2021).

Shephard, B. (2014). *Headhunters: The search for a science of the mind.* London: The Bodley Head.

Smith, A. (2020). *The Rock: Looking into Australia's 'Heart of Darkness' from the edge of its wild frontier*. Melbourne: Transit Lounge.

Smith, I., & Smith, J. (1979). *The Die-Hard*. Sydney: Harper & Row.

Stapleton, A. (1981). *Lasseter Did Not Lie!* Hawthorndene: Investigator Press.

Stapleton, A. (1992). Willshire of Alice Springs. Perth: Hesperian Press.

Such, L. (1939). Cartoon. Man Magazine, 5(5), 41.

Synge, L. (2001). *The novel: Precious. The critical essay: Men, Women and Gold: the Problem of Desire in the Writing of 'Precious'*. Thesis for Master of Arts (Creative Writing), University of Queensland, Brisbane.

Talbot, H. W. B., Chambers, M., Central Australian Gold Exploration Co, & South Australia Department of Lands Survey. (1985). *Central Australian Gold Exploration Co, 1931 Expedition to the Petermann and Rawlinson Ranges*. Adelaide: Department of Lands Survey.

Tennant, K. (1963, December 22). *Letter to Ion Idriess*. Lot 100, Sydney Rare Book Auction, 4 February 2022: https://www.invaluable.com/auction-lot/kylie-tennant-to-ion-idriess-100-c-2214b8ab27.

Tennant, K. (1976). No good at lying - Two views of Australian writer Ion Idriess. *Hemisphere, 20*(12), 27-31.

Terry, M. (1936). Does Lasseter's Reef exist. *Walkabout* (August 1st), 16-21.

Terry, M. (1974). *War of the Warramullas*. Adelaide: Rigby.

Terry, M. (1979, January 30). *A typed letter signed with manuscript additions and corrections by Michael Terry, written in response to a letter from a reader of an article about Lasseter's reef, published in Brisbane 'Courier-Mail' in January 1979*. Michael Treloar, Antiquarian Booksellers - website. https://www.treloars.com/pages/books/114407/michael-terry/a-typed-letter-signed-with-manuscript-additions-and-corrections-by-michael-terry-written-in/?soldItem=true (accessed July 5, 2020).

Testa, A., & Decarli, B. (2005). *A Dead Man's Dream: Lasseter's Reef found*. Perth: Hesperian Press.

Thompson, T. (Ed.) (2020). *Lasseter's Diary: Transcribed with Mud-Maps*. Sydney: ETT Imprint.

Thomson, A. (2000). *The Singing Line*. London: Vintage.

Tonkin, D. (2001). *A Truly Remarkable Man: The Life of H.H. Flinlayson, and his Adventures in Central Australia*. Adelaide: Seaview Press.

Trezise, P. (1973). *Last Days of a Wilderness*. Brisbane: William Collins.

Vallee, P. (2004). God, guns and government on the Central Australian frontier. Canberra: Restoration.

Various authors. (1931). *Correspondence relating to death of H.L.B. Lasseter*. Central Australian Gold Exploration Synd. Assistance to Prospect. National Archives of Australia: NAA: A431, 1948/1143, pp.68-95; https://recordsearch.naa.gov.au/SearchNRetrieve/Interface/ViewImage. aspx?B=68988.

Various authors. (1958-1978). *Burial L.H.B. Lasseter*. Correspondence, District Office Alice Springs. National Archives of Australia: NAA: F706, 1960/39; Series number F706; Barcode 1841638; https://recordsearch. naa.gov.au/SearchNRetrieve/Interface/ViewImage.aspx?B=1841638.

Walker, L. (Writer). (2012). Lasseter's Bones. In L. Walker (Producer). Australia (Melbourne): Scribble Films.

Walsh, G. P. (1983). Lasseter, Lewis Hubert (1880-1931). In *Australian Dictionary of Biography*. National Centre of Biography, Australian National University, http://adb.anu.edu.au/biography/lasseter-lewis-hubert-7039 (accessed online 9 April, 2020).

Wauchope, A. (1931, Saturday September 19). Was Lasseter "Hoodooed"? Theory in Book on Expedition. *The Mail (Adelaide)* p. 16. https://trove.nla.gov.au/newspaper/article/61565050.

Wise, P. (2017-2020). Historical Locations Connected with Lasseter's Grave, Petermann Ranges, Central Australia. *XNATMAP*. Retrieved from https://www.xnatmap.org/adnm/docs/1genmap/LASSETER/LHLasseter.htm (accessed 18 January 2020).

Lot 1000: LASSETER IDRIESS ORIGINAL PHOTOS

7,500 AUD (Competing Bid)
Fair Warning!
8,000 AUD (Online)
Fair Warning!
Fair Warning!
Fair Warning!

Register to Bid

1 of 20

375 bidders viewing
Estimate: 4,000 - 5,000 AUD
Current bid: 8,000 AUD

DESCRIPTION
Seventeen original photographs all used in the book Lasseter's Last Ride by Ion Idriess. The photos are original prints and mounted on board. They measure 29 x 39 cm. Images are sharp, clean and clear. Most of the mounts are grubby and stained. On each mount is the title of the photo: A Girl of the Spinifex 2) Her First Looking Glass 3) A Warrior Bold 4) Lasseter's Cave Where He Lived For Many Days 5) Ayer's Rock 6) A Warrior Who Has Killed His Men 7) A Dessert Warrior 8) A Central Australian Belle 9) Lasseter's Diary Uncovered When Found 10) Mt Olga In The Distance 11) Marked Tree at Entrance to Lasseter's Cave 12) A Close Up of Mt Olga 13) My Baby 14) NO title but is a group of Aboriginal

*... the only items directly related to **Lasseter's Last Ride**, Lot 1000 – Lasseter Idriess Original Photos ...*

ENDNOTES

FOREWORD

1   (Hogan, 2021).

2   Petrina Osborne's thesis exemplifies *middlebrow* writing in the works of Ion Idriess, Arthur Upfield, Ernestine Hill and John K. Ewars in the magazine *Walkabout*, published from 1934 to the mid-1970s (Osborne, 2014).

3   Page 417, in: (Hill, 1951).

4   There are Aboriginal variants. In her dual biography of Daisy Bates and Ernestine Hill, Eleanor Hogan recalls a campfire conversation: *I was fascinated to hear how Lasseter had become a skein of local mythology: that this tale had another life among Anangu as a story about a white man failing to survive in the country's centre.* Page 272, in: (Hogan, 2021).

5   The text was only significantly altered once, with the inclusion of material from the Second Expedition from 1932. Whether reprintings or editions, the latter term has been commonly used by collectors and writers and is used here.

6   Thanks to Jim Bradly for identification of these pseudonyms.

7   (Thomson, 2000).

8   (Wise, 2017-2020).

CHAPTER 1 – Adelaide

9   Page 226, in: (Ion L Idriess, 1931).

10   Archaeologist Kate Holmes cites Central Australian historian, Dick Kimber, that Arltunga is a corruption of *Aldolanga*, meaning 'Easterners' in Aranda (Holmes, 1983).

11   Page 190, in: (Marshall-Stoneking, 1985).

12   (Australian Military Forces, 1917).

13   (Australian Military Forces, 1920b).

14   (Kaplan, 2019).

15   (Hodgetts (nee Lasseter), 1960).

16   Page 20, in: (Kaplan, 2019).

17   Page 150, in: (Cawte, 1998).

CHAPTER 2 – Witnesses

18   Page 1, in: (J. Bailey, 1947).

19   Foreword in: (Ion L Idriess, 1931).

20   Phillip Scherer, who interviewed various people in this saga including Albrecht and Taylor, points out that the correct spelling should be Paul John. However, it is consistently spelled as Johns and will be so here (P.A. Scherer, 1994).

21   (P.A. Scherer, 1994).

22   (Coote, 1981 (1934)). When first published by Peterman Press in 1934 the title was **Hell's Airport: The Key to Lasseter's Gold Reef.** The later edition, published after his death, was edited by Austin Stapleton to accompany his own book **Lasseter Did Not Lie!**

23   (Johns, 1932). This was republished as a signed, limited edition series – **About Lasseter** – by Ernestine Hill through Scrivener Press in 1968.

24   (Johns, 1934, Sunday December 9).

25   (Johns, 1935, Wednesday August 7).

26   (J. Bailey, 1947).

27   Kindly provided by Robert Ross of *lasseteria.com,* the original at: (Blakiston-Houston, 1947).

28   (Rodd, 1973).

29   While his assistant and editor, Mary Mansfield, stated in the published version that there were limited changes from Blakeley's original text, some comments about tribal Aboriginal people, and strong criticism of Coote and Bailey were removed. See: (Synge, 2001).

30   (F. Blakeley, 1948).

31   (F Albrecht, 1967, Sunday April 1).

32   Page 2, in: (F. Blakeley, 1984 (1972)).

33   In the late 1930s Blakeley corresponded with a friend of Lasseter's father, identified as *Cubby.* He recalled first meeting *Lewis, a wee-lad, wild but not bad* in 1887 at Meredith, adding: *He ran away from "where there is no place like it" made for Geelong, got aboard a schooner for the South Sea Islands where he remained about 2 years – then he managed to ship to America where he spent the greater part of his life – Reaching Sydney in 1911.* The letter continues that at that time Lasseter, with his American wife and daughter Ruby, sought out *Cubby* in Drake, and that he was in contact once more in the late 1920s after Lasseter married Irene. He noted: *Lewis was a short, thick set, powerful chap, swarthy appearance, having a constant unforgettable smile and a decided Yankee accent and style of speech – An atom of Great Pluck and Perseverance.* On the back of the last page and in what looks like Blakeley's writing, is the following: *This matter re Lasseter I sent on to Mr Ion Idriess author of Book "Lasseter's Last Ride". ... Mr Idriess' reply thanked me and regretted not having the information before he published the book.* Blakeley tracked down Lasseter's sister in Adelaide and the last two letters in the same file are from Lillian McGrath in early 1940 with general comments about her brother and apologising for not being able to give specific dates. Blakeley was trying to hone in on where Lasseter was in 1897 – the closest he got to what emerged half-a-century later, is *Cubby's* puzzling statement: *He ran away from "where there is no place like it"* (Anonymous, n.d.).

34   (E. Bailey, 1930, May 22).

35   Pages 425-430, in: (Anonymous, 2011).

36   (Morley, 1930, July 10).

37   (A. Blakeley, 1930, July 11).

38   (Anonymous, 1935, Friday March 15).

39   (Australian Military Forces, 1919).

40   (Coote, 1930, June 21).

41   See note at the beginning of Chapter 3.

42   (Brinsmead, 1930).

43   Page 37, in: (FW Albrecht, 1964).

44   Page 6, in: (Stapleton, 1981).

45   (Johns, 1932). Johns actually arrived at Ilbilba two days before *Golden Quest II* was flown in by Pat Hall.

46   (F. Blakeley, 1930, September 13).

47   Page 76, in: (Marshall-Stoneking, 1985).

48   (Kimber, 1982).

49   Page 86, in: (Kimber, 1986).

50   Page 35, in: (FW Albrecht, 1964).

51   Page 127, in: (Coote, 1981 (1934)).

52   It may be that the recollection of Albrecht and the account of Marshall-Stoneking confuse this episode with the first departure of Johns from the mission. This section of Taylor's diary on, page 47, in: (P.A. Scherer, 1994).

53   Carl von Czarnecki was interviewed by Philipp Scherer in 1973 and 1983 (Philipp A Scherer, 1996).

54   (Foy, 1936, March 16).

55   (Johannsen & Palmer, 1992).

56   (Kell, 1940, March 20).

57   Page 147, in: (F. Blakeley, 1984 (1972)).

CHAPTER 3 – The Expedition

58   Entry 161 – Lasseter's Reef – on Lasseteria.com.

59   Lasseter initially wrote to Texas Green on 14th October 1929 offering *fraternal congratulations on Labor's Victory* and seeking support for a water supply venture in Western Australia that would be funded through what later became the whole focus – the reef of gold. The trail of correspondence culminated in a letter on 2nd December from Herbert Gepp, Chairman of the Development and Migration Commission who, with the Government Geologist of South Australia, had interviewed Lasseter in Sydney on 14th November. That letter, subsequently known as the *Gepp Report,* to Senator J.J. Daly, Minister assisting the Prime Minister and Vice President of the Executive Council, was not

promising but not entirely dismissive (Gepp, 1929, December 2). Lasseter had also been in correspondence around that time with M.J. Calanchini in the Department of Mines in Perth who, four months later with things speeding up on the other side of the continent, received a letter from Mining Geologist Charles Gibson written on 4th May from Turramurra, Sydney, which starts: *Some friends of mine have been attracted by another lost lode story* (Gibson, 1930, May 4). He was after anything to support Lasseter's story (which he records as having been in 1895). By that time reports in the press were mounting, and on 21st May Lasseter himself wrote to Herbert Gepp commenting: *the media attention was really a surprise to me as I was asking Bailey's assistance to get the Minister's consent to prospect in the Abo reserve in Central Australia, and he took the initiative in forming a syndicate.* Lasseter insisted that it was Bailey who *spilt the beans,* and concluded: *If you care to have a finger in the pie the Syndicate consists of 50 shares of £50 each paid to £20 with calls of £5 as required* (L. H. B. Lasseter, 1930, May 20). The next day, Ern Bailey wrote as newly installed Secretary of the CAGE Syndicate to Minister Blakeley seeking *a subsidy of £1 for £1* from the Commonwealth (E. Bailey, 1930, May 22). It was hardly news to Minister Blakeley.

60   For reasons outlined in the previous chapter, Fred Blakeley's account is used as the primary source unless otherwise noted.

61   There was a well-publicised ruby rush in the 1880s that, coincidentally, resulted in gold finds around Paddy's Rockhole – now Arltunga. The rubies turned out to be garnets and by 1888 – a decade before Lasseter reported heading to the Centre – the ruby claims were deserted (Holmes, 1983).

62   Transcriptions of these three letters are in Blakeley's unedited manuscript – *Dream Millions* – in the Mitchell Library: Pages 3-4 in: (F. Blakeley, n.d.-a)

63   The document was sealed on 14th June 1930. After news of Lasseter's death Bailey sought access but was initially blocked. Eventually the documents were inspected; neither that written *en clair* nor the other with invisible ink provided guidance. For transcripts of the *open* and *secret* messages see (Anonymous, 1931, Sunday August 16).

64   (Anonymous, 1930, Friday July 18b).

65   Page 55, in: (Blakiston-Houston, 1947).

66   Page 3, in: (L. H. B. Lasseter, 1930, June 1). Quinlan's response in same file.

67   Fred Colson's brother, Ted, was with the Endeavour expedition under Michael Terry that set out just weeks earlier.

68   Page 61, in: (Blakiston-Houston, 1947).

69   In Blakeley's hand with the original note is another: *Harrold. This is a mistake by Colson for Errol & refers to Errol Coote.* These are with Blakeley's papers in the Mitchell Library and on the reverse Blakeley records: *Insufficient experience was the main cause of the plane crashing.* He also noted: *Coote was badly hurt. He was lucky to have a man like Fred Colson with him who was on his way inside 30 minutes to Alice Springs 240 miles away. He did a wonderful job in saving Coote's life doing the 240 miles in 22 hours without stopping and no road a wonderful feat of driving and endurance.*

70   (Coote, 1930, August 27).

71   Marshall-Stoneking's informant, Nosepeg Tjupurrula, and George Tjangala told historian Dick Kimber that from early in the First CAGE Expedition Pintubi had

been close by – out of sight but tracking its progress (Kimber, 1982).

72   (F. Blakeley, 1948). In his statement Blakeley added that in the trunk he found what appeared to be Lasseter's United States naturalisation papers and a passport in the name of *Frederick Harold Bell.*

73   Pat Hall was a pilot in Morley Cutlack's 1936 expedition to find the reef following which there were sensationalised reports of an *attack by natives* (Anonymous, 1936, Tuesday June 23).

74   Page 84, in: (Coote, 1981 (1934)).

75   The following day Lasseter wrote a letter to the Chief of Police in Alice Springs noting: *it has been decided to send me on by Camel team owing to the failure of our motor transport.* He requested that the police take responsibility for a tin trunk returning with Blakeley. Lasseter signed off with: *LHB Lasseter. At present in search of my lost reef* (L. H. B. Lasseter, 1930, September 14). The trunk was delivered to the police in Alice Springs two weeks later. That trunk and its contents, which may have also included some of the objects found by Bob Buck near Lasseter's body, ultimately made its way to his wife, by then Irene Green, in 1942, the year before she died.

76   The letter is reproduced in editions of **Lasseter's Last Ride** from February 1932.

77   Page 43, in: (FW Albrecht, 1964).

78   (Nandan, 2000).

79   (Gill, 1968). Written decades after the events, Gill's dates vary by a few days from other sources.

80   (Anonymous, 1931).

81   In his narrative of another Territory tragedy, Mark McKenna quotes Charles Mountford's observations of the ubiquity of firearms at Buck's homestead at Middleton Ponds, including a revolver at the foot of every bed (McKennna, 2021).

CHAPTER 4 – Seven Hills

82   (Walker, 2012).

83   As reported in the press in January 1931, in one of the last letters received by his wife, Irene, Lasseter described how he had frightened *the emu that Bobby wanted* away so that Johns could not shoot it (Anonymous, 1931, Friday February 20).

84   The Douglas Mawson was a coastal steamer which was lost in the Gulf of Carpentaria and the story of surviving women *seized by wild tribesmen* fed into a genre of writing exemplified by Frank Reid who, in mid-century, collated such stories of northern shores, including that of Barbara Thompson (Reid, 1954) who features in Idriess' Torres tales.

85   Porteus, whose name lives on in the Porteus Maze Test, was blindsided by his medical colleague in the use of the film footage. His attempts to prevent release and, later, to undo the damage weren't successful and the controversy resulted in ethnopsychological research being resisted for decades (Gray, 2006).

86   Footage from the 1957 *High Adventure* episode was used in Robinson's 1979 documentary, ***The Legend of Lasseter***.

87   The skull shows two canines in the mandible and, possibly, a right molar which may not have erupted when Lasseter was fitted with dentures in the military in 1917. There are no upper teeth. His military record details that he had three *Teeth Natural* on the right and left and four *Artificial Teeth Required* – giving a total, when *Wearing Artificial Teeth* of s even on each side. While his upper teeth may have been lost or extracted subsequently, it is possible that they were already absent and he had an existing upper denture in 1917. Regardless, the image is entirely consistent with his military record – he had a few remaining lower teeth when his denture was supplied. This also may resolve Nosepeg Tjupurrula's comment: *"Not false teeth! True one! Inside."* I am grateful to Dr Michael Kevin for this forensic dental opinion. The story is further complicated by the disappearance of the dentures that Bob Buck retrieved, displayed at Hermannsburg and delivered to Alice Springs. While the other items found near the body were itemised by the police in Alice Springs, the dentures were not recorded. When the Lowell Thomas circus returned to Alice Springs with the disinterred skeleton, Lee Robinson and another member of the team, Alton (Curly) Frazer, were arrested (though quickly released) for desecration of a grave (Anonymous, 1958, Saturday June 21).

88   In 1977 Nosepeg was with Bob Lasseter overflying the region with Dick Smith's *Lasseter's Reef Expedition* (Clark, 2019).

89   Alison Anderson, personal communication, May 2019.

90   At the supposed site that Lasseter's body was found there is a rough bush monument that incorporates a stone that had been inscribed by the truck driver of the Lowell Thomas team in 1957 which read: *Harold B Lasseter, died was buried here Jan 1931.* The current and more substantial monument includes a brass plaque that was added in 2003 reading: *Harold B Lasseter. Perished and was buried here Jan 1931. "His death gave birth to a legend." This plaque provided by members of The Australian Geographic Society 2002 Expedition.* See: http://xnatmap.org/adnm/docs/1genmap/LASSETER/LHLasseter.htm.

91   (Hubbard, 2017 (1993)).

92   (Hodgetts (nee Lasseter), 1960).

93   Page 28, in: (Hubbard, 2017 (1993)).

94   (J. Bailey, 1947).

95   (Anonymous, 1931, Sunday May 10).

96   (James, 1999).

97   (Ferguson & Lasseter, 1958).

98   These related to contracts for a steam raising plant at Bunnerong Power House, and the Arnhem Gold Development Company (Anonymous, 1935, Friday March 15).

99   (L. H. B. Lasseter, 1927, March 28).

100   The letter was written to Harry Chaplin, a dentist who was foundation president of the Book Collector's Society of Australia and amassed an enormous collection of Australiana that now resides in the National Library. Erle Cox apologised that he

hadn't kept the letters (Cox, 1948).

101   (Cox, 1925).

102   (Blackford, Ikin, & McMullen, 1999).

103   (Cox, 1934, Tuesday October 30).

104   (L. H. B. Lasseter, 1930).

105   Patenting the *Roberts alluvial washer and gold-saving machine* decades earlier (Anonymous, 1894: Saturday August 25).

106   (Commonwealth of Australia: Home Affairs Department, 1929-1930).

107   (L. H. B. Lasseter, 1929, November 6).

108   (Graham, 1988).

109   Page 27, Saturday March 1, and page 27, Wednesday March 5, 1930.

CHAPTER 5 – The story

110   Page 161, in: (Eley, 1995).

111   Tape 5 in: (Ion L Idriess, 1974, November 25).

112   This document and uncited quotes following are from the file: (Central Australian Gold Exploration Syndicate, 1930).

113   Page 158, in: (Eley, 1995).

114   So named after the 1900 British music hall song of the same name by Harry Norris, or its 1905 imitator – *Burlington Bertie from Bow* – by Willliam Hargreaves, parodying silver-tailed and silver-tongued, West End and East End swells respectively. Much imitated musically, it also passed into gambling argot.

115   Page 57, in: (Bell & Shadbolt, 2002).

116   Page 378, in: (Greeves, 1979).

117   (Ion L Idriess, 1932, Wednesday December 14).

118   Page 191, in: (Ion L Idriess, 1947 (1933)). According to Territorian and Lasseter historian, Barry Allwright, Ray Parer (a distant relative), a distinguished pilot who was flying in New Guinea at the time, had also been considered for the Expedition (personal communication, July 2021).

119   On 29th July 1932 E.J. Stackpole Sr., President and Editor-in-Chief of the *Harrisburg Telegraph* in Pennsylvania wrote from a Matson Line steamer to Lexius-Burlington at 14 Spring Street Sydney with a draft review of ***Lasseter's Last Ride***. (Letter and draft part of the Idriess estate, inspected at Sydney Rare Book Auctions on 2nd February 2021).

120   (Anonymous, 1934, Monday May 14).

121   (J. Bailey, 1947).

122   Idriess' contract was signed on 1st September 1931, witnessed by William Frederick Dibley, the Secretary of Angus & Robertson Limited. Within two weeks copies were ready for distribution.

123   (W. Cousins, 1931, September 21).

124   Last rites were performed on 30th September 1932, just a couple of months after Ernest Bailey's letter to the minister, with £20 in the bank account.

125   (E. Bailey, 1932, October 25).

126   (J. Bailey, 1936, Friday July 10).

127   (Various authors, 1931).

128   Lasseter's first death certificate was issued by H.A. Heinrich in Hermannsburg on 25th April. Buck reported finding Lasseter's body on 29th March at which time it was covered with brush and sufficiently intact that it could be interred nearby albeit, as he related to Walter Gill, *"I just dug a hole an' poured th' poor bastard in"*. The reason for the 30th January date on Carrington's certificate, two months before the body was discovered, is unexplained, perhaps to avoid the conclusion that Lasseter could have been saved but for conflicted priorities and unnecessary delays.

129   (Hodgetts (nee Lasseter), 1960).

130   Page 179, in: (F. Blakeley, 1984 (1972)).

131   Page 221-222, in: (F. Blakeley, n.d.-b). Blakeley's early manuscript includes:

> *"The dingoes howl........the gold bugs crawl.....a dead man's bones on a bag of stones from a Reef that was never found.*
> *Cross bones and skull of old pirate days that dead men tell no tales, but dead men's bones with a bag of stones*
> *Are talking all the day, of reefs they found, on a burning plain, a bag of stones that gold bugs found on a burning plain,*
> *a bag of stones that gold bugs found, on dead man's bones,*
> *Gold fever raged in white man's soul, his dreams, his hopes, then despair*
> *So gold bugs peg another claim on dead man's bones."*
> *So the Gold Fever Company carried on.*

132   For instance, and despite inaccuracies in the reporting, see: (Anonymous, 1931, January 26.

133   (A. H. Chisholm, 1936, May 6).

134   The hand-written draft was inspected at the premises of Sydney Rare Book Auctions on 2nd February 2021.

135   *The Camel-man rode alone – or so it seemed! His back suggestively humped to the monotonous sway of the camel he gazed with eyes dream laden as the long miles crawled by.* The story of **Flynn of the Inland** begins with camels and ends with planes. The Cage Expedition, of course, did the opposite. See, page 7, in: (Ion L Idriess, 2019 (1932)).

136   Page 26, in: (Ion L Idriess, 1931). Subsequent quotes in this section on pages 94, 154, 169, 182 & 110.

137   (Anonymous, 1931, Monday January 12).

138   In the 1970s he told journalist Tim Bowden that for his trip through the Kimberley and the Northern Territory in the mid-1930s – the basis for **Man Tracks** – he had been provided with a camera and a Zeiss Icon lens. Recorded in: (Ion L Idriess, 1975). Idriess' Zeiss Ikonta camera was Lot 99 in the auction of his estate on 13th February 2021, selling for $300. He became a photographer.

139   There are three files with photographs from the Expeditions in the Mitchell Library. The first – *1930 'CAGE' expedition led by Lasseter, Central Australian Gold Exploration [and the later search for him]* – has pictures from the First and Second 'CAGE' Expeditions but contains most of the images used by Idriess. The second – *John Bailey collection of photographs showing Bob Buck leading the expedition to recover Lasseter's body in Central Australia* is largely from the Second Expedition. The third – *Errol Hampton Coote photographs, 1929 to 1932* – is a mixed bag with some extraneous photographs including from the 1932 West Centralian Company air search with Coote and Keith Farmer undertaking seven flights from Warburton. Idriess had access only to the photos of the original Expedition for the first four editions of **Lasseter's Last Ride** but includes images from the Second Expedition in subsequent editions. I am informed by Robert Ross that he had a conversation with Taylor's son who noted that Taylor had provided photographs that Idriess had agreed to pay for – but did not (personal communication, April 2020).

140   Page 134, in: (Eley, 1995).

141   Hand drafts of letter written by Idriess from 5 West Street, Paddington on 12th August, 1931. Original found among Idriess' documents in Narrandera on 30th November 2019.

142   The Second CAGE Expedition, which did use camels, had not left. These photos may also have been of Bob Buck's first trek to locate the prospector (labelled *trekking towards Ilbilba*). However, one photo shows five camels at a water hole and Paul Johns had five camels.

143   Page 102, in: (Ion L Idriess, 1931). Subsequent quotes in this section on pages 26, 7,24, 25, 26, 21, 22, 17, 13, 39, 71, 39, 69, 73, 70 & 92.

144   Presumably sent by Angus & Robertson, the draft in Idriess' own handwriting includes: *Rather surprised to know too that such names as "Rip Van Winkle" are Mr Idriess' own names.*

145   Page 107, in: (Gill, 1968).

146   Page 49, in: (Gill, 1968).

147   Not to be confused with Gwoya Tjungarrayi, also known as One Pound Jimmy, a Walpiri-Anmatyerre man whose photograph by Roy Dunstan in 1935 was used on the cover of *Walkabout* in 1936 and 1950, was adapted for postage stamps and inspired the design of the two-dollar coin decades later. He died in 1965 having worked at the same station where two years later Hugh Sawrey, founder of the Stockman's Hall of Fame in Longreach, painted *Lassiter's Last Ride* onto the wall of the homestead.

148   (Marshall-Stoneking, 1985).

149   Page 34, in: (FW Albrecht, 1964).

150   (Anonymous, 1932, Thursday September 15).

151   Opposite Page 63, in: (Henson, 1994). Although the biography notes that the events dated to October 1930, which would have been soon after his return from Ilbilba, it may have been two years earlier. It involved the public removal and display of *Tywerrenge* – sacred objects – at a culturally restricted cave site – *Manangananga*. The initiative occurred in the context of other issues including the monetising of sacred items as artifacts, and a recent court case of such objects being removed, but Albrecht's intent seems to have been to confront and undermine the power of traditional beliefs through forcing community members to make a choice – *"Churinga or Christ"* (Barry, 2014).

152   (Anonymous, 1931, Saturday November 21).

153   (Ion L Idriess, 1931, October 4).

154   (Wauchope, 1931, Saturday September 19).

155   (Ion L. Idriess, 1931, Wednesday September 16). The *Trove* image of this page of the *Sydney Mail* is assembled for completeness from different sources. The same page appears in *Lasseteria* in what appears mint condition with one difference; the title to the rondelle on *Lasseteria* reads: *They knew that when the native pointed water as being north...* See: http://www.lasseteria.com/CYCLOPEDIA/sydmail.htm. On this being pointed out, webmaster Rob Ross admitted his technical deftness in both returning the page to its original integrity, and protecting the integrity of the website by editing out demeaning terms which, it is worth noting, were in sufficiently common use to be acceptable in mainstream newspapers in the 1930s.

156   Page 147, in: (F. Blakeley, 1984 (1972)). Subsequent quotes on pages 155 & 156.

157   The transcripts are with relevant CAGE materials in the National Archives: (Anonymous, 1931-1938).

158   (H. B. Lasseter, 1931). This version is from the transcribed copy in the National Archives and the 'original', which turned up in the estate of Richard and Jillienne Stalley of Turramurra and was donated in September 2015 to the Mitchell Library.

159   Page 161, in: (Gill, 1968).

160   Page 143, in: (Marshall-Stoneking, 1985).

161   Page 132, in: (Ion L Idriess, 1931). Subsequent quotes from pages 139, 184, 195, 199, 220, 222 & 227.

CHAPTER 6 - Narrandera

162   (Ion L Idriess, 1915-1916)

163   Provided by Tom Thompson, November 2019.

164   Page 147, in: (Ion L Idriess, 1979 (1958)).

165   Page 222, in: (Ion L Idriess, 1934 (1932)).

166   (Hamilton, 2008).

167   *Glimpses of Romance*, draft of an address for broadcasting on Radio 2KY in July 1936, Sydney Rare Book Auction, lot No 72 of Idriess estate auctioned on 13th February 2021.

168   Will of Ion Llewellyn Idriess certified at The Public Trust Office, Sydney, on 30th October 1933. Inspected on 2nd February 2021 at Sydney Rare Book Auctions, part of Idriess estate.

169   Eta Lax (the name on her death certificate) was still residing in Sylvania Heights when she died of a stroke complicating metastatic breast cancer aged 80 years in December 1981 – in Kogarah hospital (New South Wales Register of Deaths).

170   Interview with Tom Thompson 25th November 2019.

171   Book and annotations in the collection of Jim Bradly and photographed on 10th January 2021 at Bolton Point.

172   Page 5, in: (Bowden, 2020 (1975)).

173   (Ion L Idriess, 1975).

174   Led by Alfred Cort Haddon, the 1898 *Cambridge Expedition to the Torres Straits* included four psychologically-oriented doctors – William McDougall, Charles Myers, Charles Seligman and W.H.R. Rivers. During the First World War all were pioneers in addressing the needs of traumatised soldiers and Charles Myers coined the term *shell shock* in 1915. Rivers served at Craiglockhart Hospital near Edinburgh, his patients including First World War poet Siegfried Sassoon. **The Reports of the Expedition** were released from 1901 to 1935 and Idriess drew on them for his books about the Torres Straits, particularly **Drums of Mer**. *Volume 6: Sociology, Magic and Religion of the Eastern Islands* was Lot 16 among Idriess' effects auctioned in Sydney on 12th December 2020 (See Epilogue). For information about the expedition see: (Herle & Rouse, 1998). About the team members and their influence on psychology and anthropology see: (Shephard, 2014). As 1917 closed and Jerusalem fell to allied forces, three of the most talented soldier-authors of the First World War – all of whom bear a relation to the Idriess/ Lasseter story – were in Palestine. Rivers' patient, Sassoon was with British troops in reserve, and would be redeployed to the Western Front following the German breakthrough in 1918. T.E. Lawrence was further east and Lowell Thomas would soon leverage interviews with him to a media career that took him to Lasseter's grave four decades later. And Ion Idriess, Trooper 358 of the 5th Light Horse Regiment, was to the west in the region of Jaffa. He had been fighting for three years and had sustained multiple wounds and contracted malaria. In December 1917 he was hospitalised again, only for the field station to come under fire. Evacuated to Egypt, he recorded on 7th February 1918: *I am told officially that I am going to Australia for six months. Enough said*, page 70, in: (Ion L Idriess, 1917-1918). His diary for the previous year ends with an address for the document to be sent in the event of his death and a final statement: *And Damn the World*, page 89 in: (Ion L Idriess, 1917).

175   (Anonymous, 2013, November 5). The launch attracted an audience of about a dozen to hear the author (Jim Bradly, personal communication January 2021) and the *Singleton Argus* website article provided this author with the link to the Library, where Wendell had been working, and on to Narrandera.

176   Idriess set up a company that morphed into Idriess Enterprises in the 1950s. In the 1970s Wendy Idriess, by that time caring for her father in Mona Vale, met Beverley Eley who facilitated the valuation of his archive in 1977. Following Idriess' death in June 1979 Wendy, executor of the estate with Margaret Oldenburg, solicitor, assumed control

of the company with Eley as a co-director. Through the late 1980s the relationship between the half-sisters, Wendy and Judy, soured (and thus, also, Judy and Eley). It was at the end of the 1980s that Tom Thompson met both Wendy and Eley, who was working on the Idriess biography. In 1994, just before **Ion Idriess** was released, Wendy died. Beverley Eley was the executor of the estate which was left to Judy who, with her children, enlisted Ross Burnet, a bookseller from Uralla (who declined to be interviewed), to develop the potential of the estate. The family relationship with Burnet eventually soured around 2006 over issues to do with film rights.

177   (Charnley, 1935; 1936).

178   (Anonymous, 1936).

179   Not a winner; rejected under the New South Wales Cinematography Films (Australian Quota) Act on the basis of quality. It was so bad Foy blocked its distribution. It also led to a lawsuit from Angus & Robertson.

CHAPTER 7 – Revision

180   Page 42, in: (Avery & Heath-Stubbs (translators), 1981 (1979)).

181   (Richardson, 2016).

182   Including by Walter Gill who travelled with Bob Buck to the Petermanns in 1931, and who began the chapter covering Thursday 28th May of that trip – just two months after Buck had been led to Lasseter's body - with: *"Dawn's left hand was in the sky," when I rolled out. I woke Buck, who roused the others…*

183   And by late 2020 to an auction house in Sydney (personal communication, Paul Feain, November 12th 2020).

184   (Anonymous, 1934).

185   (Carrington, 1934. October 28).

186   Idriess, writing as *I.I.*, cited Green in an early-1932 piece boosting mineral and pastoral possibilities in Central Australia (see Chapter 15).

187   Membership of the Second CAGE Expedition: *The party which consisted of eight whites comprised Robert Buck, Leader; H.W.B. Talbot, Assistant Geologist and Mining Surveyor; B. Brandon Cremer, Photographer; F. Green, Prospector; W. Felton, Wireless Operator; E. Cooper, Assistant Wireless Operator; P. Worth, Cook; the writer as Geologist. In addition a half caste Johnstone and a black "Paddy" acted as camel men.* Page I, in: (Blatchford, 1932, February 18).

188   (Talbot, Chambers, Central Australian Gold Exploration Co, & South Australia Department of Lands Survey, 1985). The copy inspected was provided by Robert Ross and has the following inscription: *H.W.B. Talbot's diary transcribed for the Department of Lands and Surveys by Mark Chambers in April 1984. Original held privately by Kevin Bullivant of Carine.*

189   Page 3, in: (Blatchford, 1932, February 18).

190   (Anonymous, 1932, Saturday January 30).

191   That is, half of what is in the Mitchell Library; there is no way of knowing if that is all that Green brought to Sydney.

192   That letter was probably obtained by Idriess in mid-1931. It was included with the material sold to the Mitchell Library, but is written on different paper, the reverse showing a Miner's Right application, and is folded vertically, the writing in two columns as was the case with one of the *fragments* sent to the CAGE Directors with which it was, of course, originally found. The letter does not appear in the facsimile edition published by Angus & Robertson in 1986, nine years after it was sold to the Mitchell Library (Lasseter, 1986 (1930-31)). It does appear in the transcription produced by Tom Thompson (Thompson, 2020).

193   Page 12, in: (Coote, 1981 (1934)).

194   (Biggers, 1930, Monday February 17).

195   (Australian Military Forces, 1920a).

196   (Australian Military Forces, 1917).

197   (Biggers, n.d.).

198   Page 120, in: (Ion L Idriess, 1979 (1958)).

199   Cited on pages 119-120, in: (Hubbard, 2017 (1993)).

200   Digital copy with: (H. B. Lasseter, 1930-ca.1931).

201   The letter was found in Idriess' papers by Beverley Eley who does not provide a date, but probably September or October 1931 given the amount of prepublicity, page 135, in: (Eley, 1995). It also raises the possibility that it was Idriess who was responsible for passing on this information to John Bailey and the CAGE Directors. Eley records Lewis Herbert Lasseter rather than Lewis Hubert.

202   That year her eldest daughter, Lillian Agnes (Ruby), met Bob Buck at the City Club Hotel in Melbourne when he was on his way to Sydney (Hodgetts (nee Lasseter), 1960). She lost both parents, her father for the second time.

203   Perhaps to encourage sales, photographs were changed from one edition to another from 1932 on. For the purposes of this discussion I have compared the first 1931 edition with the thirteenth edition – August 1933.

204   This image does not appear in the Mitchell collections raising the possibility that Idriess retained it or staged the 'just found' setup. An enlarged print was among the materials found at Narrandera and was subsequently auctioned with Idriess' estate in December 2020 (see Epilogue).

205   Page 229, in: (Ion L Idriess, 1933 (1931)). Subsequent quotes on pages 23, 241, 243 & inside back cover.

206   Page 48, in: (FW Albrecht, 1964).

207   The likely identity of Johannsen – Olof Johanson – is discussed in Chapters 17 & 18. However, it remains contested and Robert Ross gives an account of the other likely contenders and of the rumours about the spearing of two miners in the Rawlinsons which, as it turns out, were simply that – see *Lasseteria.com*.

208   Page 151, in: (Marshall-Stoneking, 1985).

209   Page 149, in: (F. Blakeley, 1984 (1972)). The trunk that Blakeley searched was probably the same that Blakeley transported from Ilbilba to the Police Station in Alice

Springs in September 1930. What was lost when Lasseter's camels bolted is different, and from what was itemised in the former in 1942 (see *Lasseter's Tin Trunk* on *Lasseteria*), there must have been repacking before Lasseter set out. All one can say is that what is now known as *The Diary* may have also been elsewhere when Blakeley was sleuthing.

210   http://www.lasseteria.com/CYCLOPEDIA/153.htm (accessed May 1, 2020).

211   Draft letter found with the remains of Idriess papers in Narrandera and photographed on 30th November 2019.

CHAPTER 8 – Victoria Park

212   Page vi, in: (P. J. Bridge, 2020).

213   Page 18, in: (Ion L Idriess, 1959).

214   Page 21, in: (Terry, 1936).

215   Page 102, in: (Drayton, 2013).

216   (P. Bridge, 1999).

217   (P. J. Bridge, 2020).

218   Jim McKeague, in researching the life and Central Deserts prospecting and exploration of Sam Hazlett (1872-1942), collected a trove of Lasseter information, including the schemes and scams of Stan Hummerston and Morley Cutlack. See https://hazlettgold.wordpress.com/text/ (accessed March 2021).

219   Page 353, in: (Keesing, 1967).

220   (Anonymous, 1935, Saturday October 26).

221   Page 30, in: (Ellis, 1937).

CHAPTER 9 – Magnetic Island

222   Page 14, in: (Terry, 1974).

223   Page 287, in: (Parking, 2003 (second edition)).

224   Page 106, in: (Ion L Idriess, 1957).

225   Hiddens grew up in north Queensland and spent time in the Escape River area retracing Kennedy's journey. He was responsible for the facsimile of William Carron's narrative (Carron, 1996 (1849)), and Byerley's edited journals of the Jardine brothers' trek (Byerley, 1994 (1867)).

226   Page 155, in: (Ion L Idriess, 1957). See also Chapter 14.

227   This is probably as much generational as it is about age appeal. As journalist Aaron Smith observes of Idriess' tales of the Torres Straits – ***The Wild White Man of Badu*** specifically: *Idriess's tale of Badu and its eternal feud with the neighbouring island of Moa, each making headhunting raiding parties on the other, sparked a boy's-own-adventure intrigue within me that belonged to my father's generation more than my own.* Page 148, in: (A. Smith, 2020).

228   (Hiddens, 1996).

229   Well received in Australia, in the UK it was released in a shortened form and neither there nor in the USA did returns live up to expectations (Kevin, 2020). Nosepeg Tjupurrula had a cameo role in the film (see notes to Chapter 13). Another character in the film, Peter Wallis, was played by Tas Fitzer who, as a Mounted Policeman stationed at Timber Creek, Idriess wrote into *Nemarluk: King of the Wilds* and *Mantracks*. Charles Chauvel recruited him for *Jedda*. Chauvel had form with desert dramas; Idriess collector, Duncan Quarterman, has a copy of Chauvel's 1936 book, signed by the author and published in Sydney, ***Uncivilised*** (possibly written by E.V. Timms) released as a film that year (and in the USA as Pituri). The *Wikipedia* entry for the film captures a vibe that is not dissimilar to ***The Blond Captive*** (which had voiceover by Lowell Thomas (Chapter 4)). Chauvel was covering all bases:

> *Successful author Beatrice Lynn is commissioned by her publisher to go to the Outback and locate the legendary white man, Mara, who heads an aboriginal tribe. Travelling by camel, she is abducted by an Afghan, Akbar Jhan and his group of aboriginals who provide pituri, a narcotic to aboriginals. Previously not allowed into Mara's tribal land to sell his wares, Akbar Jhan has schemed to use Beatrice, a white woman to arouse Mara's interest. Meanwhile, the Australian Mounted Police has its hands full with a missing Inspector, an international drug ring, and a tribe of hostile aboriginals led by the savage Moopil who have killed two prospectors as well as searching for the missing Beatrice. Mara buys Beatrice from the Afghans and the two fall in love.*

230   Pages 159-160, in: (Trezise, 1973).

231   Flyleaf of: (Ion L Idriess, 1969).

CHAPTER 10 –
Corroborators

232   Page 11, in: (Miller, 1940). Subsequent quotes on pages 66, 94, 12 & 10.

233   Idriess had a longstanding relationship with Jonathan Cape. On 5th April 1974, the company forwarded a lengthy letter with the following cover note: *Dear Mr. Idriess, We have received the enclosed letter and with much difficulty have read most of it. It seems that Miss Thiede would like your assistance in contacting some Sufis who would be willing to judge the veracity of some alarming prognostications. As you see, we did not give her your address.* (Letter in the Idriess Estate inspected at premises of Sydney Rare Book Auctions on 2nd February 2021).

234   (Miller, 1935).

235   (Ion L Idriess, 1930).

236   There are various possible writers other than Clune, including Ernestine Hill – both had relationships with Idriess and interest in the story, Hill having ghost-written Johns' account. With a degree of wariness, Hill and Idriess cooperated; *on hearing that he was heading to the Kimberley, Hill wrote on 18th November 1933 suggesting that they get together: Any help in the way of information or bright ideas in general, I shall be glad to give you – two old bagmen discussing the state of the tracks over the billy fire, as it were* (Hill, 1933, November 18). But it was a small pond; in her dual biography of Ernestine Hill and Daisy Bates, Eleanora Hogan records that around that time Idriess contacted Bates about writing her story (Hogan, 2021). The Daisy Bates story was complicated enough and it's hard to imagine Idriess faring better than Hill. In relation to The Lost Reef, Idriess expert Jim Bradly suggests that the author may be Charles Leslie

Barrett (1879-1959). An interesting possibility; a journalist who visited Central Australia, Barrett had been with the Camel Brigade Field Ambulance in Egypt and Palestine towards the end of the First World War, and it's possible his path crossed that of Idriess who was evacuated in late 1917; if not then, perhaps afterwards. Barrett is remembered as an ornithologist and naturalist, and his entry in the *Australian Dictionary of Biography* was by Idriess' friend, Alec Chisholm (A. Chisholm, 1979). And Barrett's *Koonawarra: A naturalist's adventures in Australia* (1939) and *Australia: My Country* (1941), were published by Oxford University Press which was also responsible for *The Lost Reef* in 1941.

237   Page 15, in: (Clune, 1944). Subsequently released as *The Red Heart: Sagas of Central Australia.*

238   This photo also at https://nla.gov.au/nla.obj-148889912 – whether it was camaraderie or canny cross-promotion, Clune and Chisholm wrote appreciations of Idriess (cited in this book) and Colin Roderick wrote the glowing introduction to Angus & Robertson's *Gems From Ion Idriess* in *The Junior Library of Australian Books* (Roderick, 1949).

239   (Griffen-Foley, 2016).

240   On the Lasseteria website there is a comment that Lasseter wrote directly to Donald Mackay in May 1930 looking for a ride to Ilbilba and on to somewhere unspecified to peg some claims. If so, it was around the same time that Lasseter received a letter in Kogarah from Johannsen/Johanson (https://www.lasseteria.com/CYCLOPEDIA/87.htm).

241   Clune described this trip in a 1939 article with a photograph of himself with an Aboriginal group: *the author with members of the Laritja tribe, who succored [sic] Lasseter prior to his death in the Petermann Range* (Clune, 1939, Saturday December 2).

242   (Anonymous, 1939, Saturday December 9).

243   Frank Clune was not the only member of a Cutlack expedition excluded from the pointy-end of finding the reef. A decade later Max Cartwright reported similar paranoid behaviour. And like Lasseter, Cutlack also slept in the locked cab of an expedition vehicle with loaded firearms (Cartwright, 1991). Clune quotes on pages 49-56, in: (Clune, 1957).

244   Clune was not blind to Idriess' tale-telling liberties and in a 1948 letter notes, in relation to Ernestine Hill, that like Ion Idriess: *she never worries about the truth*, quoted on page 108, in: (Hogan, 2021).

245   (Cahill, 1990). There is another parallel with Clune, some of whose books were ghost-written by P.R. (Inky) Stephensen. Communist, Rhodes Scholar, Aboriginal advocate, anti-Semite, cofounder of the Australia First Movement, interned Axis-sympathiser – Stephensen was a complicated man in a tense understudy role. Rodd shared Stephensen's early left-leaning political inclinations but his radicalism was confined to educational reform, and he relished his role supporting his wife's writing career. Just a couple of years after Rodd's Quadrant article his wife, Kylie Tennant, interviewed Idriess and published No good at lying - Two views of Australian writer Ion Idriess (Tennant, 1976).

246   Page 67, in: (Rodd, 1973). Subsequent quotes on pages 77 & 71.

247   Anonymous ("Verax"), 1932, March 2). Also quoted in: (Rodd, 1973).

248   Page 175, in: (Marshall-Stoneking, 1985).

249   Quoted on page 75, in: (Rodd, 1973).

250   Page 6, in: (Stapleton, 1981).

251   Aboriginal trackers were a supplement to a policeman's salary; pay and ration allowances went directly into Willshire's personal account (Vallee, 2004).

252   Quoted in: (Mulvaney, 1990). Willshire had a way with words and it is argued that the focus on his violence has eclipsed what, in other times, might be considered ethnography: *his history, and his writings are of valuable interest, and a vehicle for the revelation of traditional culture at an important time for Arrernte and other clans. They do not contain weather observations, or technical geographical or topological information. They are a striking oddity in the archive of Australian, Aboriginal, and colonial history. It would be easy to incinerate Willshire and his writings, but I argue that by doing this we erase a patchworked cultural storehouse, a nuance that does not appear in any other colonial stories of the time,* page 156, in: (Boyack, 2020).

253   Quoted on page 298, in: (Vallee, 2004).

254   There had been enormous economic investment in the newly opened Overland Telegraph and there had been episodes of 'dispersal' of local tribal groups by employees prior to the attack (Vallee, 2004).

255   Alice Thomson, named for her great-great-grandmother, wife of Charles Todd who was the driver of the Overland Telegraph, relates that it was Todd who enabled the telegraphic communication with Stapleton's wife (Thomson, 2000). Ernestine Hill gives a graphic account of the attack, and of the retaliation raids that followed, noting: *Out there a range, for grim and sufficient reason, is on the map for ever with the name of Blackfellow's Bones.* Page 133, in: (Hill, 1951). Idriess took note too: *Lot 4, Idriess 1874 Barrow Creek Murders,* in Sydney Rare Book Auctions on April 16th 2021, was a nine page note by Idriess: *from report of Constable Sam Gason day after affray.*

256   Page 11, in: (Gillen, 2019 (1995)).

257   Page 48, in: (Stapleton, 1992). Following quote on page 48.

258   Page 181, in: (Nettlebeck & Foster, 2007). Just to the north and some four decades later the trials in 1928 and 1934 of Constables William Murray following the Coniston massacre, and William McKinnon for the killing of Yokununna at Uluru also resulted in exonerations – and similar post-hoc rationalisations (McKennna, 2021).

259   Page 11, in: (Stapleton, 1981). Subsequent quotes on pages 25, 24, 57, 33 & 56

260   Page 205, in: (Synge, 2001).

261   There have been repeated calls for Willshire Street in Alice Springs to be

renamed, most recently to honour Charles Perkins. As of July 2021 the council had demurred (David Hewitt, personal communication).

262   Page 236, in: (Ion L Idriess, 1934 (1932)).

263   Personal communication, Desmond Clacherty, 31st July 2020. A few weeks after speaking with Desmond by phone I was informed by his daughter that he had died. He maintained his interest to the end.

264   The month after the Second CAGE Expedition returned empty-handed, articles appeared about a *cave of gold*. A London paper is quoted that Herbert Basedow was: *returning to Australia to lead a fully-equipped camel expedition in search of a cave of gold. This cave has been fruitlessly sought by previous explorers. The "Daily Express" says that a sketch showing the spot where an old prospector named Earle located the cave but who died before he was able to lead the expedition to the spot, has now come into Dr. Basedow's hands* (Anonymous, 1931, Friday December 11).

265   Page 7 in: (Clacherty, 1989). Subsequent quotes on page 49, 51, 45, 77, 65 & 87.

266   Page 181, in: (Marshall-Stoneking, 1985).

267   Facebook post, February 9th, 2020 - https://www.facebook.com/Desmond Clacherty/- accessed July 27th 2020.

268   (Anonymous, 1930, Friday July 18a).

269   (Anonymous, 1930, Friday July 18b).

CHAPTER 11 – Happy Valley

270   See the entry for *Lasseter's Cave* at *Lasseteria.com*.

CHAPTER 12 – Woollahra

271   Page 322, in: (Eley, 1995).

272   Beverley Eley, personal communication, July 2020. There have been other medical conditions suggested.

273   Tape 6, in: (Ion L Idriess, 1974, November 25).

274   (Coutts, 2013).

275   (Ion L Idriess, 1946).

276   (Anonymous, 1954, Monday August 16).

CHAPTER 13 – Sleuths and decoders

277   Page 202, in: (Hubbard, 2017 (1993)).

278   Page 9, in: (Marshall-Stoneking, 1985). Subsequent quotes on pages 143 & 190.

279   For the full poem visit the Australian Poetry Library at https://www.poetrylibrary.edu.au/poets/marshall-stoneking-billy/poems/singing-the-snake-0390001.

Nosepeg Tjupurrula had an impressive career as a cultural intermediary, actor, and was active in the early art movement at Papunya. As well as a documentary directed by Billy Marshall-Stoneking he acted in several films – including a cameo role in *Jedda*. In 1954 he was presented to Queen Elizabeth in Toowoomba, allegedly confidently asserting: *I am king of the Pintupi*, and in later life was esteemed as a friend by Gough Whitlam and Malcolm Fraser. See: https://www.daao.org.au/bio/nosepeg-tjupurrula/biography/.

280   Quoted on page 205, in: (Hubbard, 2017 (1993)).

281   Page ix, in: (Hubbard, 2017 (1993)). Subsequent quote on page 200, 202 & 183.

282   Walker's source was the fragments of correspondence from Johanson to Lasseter that, following Irene's death, passed to Bob Lasseter, who in 1959/1960 sought to find out who the Johanson mentioned in dispatches was from the address given - 193 Piesse Street, Boulder (Sharp, 2021, September 25).

283   Supposedly; Dick Kimber reported that he had been told by Paddy Tucker that he had "found a note at Ayers Rock which had been left by Johannsen and Smith" – see page 93, in: (Kimber, 1986).

284   (Clark, 2015).

285   Page xii, in: (Brown, 2015). Second quote on page 235.

286   Foreword, in: (Clark, 2019). Second quote on page 2.

287   Cutlack had been well-mentored; he was with Stan Hummerston on expeditions earlier in the 1930s and a co-conspirator in the 1936 swindle based on what were claimed to be messages left by the dead prospector.

288   Page 109, in: (Cartwright, 1991).

289   Page 44, in: (Testa & Decarli, 2005). Subsequent quotes on pages 1, 5, 28 & 89.

290   There is only one written reference to Harding by Lasseter in a letter dated 14th February 1930 (quoted on page 177, in: (Clark, 2019)).

291   Page 187, in: (Hiddens, 1996).

292   After an introductory conversation we scheduled an interview which, I explained, would be recorded. I emailed a copy of the transcript on the same day as I mailed a copy of Vicarious Dreaming – which was returned to Cairns unopened.

CHAPTER 14 – Oak Flats

293   (Rowlands, 1995).

294   My first interview was by phone but as COVID-19 restrictions eased I visited John and sighted his extraordinary collection.

295   Page 86, in: (Ion L Idriess, 2019 (1942)).

296   Project Gutenberg Australia: http://gutenberg.net.au.ebooks06/0608291h.html (accessed July, 2020).

CHAPTER 15 – Bolton Point

297   Dedication to: (Bradly, 2008).

298   (Clouten, 1988 (1967)).

299   He may have been the son of one of the *Three head men of Mer* who appear in a photograph in ***Drums of Mer***. Idriess' appropriation of material from the 1898 Cambridge Expedition Reports (see notes to Chapter 6) into the narrative of ***Drums of Mer*** has been influential both in terms of popular understandings of Torres Strait Islander cultures and of local representations of traditional practice – blurring the lines between ethnography and fiction (Febuary, 1997).

300   (Anonymous, 1939, Saturday September 23).

301   Pages 3-5, in: (Ion L Idriess, 2020 (1938)).

302   Page vi, in: (Feain & Aroney, 2016). On 13th February 2021 Paul Feain, with Ellie Aroney in support, conducted the second Idriess Estate auction at Sydney Rare Book Auctions, lot 86 of which was a letter written by Alex Chisholm under the header of *Daily Telegraph Newspaper Company* on 23rd September 1924 to Ion Idriess who was visiting Sydney: *Dear Mr Idriess. Have you the MS of your northern novel with you? I mentioned this casually to a publisher yesterday & he expressed a desire to see your work. If you have the story drop in here and I will give you an introduction.* That MS became ***Madman's Island*** and the introduction was to Angus & Robertson. The letter was purchased by Jim Bradly.

303   (Midford, 1937, February 10).

304   (Bradly, 2013).

305   Page 207, in: (Bradly, 2008).

CHAPTER 16 – Mythbusters

306   Page 126, in: (Finlayson, 1946 (1935)). Subsequent quote on page 127.

307   Page 203, in: (Tonkin, 2001). Subsequent quotes on pages 168, 200 & 205.

308   There is a startling similarity to the plot device of Ian Miller's ***The Lost Reef*** (see Chapter 10) and this Hummerston confection. In 1934 he lured gullible investors with the story that, having shot at but missed a dingo, he sought to check the accuracy of his rifle by aiming at a mark on a tree which, he discovered, was a message from Lasseter which led him to find buried nearby: *a bottle containing several sealed letters and map* (Anonymous, 1934, Saturday December 15).

309   Page 157, in: (Rothwell, 2009).

310   (I. Smith & Smith, 1979).

311   The parallels to Jason and the Argonauts are numerous, not least that both Jason and Lasseter die alone, crushed by the rotting vessels of their journeys – in the case of Jason it was the *Argo* and for Lasseter, the CAGE Company.

312   Page 19, in: (O'Brien, 2019).

313   ***Flynn of the Inland*** (1932) and ***The Cattle King*** (1936) might also be considered

but were largely about events beyond the Northern Territory and mainly written from interviews and archival research.

314   Page 53, in: (Dewar, 2019 (1997)). Subsequent quotes on pages 101, 138, 122, 131 & 125.

315   Such, 1939).

316   He made a formal submission to the Select Committee on the Administration of the Aborigines Protection Board on Wednesday 24th November 1937 with recommendations regarding leprosy and venereal diseases. Draft found in papers of the Idriess estate inspected at Sydney Rare Book Auctions on 12th December 2020.

317   (Synge, 2001).

318   See: https://www.lesleysynge.com/.

319   A daughter out of wedlock is plausible. In 1960 Lillian Agnes Hodgetts, his eldest daughter, wrote of the restlessness and other changes that her father showed after the beginning of the First World War: *From some reason women who had been quite respectable became fascinated by him. I could name several who had children by him – one he got a mate in camp to marry before her son (Kevin) was born – another one (an artist's model) and quite prominent was so enamoured of him that she followed from camp to camp in several states and my mother received a letter from her brother threatening to shoot him if he went near his sister again. She eventually married one of her brother's friends before her son (Lewis) was born* (Hodgetts (nee Lasseter), 1960). Synge discusses information from a granddaughter of Lasseter that he had had a relationship with a woman who was an artist's model – the basis for Scarlett Musgrove. That woman may have been Pearl Bell; in 1920 Lasseter was trying to trace her and placed an advertisement in the *Kalgoorlie Miner* under the header *MISSING FRIENDS*, which read: *Pearl Bell, last heard of at Tower Hotel, Kalgoorlie, June, 1917, or anyone knowing her address please communicate with Lewis H. Lasseter. Fullers Hotel, Bourke st., Melbourne* (Anonymous, 1920, Monday July 5). If they had met it was probably briefly in Adelaide in 1917 and she was, by then, recently married – Mrs Pearl Sharkey. In 1920 she was living in Boulder and died following the birth of her fourth child in 1924 (Sharp, 2021, August 14).

320   Both the trunk and the tale have become woven through the myth. Without providing a source Billy Marshall-Stoneking (1985) asserts: *One of the few, almost overlooked, items that was found on Lasseter's body was a small, furry-covered edition of **The Rubaiyat of Omar Khayyam*** (p. 169). In the section *Lasseter's Tin Trunk* on *Lasseteria* Rob Ross documents the history of the trunk that Blakeley searched during the expedition and which he delivered to the Police Station in Alice Springs in September 1930. He finishes that entry by noting: *and to settle yet another rumour that has grown up with the Lasseter legend, there was no copy of The Rubaiyat of Omar Khayyam found with Lasseter's body or in the trunk*. Which is not to say that a copy of ***The Rubaiyat*** may not have been among the possessions he lost with his camels – unlikely but it would be a nice touch.

321   Page 238, in: (Synge, 2001).

322   (Ryan, 2015). Subsequent quotes on pages 382 & 394.

323   Page 208, in: (Ryan, 1996).

324   (Ryan, 2013).

325   The defeat of technology by the desert and quasi-supernatural forces framed

as a series of *neo-Gothic occurrences* had been anticipated nearly two decades before (Haynes, 1998).

CHAPTER 17 – Northcote

326   (Hannaford, 2013, Thursday October 31).

327   Page 188, in: (Marshall-Stoneking, 1985).

CHAPTER 18 – Docklands

328   (Clark, 2018).

329   (Walsh, 1983). Walsh was also responsible for the Lasseter entry in the Northern Territory Dictionary of Biography (https://www.territorystories.nt.gov.au/jspui/handle/10070/260154).

330   Page 63, in: (Clark, 2015).

331   Page 102, in: (Ion L Idriess, 1931). Subsequent quotes pages 113, 114 & 202.

332   Page 233, in: (Ion L Idriess, 1933 (1931)).

333   (Clark, 2015).

334   (Clark, 2019).

335   (Brown, 2015).

336   Page 21, in: (Clark, 2019). Second quote on page 33.

CHAPTER 19 – One more river to cross

337   (Terry, 1979, January 30).

338   (I. L. Idriess, 1932, April 15).

339   (Price, 1932, August 11).

340   (W. G. Cousins, 1939, October 13). Idriess didn't waste time in reaching out; in the same month that General Douglas MacArthur arrived in Australia Idriess received a letter from Colonel L.A. Dieles, Aide-de-camp to the General: *Mrs MacArthur has asked me to express her deep appreciation for the splendid gift to little Arthur. It was thoughtful of you to autograph each volume. Arthur will some day appreciate them and be reminded of his pleasant experiences in Australia.* (Letter dated 30th March 1942 in Idriess estate examined in the premises of Sydney Rare Book Auctions on 2nd February 2021).

341   (Anonymous ("The Gossip"), 1931, Wednesday August 12).

342   (Anonymous ("Warrigal"), 1931, Friday September 18).

343   Draft typed letter written by Walter Cousins to Idriess on 13th July. Originals found among Idriess' documents in Narrandera on 30th November 2019. Cousins refers to Bob Buck as the *owner of Tempe Downs Station* but In 1930 Bob Buck had moved from Tempe Downs to Middleton Ponds.

344   Typed draft of letter to Idriess, 12th August 1931, among Idriess' documents

found in Narrandera on 30th November, 2019.

345   Page 67, in: (P. Bridge, 1999).

346   Page 191, in: (Clark, 2019).

347   After his father's death Aubrey Cousins also worked at Angus & Robertson and went on to a life in publishing. The letter written by Idriess on 10th February 1968 was part of the 'Cousins Auctions' held in Sydney in September and November 2011, this item among several purchased by Duncan Quarterman and described on the Idriess website set up by Rob Coutts. See: https://www.idriess.com.au/thecousinsauctions.htm (accessed 1st January 2021).

348   Walter Cousin's estate was auctioned in 2011 and among the items purchased by Duncan Quarterman were two work journals that Walter Cousins maintained during a trip to the UK and US in 1937. He was in New York in mid-April and wrote: *I can't understand why Idriess cannot get a start here. ... Told Harpers that I could probably get Hoover, former President, to write a foreword to Lasseter, but that did not click. Shaw could have got the Foreword as he is a personal friend of Hoovers. Hoover spent his younger days in WA. ... Feel sure Idriess will come into his own here sooner or later. The schools & colleges I feel certain will buy his sets in big numbers.* (page 8 in second journal, inspected in Canberra, 30th January 2021).

349   Lasseter was in Canberra from the mid-1920s, initially at the Northbourne Camp for single men and, after Irene and their children arrived, at the Russell Hill Settlement. He was Secretary of the Progress Association at the former and President of the Social Service Association at the latter – as well as working and maintaining his *Gleaner* contributions.

350   (Anonymous, 1926, Monday October 11).

CHAPTER 20 – Manunda

351   Page 202, in: (Hubbard, 2017 (1993)).

352   (Anonymous, 1935, Tuesday March 26).

CHAPTER 21 – The Promised Land

353   (Eley, 2007, Saturday February 10).

354   (Anonymous, 1938, Thursday September 29).

355   (Ion L Idriess, 1975).

356   (James, 1999).

357   Page 28, in: (Tennant, 1976). At the end of the copy of the article owned by Jim Bradly, in Idriess' handwriting is written: *keep the machine going while she had such good copy she said after all there was plenty of time to revise. There wasn't! and I suppose her contract ran out while my malaria has dragged on ever since.* In 1963 Tennant had written to Idriess seeking a contribution to a proposed series – *Great Stories of Australia* – beginning: *I have been one of your readers and admirers ever since I read **Lasseter's Last Ride** in Coonabarabran over 30 years ago (Tennant, 1963, December 22).*

358   (Eley, 1995).

359   Beverley related that George Ferguson also went to Kogarah with Idriess; there was probably more than one trip and the comment by Idriess in correspondence to

Cousins regarding a *photo you took a liking to* (the family photo) suggests that Cousins was present on an early trip before *The Diary* arrived in Sydney.

360   Page 1, in: (F. Blakeley, 1984 (1972)).

361   Letters inspected among Idriess estate at premises of Sydney Rare Book Auctions, 2nd February 2021.

362   Idriess probably had advanced cerebrovascular disease by the time of the interview, his death certificate registered on the 12th June 1979, six days after he died, records *Cause of death* as: *I (a) Bronchopneumonia – 7 days; (b) Senility – years. II Cerebral arteriosclerosis – 10 years; Cerebral thrombosis – 10 years; Left hemiparesis – 10 years* (New South Wales Register of Deaths).

363   Tape 6, in: (Ion L Idriess, 1974, November 25). Sections of de Berg's interviews with Idriess are presented in a compilation of her work (de Berg, 1991).

CHAPTER 22 – Visions of soul's future gold

364   Page 29, in: (Tennant, 1976).

365   Back cover: (Gregor, 2016).

366   The plaque set up with the assistance of David Hewitt (personal communication, July 2021). Docker River has a children's playground set up by the MacDonnell Regional Council – *Lasseter Park* (Marcus Tabart, personal communication).

367   Lasseter trees are like Lasseter maps – some may be the real thing. For a review see the entry for *Lasseter Trees* on *Lasseteria.com*. However, there is another Lasseter tree that is thousands of kilometres from the others. The photograph of Lasseter, Irene and the kids that was included in the first two editions of **Lasseter's Last Ride** was taken around 1927 at the Russell Hill Settlement for workers on the nation's capital. Canberra historian, Alan Foskett, has written a history of Campbell which now covers the area which was the Russell Hill Settlement, including Lasseter connections (Foskett, 2008). At the back of the Campbell shops is a park with a long dead gum tree with a bifurcating trunk (as have many others in this saga). After interviewing Alan I was taken by Duncan Quarterman to view that tree which supposedly was in the background as that photograph was taken 95 years earlier. Perhaps.

368   (Various authors, 1958-1978).

369   Robinson used footage from the Lowell Tomas *High Adventure* episode two decades earlier which had not been released in Australia because of the desecration of Lasseter's grave. He may have been attempting to cover all bases – Indigenous interests, family interests and, through Mike Willesee, media interests.

370   (Anonymous, 1976, Sunday September 5).

371   This is an inaccurate rendition of *The Man in the Arena* section of a speech delivered by Theodore Roosevelt at the Sorbonne in Paris on 23rd April, 1920 – after his presidency ended.

372   *The Legend of Lasseter's Reef* – written by musician turned writer and educator, Mark Greenwood, which won a 2003 Western Australian Premier's Book Award and for which there is also a set of *Teacher's notes* on the author's website: http://www.

markgreenwood.com.au/index.html.

373   (National Library of Australia, 2005).

374   (I. Smith & Smith, 1979).

375   (Reed, 1929, Saturday March 23).

376   Cited on page 12, in: (Lawton, 2007).

377   (Pearson, 2020, September 5-6).

378   Page 201, in: (Conrad, 2017).

379   Betty Riddell (1910-1988) was a journalist and an acclaimed poet. A cutting containing this poem was found in a box of Idriess ephemera auctioned through Sydney Rare Book Auctions on 13th February 2021 and was purchased by Jim Bradly. It appeared in *The Daily Telegraph* (Sydney) on Thursday 28th May 1931 (Riddell, 1931, Thursday May 28).

380   (Kinsella, 1989).

EPILOGUE – Ultimo

381   Page 96, in: (I. L. Idriess, 2020 (1975)).

382   While Idriess was still alive the Mitchell had made its own pitch. Mixed into a box of *ephemera* swept together for auction I found a letter from R.F. Doust from the Mitchell Library dated 14th December 1973 which begins: *Dear Mr. Idriess, During your long career as a writer you will no doubt have accumulated a considerable quantity of papers, photographs and other material of documentary interest. I write now to ask if you would consider placing any such material in the Mitchell Library.* (Inspected at the premises of Sydney Rare Book Auctions on 2nd February 2021).

383   Those photographs are also in the Mitchell Library, donated by John Bailey and with a note indicating that Ernest Brandon-Cremer was the official photographer with the Second Expedition. The Bill Davis mentioned in the catalogue worked for Angus & Robertson and made the enlarged images that remained with Idriess. The image of *Lasseter's Diary Uncovered When Found* is in *Lasseter's Last Ride* but not in the Mitchell collections.

384   (Feain & Aroney, 2016).

Lightning Source UK Ltd.
Milton Keynes UK
UKHW042335230522
403422UK00005B/162